Pacifist Prophet

Pacifist Prophet

Papunhank and the Quest for Peace in Early America

RICHARD W. POINTER

University of Nebraska Press
Lincoln

Portions of this book originally appeared in "An Almost Friend: Papunhank, Quakers, and the Search for Security amid Pennsylvania's Wars, 1754–1765," by Richard W. Pointer, in *Pennsylvania Magazine of History and Biography*, 138 (2014): 237–68. Manufactured in the United States of America ♾

Library of Congress Cataloging-in-Publication Data
Names: Pointer, Richard W., 1955–author.
Title: Pacifist prophet: Papunhank and the quest for peace in early America / Richard W. Pointer.
Other titles: Papunhank and the quest for peace in early America
Description: Lincoln: University of Nebraska Press, [2020] | Includes bibliographical references and index. |
Identifiers: LCCN 2020001887
ISBN 9781496222862 (hardback)
ISBN 9781496223562 (epub)
ISBN 9781496223579 (mobi)
ISBN 9781496223586 (pdf)
Subjects: LCSH: Papunhank,–1775. | Moravian Indians—History. | Indians of North America—Religion. | Pacifists—United States—Biography. | Munsee Indians—Biography.
Classification: LCC E90.P18 P65 2020 |
DDC 970.004/973450092 [B]—dc23
LC record available at https://lccn.loc.gov/2020001887

Set in Adobe Caslon by Laura Buis.

For Katie, Kristy, and Julie, with love

If it is possible,
so far as it depends on you,
live peaceably with all.

ROMANS 12:18

Contents

Figures

Acknowledgments

Writing another's life is a humbling experience. At least it has been for me. "Seeing through a glass darkly" only begins to convey what I regularly experienced in piecing this complex historical puzzle together. Like so many other research projects, this one began with a different goal in mind. But Papunhank kept showing up as the most compelling part of what I was investigating, and before long he had my full attention. Deciding to write a biography of him took a bit longer and the encouragement of a number of the people identified below. Once off on that journey, I came to realize in a far more profound way how much biographers owe to their subjects. If what follows in this book provides a family resemblance to the lived reality of Papunhank and his people, I will have begun to repay that debt.

I have accumulated many other debts along the way. Fortunately, Westmont College graciously covered the fiscal ones through grants from the offices of President Gayle Beebe and Provost Mark Sargent and the very generous research funds that accompanied my tenure in an endowed chair underwritten by the Fletcher Jones Foundation. That support allowed me to make numerous trips to east coast repositories and to employ the services of three highly skilled translators of eighteenth-century German language materials. Pastor Roy Ledbetter, Julie Tomberlin Weber, and Edward Quinter literally made this book possible. The care and expertise they poured into their work is evident in every Moravian letter and diary entry they translated. Without their assistance, much of Papunhank's later life and surrounding context would have remained hidden.

Numerous librarians and archivists also provided essential assistance, including my colleagues at Westmont's Voskuyl Library and those nearby at the University of California, Santa Barbara. Special mention must be made of the staff at the Moravian Archives in Bethlehem, Pennsylvania. Over the course of multiple visits and email correspondence, director Paul Peucker and assistant archivists Lanie Graff and Thomas McCullough graciously and efficiently accommodated my every request. They also kindly put me in contact with the translators mentioned above.

Once I began to put something about Papunhank in writing, valuable feedback came from many quarters. Greg Dowd, Rachel Wheeler, Jim Merrell, Dawn Marsh, and Julius Rubin read the entire manuscript and offered helpful critiques and much needed encouragement along the way. Michael Goode, Scott Paul Gordon, Erik Seeman, Katharine Gerbner, John Grigg, Tammy Gaskell, Cathy Brekus, Jennifer Graber, and Steve Pointer read one or more chapters and likewise provided good advice on how to make them better. Very early on colleagues in a small writing group at Westmont—Greg Spencer and Gary Moon—told me, perhaps simply to be polite, that they saw potential in my rather ill-defined and inchoate project ideas. I took them at their word and kept plowing along. During a sabbatical year's leave, I drafted a good chunk of the manuscript and benefitted greatly from the listening ear of friends John Sider and Erica Camardella. Their patient and gentle responses steered me and the book into better places. I was also fortunate to have a series of excellent undergraduate research assistants including Matt Browne, Emilie Whitman Martin, Thea Brentlinger, John Detrich, Jayne Avendano, and Cassidy Rea. Julie Pointer Adams willingly lent her professional photographic assistance to the preparation of a number of the images included in the book. At the University of Nebraska Press, Senior Editor Matthew Bokovoy and his assistant, Heather Stauffer, provided enthusiastic support and strategic wisdom. They shepherded the book to its completion.

Over the past twenty-six years, I have been privileged to work alongside a group of stellar historians at Westmont. I would be remiss not to mention them here. During the decade this project has been in process, Marianne Robins, Chandra Mallampalli, Alister Chapman, Heather Keaney, and Rachel Winslow cheered me on at various critical moments. They are cherished colleagues and friends.

This book is dedicated to my three daughters, Katie Pointer, Kristy Pointer Hyres, and Julie Pointer Adams. Long past are the days when Dad needed to excuse himself from dinner or play time to go work in his bedroom office. But the same love they extended to me then has continued unbroken, and has been made all the sweeter with the addition of our sons-in-law, Alex Hyres and Ryan Adams, and grandchildren, Elodie, Oliver, and Lucia. As I have written before, they are all a source of unspeakable joy. So, too, is their mother and grandmother, Barb. She has endured endless conversations and rewrites. I see her touch upon every page. For that and so much more, hers is the debt I will never be able to repay.

Pacifist Prophet

Introduction

Long before dawn on the morning of February 6, 1764, Philadelphia's bells sounded the alarm. For weeks rumors had circulated that hundreds of disgruntled Pennsylvanians were on the march toward the city. Now they had reached its edge, poised to repeat the deadly violence waged upon unsuspecting Indians at Conestoga six weeks earlier. "Citizens were summoned to the Courthouse. Weapons and powder were distributed. . . . [Men] were formed into companies and officers appointed for the common defense."[1] Meanwhile, roughly 140 Native persons—men, women, and children—the principal targets of the rebels' wrath, nervously paced within the British army barracks wondering if they would ever see the sun rise again and praying for God's protection. Mahicans huddled alongside Delawares and Munsees waiting for the day to break.

Most of those Indians were Moravian Christians, a German Pietist movement whose missionary outreach to Native Americans had been unusually successful during the prior two decades.[2] Johannes Papunhank was one of its fruits.[3] A relative newcomer to Moravian ranks, his baptism eight months earlier provided him a Christian name and a new Native community. In return, he brought his prophetic voice, diplomatic skills, and unflagging commitment to peace. A dramatic adult vision fifteen years earlier had made him a determined pacifist. Many of the Indians who surrounded him and his family that night shared his love of peace. They were all in Philadelphia as war refugees, testaments to a world too often void of peace and a place for Indians like Papunhank to call home.[4]

His life before and after the upheavals of early 1764 was a long quest for such a homeland. He wanted a space, however modest, in which the communities he formed and typically led could live independently and peaceably. That goal proved elusive for him and dozens of other Native peoples in eighteenth-century America. In that respect, his story was their story. They commonly struggled to maintain or regain a measure of autonomy amid a range of countervailing forces. Yet Papunhank did it his way, a decidedly peaceful way, and that set him apart from most, though not all, of his Indian counterparts. Faced with the onslaught of colonial peoples and pressures, scores of Native leaders eventually led their communities into war. But contrary to longstanding popular impressions, some Indian headmen sought to resolve conflicts, or at least to protect their own peoples, through strictly peaceful means. Few did more or tried harder along those lines than Papunhank. In so doing, he exemplified a heretofore largely overlooked Indian peacemaking tradition.

That meant nothing to the so-called Paxton Boys as they made their way toward the City of Brotherly Love on that cold February night. In fact, if anything, it made Papunhank a special target of their rage, for among other things he complicated their increasingly one-dimensional view of Native peoples as threatening, warlike, and evil. A virulent racial hatred sown amid a decade of frontier warfare fueled their advance, as did a religious creed that condoned extralegal actions against governments that failed to protect and promote the public welfare. After the latest round of carnage during the summer and fall of 1763 (what came to be known as Pontiac's War), when hundreds of settler lives had been taken by raiding Natives, the Paxton Boys and many other Pennsylvanians had no trouble concluding that all Indians, of whatever stripe, were their enemies. How could their colonial government offer succor and defense to any Natives after having failed so miserably to provide the same for frontier whites? There was no such thing as "peaceful" Indians; they were all deceivers, in league with the perpetrators of brutal attacks. Peace would only be possible in Pennsylvania when Indians as a race were "defeated, removed, or decimated." That meant eliminating the Conestogas—mission accomplished—and removing from the province the Moravian Indians now hiding behind government walls and waistcoats.[5]

Moravians, whether Euro-American or Native American, were unfortunately accustomed to facing violent opposition. They traced their origins back to the persecuted followers of Czech religious reformer Jan Hus in the fifteenth century. The movement revived in the early eighteenth century amid central Europe's Pietist renewal and the patronage of Count Nicholas von Zinzendorf in Herrnhut in what is today the eastern part of Germany. He inspired a strong missionary impulse among the Unitas Fratrum (United Brethren or Church of the Brethren as the Moravians were called) which they brought to Britain's North American colonies in the 1730s. They soon began evangelistic work among Indians in the Housatonic Valley on both sides of the New York-Connecticut border and in Pennsylvania from their "headquarters" in Bethlehem. Scores of Indians responded positively to the Moravian emphasis on the love and sacrifice of Jesus. Moravian theology focused on the shedding of his blood and proclaimed his side wound as a symbolic opening through which believers might enter into intimate union with the Savior. Such a message resonated far less with most colonists (Protestant in orientation), who considered it too "Catholic" or too sensual and labeled Moravians as theologically heterodox and politically dangerous as possible French spies. That was enough to persuade New York's and Connecticut's governments to expel (temporarily) Moravians from their colonies in the 1740s and to breed a widespread mistrust of their intentions.[6] Even many Indians distrusted the Brethren's outreach as they observed their Native communities become divided between Christians and non-Christians, and witnessed the out-migration of many of the former to Moravian towns such as Gnadenhütten, Pennsylvania. That village felt the full brunt of Indian rage in 1755 when amid the Seven Years' War Natives attacked and killed a dozen peaceful whites. The Paxton Boys' march on Philadelphia eight years later was one more episode in what had become a long history of retaliatory violence within which pacifist Moravians were sometimes caught in the crossfire.

Papunhank had no hand in getting the Paxton Boys to stand down. Benjamin Franklin and others cared for that work. But he surely would have been willing to lend his voice to the negotiation if he had been asked. His interest would have been in finding some just settlement of Paxton grievances, altering their views of at least his band of Indians, and securing for his people some peaceful place to go. His conviction that affording justice to all was the surest road to social harmony was a critical element of his larger vision of peace. Peace was more than simply the absence of war; it was a condition in which equity and a wide measure of self-rule prevailed, a place without violence where men and women were free to act in ways consonant with the Creator's desire for human well-being.[7] Such views placed him in the ranks of a small minority. Not surprisingly, then, he was rarely in a position to exert substantial influence over large colonial affairs. Moreover, relatively few contemporaries knew him outside Pennsylvania, New Jersey, New York, and the Ohio Country, even if for a few decades his fame reached the British Isles and the European continent. Little wonder, then, that virtually no Americans today have heard of him. Even most historians of early America don't recognize his name. Yet in this case, obscurity should not be equated with insignificance or imply a life of no interest or worth to modern readers. As one recent scholar has succinctly noted, Papunhank was an "extraordinary man."[8]

How so? *Pacifist Prophet* explores Papunhank's life as reformer, prophet, preacher, diplomat, and community leader, a life marked by personal and corporate struggles, disappointments, tragedies, and loss. But one also marked by courage, perseverance, survival, spiritual quest, religious faith, integrity, and a willingness to do the unexpected. The narrative flow of his story and my portrait of him may be summarized briefly. I begin by painting his first forty-plus years with broad strokes in an opening chapter, situating him within his people's (the Munsees) increasingly challenging world in Pennsylvania in the first half of the eighteenth century. Then I explore the great turning point in Papunhank's life—an adult vision quest that brought a radical encounter with the supernatural and a newfound sense of purpose and vocation. He became a prophet determined to fulfill the divine calling he received.[9] Over the next decade and a half, he preached a peace and justice message in the midst of a world at war, gathered a substantial band of followers, and pursued a host of strategies to keep them alive and comparatively autonomous. When violent forces finally threatened to destroy them all, his company splintered; he and a small minority joined with fellow pacifists—Native and white Moravians—and sought protection in Philadelphia. For sixteen months they suffered as war refugees, losing a third of their members to disease even while narrowly escaping attack from the Paxton Boys. During those difficult days, he became immersed in Moravian ways and began to combine Christian elements more thoroughly into his Munsee identity. When finally released from the city, Papunhank led his new Native community back to his former town along the North Branch of the Susquehanna River, where they spent the next seven years mostly prospering as a Moravian town, but all the while struggling to secure a more permanent right to live in that place. By 1772 their fight had been lost, and the entire community was forced to move west to the Ohio Country in search once more of a safe and peaceful homeland. Papunhank persevered three more years in that work and then died in May 1775 just as a whole new conflagration, the American War for Independence, was breaking out. He had spent the last three decades of his life fighting his own Native war for independence, not with guns or tomahawks but with a powerful peace discourse. Through word and action, he showed Indians and whites alike what it meant to live upon the conviction that "when God made men, he never intended they should kill and destroy one another."[10]

In a range of ways, Papunhank was a surprising, countercultural figure in the eighteenth century, fitting neither the stereotypes of Indians held by whites nor the expectations other Natives had for one of their own. Perhaps that is why when prominent Quaker social reformer Anthony Benezet, a radical nonconformist himself, decided to defend American Indian character, Papunhank came to mind. Against increasingly virulent cries during the American Revolution for the "universal extirpation of all Indians from the face of the earth," Benezet drew upon his earlier friendship with the Munsee prophet and held him up as an exemplary man, a preacher of peace and justice, and a human being worthy of esteem, not murder.[11]

Benezet included those reflections in his 1784 work, *Some Observations on the situation, disposition, and character of the Indian natives of this continent.* As he arranged for the distribution of some 2,500 copies, including ones to be sent to Congress and General George Washington, he expressed the hope that his words would "soften the spirit of all who read it towards Indians, even, I hope some of their murderers."[12] The pamphlet linked Papunhank to broader numbers of Indians, past and present, committed to peace, but lamented that they had been distrusted, discounted, or simply ignored. Now amid the fury of the late eighteenth century, it seemed that more and more white Americans were convinced, as the Paxton Boys had been, that all Native Americans were warlike and cruel. Papunhank belied those claims according to Benezet. He explained that about thirty years earlier, his subject had gathered a group of Indians "into a good degree of civil and religious order" and "declared their particular disapprobation of war, and fixed resolution to take no part therein"[13] That was no easy path to follow in the 1750s. England's and France's longstanding contest for imperial domination in North America was reaching its climax. Most Native communities from the Atlantic coast to the Mississippi River felt great pressure to line up on one side or the other and join the fight. Those who did so always had the interests of their own peoples principally in mind. So did Papunhank. But in contrast he, if not all his followers, managed to stay the peaceable course and as that imperial war (Seven Years) concluded and a new Indian war (Pontiac's) began in 1763, he joined the Moravians. Within another decade the colonies were poised for revolution, and Native Americans would prove to be among its greatest losers.

Few Indians suffered more than Papunhank's own community of Moravian converts. Falsely suspected by both sides of aiding their enemies, they eventually became victims of an American militia unit. In March 1782 roughly 160 soldiers gathered up more than ninety Native

Moravians at Gnadenhütten in the Ohio Country and, after giving them a night to say their prayers and sing their hymns, slaughtered them all. Benezet called it a "deliberate massacre" and denounced both it and those who sought to defend "the grievous transaction." Charges that these peaceable Indians, like all others, were treacherous and by implication appropriate targets for destruction, were false and failed to recognize that it was "not the colour of our skins, outward circumstances or profession, but the state and temper of the mind and will" that determined a people's identity and character. The whole tragedy illustrated the disturbing truth that more often than not, white injustices were responsible for the frontier violence that had plagued Pennsylvania and other colonies for a generation.[14] Papunhank was all too familiar with that reality and had long endeavored to keep his people from suffering its worst effects. The Gnadenhütten massacre demonstrated how difficult a task that was. Mercifully, Papunhank did not live long enough to witness the slaughter. Otherwise he likely would have been another of its victims, alongside his son-in-law, a grandson, two of his granddaughters (ages sixteen and fourteen), and a great-granddaughter (age seven) bludgeoned, scalped, and burned with the rest of their village.

In the 1780s Benezet's pamphlet, however passionate or well-reasoned, largely fell on deaf ears. It could do little to abate the new nation's surge to run over or push aside Indians of Papunhank's type or any other type. White Americans built their new republic upon the presumption that Indian dispossession would continue, and their Indian-hating was simply too powerful an impulse to be complicated by the likes of Christian pacifist Natives. It was far easier to assume that all Natives ultimately desired to kill whites, so it was going to be us or them in the fight to control the continent. Overall, American historical memory has suffered from the same blind spot, allowing little room for Indians who didn't "go on the war path." It has likewise allowed little room for "narrative histories of peace." We are far more accustomed to rehearsing stories of war. No great surprise, then, that Papunhank faded rather quickly from view, though it is likely his Munsee descendants kept his memory alive for at least a few generations after his death. In the late

1780s Moravian George Henry Loskiel gave the Munsee reformer considerable coverage in his history of Moravian missionary work among Native peoples. And once translated into English, portions became the basis for an evangelistic tract entitled *John Papunhank, A Christian Indian of North America. A Narrative of Facts*, published in Dublin, Ireland, in 1820.[15] Like numerous indigenous converts before him, his life and death were held up as proof of the transforming power of Jesus and as impetus for readers to choose Christian salvation. Thereafter, apart from brief mentions in denominational publications and local histories, Papunhank essentially disappeared.

So why resurrect him now? Why might his life be worth retelling? For one thing, several strands of recent scholarship have already begun to breathe new life into him. Studies of what has been called the "Indians' Great Awakening" have taken note of Papunhank as one of a wave of Indian religious reformers from the 1730s to the 1760s who drew on sacred sources of power to renew and protect their peoples. These Native visionaries, particularly in the mid-Atlantic region, inspired resistance efforts of various kinds against the onslaught of Anglo-American forces, or what is collectively called "colonialism."[16] Other studies have reexamined the resulting conflicts over land, liberty, and liquor and have briefly highlighted Papunhank's leadership in trying to orchestrate peaceful resolutions. They have introduced some of the ways he stood against the grain in war-torn Pennsylvania.[17] Moravian and Quaker scholars have likewise given some attention to the Munsee's role in the religiopolitical affairs of their subjects, including the warm relations he established with both sets of Christians during his final fifteen years (1760–75).[18] Yet no comprehensive effort has been made to reconstruct his life or take full account of his significance within early America. Nor do existing interpretations, however brief, adequately capture him. One scholar, for example, implies that Papunhank was an "accommodationist," a term that can imply a capitulation to European ways. The Munsee prophet was instead a sharp critic of much Euro-American practice even while engaging in a strategic and creative adoption of particular European beliefs, ideas, and actions. Another view posits that the heart of Papunhank's message was a call for "the restoration of a traditional economy grounded in communal sharing and modest utilization of native resources." But his economic plan was more a means than an end; it was designed to counter fraudulent practices, inhibit Indian greed, and promote economic justice, all for the sake of the larger goal of reducing the likelihood of violent conflict and maintaining peace. A third historian accurately portrays Papunhank's strong stance against the alcohol trade and other forms of "moral corruption." But here again those efforts must be situated more fully within his larger overriding concern for orchestrating peace.[19]

These studies have been helpful in drawing attention to Papunhank but haven't provided the robust treatment he deserves. At best, they have whetted our appetites to know more about this extraordinary character. Part of his intriguing story entails his choice to embrace Moravianism. Fortunately, broader work on the history of Native American Christianity has supplied new conceptions of how Indian persons appropriated that faith and made it their own. Interpretations have moved beyond earlier presumptions that Natives somehow gave up their Indian identities whenever they embraced Christianity.[20] Those insights on Native religious history are part of a larger renaissance of scholarship on Indians in early America that has flowered since the 1980s. Hundreds of articles and dozens of books have together altered not only how best to understand the Native experience but shown how crucial Indians were for virtually every aspect of life in sixteenth-, seventeenth-, and eighteenth-century America. Together they have largely fulfilled one historian's call to re-place Indians at the center of early American history.[21] That scholarship includes a growing number of biographical accounts of Native men and women.[22]

All that good work is to be applauded for it lays the groundwork for writing a life of Papunhank. Still, major holes in the literature remain. For example, interpreters of Indian prophets have been drawn overwhelmingly to reformers whose messages inspired and sometimes explicitly endorsed violent resistance to Anglo-American authority, the antithesis of what Papunhank proclaimed. As a pacifist and eventually a Moravian Christian, Papunhank has consequently escaped the level of sustained attention accorded men like Neolin (the Delaware Prophet) and Tenskwatawa (the Shawnee Prophet). Moreover, for all the gains made in conceptualizing Native religious experience, additional efforts are needed to narrate the lives of Christian Indians, including those who rejected warfare. There are no biographies, for instance, of any of the several thousand Native Americans who became Moravians in early America with the exception of Delaware leader Teedyuscung, and he left that fold after only a few years. Such a lacuna is indicative of the reality that early American biography remains overwhelmingly populated by the lives of white men. As two historians have recently put it, "biography has rarely favored the Indigene." Yet they also remind us that biography "through its emphasis on whole lives [can] help bring the historical moment of imperial encounter for Indigenous people down to more modest size."[23]

An even larger gap exists within the general American public's knowledge of Indians before 1820. When most of us think of Indians in early America, our minds usually go first to Squanto and Pocahontas. They became famous figures, but they were hardly representative of the lives of most Natives. So, too, with the Indian leaders we might remember, men like Metacom, Pontiac, and Tecumseh. They were important, but they were all war captains and have contributed to the impression in the popular mind that Indians everywhere and always were warlike. It turns out, however, that most Native peoples across the long span of early American history avoided war whenever they could. Instead, they more quietly pursued peaceful ways to cope with the new realities facing them after the Europeans' arrival.

There are of course many reasons why historians choose their subject matter. For generations, combinations of prejudice, lack of interest, and paucity of sources kept biographers from imagining, let alone executing, reconstructions of Indian lives. Today changes in racial attitudes and new methods of historical inquiry have brought studies of indigenous peoples into the forefront of early American histories. Yet enormous challenges remain for those interested in capturing the complexities and detail of any particular life. Papunhank's biography is no exception. As chapter 1 makes clear, the historical record is essentially silent on him for his first forty-five years. Educated guesswork and a wide-angle lens are necessary to place him within the broader world of Munsee peoples in New York, New Jersey, and Pennsylvania. Knowledge of their land deals, demographic trends, political alliances, and geographical migrations allows for a plausible situating of Papunhank into their rapidly changing and in most respects, increasingly distressed circumstances during the first half of the eighteenth century. Then once he appears in colonial documents, all of his words, thoughts, and actions are mediated to modern audiences through a range of Euro-American translators, transcribers, diarists, letter writers, and editors. Papunhank himself left no diary, sermons, speeches, letters, memoirs, or any other form of communication in his own hand. Able to speak several languages, he never learned how to write any of them. The only direct writing we have from him is his Munsee clan symbol (a turkey) on several documents (see figure 1—his name and symbol appear at the bottom right of the document). Given these realities for him and the vast majority of other Indians, numerous scholars have pointed out that discerning what is an "authentic" or faithful representation of Native American expression is very difficult, so difficult in fact that some believe it to be impossible. But that view seems too extreme in this case, for there are ways of judging what is more and less reliable in colonial sources purporting to contain Indian voices.[24] Getting behind or beyond the cultural misunderstandings, mistranslations, and private agendas of Papunhank's Euro-American interlocutors is tricky work and subject to imprecision and error. Along with filling in the gaps in the historical record on Papunhank, it results in a retelling of his life story often in terms of probabilities, possibilities, and likelihoods rather than absolute certainties. But such an incomplete account, if based on thorough research and detective work, seems better than no account at all.[25]

Most of what can be known about Papunhank comes from government documents—minutes of treaty conferences, letters to and from political and military officials, legislative proceedings, and diplomatic dispatches—and from religious sources, such as Quaker and Moravian letters, diaries, petitions, pamphlets, and meeting minutes. As might be expected, such materials offer particularly good bases for tracking

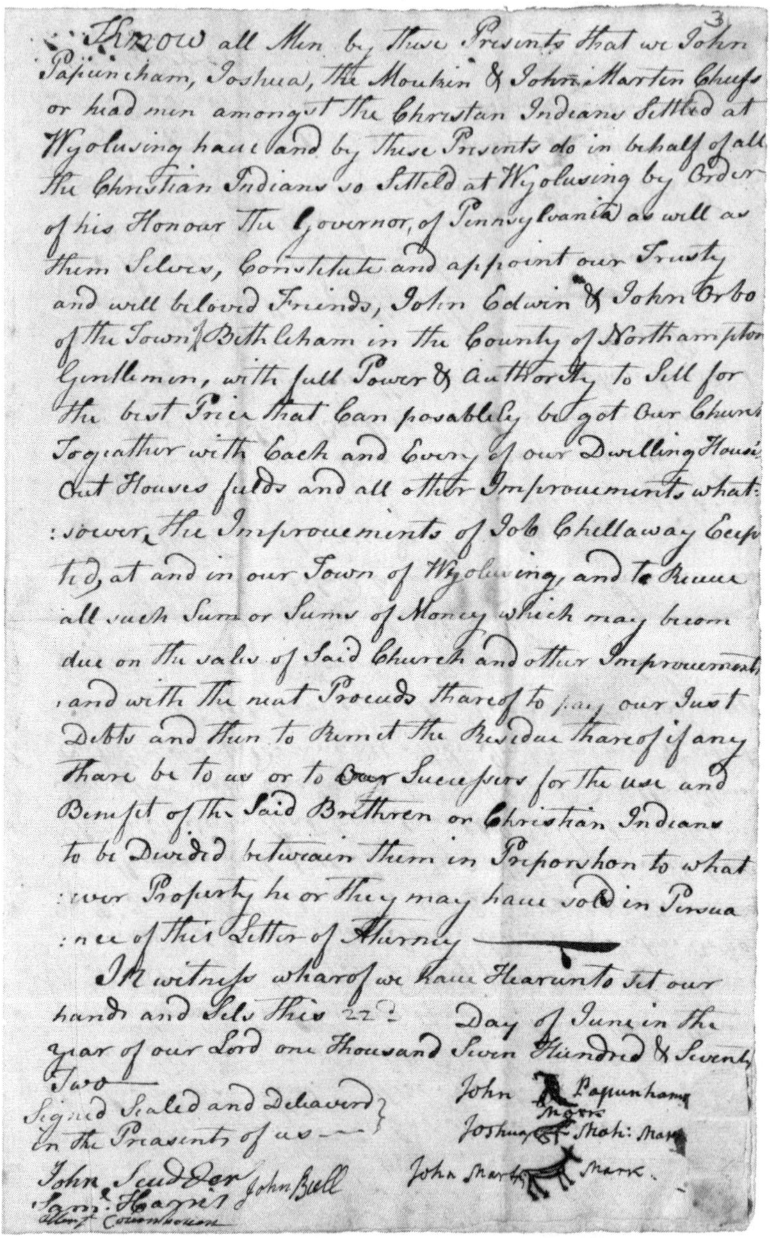

Know all Men by these Presents that we John Papunham, Joshua, the Moukin & John Martin Chiefs or head men amongst the Christan Indians Settled at Wyolusing have and by these Presents do in behalf of all the Christian Indians so Settled at Wyolusing by Order of his Honour the Governor of Pennsylvania as well as them Selves, Constitute and appoint our Trusty and well beloved Friends, John Edwin & John Arbo of the Town of Bethleham in the County of Northampton Gentlemen, with full Power & authority to Sell for the best Price that Can posablely be got our Church Togeather with Each and Every of our Dwelling Houses Out Houses fields and all other Improvements what:sower, the Improvements of Job Chellaway Excepted, at and in our Town of Wyolusing, and to Receive all such Sum or Sums of Money which may becom due on the sales of Said Church and other Improvements, and with the neat Proceeds thareof to pay our Just Debts and then to Remit the Residue thareof if any thare be to us or to our Successors for the use and Benefit of the Said Brethren or Christian Indians to be Divided betwean them in Proporshon to what:ever Property he or they may have sold in Pursua:nce of this Letter of Attorney

In witness wharof we have Hearunto Set our hands and Sels this 22d Day of June in the year of our Lord one Thousand Seven Hundred & Seventy Two

Signed Sealed and Delivered in the Prasents of us—

John Scudder
John Bull
Saml. Harris

John Papunhank mark
Joshua Shoh: mark
John Martin mark

Fig. 1. Power of attorney from Johannes Papunhank, Joshua (alias Nanhun and Tassawachamen), and John Martin to Johannes Ettwein and Johann Arbo, June 22, 1772. Moravian Archives, Bethlehem, Pennsylvania.

his political and diplomatic dealings as well as his religious thought and practice. But thanks to the Moravian disciplines of having their congregations keep daily diaries and their missionaries write frequent letters, there is also much rich information about the practical realities of Papunhank's life from 1764 to 1775. From them, for example, we learn not only of his piety but of his prowess as bear hunter and his frequent preference for being in the woods, on the move, rather than at home in his village. As rich as they are, these sources still leave us wishing for more—more about his personality, more about his interior spaces, much more about his earlier life. The type of full-bodied biography possible for better known or more recent historical figures is simply not feasible in Papunhank's case. Still, the available sources allow a portrait to be drawn that consists of more than a few impressionistic lines and shapes. The colors of his mind and personality, as well as the details of his political and religious maneuverings, at least for the final third of his life, can be filled in with reasonable confidence.

Regrettably, we cannot fill in what he looked like physically with any specificity. No artistic portrayals of Papunhank exist, at least none produced in his lifetime. Renditions of other area Natives give hints of his possible appearance, as do snippets of written description scattered throughout the archival record. In particular, Gustavus Hesselius's portrait of Delaware sachem Tishcohan from 1735 (figure 2) provides a starting point for conjuring an image of the Munsee reformer. The two men may have even known one another since both operated in the Forks of the Delaware region of northeastern Pennsylvania. Hesselius depicted Tishcohan as a strongly built man, apparently fully capable of doing demanding physical labor well into his later years. More telling yet is the artist's effort to capture the sachem's serious and wearied countenance, here deep in thought and unadorned by any paint or tattoos (according to Moravian missionary John Heckewelder, Tishcohan's name meant "he who never blackens himself"). All of that fits well as a description of Papunhank. He did the strenuous work of younger men right up until his death at age seventy, and once he became a Moravian Christian gave up wearing paint or other previous forms of adornment.[26] Like Tishcohan, he wore nothing to hide the naked truth of life's toil. His face, old and worn, would have shown the stresses and strains of fighting against the destructive effects of colonialism for many decades. Each wrinkle and line bespoke the toll that alcoholism, war, disease, displacement, and death took upon him and so many other Native persons.[27]

A century later (1862), Philadelphia painter Christian Schussele sought to capture the drama of Moravian missionary David Zeisberger's evangelism in the Pennsylvania interior (figure 3) in a portrait entitled *Zeisberger Preaching to the Indians* (also known as *The Power of the Gospel*). Schussele likely based his work on historical accounts of the action he sought to depict—Zeisberger's 1767 visit to Goschgoschunk, a multiethnic Indian town on the Allegheny River—and therefore knew to include Papunhank in the picture. He was one of two Native assistants who accompanied the missionary on the journey and played a crucial role in evangelizing Indians there. Most likely, Schussele depicted the two of them as seated on either side of Zeisberger. They listen with rapt attention and gaze upward into the light illuminating Zeisberger's face and hands. But there is no hint here that they too will speak, which they in fact did at length. Nor are there many clues for nineteenth-century viewers that Johannes and Anton are already Christian believers. At best, they are bit players or worse, stage props, partially hidden in the shadows, cast in a drama in which they can do no more than kneel at the feet of its star and sit at the edge of its action.[28]

Unfortunately, this comes close to capturing metaphorically where Papunhank remains within early American historical consciousness. This will not do. He is too important a figure to remain so obscure. His story is simply too interesting and dramatic not to be better known. Full of moments of spiritual awakening, violent conflict, political negotiation, moral condemnation, racial attack, wartime captivity, epidemic disease, witchcraft accusations, and overland journeys, Papunhank's life offers a rich window into the predicaments and perseverance of Indians in the mid-Atlantic region in the eighteenth century. They faced unprecedented pressures upon their lands and sovereignty as white settlers pushed westward, imperial rivalries intensified, and the racial divide widened.

Fig. 2. *Tishcohan* (1735) by Gustavus Hesselius (1682–1755). Oil on canvas. Philadelphia History Museum at the Atwater Kent. Courtesy of Historical Society of Philadelphia Collection, Bridgeman Images.

Fig. 3. *Zeisberger Preaching to the Indians* (1862) by Christian Schussele (1824–79). Oil on canvas. Moravian Archives, Bethlehem, Pennsylvania.

Under those conditions, most area Indians chose to engage in a series of "wars of independence" from British and then United States rule between the 1750s and the 1790s.[29] Papunhank likewise sought some measure of autonomy for the Native community gathered around him. But as an adamant opponent of war, and violence in general, he needed to devise alternative means for achieving those ends. Religious reform, geographic mobility, political neutrality, strategic alliances, diplomatic service, and an eventual embrace of Moravian Christianity all proved critical pieces in his quest to secure self-rule and peace for his people, and by extension, for other Natives and whites. At times, those efforts achieved their goals and yet ironically, their very achievement sometimes proved a source of their undoing. Throughout the middle decades of the eighteenth century, his labors repeatedly swam against a strong tide of opposition from most colonists and many other Indians, and in the end, could not prevent geographical removal and after his death, wholesale massacre. Still, he managed partial success, no mean accomplishment given the long odds he faced in the midst of the Seven Years' War, Pontiac's War, and persistent frontier violence in Pennsylvania and the Ohio Country. Papunhank's story therefore promises to broaden our view of Native responses to the crises of the mid-eighteenth century while also revealing the stuff of an ordinary Indian life—the daily rhythms of finding food, building shelter, trading goods, caring for the sick, loving a family, and practicing religion.

It also offers an opportunity to illuminate a different type of Native ideology. As noted above, for far too long, the American public has been inclined to embrace an image of most if not all Indians as "warlike." The usual presumption has been that all Native groups were predisposed to resort, sooner or later, to violent conflict to protect their lives and livelihoods. Tragically, in the long, painful history of Indian-white relations in America, the presence of Europeans and their weapons precipitated more violent and deadly warfare, and most indigenous peoples found it necessary to use force at various points to defend themselves or further their interests. Recent studies have made it clear that Pennsylvania Indians were no exception. After a generation or two of comparatively peaceful relations following the establishment of an English colony in the region in the early 1680s, Indian circumstances grew increasingly dismal. Mutual accommodations and common ground dissipated as white population and territorial growth, imperial rivalry, racism, economic fraud, land speculation, and intercolonial competition impinged on Native lands and sovereignty. Indian fortunes were so bleak that periodic resorts to war were seemingly inevitable.[30] And yet not all Indians chose that path. Largely overlooked in this prevailing narrative are Indian individuals and communities for whom "the way of war" was no way at all. Anthony Benezet tried to alert the new American nation to this Indian "peace tradition" in the 1780s but few would listen.[31]

Now, after more than two centuries, some early American historians are beginning to heed Benezet's call and take more careful notice of Indian peace advocates and peacemaking efforts. Collectively, they are helping us to see that "peace—what it meant, how it was created, how it was maintained—played a central role in shaping colonial and imperial relations in the Americas from the first era of European exploration and conquest through the 'age of revolutions' in the late eighteenth and early nineteenth centuries."[32] For example, studies of Ohio Indians in the 1740s, 1750s, and 1760s have highlighted the work of Tamaqua, headman of the Delaware peace faction. For two war-torn decades, he labored diligently to sow peace through shrewd negotiation and for a time enjoyed considerable influence.[33] He embodies a tradition of pragmatic pacifism practiced by other Indian leaders as they assessed what was best for their peoples. In the same era, Shabash, one of the first Mahican (Mohican) converts to Moravian Christianity, accepted an appointment as "war captain" for the mission Indians at Stockbridge, Massachusetts. In that role, Abraham (his baptized name) continued his longstanding endeavors to "preserve peace and keep his people out of war." For him "Moravian pacifism, coupled with the Moravian understanding of communion, offered a way out of warfare while presenting a spiritually compelling substitute for some of the traditional benefits of war."[34] A pacifism that began as a pragmatic policy for Abraham may therefore have developed into an ideological conviction.

Growing evidence suggests that Tamaqua and Abraham were not isolated instances of Indian peacemaking but were instead connected to a wider and longer set of Native ideas and actions aimed at cultivating peace and "right order."[35] Seventeenth-century lower–New York Indians used historical memory of a peaceful past to preserve their place on the land amid Dutch and English settlement. Hudson Valley Indians subtly resisted demands from the English and the Iroquois for military assistance through evasion and delays. The Iroquois themselves and other northeastern Native peoples employed elaborate condolence ceremonies as an essential means of conflict resolution that avoided retaliatory violence. Lenape and other Delaware Valley Indians orchestrated their own myths, gestures, alliances, and symbols to preserve social harmony. Further south and west, Chickasaw headman Payamataha turned his people away from war in the late 1750s and over the next two decades led them "in systematically making peace with a startling array of old enemies." Like Papunhank, "his exhortation to make peace was based on a spiritual calling to avoid war."[36] In these ways and others, large numbers of Natives fought against war. When war couldn't be prevented, they worked to keep their own people safe and out of the fighting. They also worked to find means to end the fighting, design a new-found peace, and maintain it by not allowing new instances of violence to escalate. For his part, Papunhank developed a distinctive principled pacifism that drew upon these indigenous streams of peace-craft and other sources, and became the driving force of his life and leadership. Few if any aspects of his final twenty-five years were not profoundly affected by it. Other Native Moravians were pacifists but none articulated that commitment so fully, so often, or so well. As he communicated his ideological pacifism in word and deed to Natives and whites, he voiced an important element of eighteenth-century Indian thought and represented a prime example of the Native peacemaking tradition. Reconstructing his story, then, provides a key opportunity to examine that tradition in a time and place of great testing. Like many of his Native contemporaries, Papunhank yearned for his people to enjoy enough independence to live, work, and worship where and as they pleased. Unlike most of them, he would not resort to armed conflict to gain those results and asserted a leadership committed to making peace the instrument of Native well-being. That was an uphill battle to say the least in an early America fraught with bloody violence and racial hatred. But that is all the more reason to give someone like Papunhank his due.

Finally, telling his story allows us to personalize the odyssey of mid-Atlantic Indians in the middle decades of the eighteenth century. In recent years a host of excellent studies have deepened understanding of the web of relationships among Native and European peoples in that region and others.[37] Earlier one-sided accounts have been replaced with nuanced treatments that capture more effectively the complex dynamics of Delaware, Susquehanna, and Ohio Valley histories. Each of them provides glimpses into particular Indian lives while rehearsing more sweeping developments. Fixing our eyes with a sustained gaze upon one Native man offers a different angle of vision with which to see this eighteenth-century world. It won't show us everything, but it may reveal some of what has been too long hidden or forgotten in the historical record and will surely show us that Johannes Papunhank is someone worth remembering.

In his magisterial life of colonial pastor and theologian Jonathan Edwards, historian George Marsden has suggested that the "first goal of a biographer . . . should be to tell a good story that illuminates not only the subject, but also the landscapes surrounding that person and the horizons of the readers."[38] Those words capture well my intent for this work. It is interesting to note that Edwards and Papunhank were born within two years of one another, possibly separated by less than a hundred miles. In most respects, their lives would take very different turns, in the one case leading to great renown, in the other virtual obscurity, the one marked by substantial privilege, the other by substantial want. Yet the two men shared a surprising amount in common. Both matured within volatile frontier environments, both experienced profound personal religious awakenings, both felt a strong divine call to preach, both were rejected by the communities they had long led, both crossed racial boundaries to form new communal bonds, both found ultimate meaning and peace in Jesus the Savior and Redeemer. Edwards's life has been told often and well. Now it is Papunhank's turn.

I

The Munsees' World

Papunhank was laid to rest on a spring day in May 1775 by his Moravian Indian brothers and sisters. Dozens of Munsees, Delawares, and Mahicans gathered to mark the going home of Brother Johannes, the Christian name given him at his baptism in 1763. Native men, women, and children slowly processed by Schönbrunn's buildings, passing Papunhank's log cabin (figure 4) on the left and their meeting house on the right. Then they turned north and solemnly walked the final two hundred yards to the small, grassy plot where they buried him alongside other baptized members of their Ohio Country community. There his remains resided with thirty or more Native sojourners, many of them children, deceased since Moravian Indians had established Schönbrunn three years earlier. God's Acre (figure 5), their cemetery, now had a senior statesman in its midst. His comparatively short-term illness and peaceful passing belied his long struggle to craft a more peaceful and stable world.[1]

As was the Moravian custom when one of their own passed, Papunhank's life was quickly inscribed on paper. Veteran German missionary David Zeisberger wasted little time in penning Papunhank's *lebenslauf* (life story). Within hours, or at most, days, of his long-time Native associate's death, Zeisberger wrote into the Schönbrunn congregational diary for May 16 (the day of the burial) a roughly five-hundred-word biography. It began with the Munsee headman's Christian baptism, administered by Zeisberger himself twelve years earlier, and

Fig. 4. (*top*) Papunhank's cabin at Schönbrunn, Ohio. Photo by author.

Fig. 5. (*bottom*) "God's Acre" burial ground at Schönbrunn, Ohio. Photo by author.

then described him as a man who "served the congregation and the Brothers faithfully according to his abilities." Most of the missionary's remembrances focused on Papunhank's state of heart and mind only since his arrival in Ohio in 1772. Fresh among his memories of Papunhank was what he had just witnessed from the Indian brethren. So he closed the *lebenslauf* confidently with the claim that Johannes "died with the blessing of the congregation, at about 70 years old."[2]

Zeisberger shared something about Papunhank's ending but nothing about his beginning. For him, the Indian's *Christian* beginning at baptism was the only beginning worth mentioning. Everything prior to it was veiled in the mists of a foggy Native American past. More than two centuries later, historians are still more or less in the same boat, at least when it comes to the specific details of his early years. In fact, reconstructing Papunhank's world for the first half or even two-thirds of his life requires painting with broad and rather impressionistic strokes. There is simply too much silence in the historical record to portray him with any finitude. Still, the wider story of the Munsee peoples provides an appropriate canvas upon which to work. His story may be fit within the broader contours of their history, a history wrought with instability and declining fortunes.

Munsee Challenges

The missionary's final three words about Johannes, "*etwa 70 Jahr*," provide a place to start. At threescore and ten years in 1775, Papunhank had lived longer than most Munsees of his generation, but it had not been easy. He had long been showing the wearying effects of a difficult life. Struggles with alcohol, numerous migrations, disruptive wars, economic want, epidemic diseases, and painful community divisions—all layered on top of the constant physical and mental challenges of living as a Native on the eighteenth-century mid-Atlantic frontier—weathered the Munsee. On numerous occasions in the 1750s and 1760s, friends and strangers described him as "the old man."[3] He resorted to a similar description of himself in 1760 when he declined an offer to be part of an arduous diplomatic mission to the west. "I am weak & Poor & cannot go," he claimed.[4] Yet throughout his last fifteen years of life, he was very much a man on the move. He traveled thousands of miles, most of it on foot and much of it through difficult terrain; he regularly hunted bear and other large game; and he cleared land and built houses. Papunhank may have looked worn out but he had the body of a bull and a tenacious spirit to match. Zeisberger's estimate of seventy years for Johannes's life therefore seems a reasonable approximation if descriptions of his physical appearance are balanced with what is known of his actions, and the likelihood that at some point in their twelve-year relationship, the Native actually told the missionary his own sense of his age.

If born, then, around 1705, Papunhank essentially lived through the entire span of the first three quarters of the eighteenth century. Doing so in early America was to have experienced monumental change regardless of whomever and wherever one was. Native Americans, Africans, and Europeans all saw their worlds turned upside down more than once. Few developments mattered more than the rapid population growth of Britain's mainland colonies. Natural increase and immigration, both voluntary and forced, was doubling the size of the non-Indian population every twenty to twenty-five years. There were simply many more people on the colonial American landscape by the time Papunhank died than when he was born. And those people needed, or at least wanted land—land to live on, land to work, land to call their own, land to give them status and wealth. This was no new story in the eighteenth century. Ever since the earliest colonial settlements were established up and down the Atlantic seacoast in the first half of the seventeenth century, newcomers had continuously set their sights on acquiring more land through one means or another. Fueled by personal needs and desires and the imperial designs of various competing European powers, colonial territorial expansion invariably complicated relations with Native communities. The results were not always violent; complex relationships between Indian peoples and Euro-Americans constantly evolved and contained elements of cooperation, negotiation, exchange, borrowing, alliance, and mutual dependence. But they typically also included moments of tension, antagonism, and outright conflict. And in the end, in most cases, sooner or later Euro-

Americans got what they wanted. They spread themselves farther and farther into the American interior, placing ever greater strains on the Indian peoples they encountered and often displaced.[5]

Native Americans were no mere bystanders or helpless victims in how that story unfolded. They usually looked upon the colonial presence as both opportunity and challenge. On the bright side, new chances for trade could give their communities access to goods that might enrich their lives physically and metaphysically or enhance their position vis-à-vis Indian neighbors or rivals. Land sales to settlers or governmental bodies might bolster their economies, afford them some legal protections, and satisfy the land-hungry colonists long enough to give Indian communities some relief. Carefully constructed diplomatic connections with one or more European powers could afford them new advantages in their existing political and economic relationships with other Native peoples. Even the strange religious ideas and practices of the newcomers might offer them additional spiritual resources to cope with their rapidly changing worlds. On the other hand, there were good reasons to be cautious. Christianity could draw them away from their ancient ways and cause division in their ranks. Trade with whites was risky because it could make them too dependent on what the Euro-Americans could supply, and some of those items, such as firearms and liquor, were at best mixed blessings. Moreover, white traders regularly proved to be unscrupulous. Somebody often ended up dead as a result, events which usually precipitated wider violence. Selling land almost always meant having to move or at least having less access to traditional hunting, fishing, and foraging grounds. And agreements crafted with the Dutch, French, or English had a way of meaning something different after the Europeans wrote them down from when the treaty words had been spoken.[6]

All these patterns played out in the history of Papunhank's people, the Munsees. On the eve of contact with Europeans in the sixteenth century, the homeland of his ancestors encompassed "the westernmost reaches of Long Island Sound and present-day Connecticut, extended across New York Harbor and its adjoining hinterland, and reached over the Hudson Highlands and through the Great Valley of southeastern New York and northern New Jersey to northeastern Pennsylvania's Pocono Plateau and Lehigh Valley."[7] Less well known than their Mohawk and Mahican neighbors to the north and their Lenape or Delaware neighbors to the south, the Munsees only acquired that name in the 1720s. It came from the language they spoke, Munsee, a dialect of the Eastern Algonquian language known as Delaware. Other Delaware dialects were spoken in southeastern Pennsylvania and northern Delaware (Unami) and in southern New Jersey (Unalachtigo). Prior to the eighteenth century, the Munsees were referred to by more regional or localized labels such as the Manhattans, Massapequas, Esopus, Wappingers, and Minisinks. Whatever their name, these peoples typically lived in small settlements linked together through kinship networks. They situated their villages in advantageous locales, often along rivers and creeks or on islands such as Minisink in the upper Delaware River or Manhattan in the lower end of the Hudson. There they planted fields of corn, beans, and squash, foraged for herbs and berries, and hunted forests well-stocked with game. Like other Native communities situated in the woodlands near the Atlantic Ocean, they augmented their food supply through seasonal migrations. Each spring they moved nearer the coast to gather clams and other shellfish and to find the marine shells that could be used to manufacture wampum, the strings of highly valued beads that were used as a means of exchange.[8]

In the seventeenth century the Munsees were arguably the most important Native group with whom the Dutch interacted in New Netherland, and the people who felt the Dutch presence most acutely. A set of evolving exchanges characterized Dutch-Munsee relations from the time of the latter's first contacts with explorers in the 1500s through eras of trade, settlement, and warfare in the decades between 1610 and 1664. Over time, the Munsees faced a worsening crisis as the Dutch increasingly expanded into their geographical and cultural space. With each successive stage of Dutch intrusion—initial contacts, trade, and settlement—the Munsees' challenges mounted. Like Natives elsewhere, their responses varied across a spectrum of resistance, accommodation, and acculturation. Relations with the Europeans turned far more violent in the early 1640s when there was a "shift in Dutch colonial practice from a focus upon trade to a focus upon intense European settlement." The First Dutch-Munsee War began a process in which most of this Native group came to accept the military and political sovereignty of the Dutch and to accommodate themselves, at least partially, to the Europeans' economy and culture. More resistant Natives participated in Second and Third Dutch-Munsee Wars. By the end of the Dutch era (1664), much of the Munsees' exterior world had been substantially altered. They had deeded over to colonists about 10 percent of their lands, including their most valuable saltwater territories. More important, the toxic combination of European diseases and deadly warfare with both the Dutch and other Natives had reduced the Munsee population from roughly fifteen thousand at the beginning of the century to less than three thousand. Munsees could no longer be found on Manhattan and Staten Islands, and all of their settlements, but especially those closest to the Dutch presence, had been reduced in size. Still, among many of the Munsees, their interior worlds showed more continuity than change. Many of them held on to traditional belief and value systems and retained the ways of life to which they were long accustomed.[9]

Such cultural sustenance became more difficult with the English takeover of New Netherland in the 1660s and their establishment of the new colonies of East and West Jersey and Pennsylvania in the 1670s. Holding on to Munsee lands—and life itself—also became harder. By the first decade of the eighteenth century, sales of additional territory during the prior forty years had cumulatively divested Munsees of huge tracts of land northward along both sides of the Hudson River, westward as far as the Catskill and Kittatinny mountain ranges, and southward along the west bank of the Delaware River. As a result, more and more of them moved farther inland to areas where it was tougher to sustain themselves.[10]

Throughout the seventeenth century, Munsee headmen employed a variety of strategies to mitigate the effects of an increasingly *settler* colonialism. Few leaders proved more resourceful than Tackapousha, a Massapequa sachem on western Long Island. He likely inherited his position from his father and his father's cousin in the 1640s and eventually passed it on to his own sons, who carried it into the eighteenth century. For at least fifty years Tackapousha used kinship ties and marriage to build an impressive power base from which to navigate relations with Europeans and other Indians. But family connections alone do not explain his prominence. His authority instead depended largely on his diplomatic skills. "Mediation was a highly visible feature of intergroup relations" among Munsees and neighboring Indians, and Tackapousha proved remarkably adept at it. In May 1645 he was the principal peace negotiator for all Long Island Indians with the Dutch at the conclusion of Kieft's War; three months later he did the same for Hudson Valley Natives who had been reluctant to end the long three-year conflict. Thereafter he finessed his people's relationship with the Dutch, acknowledging their need for protection from outside attack but stopping short of handing sovereignty over to the Europeans. When some Natives resumed war with the Dutch in 1655 (the so-called Peach War), he critiqued them and promised not to break the peace as long as the Dutch held up their end of the bargain. Forging tactical alliances carried on into the English period but became joined to other approaches. When settlers grabbed more and more land, Tackapousha resorted to filing legal complaints in English courts in the 1670s and 1680s and even made direct complaints to the colonial governor. He and other sachems also made strategic land sales, sometimes intentionally selling overlapping tracts to rival colonial interests who they hoped would get bogged down in legal disputes that delayed their occupation of the land and left the Munsees with some sliver of hope that a reversal of fortune would one day come.[11]

Unfortunately, that was not to be. Munsees had many motives for negotiating land deals but none more painful than needing the money to pay for funeral goods. Like other Native peoples, they buried their kin with appropriate items for the next life. When a fifteen-year lull in the ravaging effects of smallpox ended in 1679 and whole new waves of community members succumbed, they had to turn some of their real estate earnings toward those costs. Largely due to disease, Munsee numbers dwindled to about thirteen hundred or less by the turn of the century, a small force compared to what they had been just a hundred years earlier and to the more than fifty thousand colonists who now populated the Middle Colonies.[12]

Munsee demographic losses were much more than a matter of numbers. They thinned the ranks of leaders, laborers, warriors, and healers, and left their communities far more susceptible to the forces of European colonialism. For example, fewer skilled artisans in their villages dictated that the Munsees had to rely increasingly upon the manufactured goods supplied by white traders. It did not take long for a debilitating Native dependence to develop. In exchange for what they wanted and needed from settlers, Munsees gave up more and more of their primary asset, their land. Land sales temporarily eased the Indians' need for capital with which to purchase European items. But with each new property cession, they had fewer tracts to offer and were forced to live on less productive lands. That in turn meant that their need for European stuffs only grew greater. And so the cycle spun.[13]

As the eighteenth century began, then, Munsee sachems had their hands full. Within a short period, their communities had become "smaller, scattered, and increasingly isolated."[14] What is more, they operated within a broader political, military, and diplomatic environment usually fraught with danger. King William's War raged between French and English forces from 1689 to 1697. Each side enlisted powerful Native allies including rival factions from within the Five Nations of the Iroquois. Most Munsees lived within the shadow of Iroquois authority during the late seventeenth century. Like other Native peoples living in the vicinity of the Mohawk and Hudson Rivers, the Munsees were considered a "lesser link" in the Covenant Chain that from the English point of view, bound the Iroquois to them. That alliance or set of diplomatic understandings and procedures had been solidified in the 1670s as a means of normalizing relations between the English colonial governments and the Five Nations. With their position more secure and their confidence bolstered, Iroquois leaders looked upon Munsees and other area Native groups as tributaries and felt empowered to act on their behalf in both war and peace, though they often left them alone to manage their internal affairs. The Iroquois also felt emboldened to claim hegemony over wider territories and peoples, including lands in Pennsylvania's Susquehanna Valley that in the future would become central to the Munsees' and Papunhank's story. In the imperial violence of the 1690s, Munsees, given their modest size, generally managed to keep their warriors at home and their people out of the fray. Survival called forth a pragmatic pacifism in this instance. Nevertheless, the decade's persistent warfare only made their situation more tenuous. A wider peace came in 1701 when Five Nations diplomats negotiated treaties in Montreal and Albany that established Iroquois neutrality between the English and French colonial empires. Munsees surely welcomed that news even though they received no direct consideration in the agreements. They may have actually preferred it that way, however, since they were now long accustomed to dealing directly with European or colonial officials and likely wished to continue exercising that freedom as much as possible.[15]

During the relative calm that prevailed in the next decade, Munsees exercised another type of freedom: they dispersed ever more widely across their homeland. Minisink and its surrounding territory lying just west of the Kittatinny Mountains in northwestern New Jersey hosted the biggest concentration of their people. Perhaps as many as four hundred Munsees were congregated there, as refugees merged with already resident Minisinks. Cochecton was another sizeable Munsee town situated north of Minisink on the upper Delaware River. Other Munsee communities of one hundred to two hundred persons were located in central Long Island, the Berkshire Mountains east of Albany, the Fishkill and Esopus areas in the Hudson Valley, and central New Jersey. Small numbers of Munsees chose to leave their homeland altogether and migrated to other Native communities in as faraway places as Maine and Michigan. Meanwhile, beginning in the 1690s, as many as three hundred Shawnees moved into Munsee territory above the Delaware Water Gap at Pechoquealing in northeastern Pennsylvania. Soon after, Tuscarora refugees from North Carolina began streaming into Pennsylvania and New York fresh from their warfare with colonists and an assortment of southeastern Indian tribes.[16] Most of them eventually settled along the Susquehanna River on Munsee lands.[17]

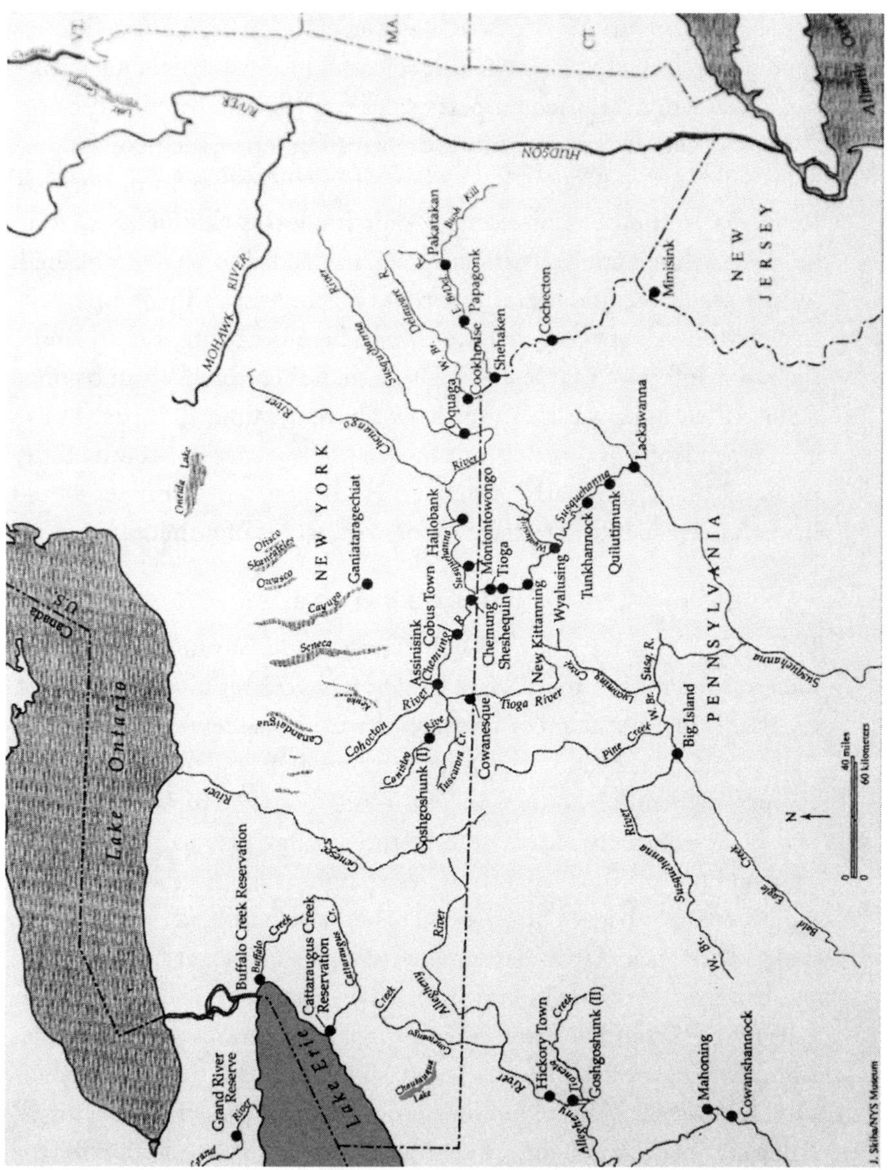

Fig. 6. A map of eighteenth-century Munsee towns in Pennsylvania and New York, drawn by John Skiba. Courtesy of New York State Museum.

Amid these various migrations in the early 1700s, Munsee leaders generally managed to keep their peoples out of the limelight and crossfire. Even while Munsee property sales went on unabated and Euro-American settlers streamed into their former lands, sachems focused primarily on solidifying their communities whether in old or new locations. In the wake of recent population losses, families needed to be reconstituted and subsistence patterns needed to be reestablished. Wider security could seemingly best be achieved by living unobtrusively. Munsees of this generation were therefore content to fly under the radar and took a far less active role than their forebears in colonial affairs. Their hope was that they would have the time and space to live as independently as possible. But those were two precious commodities in an ever-evolving early American landscape, and Munsees would have to keep adapting to have modest measures of either.[18]

Papunhank's Arrival

Papunhank was born into this Munsee world of rapid change and uncertainty. Yet his arrival date of 1705 was comparatively fortuitous. By that point his chances of survival were considerably better than they would have been twenty years earlier when epidemic disease was rampaging through Native villages. Young boys and girls in the 1680s had been especially susceptible to the scourge of smallpox because they had not yet built up antibodies to fight it off. By the early eighteenth century, battles of other sorts had also subsided. The Iroquois had secured their "Great Settlement" with the French at Montreal and the English at Albany in 1701. That same year, further south in Pennsylvania, William Penn and representatives of various Indian peoples from the lower Susquehanna Valley signed a treaty that set intercultural relations in that region on a comparatively peaceful trajectory.[19] All things considered, then, Papunhank arrived in a world that for the time being was quieter and calmer than it had been.

But where Papunhank entered that world and to whom largely remain mysteries. One proposal is that Papunhank was the son of important Munsee sachem Dostou and her husband Harman Hekan.[20] They lived in Esopus country, lands lying just west of the Hudson

River and a bit south of present-day Kingston, New York, about one hundred miles north of Manhattan. Esopus Indians (one of the many groups of local Natives that came collectively to be called Munsees) had enjoyed relative isolation from European colonization until the 1650s. Then Dutch settlers began moving into their fertile territory, some on land purchased from Hekan himself. Dutch-Esopus relations worsened by the end of the decade and war ensued in 1659–60 (the Third Dutch-Munsee War). Its causes were a set of conditions that would be all too familiar to Papunhank a century later: Dutch traders illegally sold liquor to the Esopus or paid Indian laborers in brandy. Native use and abuse of alcohol sooner or later precipitated violent and often deadly encounters with settlers. Arguments also arose over land deals, land use, stolen crops, fraudulent trading practices, and hostile threats of attack. Esopus sachems signed a peace treaty with the Dutch in 1660, but warfare resumed three years later. When the fighting finally stopped in 1664, the Dutch were in a position to impose stricter terms on the Esopus, including forced land cessions and limits on trade.[21]

Dostou's mother, Mamanuchqua (or Mamaruchqua), was among those Esopus leaders needing to adjust to the enlarged European presence. She was likely one of the women who, along with a group of young men, pressured Esopus war captains to make peace with the Dutch in 1664. From 1675 to 1682 her name appears alongside other sachems on land deeds and other colonial documents. Such evidence suggests that however wide and deep the impact of European colonialism, Munsees persisted in affording some of their women key leadership responsibilities.[22] In her case that meant being among the decision makers who determined that the Esopus would be enhanced through land sales. Dostou continued that tradition. From at least the 1690s until the early 1720s, she was active in Esopus land transactions. So, too, were two of her sons, Maringoman and Hendrick Hekan. They played critical roles in the late seventeenth and early eighteenth centuries in selling to the English major portions of Munsee lands farther south in what has become Orange County, New York, and an elderly Hekan was still the principal signatory on two land sales in 1746. He likely lived at Papagonk, one of the two main Esopus settlements on the East Branch of the Delaware River in western Ulster County, New York (see figure 6). From there, Esopus Indians had frequent contact with Munsees at Cochecton and Minisink.[23]

By the early 1700s those two possible elder siblings of Papunhank would likely have been in their twenties or older. One of them may in fact have been the baby English traveler Charles Wolley heard about during his travels in New York in 1679. Wolley marveled at Dostou's seeming ease in delivery, no doubt mistaking her composure for a lack of pain. Eastern Woodland Indian women were expected to endure the pangs of childbirth in stoic-like fashion. Dostou apparently perfectly fulfilled that expectation, another indication of Munsee cultural persistence and perhaps a sign as well of a determined character. The latter may help to explain why she was willing and able to give birth again as late as twenty-six years later.[24]

These fragmentary glimpses of Dostou suggest that she held her own alongside husband Harman Hekan. That was no small accomplishment given his stature. Like other Esopus leaders, he sold lands to the Dutch and English on numerous occasions. But he also bought land from the colonists, the first Esopus Indian to do so, and he figured prominently in Munsee contacts with colonial officials over a long span of years stretching from the 1650s to the 1720s. No wonder he became well known among settlers. They called him by a nickname, Ankerop, and became accustomed to doing business with him. For his part, Hekan proved willing to meet the Europeans more than half way. In the 1670s, after purchasing two twenty-acre lots, he became the first Indian in the region to agree in writing to "pay all village taxes and obey the laws, and to behave as well as any Christian man."[25]

If all these men and women were indeed Papunhank's kin, he belonged to an especially powerful Munsee lineage. Within Esopus country, no other family shows up as prominently in the historical records of the late seventeenth and early eighteenth centuries. Leading families within Munsee society often used marriage as a means to enhance or maintain their authority. For that reason, it is likely that Harman Hekan, like Dostou, came from a well-positioned line.

Munsee sachems were typically "drawn from particular families and lineages . . . with proven track records for leadership." In other words, for Munsees heredity and ability both mattered in determining who would lead them in the next generation. Papunhank's kin apparently had both going for them. Since children within Munsee society belonged "to their mother's lineage and would inherit the rights and privileges of their mother's brothers," it is noteworthy, too, that several of Dostou's brothers were also prominent figures among Esopus Indians. Surrounded by such a network of influential kin, Papunhank almost certainly grew up expecting to assume a leadership role within his community. And correspondingly, his community likely presumed that the young Papunhank would someday take his place among its sachems.[26]

Since Papunhank eventually became a Munsee leader, it tempting to presume that the foregoing genealogy for him is accurate. Moreover, the family tree it draws points to some intriguing connections among future generations. For example, one of Mamanuchqua's other daughters, Manhigh or Manhat, purportedly had a son, Shabash, who, as mentioned in the introduction, became one of the first Mahican Indians to be baptized (renamed Abraham) by the Moravians in 1742 in Shekomeko, New York. He was actively involved in disputes over Mahican lands with local whites from the 1720s through the 1740s. Another supposed son, Tataemshatt, had a great-grandson, Joshua, who was born in 1740 and married Sophia in 1764. She happened to be Papunhank's daughter. Their union would have brought two lines of Mamanuchqua's descendants—one Mahican and one Munsee—back together.[27]

As fascinating and appealing as all this is, other evidence casts doubt on the plausibility of this proposal regarding Papunhank's parentage. As already noted, the likely ages of Dostou's other children would require her to have been unusually old when bearing Papunhank. Even trickier is the chronology for Harman Hekan. If he was selling a land tract as early as 1652, it seems unlikely that he was still fathering children in 1705. More telling is the fact that Papunhank related in 1760 the story of his father's death and implied that it occurred in the not too distant past, perhaps in the late 1740s or 1750. That event led him to begin preaching and gathering a set of followers around 1752. A death that late would seem to preclude it from being the passing of Harman Hekan. Moreover, he stopped appearing in European records around 1715 or 1720. In addition, Papunhank unexpectedly met a sister of his father's when he moved to the Ohio Country in 1772. Though he described her as very elderly, she almost certainly could not have been of the same generation as Harman Hekan. All this makes it problematic to claim Hekan as Papunhank's father.[28]

From a pure chronology standpoint, the math works out better if we instead imagine Papunhank as Hekan and Dostou's grandson. Evidence suggests that those two had offspring in the 1660s and 1670s. One of those children could easily have had a son in 1705, die or have a spouse die in 1750, and have a very old sister or sister-in-law still living in 1772. Could he for example have been a son of Hendrick Hekan, who was still alive in 1746 but elderly enough to likely pass away within the next few years? From his location in western Ulster County, with its close contacts with Munsee towns in northwestern New Jersey, Hekan's offspring could have easily migrated into those regions and later moved westward into Pennsylvania where Papunhank would eventually appear.

Unfortunately, however plausible that proposal might be, no other evidence has been found to confirm Papunhank's link to Hekan and Dostou's line. Still, that alone does not rule out the possibility. Nor does it mean that he did not spend his early years in Esopus country or possibly remain there into midlife. Papunhank has been associated with five land sales made by Esopus Indians in that region from 1745 to 1750. Based on Native naming practices, the claim has been made that individuals listed on the land deeds as Teweghtemap, Tamacapawain, Tewightemon, and Tewightamon were all in fact Papunhank. Natives often used nicknames and aliases since their given names were thought to have special spiritual significance. Hence, "differently spelled but broadly similar names not appearing in two places in the same document or in different documents signed in different places at the same time can be provisionally assigned to single individuals."[29]

Apparently employing that method and one government document from 1761 that lists Papunhank's alias as Toughachena, he has been linked with these earlier transactions.[30] Papunhank has also been described as a "Moravian convert" of the early 1740s at Shekomeko, the Moravian mission east of the Hudson in present-day Dutchess County. Most of the Natives in Shekomeko were Mahicans, but there were some Esopus Indians there as well. Yet it seems highly unlikely that Papunhank was among them in light of his absence in Moravian records from that time and place and his later extensive interactions with the United Brethren, which never make any reference to earlier, formal associations.[31]

So a good deal of uncertainty remains about Papunhank's parentage and locale. If he originated or grew to adulthood somewhere outside Esopus country, the odds are it was in Minisink in northwestern New Jersey. As noted earlier, by the early 1700s, more refugee Munsees had congregated in that area than anywhere else. They merged with resident Minisinks and over time, lost their earlier, more localized identities.[32] Larger numbers of people, among other things, created a need for more sachems in Minisink. Papunhank's later rise to supreme leadership in a mixed community of Munsees, Delawares, and other mid-Atlantic Indians was built upon his dramatic spiritual experiences, impressive speaking ability, and powerful prophetic message. But given traditional Munsee means of choosing leaders, it was also likely built upon his personal know-how and family connections. The skills he exhibited as a leader suggest that he and other members of his family had served as sachems. He knew diplomatic protocols, was comfortable interacting with Euro-American traders and missionaries, and garnered respect for both his political and religious authority from persons inside and outside his following. All that bespoke someone familiar, or even long familiar, with exercising power. With its growing population, a likely place for that to have begun was Minisink.

Papunhank's later movements also square well with a possible Minisink beginning. As will be discussed in greater detail below, the geographical world the adult Papunhank knew best was northeastern Pennsylvania and more specifically the Susquehanna River Valley. In the mid-1720s a good portion of the Munsees at Minisink moved into that region and settled where the Lackawanna Creek flowed into the North Branch of the Susquehanna, just north of present-day Pittston. Papunhank could have been among those migrants who established or populated two villages, Adjouquay and Asserughne (also known as Lechaweke, or collectively as Lackawanna). Another possibility is that he was among other Munsee refugees from New York and New Jersey who gathered somewhat farther east at the village of Cochecton on the upper Delaware River by the 1730s or 1740s. Pathways made regular contact between these Munsee villages comparatively straightforward, so it is conceivable that Papunhank spent time in all of them. From the new Munsee settlements by the Lackawanna, for example, a major Indian path headed north all the way into southern New York. Smaller footpaths headed off of it to the east to both Minisink and Cochecton. It is easy to envision Papunhank traversing these trails as a young adult. We know that he was still in their vicinity in the early 1750s when he began preaching.[33]

Munsee Manhood

Wherever Papunhank spent his youth, he imbibed the lessons of what it meant to be a Munsee man. Like other northeastern Algonquian peoples, the Munsees reared their children along highly gendered lines. The worlds of men and women intersected but were clearly distinct. From early childhood boys and girls began to be socialized into male and female adult roles, respectively. When he was as young as four or five, Papunhank would have been given his first schooling in hunting, one of the primary responsibilities of Munsee men. He and other boys would have been taught to use bows and arrows and introduced to "war games" to begin to know what it meant to be a warrior. Throughout his youth, he would have been told to listen to seasoned hunters to gain wisdom and insight from their years of experience. And as he grew older, alongside such oral instruction, he would have been taken into the woods more frequently and progressively given more responsibility for the hunt.[34] According to later Moravian missionaries, a Native boy's first large kill (typically a deer or a bear) was an important rite of passage. It occasioned reverential community celebration in what was known as the "first fruits ceremony." The youth would be praised for having "listened attentively to the aged hunters" and given "proof that he will become a good hunter himself." The kill was presented to the village's oldest man and woman and a feast followed in which the meat was offered as a sacrifice to Native deities. The ceremony bestowed a new name on the boy to mark his coming of age and included prayers for him and admonitions that he would learn the wisdom his elders had to offer. This day and ritual were then celebrated each year of the boy's life so that he would be successful in the hunt.[35]

The male journey from youth to adulthood also included a vision quest. Around puberty, Papunhank would have been sent off by himself into the forest for several days of solitude and fasting. He might also have been given powerful potions to consume. The hope was that the combination of isolation, little food, and strong drink would elicit visions or trances in which the youth would encounter a spiritual guardian or manitou who would provide guidance and protection for the rest of his life. The manitou might also inform him of his life's "calling" or work. For many Native men it was to become a warrior, but others were to be "physicians, sorcerers . . . or devoted to some other civil employment." Overall, the vision quest was intended to link a young man more profoundly to the spirit world and was no childish game. Boys who left villages came back as men, aware as never before of how the natural and the supernatural were one. Some of those boys, including Papunhank, would find reasons to repeat the quest later in life as mature men.[36]

By late adolescence Munsee males moved fully into the work tasks and rhythms assigned to their sex. While women were to grow vegetables and gather other foodstuffs such as berries, nuts, and fruits, men were to supply meat and fish. Fulfilling those male duties meant regularly being away from villages. Seasonal patterns of coming and going became well engrained as one year flowed into the next. For Indians living within the Hudson, Delaware, and Susquehanna Valleys, the most important hunt came in the late fall and early winter on the heels of the corn harvest. From October or early November through sometime in January, Papunhank and other able-bodied men of Native communities would spend six or more weeks at a time in the woods, wandering far from their homes. Sometimes women and even children went with them to aid in the work. Winter snows made it easier to track game needed for both food and clothing. Bear, deer, foxes, fowl of various sorts, and other small game provided meat to eat and pelts to wear. More localized hunting would continue throughout the winter. In February or more often March, both men and women headed into the forest to collect sap from maple trees. Temporary camps were set up for several weeks each spring to boil down maple sugar and syrup. Spring was also the best time for fishing. As temperatures warmed, hunters were away again during portions of June and July while women did the arduous tasks associated with producing the year's crop. Before long it was harvest time again and the cycle began anew.[37]

Hunting kept Munsee men on the move as did their responsibilities to engage in trade, diplomacy, and warfare. Absences of a few or many weeks could ensue while goods were exchanged, treaties held, or raids perpetrated. Munsee Indians were not nomadic, but their lifestyles, and especially those of their men, could be peripatetic. Papunhank's near-constant travel during the last fifteen years of his life bears testament to this pattern. There is no reason to think that his earlier adult years had been any different.

Expanding Whites and Iroquois Uncles

Almost anywhere Munsees went in the quarter century from 1725 to 1750, they were bound to run into increasing numbers of whites. Or to put it more accurately, whites were running into (and over) them and their lands. The Euro-American presence in the mid-Atlantic colonies grew thicker and thicker, and Native peoples had to adjust accordingly. In most instances that meant having to move. In Pennsylvania, Unami-speaking Delawares in the vicinity around Philadelphia and then in the upper Schuylkill and Brandywine river basins had been displaced by the early 1700s to the lower Susquehanna Valley. But they weren't there very long. By the 1710s and 1720s waves of Ulster and German settlers forced them to move farther up the Susquehanna River to places such as the burgeoning Indian town of Shamokin. It served as a major crossroads of intercultural activity until abandoned in the early stages of the Seven Years' War in the mid-1750s.[38] Other Delawares in New Jersey and in the Lehigh Valley similarly had to migrate due to white squatters and illegal land settlements. They came westward to the North Branch of the Susquehanna and settled around Wyoming. As noted earlier, Munsees from Minisink moved to that area as well, forming their own villages about ten miles north at Lackawanna Creek in the late 1720s. On the southern side of Wyoming, Nanticokes, an Indian people originally from Maryland, took up residence in 1748 and remained there until 1753.[39]

With the upper Susquehanna Valley filling in, some Delawares and Shawnees took the more dramatic step of leaving eastern Pennsylvania altogether between the 1720s and the 1740s and started over in villages along the Allegheny River in western Pennsylvania. Before long, some of them went farther west into the Ohio Valley. They were joined in both places by southwestward-moving Iroquois, mostly Senecas, from western New York. Members of all three Indian peoples saw the move west as a chance to gain a measure of greater autonomy from colonial officials and perhaps some greater leverage in their relations with the European powers (France and Britain) lurking on either side of them. They also hoped to have more elbow room from the Iroquois Confederacy centered at Onondaga.[40]

Relations with the Six Nations (the Iroquois Confederacy of Mohawks, Cayugas, Oneidas, Onondagas, and Senecas now included the Tuscaroras who had migrated north from the Carolinas) proved complicated for the Delawares and Munsees wherever they were. The Iroquois continued to make bold claims of ownership of lands across Pennsylvania and the Ohio Country and to assert their sovereignty over all the resident Native peoples. By the 1720s and early 1730s Pennsylvania's proprietors—William Penn's sons John, Thomas, and Richard—concurred with provincial secretary James Logan that their interests would best be served by endorsing Iroquois claims over Delaware ones and supporting Iroquois hegemony in the region. The proprietors' ultimate goal was to displace the Delawares; aligning with the Iroquois might help get that done. Meetings in 1732 sealed the new partnership. Four years later, the two sides reached an agreement in which the Six Nations gave Pennsylvania the lands of the lower Susquehanna Valley. Next the proprietors set their sights on the Lehigh Valley and the territory around the Forks of the Delaware. They were intent on expelling Munsees and Delawares still living in the region and were prepared to use most any means to accomplish it. In the end the main tool was the infamous Walking Purchase of 1737. Under pressure, Delaware leader Nutimus and other sachems, including Tishcohan, agreed to an arrangement in which area Natives would relinquish all the land "walked" in a day and a half. Thomas Penn made sure to maximize his gain by using three walkers well-supported by supply horses and Indian guides. For Indians collectively, the land loss totaled eleven hundred square miles, probably four or five times what they anticipated losing. For Munsees in particular, the lost land amounted "to nearly all they had left in Pennsylvania."[41]

Disappointed and disgruntled, Forks Indians succumbed to the reality of the Walking Purchase but not before putting up some measure of resistance. They dragged their feet in leaving the area. They issued threats of violence against colonists eager to get access to their lands. And most significantly, they appealed to the Six Nations to intervene on their behalf, even while the proprietors were pressuring those same Indians to use their clout to get the Forks Indians removed. The issue came to a head in 1742. Close to two hundred Delawares, Munsees, and Iroquois met with colonial officials in Philadelphia to resolve the problem. Onondaga speaker Canasatego's opening speech left no doubt as to which side the Iroquois were supporting. He lashed out at the Forks Indians for their uncooperative behavior, told them they had no rights to sell or stay on their lands, and ordered them to remove immediately to Shamokin or the Wyoming Valley. His harsh words must have stunned Delaware and Munsee leaders: "You ought to be taken by the Hair of the Head and shak'd severely till you recover your Senses and become Sober; you don't know what Ground you stand on, nor what you are doing." Not yet done, he delivered a final blow: "We conquer'd You, we made Women of you, you know you are Women, and can no more sell Land than Women."[42]

Calling the Delawares women had more meanings than it might at first appear. In some instances it could even have a positive connotation.[43] But in this case, it is hard to escape the conclusion that Canasatego meant to humiliate them and to indicate their inferiority to the Six Nations. Nor is there little doubt that the events of 1742 worsened Iroquois-Delaware relations. Yet it is important to remember that those relations were complex and hardly one-dimensional since neither group was monolithic: "Many *relationships* as opposed to one *relationship* between the Iroquois and the Delawares operated at any given time, and . . . shifted over time in response to rapidly changing circumstances."[44]

Papunhank's diplomatic dealings after the mid-1750s would bear out that truth on many occasions. What he thought of the Iroquois fifteen or twenty years earlier, however, is hard to know. One intriguing possibility is that Papunhank became acquainted, either personally or by reputation, with Shickellamy. He was an Oneida "go-between," one of those valuable people in early America who could bridge the cultural divide between Natives and Euro-Americans. Though his exact responsibilities for the Six Nations are not clear, from the late 1720s into the 1740s he served more or less as their representative in Pennsylvania. Arguably no Iroquois person played a more crucial role in binding them and the colony together. He and his family lived along the West Branch of the Susquehanna River at a village that came to be called Shickellamy's Town. From there he ventured far and wide cultivating collaborative relationships with key Pennsylvanians such as James Logan and Conrad Weiser and smoothing the way for Indian-colonial dialogue. His constant travels must have regularly, or at least occasionally, taken him through Lechaweke or Cochecton where Papunhank likely lived in those years. Both men visited Shamokin. Given Shickellamy's prominence, might the two have conversed? Could Papunhank have been among the many Indians who stopped at Shickellamy's home? Was the Munsee taking note of the way Shickellamy got things done in spite of having little formal authority? Did he recognize the Oneida's "patience, persuasion, and . . . shrewd sense of the possible"? Might he have admired him for his successes despite what it meant for the Munsees and Delawares in the colony? And what did he make of Shickellamy's aversion to liquor and the liquor trade at a point in his life when he struggled with drunkenness? Even more, what might Papunhank have thought of the Oneida's increasingly close relationship during the final six years of his life with an odd group of immigrant German Christians (Moravians) who had now established settlements in the Lehigh Valley and were eager to share their faith in a crucified god?[45]

Answers to those questions are frustratingly elusive. What can be said is that both some of the broad contours and particular circumstances of Shickellamy's life during his final twenty years (1728–48) bear interesting parallels with Papunhank's experience a generation later. As with Papunhank, little is known about Shickellamy's life prior to his final two decades. Not until he arrived in Philadelphia in 1728 did he begin appearing in colonial records. Thereafter he carried on a life similar to most Indians in the Susquehanna Valley through farming, hunting, and trading. But he also functioned as an important messenger and diplomat and promoted the interests of his own people with skill and determination. He knew and practiced all the appropriate Native protocols when negotiating and won over Indians and whites alike, including the Pennsylvania government, with his gracious personality. He lamented the ill effects of the liquor trade upon Native communities and took actions to stop it. Deceptive colonial traders were among his least favorite people. When he could, he intervened to stop likely violence. In his later years, epidemic disease brought family loss, emotional heartache, and accusations of witchcraft. In the wake of those struggles, he joined the Moravians. Contact with them developed in the 1740s and included traveling to the Iroquois council fire at Onondaga with Moravian missionaries David Zeisberger and Augustus Spangenberg in 1745. The Moravians recognized his importance for their evangelistic hopes in the Susquehanna Valley and worked to gain his favor. No fool, Shickellamy knew when he was being courted. But he could also recognize genuine care, and when the crises of his life grew greatest, "one thing endured: the missionaries' generosity and devotion." So into the arms of their community and their god he fled and died in 1748.[46]

A Dim Future

Papunhank would have read Shickellamy's actions in the 1740s against the broader backdrop of Munsee struggles, Pennsylvania's duplicity, the Six Nations alleged hegemony, and renewed imperial conflict. None of those contexts offered much cause for hope. In the wake of the 1742 conference, most of the remaining Munsees and Delawares in the Lehigh Valley scattered elsewhere. Many moved to the Ohio Country or to Indian communities along the North and West Branches of the Susquehanna River. Consequently, there were few Natives still living in the vicinity of the Forks of the Delaware when Presbyterian missionary David Brainerd arrived there in the summer of 1744. Brainerd lamented both the small numbers of Indians and the growing numbers of whites, most of whom proved more hindrance than help to his evangelistic efforts. The few dozen Natives who remained at the Forks lived in scattered villages and struggled to maintain some semblance of the life previous generations had enjoyed while also taking on some of the trappings of European culture. What in recent memory had still been Indian country was now rapidly being absorbed into the Anglo-American world. Whites were pouring into the lands opened up by the Walking Purchase. The Penns had quickly had the land surveyed and were selling it to settlers and speculators for substantial profits. The new towns of Easton and what would become Allentown grew rapidly. Moravians established towns of a different sort at Bethlehem and Nazareth. It was not hard to tell that these German pietists were different from the typical settler, who was more interested in seeing Indians disappear than convert. If Natives were around, their main utility, in the eyes of such colonists, was as consumers of rum and beer. Laws against selling liquor to Indians held little sway. Amid land loss, economic deprivation, and epidemic disease, plenty of Munsees succumbed to the allure of drink. Alcohol abuse plagued their villages even along the Susquehanna, where polyglot populations were increasingly dependent on European trade goods and vulnerable to the further erosion of their traditional ways. Soon prophets would arise crying out for change.[47]

Meanwhile, with lands in eastern Pennsylvania secured, the colony's proprietors now turned their attention to the west. The territory between the Allegheny Mountains and the Ohio River (the Ohio Country) was more than a little inviting.[48] What is more, the growing numbers of "Ohio Indians" seemed interested in cultivating a relationship with the colony. By the mid-1740s Shawnees, Delawares, and Miamis, as well as the Senecas (known as Mingos) living there, wanted to keep both the French and the British at arm's length. Their goal was independence from imperial control. But they were not interested in isolation. At that moment, their link to French goods had been curtailed by King George's War (1744–48). So they were quick to encourage increasingly frequent visits by Pennsylvania traders and to welcome the items they brought, especially the deerskins that Natives prized as potential objects in the reciprocal gift-giving that was an essential part of their diplomacy with other Indians and Europeans. For their part, the traders were only too happy to exploit new Indian markets and to expand their trading zones by hundreds of square miles.[49]

Pennsylvania's political leaders looked on approvingly. Here were trade contacts that could bind the Ohio Indians, or at least some of them, more closely to Britain and its colonies and give Pennsylvania a leg up on getting its hands on Ohio Country lands. With those ends in mind, Pennsylvania officials met with representatives of the Ohio Indians first at Lancaster and then at Logstown on the upper Ohio River in 1748. The meetings proceeded smoothly, even jovially. Though the future was still uncertain, both parties left feeling good about the alliance that was emerging. All seemed to be going well.[50]

But not everyone was happy with what was happening. Some Natives in the Ohio Valley were not ready to give up their ties to the French, portending a split among Ohio Indians. Meanwhile, Six Nations leaders at Onondaga looked askance upon the growing ties between Pennsylvania and some Ohio Indians. They were upset that the proprietors now seemed to care more about winning the favor of the western nations than maintaining strong ties with them, ties that were economically and politically vital to the Six Nations. They were equally upset with the Ohio Indians' increasingly bold assertions of autonomy. Iroquois Council claims to sovereignty over the Ohio Country appeared hollow when Natives there kept acting on their own initiative. Virginians interested in Ohio Valley lands were likewise none too pleased with any sign that their rival colony to the north was getting the upper hand with area Indians. Based on a seventeenth-century charter that identified no western border for Virginia, they literally began to stake out their own claims to the territory through agents of the newly formed Ohio Company. They were hungry for land and in no mood to lose out to competing colonists.[51]

Neither were the French. Three decades of peace with the British ended in what was known as the War of Austrian Succession on the European continent and as King George's War in North America. While French and Indian raids in New England drew most of the attention within the colonies, developments in Ohio during the war foreshadowed a future showdown. The French saw British colonial inroads into the region as a threat to their imperial ambitions. In their minds the Ohio Country was "the weak link in their evolving chain of forts and trading stations designed to keep British interlopers out of the middle west."[52] Tensions boiled over into violent hostilities between British and French-backed forces in Ohio in 1747 and 1748. Once peace was restored, the French moved quickly to regain the advantage. Troops came south from New France to assert land claims, intimidate British traders, and let the Indians know who was boss.[53]

Ohio Indians didn't need to be told who was in charge of their territory in the late 1740s. As far as they were concerned, they were. And that went for Ohio Iroquois as well as all the other powerful Native peoples in the area. Of course, it also went for the Iroquois Council in Onondaga, and for colonial governments in Philadelphia and Williamsburg, and for their imperial overseers in London. Everyone wanted a piece of Ohio—in some cases a big piece—and was determined to get it or keep it. It would only be a matter of time before the biggest players in the contest, the British and the French, were willing to shoot it out to decide the issue.[54]

Once their guns fired, the smoke rippled across Pennsylvania's mountains and valleys and easily reached the Munsee communities of the Susquehanna Valley. There would be no escaping the impact of the next imperial war. For now, though, in the late 1740s, all that lay in the future. Papunhank likely heard reports and rumors of what was happening in the Ohio Country and may have grown concerned. Odds are though that most of the time he was preoccupied with more local concerns. He now had a family to feed and house. His father was very likely ailing, had little time to live, and was just one of many afflicted with disease. There is a good chance Papunhank's wife was one of its victims. If not, she surely suffered from his alcohol abuse and the likely violence it precipitated. Outside their home, hunting grounds were shrinking as more whites pushed into the area. Most of his neighbors were poor and often barely got by. Munsees had no more land to sell and depended on the largesse of their Iroquois uncles for a place to live. And they had little if any political influence in Philadelphia.

All that was a far cry from the comparative power and prosperity Munsees had enjoyed 150 years earlier on the eve of European colonization. They had no way of knowing how much change the newcomers would bring. First the Dutch and then the English and the French turned the worlds of Papunhank's ancestors upside down. For four or five generations an almost unrelenting narrative of disease, depopulation, and dislocation unfolded. Munsees did the best they could to cope. They fought when armed resistance held out some promise of success. They negotiated when they thought they could get a good deal or when necessity demanded it. They moved when it seemed wise or when there was no other choice. They regrouped and resumed as much of their familiar ways as circumstances allowed. And they mourned the loss of their loved ones and buried them with the goods they needed for the journey ahead.

Papunhank inherited all of those legacies. And he lived at a time when Munsees continued to face many similar challenges. Only now they seemed to have fewer and fewer resources with which to meet them. What could he or any other Munsee do to change their lot? Was there a way forward in a world seemingly bent against them?

2

Becoming a Prophet

The Interpreter gave me an account of the manner in which Papoonahoal was first enlightened, which was as follows. He was formerly a Drunken Man, but the Death of his Father bringing sorrow over his Mind, he fell into a thought full melancoly state in which State his Eyes were turned to behold the Earth and consider the things that are there on, & seeing the folly & wickedness that prevailed, his sorrows increased, and it was given to him to believe there was a Great Power that had created all these things and his mind was turned from beholding this lower World to look towards him that had created it, & strong desires were begot in his Heart for a farther knowledge of his Creator. Never-the-less the almighty was not yet pleased to be found of him, but his desires increasing he forsook the Town & went to the woods in great Bitterness of Spirit, the other Indians missing him & fearing evil had befallen him went from the Town in search of him, but could not find him; but at the end of five days it pleased God to appear to him to his comfort, & to give him a sight not only of his own inward state, but also an acquaintance into the works of Nature. He also apprehended a sense was given him of the Virtues, and Nature of Several Herbs, Roots, Plants & Trees and the different Relation they had one to another, & he was made sensible that Man stood in the nearest Relation to God, of any other part of the Creation. It was at this Time he was made sensible of his Duty to God, & he came home rejoicing & endeavouring to put into practice what he apprehended was required of him.[1]

With this dramatic testimony, Papunhank's "recorded" history may be said to have begun. Here the narrative conveys the earliest biographical details relayed to colonists, events probably occurring sometime between the late 1740s and early 1750s. More important, it describes the spiritual awakening that radically transformed the Munsee's life. For according to these words, Papunhank's "enlightenment" replaced his sorrow with comfort and joy, his ignorance with knowledge of self, nature, and God, and his drunkenness with dutifulness. Here was a wholesale transformation that brought a new sense of purpose and vocation. Arising from deep personal loss—the death of his father—his search for meaning and for the Creator drove him into a spiritual wilderness and literally into the woods. There he wandered in quest of powers greater than himself and was rewarded with a vision and a word. He came home a new man ready to follow the calling he had received.

That at least is how Delaware translator Job Chillaway told Papunhank's story in 1760. Or more precisely, that is how Quaker Moales Pattison recorded what he heard Chillaway say. Or more precisely yet, that is what another Quaker wrote down and printed of Pattison's account of Chillaway's account of Papunhank's narrative. Such fourth-hand testimonies are by nature suspect. When translation is involved, they become even more dubious. Something is bound to be altered or added in the progressive retellings. Each layer of redaction reflects the listening skills and peculiar concerns of its editor-storyteller and their communities. What is left at the end of the chain may look far different from its initial links.[2]

All those caveats are in order when approaching this text. Chillaway, Pattison, and other members of the Society of Friends brought their own perspectives and agendas to this piece of Papunhank's biography. Yet when compared to the vapors of information about Papunhank's earlier life, this testament seems like a veritable gold mine. At the very least, it provides something much more concrete. Even better, there are good reasons to think that much, if not all, of what was included here faithfully represents the Munsee's experience. Chillaway knew Papunhank well and by this point had probably heard him tell his story many times as part of the preaching he had been doing for the past eight to ten years. Chillaway also knew enough English to communicate clearly to Pattison. He was a fairly experienced translator, having served at several treaties. As a Philadelphia Friend, Pattison passed his knowledge directly to Anthony Benezet, the Quaker most likely responsible for writing up the narrative and someone who had just spent a week or more interacting with Papunhank. He wove the Munsee's spiritual narrative into the larger, laudatory account of Friends' interactions with him and his band. In their view he was an Indian worth highlighting, and they could not wait to get the word out on him to interested parties near and far. Under those circumstances, as will be discussed in chapter 3, the Quaker portrait of Papunhank was bound to be especially flattering. And it was likely to invoke Quaker categories of religious understanding; hence, the language of enlightenment and the image of moving from darkness to light. Still, what is most striking about this account of Papunhank's pilgrimage is not how much he appears Quaker-like, but rather how much he sounds Delaware or Munsee. What he described were mostly indigenous spiritual practices and methods, indigenous means for hearing and seeing the spirit world, and indigenous ways of comprehending reality.

Furthermore, in the midst of the crises faced by Munsees and Delawares in the 1740s and 1750s, these were the spiritual roads a number of mid-Atlantic Indians trod. What emerged was a series of religious reformers or prophets determined to save their people. Papunhank was one of them. His preaching and teaching had its own distinctive ring, and listeners could distinguish his message from other voices. But he arose, as they did, from Native worlds fraught with danger and distress. And like them, he sought a way forward for himself and his people.

Nativist Prophets

For many of the so-called Delaware prophets, the way forward was to look backward. In fact, all the way back to creation. In that distant time Indians had been created separately from all other peoples. The Creator singled them out for particular duties on earth which for generations had been performed well. Rituals had been carried out carefully to appease the powerful but often fickle spirits that animated the natural world and controlled most everything in it. As a result, ancient ways had been passed to younger members of communities and through them to their own children and grandchildren. As long as those traditions flourished, Indian peoples flourished. They had the power to endure and thrive.[3]

A quick look at circumstances in the eighteenth century, however, made it clear that something had gone awry. Natives in the region had lost much of their power. They were reeling from diseases without cures and land loss without halt. White settlers were impinging on hunting grounds, and more traditional forms of economic exchange were being replaced by a market economy. Many felt increasingly powerless to stem the tide, including most Indian spiritual leaders. According to the prophets' logic, the root of the problem was the peoples' failure to do their divinely ordained tasks. They had become lax in carrying on the ways of their fathers. They had neglected the customs, traditions, and rituals that gave meaning, identity, and power to their people. In other words, they had betrayed their spirits. Instead, Native communities had embraced alien elements introduced by European newcomers. They had foolishly allowed themselves to be seduced by new trade goods and become slaves to European-supplied liquor. They had mistakenly agreed to land deal after land deal that robbed them of ancient dwelling places. Unless something changed, the spirits and the Great Spirit would bring even greater destruction upon them.[4]

All of this had been revealed to the prophets through dreams and visions given by their manitous. Delaware religious tradition taught that in those dramatic spiritual encounters, persons might receive a particular type of healing or spiritual knowledge. Some were gifted to be caretakers of the sweat lodge (*nenpíkes*), others to practice healing remedies (*pawaw*), and still others to use their powers to harm foes (*nochíh'uwe*). Prophets (*onowutok*) were those spiritual leaders given revelations about how to ensure the well-being of the whole community. They were to share their messages with the people and urge them to heed their advice. Papunhank very likely understood his vision within this framework.[5]

Some of the prophets believed that unified action across tribal lines would rectify the Natives' situation in the eighteenth century. They promoted a pan-Indianism rooted in the belief that what Natives shared in common was more important than what kept them apart. Standing together, Indians would have a much better chance of warding off the worst effects of colonialism and regaining some of their sacred power. Their cry was less a nostalgic plea to return to some imagined past and more a call to renew and revitalize rituals and holy ways that had long served their peoples well. Practicing traditional as well as some new ceremonies and accessing the spiritual power available through them were keys to weathering the storm. So, too, was keeping an appropriate distance from the corrupting influence of Euro-Americans.[6]

Not all those "nativist" ideas were fully crystallized by 1750, when Papunhank likely experienced his adult vision quest. But evidence suggests that many of them swirled through the Susquehanna Valley and formed part of the cultural milieu he inhabited.[7] Indian agent Conrad Weiser met some of them in 1737 when he visited Shawnees and Onondagas at Otseningo (Otsiningo) in Iroquois country. They told him that one of their own had experienced a vision in which God revealed that he had punished them for trading animal skins for liquor. A few years later, Presbyterian missionary David Brainerd encountered nativism more dramatically in the mid-1740s, first at Minisink and then in the Delaware Valley. When he met with a group of Munsees in the former town, his efforts to win a hearing for Christianity were mocked by the local "King" (most likely Manawkyhickon) and rebuffed by a "rational" Indian who criticized Christianity as a destructive influence. They preferred to "live as their fathers lived and go where their fathers were when they died."[8] Brainerd heard similar claims from some Indians at the Forks of the Delaware and even more from Natives living farther into the interior. He had an especially memorable encounter with a nativist preacher along the Juniata River. Brainerd later rehearsed how upon meeting this man "none appeared so frightful or so near akin to what is usually imagined of infernal powers; none ever excited such images of terror in my mind." Dressed in animal skins and a wooden mask, and dancing about with a rattle, he "came near me [and] I could not but shrink away from him." Brainerd proceeded to see the Native's sacred space, "a house consecrated to religious uses, with divers images cut out upon the several parts of it." Despite his heightened fears, the missionary paid close enough attention to what the shaman said and did to realize that the Delaware man was "a devout and zealous reformer, or rather restorer of what he supposed was the ancient religion of the Indians." He believed his people had "grown very degenerate and corrupt," were being ruined by alcohol, and needed to resume practicing ceremonies that had given their ancestors sustaining power.[9]

Brainerd was a firsthand witness to the early stages of the nativist impulse that grew increasingly strong among the Delawares and Shawnees over the next two decades. His brother, John, got his own taste of nativism when visiting the Indian town of Wyoming in 1751. The community there was awash in visions and revelations to women and men. The message they conveyed was antagonistic if not overtly hostile to the missionary. Delawares and other refugee Indians tutored him in their separate creation theology and dismissed Christianity and the Bible as of use only to whites. They spoke with an edge in their voice and rumbled against Anglo-American arrogance and greed.[10]

German Moravians heard much the same from a Nanticoke living along the Susquehanna River who had a dream in which the Great Spirit had made known to him his creation of "brown and white people" and their distinct spiritual paths: "To the brown, he gave the Sacrifice, which they were to offer to him if they had not acted properly. . . . To the white people he had given the Bible." The revelation made clear that Indians should avoid contact with whites for "if [they] associated with them, [the white people] would devour all of them." Recent sickness and famine within Native communities were signs of the Spirit's displeasure and judgment.[11]

Another nativist began preaching in the early 1750s in Assinisink, a Munsee town along the Chemung River in what would become southern New York. Its prophet developed a robust ritual life for the village, one that Pennsylvania diplomat Christian Frederick Post dismissed as a "Stupid & Tragical way of Worship," but which apparently appealed to many Indians in the area. Post and his traveling companion John Hays spent two weeks in Assinisink in 1760, enough time to observe both the daily and occasional ceremonies that enlivened the community. Hays's diary noted the prophet's regular regimen: "the old Preast Goes Round the houses Every Morning and Eveng Sayes Sum Sort of Prayers and he hase A Book of Pickters whish he Maid him Self and there is Heaven and Hell and Rum and Swan hak [white men] and Indians and Ride [Red] Strokes for Rum and he would Read Like Mad of it in the Morning and Sing to the Sune Rising." Post's journal described the more episodic gathering of "a great Number of Indians" at Assinisink to "revive an Old Quarterly Meeting which had been many Years laid aside, in which they related to each other their Dreams and Revelations every one had had from his Infancy, & what Strength & Power they had received thereby." For twenty-four hours, participants walked, sang, danced, and wailed. Through word, illustration, and ritual, the Assinisink Prophet and his followers reinvigorated ancient ways and added their own twists. They sought the wisdom and power pregnant in dreams and visions. And they denounced the destructive effects of rum, just one of the many European things, and more especially British things, that nativists considered best left alone.[12]

Yet leaving Euro-Americans and their goods behind was easier said than done. They kept showing up one way or another and the allure, at least of the goods, was sometimes too hard to resist. Then again, not everybody wanted to resist. Plenty of Indians in the Delaware, Susquehanna, and Ohio River Valleys were not sure the nativist gospel was the true road to salvation. From their perspective, it seemed inevitable that the colonists and their governments were here to stay. Better to find some peaceful means of adjusting to their presence and reaping the best of what they had to offer than to ignore or alienate them, or worse still, have your rivals benefit instead. Just how much accommodation was never a simple calculation and became the source of much discussion. Nativists were clearly on one end of the spectrum. Other Indian voices promoted modest or substantial cooperation with

Euro-Americans. Debates and divisions predictably ensued within many Indian communities.[13]

It is likely that the heart of those debates concerned "the efficacy of sacred power." Nativists and their opponents would have agreed that Indians had lost power. The question was why. Nativists believed it stemmed from a loss of faithful practice. Others proposed that "the Indians' sacred powers [themselves] had failed them." The old "medicine" had been unable to counter the evil effects of new diseases. Depleted and weakened communities had become ill-equipped to hold their ground. A new infusion of sacred power was necessary to sustain them. Why not look to the newcomers for additional or alternative spiritual resources?[14]

Papunhank's Enlightenment

Papunhank was unsure where to look when his father died. His passing was only the latest sign that little was as it had been for him and other Munsees. They were refugee Indians living in the midst of a polyglot Native population in the Susquehanna Valley. Tensions were rising locally and internationally. Finding a center that would hold was increasingly difficult. Giving up or giving in to the pressures that beset them was hard to resist.

Like many other Natives, Papunhank turned to liquor often or at least occasionally for relief and release, as well as for the sacred power associated with alcohol. Despite Pennsylvania laws making liquor sales to Indians illegal, rum was in no short supply as white dealers plied their trade up and down the Susquehanna in the 1740s. Those exchanges "allowed Indian towns . . . access to Atlantic markets for their skins and furs, but it also signaled, in the words of David Murray, a 'failure of reciprocity—trade as exploitation and deception rather than exchange, gifts . . . that are not gifts.'" Fur traders handed out plenty of free samples in hopes of getting their Native trading partners intoxicated enough to be easily swindled and permanently indebted to them. That ploy didn't work every time, but it had sufficient success to be used repeatedly in Indian towns such as Shamokin, which became especially well-known for the exchange and consumption of alcohol.

There and elsewhere, Munsees proved eager recipients and drank to drunkenness on occasions both festive and somber. Papunhank joined in the excess, so much so he described himself as a "Drunken Man."[15]

Then death sobered him up. Word of his father's passing sent him and his community into mourning immediately. If typical Algonquian mourning ceremonies were followed, the cries of wailing women, some of whom were specially designated for that role, sounded through the village for days or, in this case, for weeks, since his father was very likely a sachem. A funeral and the burial came the day after death. Following a solemn procession to the grave site, the coffin, filled with appropriate articles needed for the next life, was opened. The grieving crowd sat silently for a long stretch, pondering their loss. Then the coffin was closed and lowered into the grave and Papunhank's mother, if still living, walked across it on a bridge formed by two poles. As she made her way into the distance, other men and women filled the hole in the ground.[16]

What they could not fill was the hole in Papunhank's heart. Native mourning ceremonies aimed to honor the dead and to give kin and community ample opportunity to grieve. Through their performance, Munsees expressed some of their most sacred convictions about the nature of this world and the next. In this case, though, they apparently didn't satisfy all of Papunhank's needs. However much he had been comforted, he came out of the experience with a sorrow he could not shake. "He fell into a thought full melancoly state" and stayed there. His depression no doubt stemmed in part from having lost his *father*. Munsees were a matrilineal people. They traced descent through the maternal line. But that did not mean that there could not be strong emotional bonds between fathers and sons. As a man in his forties, Papunhank had likely enjoyed many years by his father's side in the hunt or sitting in council. As of 1741 he would have also had the pleasure of sharing a new grandchild with him since a daughter was born that year to Papunhank and his wife, most likely at least their second child. Now those days were over and Papunhank had to come to terms with what that meant for his role among his family and kin. Would he need to behave better for the sake of his wife (if she was still alive) and children and their extended family? How much suffering had they already endured because of his alcohol abuse? And what was his current depressed state doing to them? Moreover, within a society that greatly valued the aged and their wisdom, the loss of his father also meant the loss of a community elder. What might that mean for his place within the village? Was it his time to assume more responsibility for its well-being?[17]

Those questions and others drove Papunhank to consider the world around him. When he did, his depression only worsened. Tellingly, the world's "folly & wickedness" more than anything else struck him. All he had to do was look around at the condition of Indian villages in eastern Pennsylvania to see their ill impact. But he might have been thinking of something more specific. Could his father's death have been a product of that folly—the physically destructive effects of an alcoholism brought on at least in part by the exploitative trade practices of unscrupulous whites? Or perhaps it was the product of an incident of liquor-induced violence? In any case, the prevalence of unrighteousness deepened his sorrow and seems to have left him groping for some larger source of moral order. Amid his despair, his thoughts turned to the Great Spirit, the one who had brought all things into being. But who or what was that Spirit? Traditional Native American religious beliefs typically included the idea of a supreme god, but the high god or ultimate deity was not always the creator god. Moreover, these deities tended to be aloof and distant. They were not at the beck and call of human beings.[18]

Nevertheless, in his distress, Papunhank went hunting for a new revelation. His unsettled heart would not let him alone. He needed to make some greater sense out of his broken world, and no earthly being or thing seemed capable of providing relief. He wanted to know the Great Power—Kishelëmukòng in the Delaware language—in some more direct way or have some sort of message revealed to him.[19] Yet how was this to be done? For a time, Papunhank may have engaged in a round of traditional ceremonies within his town aimed at obtaining sacred power. But whatever practices and prayers he employed apparently proved fruitless for the "almighty was not yet pleased to be found of him." That is probably a more Quaker-like than Indian way of rendering what happened. Still, the bottom line was the same—the Spirit was silent, at least in Papunhank's ears, so his spirits sank even lower.

He was not yet ready, though, to give up on his pursuit. Perhaps out of desperation or even as a last resort, he headed into the woods where somehow he seemed to always be more at home and spent five days in a new vision quest. At one level, this was a natural choice since for many indigenous peoples, dreams and visions were the most vital means of gaining individual access to spiritual power, and those who experienced them were generally accorded a strong hearing within their communities. Yet vision quests were not to be undertaken lightly. They demanded courage, self-denial, and even physical endangerment. And the results could be dramatic and life-altering. For example, those called to be shamans typically experienced extraordinarily powerful visions. Thereafter, they exercised their shamanic power in various ways including healing.[20]

All that must have raced through Papunhank's mind as he made his way to some hidden place that even his neighbors could not find. They did not know why he was gone and feared the worst. Had he left to go hunting and had an accident? Had he been taken captive or somehow killed in a fray? Had he resorted to drinking amid his sorrow and simply wandered off? His wife and children were accustomed to him being away, but this time was different. It was unexpected and unexplained. Villagers went out looking but came back empty-handed.[21]

Finally, he appeared—Kishelëmukòng, that is, and then Papunhank. On the fifth day of his solo journey, the sought-after vision came. The narrative is thin on what he actually saw or heard, or how long the vision lasted. But its impact was clear. It brought comfort to Papunhank's wounded soul, not least because it confirmed that ancient Native means of consorting with the spirits were still viable. It also confirmed that the Great Spirit knew the very nature of things and was willing to share that knowledge with Indian peoples. The Spirit first showed Papunhank his "inward state," the quality of the Munsee's character and the condition of his mind and heart. Then the revelation acquainted him with the inner workings of Nature, including secret truths about flora that were essential for Native remedies. Next he was told about humanity's place in the creation and its nearness to the Creator. Here the Spirit deviated from most traditional Native American cosmologies that placed humans on an equal plane with other beings. But Papunhank drank it all in and all things became new. Or at least he had a new vision of his world and his place in it, and a new sense of purpose for his life. He came back to his village rejoicing; the Great Spirit had spoken and he had listened. Now it was his turn to speak.[22]

Papunhank Becomes a Preacher

Upon his return, Papunhank endeavored "to put into practice what he apprehended was required of him." A change in mood seems to have been the first order of business. After a long season of bitterness and sorrow, he found reasons to be joyful again. Others likely noticed his altered disposition and realized this was not the old Papunhank. He was not getting drunk anymore. Of that type of frivolity, he no longer wanted a part. And he was more serious, but not because he was depressed. He had important work to attend to and was determined to do it well.[23]

He also felt compelled to do it. To have received a vision from Kishelëmukòng was an honor and a responsibility. It gave him a sense of duty and call. But to what? Almost certainly, it meant first telling what he had seen and heard to his kin and community. Evidence from Assinisink and elsewhere makes plain how eager Natives could be at that time to share their dreams and visions and to offer interpretations of them. There is no reason to think that Papunhank was any different. He became, in the dramatic words of historian Gregory Dowd, "swept up in the waves of visionary spirituality that had washed down the Susquehanna Valley since the 1740s."[24] Papunhank may not have divulged all that the Spirit revealed to him since some of that new knowledge likely concerned healing remedies. But it is easy to imagine him finding ready audiences for his dramatic tale within his own town and in nearby villages in the Wyoming Valley.

At some point Papunhank's narration began to slide toward exhortation. Perhaps right from the start, he was anxious to convey something more than his personal story as he realized the prophetic role he had been given. If not, the impulse to instruct developed over time and before long became the bulk of his message. In other words, he began to preach. His words took on a more didactic quality, no longer content with mere description. Now he was admonishing listeners, imploring them to heed what he said, and asking them to change their ways. He spoke with authority, an authority imputed by his vision, a religious authority he had not previously enjoyed. Exercising it was part of practicing "what was required of him" as an *onowutok*.[25]

He may also have begun to practice healing skills. Though the record is almost completely silent on this point, his vision quest testimony included important claims about what the Creator had revealed to him about the "Nature of Several Herbs, Roots, Plants & Trees," essential elements in Indian medical cures and healing practices. Natives were certainly eager for whatever remedies might be available, as evidenced by their requesting Moravian missionaries to bleed them. If Papunhank demonstrated healing capabilities, this would have surely added to his appeal.[26]

In preaching, Papunhank joined the swelling ranks of prophets, religious reformers, seers, evangelists, pastors, shamans, and healers circulating within Indian country and colonial settlements in mid-eighteenth-century Pennsylvania. Early America in the 1740s was "awash in a sea of faith," as the Anglo-American evangelical Great Awakening reached its peak in New England and had a growing impact on the Middle Colonies. Indigenous peoples living in certain regions, such as southeastern New England, responded to its egalitarian offers of salvation in substantial numbers. They embraced Christianity as part of their communal survival strategies. For them, acceptance of Christian faith and affiliation with a Christian congregation proved both "meaningful and useful." Christian missionary activity among Indians in the Delaware and Susquehanna Valleys was far less developed at that point. Presbyterians David and John Brainerd had entered the field, and Moravians were beginning to evangelize from their center in Bethlehem. Indians who found reasons to be closer to Philadelphia would have encountered many other varieties of Protestants alongside some

Catholics and Jews amid the colony's diverse population. Meanwhile, as described above, nativist efforts at religious renewal within Indian communities were gaining momentum. They were engaged in their own type of "Great Awakening" and were eager to spread its gospel.[27]

Amid this spiritual swirl, new types of religious authority and a new sort of religious personality appeared. Emboldened by the transforming power of the Great Spirit or the Holy Spirit, men and women felt unfettered to voice the truths revealed to them, even to those in high places. Their dynamic testimonies often resonated with friends and strangers alike, and could give them a newfound authority and appeal.

Under those circumstances, Papunhank gathered a following. A new religious community formed around him whose faith and practice largely conformed, and indeed was indebted to, the broader nativist revival. Their religion, said one contemporary observer, chiefly consisted "in strictly adhering to the ancient Customs & Manners of their Forefathers" because they thought it was "pleasing to God that they strictly observe & keep the same." Their commitment to traditional practices and to reversing the ill effects of colonialism made them "much afraid of being seduced and brot. off from their Ways by the White People, from whom they will receive no instruction."[28] Over time Papunhank would grow more open to benefiting from the wisdom and resources some white communities possessed. For now, though, his primary emphasis was on renewing Native rituals rich with sacred meaning. Among them were communal dances. Both sexes joined in and moved rhythmically to the pulsating sounds of the drum: "[They] had A Sort of Worship and they Dansed Round and Two Beat the Skine and Wemen and Men [did] A Religes Dance."[29] Other comparatively more sedate gatherings marked the start and end of each of their days. When they weren't scattered about hunting, the community would meet together "in the Morning before Sunrise, & in the Evening after Sunset" because Papunhank had declared that it had been "early revealed to him, from above, that Men ought daily to begin and end the Day with the worship of their Maker."[30] Those occasions provided ample opportunities for him to sound his message through preaching and prayer. His words included many admonitions to live righteously during the other hours of the day. In particular, they were to avoid using liquor and were to "[live] in Love" with others. Otherwise they would cause God "to be angry & to send dry & hot summers, & hard Winters, & also Sickness amongst the People."[31]

A strict adherence to ancient custom, an aversion to white ways, engagement in sacred dance, the use of morning and evening prayer, calls to moral uprightness, prohibitions on liquor, warnings of divine judgment—all these themes and practices echoed the wider nativist revival stirring among Delaware, Shawnee, and other Indian peoples in the mid-eighteenth century. Papunhank's vision quest surely set him off on this course. But it seems equally certain that he was listening and learning from other prophets and preachers as he led his people.

His emerging religious community in the early 1750s also bore interesting resemblances to the Protestant renewal movements that had begun within continental Europe, spread to the British Isles, and in recent years come to colonial America. In both cases there was at least a covert willingness to question prevailing religious authority and practice and to promote a faith of greater moral and spiritual rigor. Adherents were called to personal transformation, often through dramatic encounters with the divine, and they were gathered into a worshipping body that regularly sought fresh infusions of sacred power. Theirs was an awakened religion, full of possibility and promise even in the midst of crisis.[32]

Odds are that when Papunhank began proclaiming his nativist message, he was still living at the Munsee town of Lechaweke just above the mouth of the Lackawanna River where he had possibly been for the past decade or two.[33] If not before, by 1752 his preaching in the area gradually drew together a mixed band of mostly Munsee Indians along with some Delawares, Conoys, and Nanticokes. Most if not all of them came from various Native towns near or along the Susquehanna River including Nanticoke, where members of that tribe lived only from 1748 to 1753. Papunhank's company likely remained in Lechaweke until late 1755 or early 1756. When Moravian leader Johannes Ettwein traveled through the former village in 1768, he noted that "until the year '55 there had been an Indian town [there] . . . John Papunham and others, who now belong to our people, had lived there."[34]

Papunhank's leadership of this new community naturally arose from the religious authority he now could claim. His vision quest had endowed him with a powerful revelation, and he apparently had sufficient speaking gifts to do it justice. From what can be surmised about his actions in these years, it seems likely that he focused most of his attention on providing *religious* leadership. That was the heart of what he understood his new calling to be. His vision had given him a set of duties to perform that principally concerned the religious practice and moral character of his people. He was to be a preacher and a prophet. And yet neither Munsee notions of authority nor the force of wider events would allow Papunhank to limit his leadership to providing spiritual and ethical guidance alone. Munsees, like other Eastern Woodland Indians, made no separation between the sacred and the secular. All the stuff of life had a religious significance or impact. As a result, the roles and responsibilities of political leaders (sachems) and religious leaders (*metewak*) "often were combined in one person."[35] It was to be expected, then, that Papunhank would exercise some power and influence over all community decisions, including ones that extended, from a twenty-first-century perspective, far beyond religious bounds. And this would have been the case all the more if he and his family had already been sachems, as suggested in chapter 1. Munsee headmen led through consensus not by fiat. It is best to conceive of them as "authoritative, not authoritarian."[36] From later evidence, it appears that Papunhank assumed that leadership style and those broad duties as much from tradition and necessity as from any personal ambition. In the early 1760s he more than once made sure to eliminate any possible impression that he was or wanted to be an important political figure. He took on wider responsibilities with some reluctance. But he had little choice. Circumstances of war and peace over the next decade dictated that he provide astute political, diplomatic, and economic leadership for his people alongside whatever he preached to them. Otherwise they had little hope of surviving.

Some historians have proposed that in 1752 Papunhank moved his followers to Wyalusing, at that point an uninhabited spot along the North Branch of the Susquehanna River about fifty miles above Lechaweke. That claim is based on the report Christian Frederick Post wrote for Pennsylvania officials in 1760 after his diplomatic mission from Bethlehem to southern New York. Both coming and going, he stopped at Papunhank's community, which he described as an "Indian town newly laid out, where there are a company together, all of the Manyssing [Minisink] Indians, a sort of religious people, it is about 8 years when they began and Papounnahang is the beginner of the company and their minister." Published in the mid-nineteenth century in the *Pennsylvania Archives* alongside thousands of other colonial documents, Post's remarks were rendered in a kind of broken German-English dialect far less clear than what has just been quoted. Local historians in the 1870s, and some later scholars, interpreted Post to be saying that Papunhank both gathered his company and founded Wyalusing in 1752. To this day visitors to the town are greeted by a large sign declaring "WYALUSING since 1752: historic, progressive, friendly."[37]

Wyalusing may be all three of those things, but the town council may still need to order a new sign. Post's journal, upon which his report was based and which was unpublished until 1999, adds further detail about his visit that casts doubt on the 1752 founding date. His entry for May 19, 1760, stated that "About Noon we came to Machachlosung [Wyalusing], which in the Indian Tongue signifieth an Old Man. The People we found all at Work in the Woods, they are an industrious People. They begun this Place abt. 2 Years ago & now it is a large Town, and according to ye Indian Way fine Houses." Post's traveling companion, John Hays, confirmed the recent vintage of the village in his journal entry for May 20: "this town is Situated on Sisquhana, East side about twenty Houses full of People, Very Good Land and Good Indian Buildings, all New."[38]

While it is possible that the community had been in the Wyalusing area since 1752 and had more recently moved to this precise location and constructed new buildings, the likelier scenario is that they had only arrived in Wyalusing in 1758. In July of that year, Moses Tatamy and Isaac Still had breakfast with Papunhank at his settlement. They were Native diplomatic messengers sent by the governor of New Jersey to invite Munsee Indians in southern New York to an upcoming treaty. After conferring with Munsee chiefs in Cobus Town and other villages along the Chemung River, they paddled south and came to Papunhank's company. At that point they were living somewhere above Tioga, an important Indian town where the Chemung flowed into the Susquehanna, located roughly thirty miles north of what became Wyalusing. There is a good chance the Munsee reformer and his people moved to Wyalusing later that fall after peace had largely been achieved through a treaty at Easton, Pennsylvania, in October. Feeling more secure, they were ready to put down some firmer roots in a "Very Good Land."[39]

War in the Susquehanna Valley

Before that time, little had been firm or secure thanks to the upheavals of war. For four years French forces and an assortment of Indian peoples with their own motives and objectives had been battling the British. Hostilities commenced in the Ohio Country where, as described earlier, tensions had been building for a decade as the two imperial powers flexed their muscles in hopes of gaining dominance over that territory. Western Delawares, Ohio Shawnees, and Mingos (Ohio Iroquois) became increasingly caught in the middle. Their efforts to gain some advantage from the British-French rivalry proved largely futile. Once war began in the summer of 1754, almost all of them had to choose sides. Though by no means united in their choices, most sooner or later opted to support the French, at least to the extent of waging war on a common foe, largely because of the alienating actions of Pennsylvania and Virginia land speculators during the prior five years and the failure of the British government to provide their Indian allies with any protection. Western Delawares also carried into the war longstanding resentments against the Six Nations, eastern Delawares, and Pennsylvania authorities for "the loss of Delaware lands in the east." In July 1755 the British sent a large force westward under the command of General Edward Braddock to capture Fort Duquesne (at present-day Pittsburgh) and push the French out. But his defeat opened all of Pennsylvania to attack.[40] By that fall, with French support and endorsement, Ohio Delawares and Shawnees were raiding homes, settlements, and forts along the Pennsylvania, Maryland, and Virginia frontiers. As historian Eric Hinderaker has explained:

> These raids were conducted in the French style, with small, mobile forces made up of Indians and French soldiers. They combined the surprise, terror, and pursuit of plunder that were characteristic of Indian raids with a sustained and flexible strategy for pursuing key enemy targets. . . . The combination of French arms and the Delawares' and Shawnees' unerring knowledge of the landscape and population made these raids especially devastating. . . . They mutilated their victims' bodies in pointedly symbolic ways, removing or defacing sexual organs to emasculate their enemies. In one community after another, raiders brought terror and death to the colonies' exposed and largely undefended frontiers.[41]

With dozens and eventually hundreds of colonists being killed and even more being taken captive, Pennsylvania shuddered with fear. Indian raids were intended to provoke panic and to convince settlers to flee from their homes before it was too late. "The contest between the English and the French," wrote one contemporary historian, "burst at once into flames, spreading terror and confusion."[42] Whites and Natives alike were in grave danger. Raids moved progressively eastward, threatening larger centers of settlement, generating streams of refugees, provoking increasingly strident calls for the colony's assembly to do more to protect its citizens, and putting more and more pressure on Indians still living east of the Alleghenies. The latter were an easy target for a colonial government and population anxious to gain some measure of retaliation and revenge against any Native peoples. A "racial hatred and regional distrust that had been latent for seven decades" was now ready to explode amid the upheavals of war. Meanwhile, raiding western Delawares and Shawnees were anxious to gain additional warriors from among their eastern brethren. But to join in that fight against the British was no easy choice; it meant risking whatever modicum of stability these Indians' communities still had and whatever ill consequences would accompany a French defeat. It also meant risking the disapproval of their Iroquois overseers. For that reason many white Pennsylvanians imagined or at least prayed that eastern Delawares would remain quiescent. But their hopes were disappointed as numerous of their Native neighbors seized the chance to express in violence pent-up bitterness.[43]

All of this played out in the Susquehanna Valley in the fall of 1755. On October 16 Delawares and Shawnees, probably including some who lived on the West Branch of the Susquehanna River, attacked Penn's Creek, a colonial settlement a few miles south of Shamokin. They killed at least thirteen whites and took twenty-eight others captive. Soon word spread that the raiding party had sent "a hatchet and two English scalps" to Indians in the Wyoming Valley "to desire them to strike with them if they are men."[44] Some heeded the call. Area Munsees were prominent among those who attacked the Moravian Indian town of Gnadenhütten on November 24. French-allied Indians suspected the Gnadenhütten Natives to be "friends of the English government." Meanwhile, rumors circulated that fall among Pennsylvania whites that all Moravians were secretly "in league with the Indians and French."[45] Seemingly trusted by no one and threatened on all sides, the Indian Brethren at Gnadenhütten fled to the woods for safety either before or during the attack, and in the end survived. Their white brothers and sisters were not so fortunate. Eleven men, women, and children, including a fifteen-month-old, were either shot dead or burned alive, and their town was destroyed. Having wreaked their havoc, many of these Munsees retreated northward to live at recently formed Munsee towns along the Chemung River including Assinisink. Other Delawares in the Wyoming Valley only decided to join the French and engage in attacks after the Gnadenhütten massacre. Teedyuscung, a former Moravian Indian at Gnadenhütten, led the charge. He had left that town in early 1754 and brought more than sixty other Natives with him to Wyoming. From there, warriors joined forces with western Delawares and raided numerous colonial settlements in northeastern Pennsylvania and western New Jersey in late 1755 and early 1756. Eventually, as many as two hundred Susquehanna Valley Indians fought for the French and spilled blood across the countryside.[46]

Teedyuscung hoped to translate his military successes into political gain. His goal was to achieve some greater measure of autonomy over the Wyoming Valley. But he had plenty of competitors for that territory. Pennsylvania settlers, land speculators from Connecticut, and Pennsylvania's proprietors all wanted a piece of the action. And then there were the Six Nations, still intent on claiming sovereignty over Pennsylvania lands and the Natives within them.[47]

The Iroquois of the Onondaga Council assiduously maintained political neutrality during the first few years of the Seven Years' War lest they end up on the losing side. Papunhank thought that was a good strategy. Consciously or not, he paralleled the Iroquois approach in keeping his people neutral while the outcome of the war was still very much in doubt between 1754 and 1758. As with the Iroquois who could not keep all of their young men from joining one army or the other, some of his company likely disagreed with Papunhank's policy and willingly joined other Munsees and Delawares on the French side.[48] Others may have been pressured into that choice by kin. Either way, whatever attrition occurred was not substantial enough to deplete or weaken Papunhank's band beyond the breaking point. Neither was the strain of claiming to be neutral Indians. Still, that strain was substantial. As with the Moravians, Papunhank's community would have felt antagonism from all combatants. Neutrality aroused suspicions from both sides that such a policy was a mere ploy to cover up efforts to aid and abet their enemy. As one group of Wyoming Valley Indians put it, "We are in danger of being attacked on all sides by [French and Native] enemies, who are much enraged. We are no less afraid of the white people, who suspect us of having been accessary to the murders, committed in various places. . . . We are in danger of being murdered by the white people."[49]

With each new terrifying report of colonists slain or captured, white Pennsylvanians' rage grew, especially on the frontier. They increasingly hated the French and their Native allies. That was perhaps to be expected. But with few identifiable Indians on their side, sympathy evaporated for all Natives. "The white people considered every Indian as an enemy," one Moravian wrote. They were all deceitful; they were all appropriate targets for revenge. As frontier whites impatiently waited for the Pennsylvania Assembly and other provincial officials to authorize a militia and build forts for their defense, some were ready to take matters into their own hands, especially once many of their wives and children were secured in "refugee towns" like Bethlehem and Nazareth. The men of these families looked for opportunities to inflict retaliatory violence on Indian persons of whatever variety. The religious identities of Natives now made no difference. All that mattered was their race. Roaming mobs formed ready to "justify an attack on any Indian as the necessary action of men defending their families and ways of life." By year's end colonial Indian agent Conrad Weiser reported that a group of "Paxton people took an enemy Indian," and after questioning him, "shott him in the midst of them, scalped him and threw his Body into the River."[50]

Amid such violence, Papunhank knew that neutrality alone would not keep his followers safe or perhaps even alive. More blood was likely to flow in the Wyoming Valley. Claims to being "friendly" or "peaceful" Indians were not enough of a defense. Moreover, in October they had likely received word from New France's Governor Pierre de Rigaud de Vaudreuil that any Delawares unwilling to join the French attacks should "go where I cannot hurt you"—presumably that meant to the Ohio Valley or further up the Susquehanna.[51] At some point, then, in late 1755 or early 1756, in the wake of that warning and events such as the Gnadenhütten massacre and Teedyuscung's raids, Papunhank and his company got out. So did most other area Indians. War scattered Natives to the north into what is now southern New York and to the west as far as the Ohio Country. Most likely, Papunhank's band had remained near the mouth of the Lackawanna River since he had begun preaching and gaining followers around 1752. That space was no longer viable. There were simply too many threats to their well-being to stay their ground. And Papunhank had no interest in defending it if it meant using violence to meet violence.[52]

So they headed north hoping to get out of harm's way. Probably numbering between fifty and one hundred persons, they moved up the North Branch of the Susquehanna River looking for a place to be on their own. It is unclear how separate Papunhank's company had been from other Indians while living in the Wyoming Valley. They may have been part of "mixed" communities of followers and nonfollowers along or near the Lackawanna River. If so, circumstances now dictated a different approach. They wanted and needed to be set off from both hostile whites and other Natives bent on warring. That ruled out Tioga, where Teedyuscung had fled with his warriors following their raids in early 1756. It also ruled out Munsee towns farther up the Chemung River as far as Passigachkunk (Canisteo) since they were populated by strong pro-French elements (Teedyuscung eventually went there as well). As they traveled north, Papunhank no doubt took notice of the fertile flatlands around what became Wyalusing since they had good potential to sustain a population the size of his company. But for the time being that area likely felt too close to the scenes of bloodshed that prompted their move in the first place. They kept going therefore and in the end, based on Moses Tatamy and Isaac Still's testimony two years later, settled upon an in-between spot along the Chemung River, a few hours' canoe-ride north of Tioga and the better part of two travel days south from the major Munsee towns. There they remained until their move to Wyalusing in late 1758 at a point when Papunhank's prayers for peace had been at least partially answered.[53]

An Indian Pacifist

Papunhank's strategies of political neutrality, geographic mobility, and communal isolation sought to protect his people amid the storms of war. They may be seen as pragmatic responses to the rapidly changing circumstances of Susquehanna Valley Indians. Take neutrality for example. Papunhank, like the Iroquois, wished to keep his options open. For the war's first year that was not difficult since its sporadic fighting was relatively far removed from his domain. Moreover, the Pennsylvania government was slow to see this conflict as its fight and therefore did not actively recruit Indian allies. British commanders charged with carrying on the war did secure the aid of southern Indians, especially Cherokees and Catawbas. But overall, British disdain toward Natives and differences with them over how to act in war contributed to some western Indians switching allegiances to the French and to Braddock's defeat and with it, radical changes for Papunhank's world.[54] Within six months the war was at his community's doorstep. If Papunhank had committed to the British side in 1754, there would have been little price to pay. But by late 1755 everything had changed, and that choice would have exacted a very heavy toll. Pro-French forces would certainly have targeted his community for attack. Alternatively, siding with the French from the beginning was not really an option for any Natives wishing to stay in eastern Pennsylvania since those Indians were close to sources of British rule and might. Once French attacks reached the Susquehanna, Papunhank could have given the French his community's loyalties to save their skins. Yet that might have brought only short-term gains. After all, enraged area colonists represented as grave a threat as the French. No one knew how the war was going to turn out. Its fortunes could swing many more times before a clear outcome was in view. For the moment, then, neutrality, combined with retreat to a safer, isolated place, made the most practical sense for the prophet and his company.

Yet something more than pragmatic strategy factored into their policy choices and community decisions. In the 1750s, if not before, Papunhank developed a deep philosophical commitment to peace and became a devoted pacifist. Later in the war, he came to side with the British, at least to the extent of aiding peace initiatives. He was willing to give up neutrality when it no longer served his community's best interests. But he was never willing to give up his opposition to war and, more broadly, violence. He refused to condone war or to believe that violence was ever the appropriate means to resolve disputes. He did not want his followers taking up the sword no matter what it might cost them. Testimony from a few years later indicates that they heeded his message and "absolutely refused to Join the other Indians in the Prosecution of the War." When pressed by pro-French Munsees and Delawares to add to their ranks, they responded "that they would not Join them in it though they should kill or make Slaves (or as they express it) Negroes of them." Apparently they were ready to be enslaved or even die for the sake of their pacifist convictions.[55]

That level of commitment bespeaks the power of Papunhank's pacifist preaching and teaching in the 1750s. Clearly it was a key element in what drew some adherents to his message and his community, a revealed truth that had to be spoken and which forced him to change his own ways: "It has been told to my heart, that man was not made for that end, therefore I have ceased from war." However much he had engaged in the affairs of war before his enlightenment, he was done with it now. And he was prepared to suffer the consequences for his stance against violence: "From the Time God first show'd himself to my mind & put his Goodness in my Heart, I found myself in such a Temper, that I thought if the Flesh had been whipt off me with Horse whips, I could have borne it without being angry at these that did it." Such words were not an idle boast. They were an expression of how deeply he believed pacifism was a matter of moral right. Therefore, "whatever argument might be advanced in defence of war," Papunhank was "fully persuaded that when God made men, he never intended they should kill and destroy one another."[56]

While Papunhank no doubt sounded his pacifist theme more urgently and others listened more attentively once the war had spread to the Susquehanna, he chided himself as the war went on for having not "labored to bring about a peace, so much as I ought to have done." He saw his moral failure as the product of an internal spiritual struggle: "I was made weak for that work by the bad spirit striving to overcome the good in my heart; but I hope the good spirit will overcome the bad, and then I shall be strong to labor heartily to bring people from war to peace." Peacekeeping and peacemaking were difficult calls to follow even for Papunhank.[57]

Where did his call come from? Papunhank always linked it back to his original vision, back to the "Time God first show'd himself to my mind." Preaching peace was part of his "endeavouring to put in practice what he apprehended was required of him." Other Indian prophets heard a different call, however. In fact, more than anything else, Papunhank's pacifist stance set him apart from other Native American prophets of this and later generations. Arising out of the nativism of the 1740s and 1750s, by the early 1760s and off and on again into the early nineteenth century, militant pan-Indian alliances arose bent on reviving Native communities and pushing back Euro-American advances. In particular, under Pontiac's leadership in the 1760s and Tecumseh's after 1809, large-scale Indian movements waged war to resist the forces of colonialism. In each case their inspiration and blessing came from powerful religious reformers. Neolin, the Delaware Prophet, proclaimed a message that "clearly entailed armed resistance to Anglo-American expansion. As early as 1761, Neolin predicted that 'there will be Two or Three Good Talks and then War.'" Pontiac took those words to heart and fulfilled the prophecy in 1763. Tenskwatawa, the Shawnee Prophet, likewise endorsed the use of force. His visions prompted a series of violent witch hunts and greatly influenced the militant struggle of his brother, Tecumseh, to defeat the United States.[58]

Papunhank could not countenance such a path. He simply wanted no part of war. His vision quest had answered that question. Even if it was a struggle to follow through on his peace work, he knew it was the right thing to do. It was a matter of moral duty. Moreover, it was in line with the traditions of the Turkey phratry of the Munsees to which he belonged. A phratry was a "union of clans and lineages." From birth, he would have been assigned to his mother's clan and been "expected to live up to the characteristics of its clan eponym," in this case, the turkey. "The merits of the *Turkey*," according to Moravian missionary John Heckewelder, were that "he is stationary, and always remains with or about them." Here was a model of stability and persistence, a steadying influence, a tradition of talk and squawk rather than fight and flee. In embracing pacifism, then, Papunhank followed (and extended) the Turkey phratry's typical bent toward negotiation and repudiated the militant ways of Wolf phratry Munsees.[59]

Papunhank's pacifism drew as well upon wider Indian traditions of peacemaking. His actions on behalf of peace and in response to acts of violence large and small reflected his employment of well-established indigenous means of conflict resolution. Three examples are worth citing here. As a Munsee, he inherited the legacy of sachems like Tackapousha (described in chapter 1) who for half a century (1640s–1690s) used treaty-making, tactical alliances, compromise, legal wrangling, and shrewd land sales to hold onto some literal and figurative space for his people.[60] Papunhank would deploy some of the same means in his diplomacy with the Pennsylvania government and the Iroquois Confederacy. Meanwhile, farther south, the Lenapes of the Delaware Valley in the period prior to the arrival of William Penn cultivated patterns of peacekeeping with Swedish, Dutch, and English newcomers that avoided "war and violent confrontations in favor of negotiations, equitable exchanges, and a set of behaviors and customs that were mutually acceptable." Those practices continued into the early eighteenth century with an emphasis on mutual civility and reciprocal satisfaction.[61] Papunhank would likewise stress reciprocity as a key foundation for maintaining or restoring the just relations needed for peace to prevail. A third case in point is his participation in condolence ceremonies. Developed particularly among the Iroquois but adopted by northeastern Indians more broadly, these were "ritual displays of grief and mourning" performed especially at the beginning of diplomatic exchanges between antagonists. Their intent was to solicit acknowledgment from all parties of mutual grievances and loss and in that way to provide a kind of emotional salve to smooth the way toward negotiation. Natives including Papunhank welcomed overt expressions of grief; tears were an outward sign of an inner empathy and if shared, a potential bridge to reconciled relationships.[62] Emotional power, then, was not to be underestimated as a force for maintaining or restoring peace and justice. It could combine with moral power and spiritual might to heal broken relations.

Christian Contacts

Indigenous sources of Papunhank's dedication to peace were likely supplemented by Christian ones. Students of eighteenth-century Indian religious reformers have concurred that Christian influences seeped into the prophets' teachings, but they disagree over how much influence occurred. Some see those teachings as largely if not wholly borrowed from non-Native Christian sources while others argue for a much more partial impact that produced syncretic religious movements. Either way, they believe Christian ideas such as the emphasis on individual moral and ethical action and the concept of a creator God as a personal, active deity came to shape the reformers' messages.[63] Hints of those themes may be seen in the testimony with which this chapter began. Papunhank's language (or that attributed to him) spoke of interacting with the divine creator in a more relational manner than was typical within Delaware and Munsee cosmologies. And the duties he now thought incumbent upon him certainly had a strong ethical component. Might Papunhank have also picked up some Christian pacifist ideas somewhere along the way?

That seems highly likely especially as his contacts with Moravians and Quakers increased in the late 1750s.[64] His pacifism did not originate with them, but their peace witness reinforced his own and gave him potential allies in the quest to keep his community secure. Later chapters will detail his important relationships with them after 1758. For now, it is worth exploring what earlier contacts may have been pivotal in this regard.

Founders and ongoing political leaders of the Pennsylvania colony, Friends were a well-known entity among Indian communities. As just alluded to, Papunhank was likely familiar with the story of how Lenape sachems and William Penn forged a relationship of peace and justice in the 1680s. That powerful founding myth shaped the identities of most Quakers and many other colonists. Plenty of Delawares and other Pennsylvania-area Indians were equally enamored with the myth—or, at least, they found it a usable past when negotiating with colonial authorities. They may have heard stories of how earlier generations of mid-Atlantic Indians in the seventeenth century, including perhaps some of Papunhank's ancestors in New York, had used historical memory to advance their cause. Emphasizing a common past of peace, they hoped to persuade the English to respect Indian land claims and in the process, retain a measure of autonomy. Asking Pennsylvania officials in the eighteenth century to follow in the established path of harmony became more contentious after the controversial Walking Purchase of 1737. Nevertheless, the myth continued to be invoked for at least another generation.[65]

As far as we know, Papunhank was not directly involved in colonial political or diplomatic affairs in the 1730s and 1740s, nor did that change in the early 1750s. At least no evidence has been found linking the two. As a result, his contacts with Friends were likely limited to face-to-face encounters with individual Quaker traders and settlers. Many of those interactions may have been hospitable and mutually beneficial given the common needs of frontier inhabitants whether Native or Euro-American. It is even possible that Papunhank noticed a difference in the attitudes and behavior of Friends from that of settlers and squatters of other religioethnic backgrounds. For example, Quakers may have expressed their desire for peaceful relations and spoken of their tradition of nonviolence. Yet it is hard to imagine Papunhank taking away anything more than a vague sense of Quaker beliefs from such encounters. He was certainly not listening to Quaker sermons or conversing with Quaker missionaries.[66]

Some of that may have changed when the violence of the Seven Years' War infected eastern Pennsylvania. News of the Quaker-dominated colonial legislature's action or inaction and the resulting frustrations of most frontier whites surely filtered to Indians in the region. The Pennsylvania Assembly began debating legislation authorizing the formation of a militia in the spring of 1755 but bogged down on matters of funding and oversight, so nothing had been achieved by the time Indian attacks spread to the Susquehanna that fall. In the wider public's mind, Quaker pacifists were to blame for the lack of government protection. They had blood on their hands for the widespread suffering of frontier residents. Quaker assemblymen rejected those claims. The prospect of passing military legislation or even worse, declaring war against hostile Natives, surely strained their consciences. But by this point most of them had actually strayed from the total proscription on violence advocated by Friends' founder George Fox and accepted the moral legitimacy of a defensive war. They voted in favor of the act establishing a militia in November 1755 and went along with Governor Robert Morris's proclamation the following April declaring war on the

Delawares and their allies. The latter action, which included offering bounties for Indian scalps, was the final straw for a minority group of stricter Quaker pacifists. Ten of them resigned from the assembly in protest and joined the ranks of some fellow Friends committed to the principle of absolute nonviolence and the goal of finding other means of restoring peace to the colony.[67]

Like most Pennsylvanians, Papunhank probably could not differentiate between the various parties of Quakers in 1756. But unlike most frontier settlers, he would have welcomed word that someone else in the colony disavowed warfare. Over the next two years he almost certainly learned more about the stricter Quakers, for despite their small numbers, their views became well known, and they were largely responsible for initiating a series of diplomatic councils that brought together Indian leaders, government representatives, and Quaker "observers." Whether from firsthand exposure or secondhand information, Papunhank came to know something about the organization those Quakers formed to carry on their work. The "Friendly Association" was an essentially philanthropic body designed to foster peace and to address the factors that had precipitated the war. Its members were among those Quakers who believed in radical pacifism and who decided that more could be accomplished for the cause of good through private, philanthropic means than through political office holding. The new organization gave reformist Quakers an instrument to exert informal influence over colonial affairs and to distribute charity to the Delawares and others in need. Papunhank would increasingly come to look upon these Friends as potential allies.[68]

So, too, were German and Indian Moravians. Unlike Quakers, German members of the United Brethren were quick to pitch their tents in Indian neighborhoods following their arrival in British North America in the late 1730s. Missionary-minded pietists, they were eager to share with Native peoples the good news of the Savior's bloody sacrifice for all humanity.[69] That took them, among other places, to the woods of the Wyoming Valley. Sometimes they were just passing through that region, as with the missionary journeys of David Zeisberger and August Spangenberg in 1745 and Zeisberger and Frederick Cammerhof in 1750.

In both those cases they traveled up the Susquehanna River Valley en route to the Iroquois Council at Onondaga.[70] Other times they came to stay in the Susquehanna, as with Moravian couple Martin and Anna Mack's two-month sojourn in Shamokin in 1746. The Macks periodically returned there over the next decade (Anna died in 1749), though their primary work was at Gnadenhütten, the Moravian Indian town established that same year forty miles northwest of Bethlehem as a home for Mahican Moravians forced to leave upper New York and for any Pennsylvania Indians attracted to their message. Its location at a crossroads was strategic according to Cammerhof: "the Wyoming Path is here, and many strange [i.e., non-Moravian] Indians pass over it, and are thus brought to Gnadenhütten—they frequently attend our meetings."[71] A second Moravian Indian settlement emerged a few miles to the east at the Delaware Indian town of Meniolagomekah. Other Moravian missionaries evangelized in Native villages along the Susquehanna River often enough to prompt Nanticoke headmen there in 1750 to ask "why the Brethren so frequently visited their people." Cammerhof and others were only too happy to provide an answer by "preaching to those assembled . . . the will of God concerning their salvation, inviting them to Jesus, that they might be made partakers of the riches of his grace; adding, that this was the only reason, why the Brethren came into their country."[72]

Papunhank heard sermons like that by 1754 or 1755 if not before. Given the flurry of Moravian activity in the region, they could hardly have escaped his notice. In fact, they came right to his town. Missionaries Johann Jacob Schmick, Johanna Schmick, Christian Seidel, and David Zeisberger reportedly visited and preached at Lechaweke several times.[73] Moreover, some Indians associated with the Moravians started moving northwest to the Susquehanna in the early 1750s for a variety of reasons, including pressure from the Six Nations to remove there. The Iroquois wanted to reassert control over them and have them function as a buffer against white settlement. Dozens left Gnadenhütten and Meniolagomekah in 1754, including Teedyuscung. Some of them retained their Christian commitments in the Wyoming Valley, others did not. As Papunhank interacted with German and Native Moravians, their pious appeals may have begun to make more of an impression on him in the aftermath of his father's death, once he began preaching himself, or once war was afoot. As he pondered the deity that had brought the world into being, his thoughts may have included snippets of what Moravians said about the divine nature or about human responsibility to "be peace-loving people who live quietly under a calm sky."[74]

That advice was hard to follow in 1755–56 when things above and below were anything but calm. In particular, the Gnadenhütten massacre shook Moravians to the core and left them wondering what their faith required in the light of such dark violence. That was more than an abstract question. With white and Indian war refugees arriving daily in Bethlehem and Nazareth, those places became prime targets for future attacks. How were Moravians to respond? Like Quakers, they held a range of views on what pacifism meant in practice. Not all agreed, for example, with Bishop Spangenberg's decision to have the residents of those towns amass arms and post guards day and night. Spangenberg justified his measures as appropriate defensive steps to protect civilians, something he blamed the Quaker-led assembly for not doing. He believed such actions would not contradict the traditional Moravian prohibition on military service. And the guns, he said, were to be considered a means of warning and deterrence to any potential attackers rather than instruments of deadly force. In his mind all of this could be squared with the Moravians' commitment to pacifism. Others were not so sure. Moravian Indians, for example, appear to have embraced a more absolute form of pacifism. They were especially courageous in the face of their fellow Natives' traditional warrior values, for "to a society of warriors peace might be desirable, but pacifism was contemptible."[75]

Papunhank was likely too worried about protecting his own people to know much of anything about Moravian disagreements in the weeks and months following Gnadenhütten. What he did know by this point was their reputation as a people of peace. He would have understood why so many other people sought refuge with them. Perhaps he was even tempted to have his company follow suit. Yet in the end he chose a different path, moving them north rather than east. He was savvy enough to realize that removal to Bethlehem or Nazareth would only keep them in harm's way. Raiding Delawares might take out their wrath on any pacifist Natives they encountered there. Such a move might also jeopardize his authority and the autonomy of his community. Moravians, after all, were religious competitors for the adherence of his people. They might be hospitable hosts but there was no getting around the fact that living in their midst, even temporarily, would subject them to Moravian beliefs and ways. Under those circumstances, his power was likely to erode and his company might dissipate.

Other Indian prophets understood this well. In decades to come, some would battle Moravian influence over their people. The same might have been expected from Papunhank in the 1750s given his desire for his community to be "strictly adhering to the ancient Customs & Manners of their Forefathers." But there is no evidence that Papunhank considered Moravians an enemy or sought to avoid them completely. He definitely wanted to keep his company intact, and his ongoing preaching and community leadership reflect his strong desire to fulfill his "Duty to God." He did not want his people absorbed into some larger entity, told how they were to live, or estranged from ancient ways. Yet by August 1758, even before their move to Wyalusing, he took his family to the new Moravian Indian town of Nain and spent two weeks there. Their visit initiated a series of regular encounters with the United Brethren. Apparently something about them was attractive to Papunhank and he was willing to explore it.[76]

More Revelations

In this way and others, Papunhank was unafraid to chart his own path as a prophet. His growing openness not only to Quaker and Moravian ideas but to association with them set him apart from other Indian religious reformers.[77] Partially clear by the late 1750s, it became crystal clear in the 1760s. Quaker and Moravian peace testimony (however it got fine-tuned in practice) resonated with his strong aversion to violence and warfare and was surely part of what drew him to them.

And while the process of moving closer to Moravians and Quakers was a gradual one and played out more dramatically from 1758 to 1763, even in the mid-1750s, with conflict raging, Papunhank seems to have thought that any voices inclined toward peace, and even more so pacifism, might be worth a listen.

That was part of the prophetic wisdom he shared with kin and community. They had gathered around him in the wake of his life-changing vision and apparently found something compelling in the words he spoke. His preaching drew their attention; it even inspired some of them to preach alongside him.[78] Yet there was something more that turned them into followers. Part of it was his kindness and hospitality, traits noticed by a range of observers.[79] Part of it was his call to respect and renew the ways of their fathers. Part of it was the political savvy and overall assertive community leadership he demonstrated. Part of it may have been his healing skills. Running through all of it was the social crisis Munsees and other Susquehanna Valley Indians faced by the 1750s. Imperial warfare was only the latest ingredient in their stew of troubles. Area Natives were anxious, even desperate, to find something or someone who could bring relief, who could restore their spiritual power.[80] Papunhank emerged as one option to follow; those who did were brought to unknown places and to uncomfortable positions. When most of their Munsee and Delaware peers were joining the fight against the British, Papunhank convinced them to take another course. He led them to make their own way, buoyed by the sacred rituals that had served their ancestors and open to the good that might be found in other revelations.

Much nevertheless remained uncertain in 1756 and in the years that followed. His people had left the familiar hunting grounds of the Wyoming Valley. Finding enough food to sustain them in their new locale north of Tioga proved challenging. Trade with Euro-Americans had been largely if not completely cut off.[81] Warring Indians lived nearby in all directions. The neutral Iroquois had their own agendas. And more and more whites looked disparagingly on all Indians. Under those circumstances, it is little wonder that Papunhank's heart and mind were troubled or that he continued to seek supernatural help.

The Great Spirit didn't disappoint him. When "his natural Faculties were, in a Manner overcome, by something superior to Nature," a new vision appeared and gave him "some Prospects . . . of the Path he was to tread, in order to attain to happiness." In it he saw "a Fire burning before him, and a sense was given him, that he was to go thro that fire which whilst he was attentively beholding & Pondering upon, he saw, as it were, a small Narrow Path, very near the Fire, and yet which might be trod in, so as to escape the Flame. This, he was given to know, was the Path in which the wise Indians had trod in."[82] This new revelation was further divine confirmation that he was to go down the road less traveled. He and his people would need to go through a crucible of fire—a war perhaps? Their happiness lay on the other end of it or maybe even in its midst. To go around it or to sidestep it might seem wise. Many prior Indians had chosen that path. But it was second best to experiencing the refining fire itself.

And there was more. Either in the same vision or in a separate moment of revelation in 1757, his own "unsettled State" was calmed. For several years he had wrestled internally to gain some certainty that what he felt to be the "good Spirit in His Heart" was in fact that. He had become convinced that it was not enough simply to talk about the things of God. His preaching could not just be an intellectual exercise. Instead, his words needed to "proceed from the good Principle in the Heart" to be effective. But was what he felt inside that "good Principle"? Finally assurance came "that Love was good, and that he needed no farther inquiry upon it." Doubts dissipated "that it was the right way." He was persuaded that "this Spirit was a Spirit of Love" so he prayed daily "to his Maker, that it might continually abide with him."[83]

Papunhank likely prayed the same prayer for his followers and for all persons in war-torn Pennsylvania. They were part of his personal and communal spirituality. His ongoing spiritual journeying reflected the fluidity of almost everything in his world and the broader world in the mid-1750s. He had come far from his days of drunken stupor. A series of extraordinary religious experiences had transformed his perspective and his life's purpose. Now, unlike other Native prophets of his day, he had come to see the critical spiritual dividing line among persons as not a matter of racial difference or separate creations but of which Spirit—the good or the evil—directed one's path.[84] In the next few years, external threats and internal struggles would continue to imperil the peace he longed for within and without. They would bring new opportunities, new partners, and new disappointments.

3

Building Alliances

Moravians baptized Papunhank in late June 1763. As he felt the baptismal waters being poured over his head, tears ran down his face and the cheeks of the gathered crowd. All could feel the spiritual power and emotional drama of the moment. Their prophet and guiding light was taking a step no others in the Wyalusing community had yet chosen. Whatever sense they made of the new ritual, for him it represented another critical turning point in his religious journey. This time it came not at the end of a five-day vision quest but only after more than five years of pondering in his heart and mind what various Moravians had told him about his need for Jesus the Savior. Repeatedly moved by their invitational message, Papunhank finally made the decision to join their ranks:

> The 26th in the forenoon in the sermon I [David Zeisberger] spoke for the first time about Baptism and what it is and amid a palpable Presence of the Savior I baptized Papunhank and named him Johannes. There was such a movement in the service that almost everyone was weeping. Afterwards he made a beautiful confession before all the people with many tears and said how the Savior had made him feel his great misery and dissolution. He had preached to them about this and had believed that there was some goodness in him, at least he had always thought that he could find it in himself but had not known that he was such

> a bad person, indeed that he was the greatest sinner among all of them, but that they should forgive him for all that he had done until now and forget it. Now we have the Brethren he said. They talk to us about the Savior and we know that we hear the one right word of God, we want to be obedient to them and do what they tell us.[1]

With echoes of the Apostle Paul's claim that he was the foremost of all sinners (1 Timothy 1:15), Papunhank poured out a heartfelt confession with an emotional openness and sincerity that moved Zeisberger and fellow Natives alike.[2] The Munsee prophet became a Moravian, a commitment he kept for the rest of his life. But that decision arose from far more than individual choice. The newly christened Johannes made it clear right away that he hoped, perhaps even expected, his people to follow his lead in heeding this "one right word of God" and obeying Moravian instruction.[3] Behind and beyond his personal conversion lay the conviction that here was a union that could move his whole community forward, an alliance that promised religious leadership, spiritual nurture, and community support.[4] For the past half-dozen years, events had placed increasing pressure upon him to be on the lookout for partners who could provide religious and political resources to help sustain his company amid ongoing conflict. His alliance-building efforts were another key strategy for protecting himself and his people as well as for promoting peace. From 1758 through 1763 Papunhank charted new waters that drew him more fully into Pennsylvania politics, enlarged his relations with other Native communities, and increased his associations with Christian bodies that shared his pacifist principles.

Papunhank's actions in these years both conform with and deviate from broader patterns of action evident among Pennsylvania and Ohio Indians. From the Seven Years' War through the early 1790s, those Natives engaged in "a forty-year series of *Indian Wars for Independence* from rule by Great Britain and, later, the newly independent United States of America." They sought to maintain as much autonomy as they could from Iroquois, French, British, and American control and fought worldly and otherworldly (prophet-inspired) wars to try to achieve it. Papunhank's many strategies for preserving his community fit well within this "independence" movement framework. He, too, wanted independence from untoward influences, encroaching settlers, and outside authorities. His goal was always to carve out a sufficient literal and figurative space for his people to live, work, and worship as they pleased. Building alliances was one acceptable means for accomplishing that end. But resorting to war was not. There he departed from the choices most other Indians made in the 1750s, 1760s, and beyond. While they embraced warfare as a necessary means to protect or regain homelands, Papunhank's moral commitments demanded that he find other avenues to secure a peaceful place for his people.[5]

Monitoring War and Peace

Looking back from 1763, Papunhank would likely have thought that all things considered, the move of his company in late 1755 or early 1756 to the far northern reaches of the upper Susquehanna Valley had proved propitious. Their new locale turned out to be a comparatively safe haven. Once there, they were more or less out of harm's way, though fears of what might befall them undoubtedly persisted. With bounty rewards for Indian scalps being offered, claims to being "friendly Indians" did little to deter any whites bent on revenge and anxious to collect the government subsidy. Fortunately for them, few if any whites had the nerve to venture anywhere close to where Papunhank and his people had landed. There were too many enclaves of armed and dangerous Indians at Tioga and among the Munsee towns along the Chemung River for anything besides a substantial force to approach them. Until September 1756 Pennsylvania seemed incapable of producing such a force. But then a militia of 360 men under the command of Colonel John Armstrong marched west and attacked the Delaware town of Kittanning on the Allegheny River. They killed a dozen or two Natives and rescued eleven white captives but suffered higher casualty rates and left perhaps as many as eighty other captives in Delaware hands. Some Pennsylvanians nevertheless hailed the raid as a victory. Yet it did nothing to pacify the colony's frontier. Instead, western Delaware and

Shawnee warriors engaged in new rounds of retaliatory raids, coming east once again across the Susquehanna River to attack settlements in Lancaster and Berks Counties.[6]

Disconcerting as those developments were, there were some more promising signs that peace might be in the works for Pennsylvania's northern front. In May Robert Morris, the colony's lieutenant governor, contacted Delaware leader Teedyuscung about the prospect of negotiating an end to the warfare with the eastern Delawares and their allies.[7] Whatever gains or satisfactions the latter had enjoyed in the prior six months, they were now hurting for food. War disrupted normal patterns of agriculture, trade, and hunting. Peace might restore the stability needed to feed them and provide a chance to return to more familiar territory. For these reasons and the possible opportunity to secure autonomous land rights to the Wyoming Valley, Teedyuscung agreed to meet at Easton, Pennsylvania, in late July. He made bold claims there to speak on behalf of ten Indian nations, including the Munsees and even the Iroquois Confederacy, and with support from the strict pacifist wing of the Society of Friends he identified the injustices of earlier land deals as the primary cause of the Native resort to war. Not everyone, however, agreed with his point of view. For example, representatives of the Six Nations and the imperial government looked askance upon his assertions of authority. Nor were they happy with an individual colony, Pennsylvania, pursuing a separate peace. Not surprisingly, then, no formal agreement was reached.[8]

But at least they were talking. That's probably how Papunhank looked upon the first Easton treaty and word that another meeting would be held there in November. Any peace initiatives must have been welcome news to his vulnerable community. They were neither practically nor philosophically prepared to defend themselves against armed attacks from whites or from hostile Indians. Their adult men had learned warrior skills, but their choice to live with Papunhank was presumably an indication of their desire to avoid warfare, at least for most of them. They had deliberately sought geographical isolation, yet their own welfare dictated that they pay attention to the flow of events. That did not prove difficult to do. Situated on the main transportation and communication link between Tioga and Munsee settlements in southern New York, their village could not help but keep abreast of what was happening. Hearing that Teedyuscung was talking rather than raiding must have brought some hope amid reports dominated by dismal details of ongoing fighting, scalped heads, and mutilated bodies.

Interestingly, Papunhank apparently chose not to attend either Easton treaty. There is no evidence that he or other members of his community were there. He likely understood that he wielded little clout beyond the modest numbers of his own people. Whatever authority he possessed came largely from his religious leadership. It arose from the power of his vision and the spiritual and moral reform it had engendered. Moreover, it had been self-generated or follower-generated, not bestowed by some wider tribal entity or recognized by any Euro-American political body. Teedyuscung's pretensions to authority as "King of the Delawares" had also been self-proclaimed, but his actions since 1754 had given them at least a modicum of credibility. Papunhank was in no such position. No one was seeking out his help or voice for peace (yet), and he was apparently content to leave it that way. He may have also thought it was too personally risky to travel to the conferences, for during the war "peaceful Indian enclaves . . . came under great suspicion." Trusted neither by whites nor by the "enemy" Indians they were suspected of aiding, communities like Papunhank's had few natural allies in a world torn by violence and intent on demarcating sides. He seems to have concluded that for the time being, his people were better off keeping to themselves, geographically isolated, politically neutral, and diplomatically detached. Indications are that his followers concurred. They agreed that those were the "peace" behaviors that made most sense in the war's first few years.[9]

Yet from his later actions, it appears that Papunhank was taking careful notes. He was alert to the complicated web of relationships being woven among those with a major stake in how the war and any future peace progressed in the second half of the 1750s and the early years of the 1760s. In particular, the diplomatic maneuverings and "peace" activities of six key groups garnered his interest: the Quakers' Friendly Association; Teedyuscung and the eastern Delawares; the

Six Nations and their close ally, Sir William Johnson, the recently appointed British superintendent of Indian affairs for the Northern District; the Pennsylvania government; the western Delawares and their principal peace proponent, Tamaqua; and the Moravians. For the next twenty years, the Munsee reformer would carefully navigate relations with each of those bodies, even as he also struggled to manage internal relations within his community. More immediately, he monitored how these outsider groups might be helpful to his people's plight amid the ongoing conflict.

Steps toward Peace

As noted earlier, Papunhank likely became aware of the Friendly Association's activities from its beginnings. Even before it was formally organized, some of its future members spent six days in April 1756 meeting in Philadelphia with several Iroquois leaders. Their exchange of speeches, wampum belts, and medals emphasized the hope that Friends and Iroquois alike would use their influence with the warring Delawares and the Pennsylvania government to bring an end to the fighting. Each called the other to the role of diplomatic go-between, and each blessed the peaceful legacy of William Penn while also lamenting the influx into the province of many "men of different principles." As Oneida sachem Scarouady put it, "though we have been lost, to one another, a great while, we are very glad to hear you are of the same sentiment with Onas [William Penn]: since he was dead there have from time to time come new governors, one after another, and another sort of people, different from the first settlers."[10]

In Philadelphia and at later treaties, headmen of the Six Nations, Delaware, and other Indian bodies repeatedly expressed their desire to find Penn-like provincials who would pursue peaceful and just relations. In parallel fashion, the Friendly Association looked for Penn-like Natives who would bury the hatchet and once again make the colony a peaceable kingdom. At a time when Quaker confidence in the peaceful intentions of their own government was low and their political rivalry with the colony's proprietors was high, they turned their gaze toward Indians in hopes of finding an ally who could restore relations to a more positive footing. Although it was by no means their only strategy for seeking peace and justice in the divisive years from 1754 to 1765, the quest for a Native partner, or better yet, an Indian protégé, was nevertheless a critical piece of reformist Quaker efforts to revitalize the Holy Experiment.[11]

For a time Friendly Association members believed they had found their man in Teedyuscung. Wealthy merchant Israel Pemberton Jr. and other leading Friends cozied up to the Delaware leader, offering political advice and supporting his efforts to craft a peace agreement and to seek redress for past colonial injustices, particularly the land fraud perpetrated in the Walking Purchase. Strongly opposed for their interference into official diplomatic proceedings by the colony's proprietors and governor, and by Sir William Johnson, the Quakers nevertheless managed to control much of what took place at the two Easton meetings in 1756 and at a third treaty held there in July 1757. In each case, with their support, Teedyuscung seized the chance to express Delaware concerns, levy harsh criticisms, and assert his independence from other authorities, whether Native (the Six Nations, western Delawares) or Euro-American (Pennsylvania government, Johnson). Friendly Association members took plenty of heat from other Pennsylvanians for aiding Teedyuscung, especially when Indian attacks (even if by other Native groups) went on unabated before and after all of the meetings. The Friendly Association was also dismayed by the Delaware leader's too great love for alcohol. Nevertheless, the group remained enamored with the prospect that here was an Indian who could lead his people and the colony back to the ways of their forefathers.[12] No wonder they listened so intently at Easton in 1757 when, according to Quaker John Churchman, Teedyuscung gave a speech in which he told his many white listeners of his desire that "we may love like brethren" that "the sun may shine clear upon us, that we, our wives, our young men and children may rejoice in a lasting peace."[13] Those words and the Delaware's choice to pepper his talks with allusions to an overruling divine being surely fueled Quaker hopes. They were consequently ready and willing to accommodate his request in the spring of 1758 to send workers to Wyoming to help build new homes for the Delawares returning there.[14]

Even with Quaker aid, though, Teedyuscung's negotiating efforts reaped mixed results at best between 1756 and 1758. On the plus side, he managed to convince the Pennsylvania governor to recognize him as a rightful representative of "a Collection of Delawares, Shawonese, Mohiccons, and some of the fugitive Six Nations who were formerly on the Ohio." That positioned him to present Native grievances and gave him enough leverage, with Friends' support, to insist on having his own clerk record treaty proceedings lest the government's official version not tell the whole story (as had already happened at the Second Easton Treaty). Following the Third Easton Treaty, his complaints spurred a committee of provincial councilors to investigate the accuracy of his claims. At that same meeting, Teedyuscung championed his goal of gaining for his people a land reserve where they could dwell permanently in peace and safety. He wanted it to be in the familiar territory of the Wyoming Valley. The Pennsylvania government found a way to acquiesce to that demand, and by the following spring provincial laborers, funded by the Friendly Association, had built ten cabins and other accoutrements to accommodate returning Delawares.[15]

But all that puts too rosy a tint on Teedyuscung's fortunes. As already mentioned, most others repeatedly dismissed his expansive claims to authority and independence. The provincial government's investigating committee repudiated his accusations of land fraud. The Six Nations and William Johnson permitted his resettlement at Wyoming only so that his people could stand in the way of more troublesome settlers occupying that land. The truces and peace settlements he negotiated didn't hold; even one of the masons rebuilding Wyoming was murdered and scalped by Indians resentful of this new sign of English intrusion and of Teedyuscung's willingness to curry English favor.[16]

Regardless of how limited Teedyuscung's success may have been, Papunhank nonetheless was likely impressed with the Delaware's efforts at mediation. In years to come, the two would establish cordial relations. The Munsee could not have been happy in 1755 when Teedyuscung resorted to war even if he understood the reasons for it.

But his opinion of the Delaware headman surely rose when he proved willing in 1756 to adjust his policies as circumstances dictated. Papunhank may have wished that other Native leaders would embrace pacifism for philosophical reasons, but he was ready and willing to endorse their pragmatic peacemaking whenever they were inclined to do it. From that summer on, Teedyuscung presented his people as key intermediaries for the construction of a peace settlement. That is why he repeatedly insisted he was speaking on behalf of many nations. Like other Delawares, he believed that "power was acquired through alliance building among many groups." Crafting partnerships with other Native peoples not only made strategic sense, it afforded all of them the spiritual resources each brought to that union. Such collective sacred power was necessary to prosper their relations with one another and to meet the difficult challenges of laborious treaty negotiations with the British.[17]

Western Delaware sachem Tamaqua (also known as King Beaver) presented Papunhank with a similar model of Native leadership. He, too, believed that building alliances was essential for restoring peace. Tamaqua had been among those of his people unenthused about the choice in 1755 to fight the British. While many of his brethren went off to war, he stayed at home endeavoring to do something for peace. His efforts, however, had little impact until the Pennsylvania militia raid on Kittanning made more Delawares question the wisdom of continued fighting even though they had come out on top in that battle. Thereafter more of his nation and their Shawnee allies began to listen to Tamaqua and others of the peace party who wanted to avoid further losses of life and property. Even more, like Teedyuscung, they wanted to secure autonomous rule for the Delawares and neighboring tribes over lands in the Ohio Country. Tamaqua thought that far more was likely to be achieved toward that goal through diplomacy than violence. He appealed to traditional notions of his people as "women" or peacemakers and as "grandfathers," the most ancient and sage of nations, to advance his peace platform. Other western Delawares were equally determined to throw off those labels and use warfare to declare their manhood and independence as a nation.[18]

As word spread westward of Teedyuscung's negotiations with the British, the Ohio Indians' peace faction saw an opportunity to use him as a go-between with the Pennsylvania government. He was a means to open communication channels. Teedyuscung played up his role as an intermediary and even claimed to represent the western Natives. But with contact established, by mid-1758 neither the Ohio Indians nor the British seemed to need him anymore. They were the real power brokers in the emerging diplomatic equation and were willing to talk directly or at least through colonial emissary Christian Frederick Post, to advance their respective causes: Indian autonomy in the Ohio Country in return for Ohio Indian neutrality during an upcoming British assault on the French in the west. Tamaqua and his allies managed to deliver the latter, thereby helping to ensure a British victory and French retreat in November 1758. The following summer, Tamaqua took the lead in orchestrating a formal peace agreement among western Delawares, Shawnees, Wyandots, and the British.[19]

Meanwhile, back east, a Fourth Easton Treaty had taken place in October 1758. More than five hundred Natives from thirteen nations, including the western Delawares, attended along with representatives from the Pennsylvania and New Jersey governments, the British crown, and the Friendly Association. Teedyuscung and his Quaker supporters once again made their case that past injustices needed to be redressed, but their efforts went for naught. The Delaware sachem acted erratically at the conference, often inebriated. More important, George Croghan, agent for William Johnson, and Six Nations headmen pushed him and Quaker diplomats aside at the meeting. Along with the colony's proprietors, they all had had quite enough of what they saw as Teedyuscung's pretensions and Quaker interference into Indian relations and were determined to assert their own control over those matters. They proceeded to negotiate a peace settlement that recognized Iroquois sovereignty over lands stretching from the Susquehanna River into the Ohio Country and promised to reestablish trade and set a western boundary line for colonial settlement. It was enough to end hostilities in the east and pave the way for later treaties in the west.[20]

Meeting Moravians

Papunhank and his company must have greeted the news of the Easton peace accord with both relief and excitement. For three years the Susquehanna Valley had endured violent conflict and bloodshed. Families and towns had been disrupted and destroyed, and Natives and colonists alike had been scattered. The time had come to restore order and regain some semblance of home. For Papunhank's people, that meant following the example of other refugee Delawares in moving south, back to lands along the Susquehanna River closer to where they had lived prior to the war's disruptions. Within days or weeks of the latest Easton Treaty, Papunhank relocated his band in late 1758 to Wyalusing, where they remained for the next five years.

Papunhank likely scouted the Wyalusing area a number of times before deciding upon it as the right spot for them to start over. His willingness to venture outward seems to have grown by the summer of 1758 as hostilities dwindled, travel became less risky, and more normal patterns of hunting resumed. When Native messengers Moses Tatamy and Isaac Still stopped at his village in early July and extended an invitation from Francis Bernard, the governor of New Jersey, to attend a treaty at Burlington, they noted that Papunhank "was well pleased with our Message, and say'd he would come down." The Munsee pacifist naturally welcomed word of another peace initiative. But if he followed through on his promise to attend the conference, it was a likely departure from past behavior. As noted earlier, odds are that Papunhank had not participated in the meetings at Easton. In the case of Burlington, though, a different story might have been expected. For one thing, he got a face-to-face invitation to go and indicated to Tatamy that he was planning on it. For another, he had good reasons to attend. Invitations had been targeted to, among others, Munsee headmen along the Chemung River. The treaty promised to address ongoing disputes over Munsee land claims. For a leader concerned about where his people might move next and how to secure their rights to be there, it made sense to show up and at least listen.[21]

Yet the minutes from the Burlington meeting on August 7 and 8 make no mention of him being there. Still, it is likely that word of what happened at the conference would have reached him sooner rather than later. As Munsees, Delawares, and Senecas met with the governor, it quickly became obvious which Natives were calling the shots. The Munsee representative, Otawopass Benjamin, had hardly offered more than an initial greeting to the colony's officials when the Iroquois speaker, Apewyett, took over and let everyone know that the Munsees were women and could not "hold Treaties for themselves." The Seneca's speech implied that the Six Nations would care for resolving Munsee land claims and they, rather than Teedyuscung or anyone else, would be the key spokespersons for Indians at the upcoming Easton conference. As he heard about the treaty, Papunhank could not have missed the point that resettlement anywhere in the Susquehanna would depend on Six Nations assent.[22]

A week after the Burlington meeting, Papunhank and his family arrived in the Moravian Indian town of Nain for a two-week stay.[23] Their visit is telling on several counts. Apparently he now felt safe enough to bring not only himself but his family south and believed that more was to be gained by going to Nain than to Burlington. Others could attend to the politics; he preferred to spend time in a religious community from whom he might learn. His choice reminds us that Papunhank saw himself principally as a religious leader and teacher. This is what his visions had called him to be and do. He had only gathered a following because of his role as a preacher. Ever since his adult vision quest, he had remained open and eager for new revelations. He had become a spiritual seeker, hungry to know more. He saw Nain as a place where he might acquire additional spiritual wisdom and power to enhance his message.

None of that however was divorced from the Munsee reformer's need to sort out next steps for his people. Where should they go? How safe would they be? Whose trust would they need to gain? Whose sovereignty would they need to recognize? From whom might they get assistance? Where might they find a valuable ally? Those were more than abstract questions for Papunhank and his community. As a result, going to Nain and nearby Bethlehem at that moment may be viewed as extremely risky and perhaps even reckless given the potential reactions of some within his village. Since many may have wondered at the wisdom of associating with any whites or Christians at this still unsettled time, he was jeopardizing his band's unity right when he was asking them to move again. Moreover, bringing his whole family with him made it clear to all that this was no casual visit. What were they to think of their prophet's political judgment as well as the validity of the message he had been preaching if he was out sampling other truths?

Whatever the misgivings of others, Papunhank, his wife Anna Johanna, their seventeen-year-old daughter, Sophia, and their younger daughter, Anna Paulina, made their way to the mostly Mahican Moravians in Nain.[24] Papunhank's previous contacts with the United Brethren had been sporadic and mostly with German missionaries rather than with a whole community of Native Moravians, though it is possible he had visited Gnadenhütten before its abandonment. They had also most likely taken place in Indian country, not in a Moravian Indian village. Whether they originally intended to stay as long as they did (fifteen days) or adjusted their plans midvisit, their time in Nain afforded ample opportunity to observe Native Moravian ways: the layout of the village, the construction style of the buildings, the daily routines of the people, the organization of their labor, the schooling of the children, the character of their daily religious services, and the nature of their piety. For perhaps the first time in his life, he had a sustained exposure to Moravian emphases upon Jesus's love and bloody sacrifice for humankind and on the ways in which believers were to live in accord with those truths through prayer, meditation, communal worship, confession, and moral obedience. He began to see how all of that was playing out in the lives of Mahican and Delaware Moravians. Time in Nain also allowed him and his family to establish or renew relationships with those Indians. Many in the town were baptized Natives who had left the Moravian fold with Teedyuscung in 1754 for Wyoming but had now returned. Once "they had given full proof of their true repentance and change of heart . . . they were gladly readmitted to fellowship." Papunhank may have interacted with some of those folk in the months prior to the beginning of warfare in the Wyoming Valley in late 1755. Now he had the chance to get to know them and their kin better, and to be known by them. When his family arrived on August 14 the congregational diary merely noted that "an Indian arrived from the Susquehanna with his family." By the twenty-seventh the missionary diarist called Papunhank by name and explained that the Indian had confided his wartime anxieties to Joshua Senior, one of the community's Mahican leaders: "Papunham had a discussion with our Josua concerning the present disquieting circumstances. Papunham said that there were still many wild Indians who were the enemies of the English. He thought it would be a long time until there would be peace again as had been before." In turn, Joshua shared his Moravian faith and hope for another kind of peace: "[he] took the opportunity to tell him about the eternal peace that we can have when we have the Blood-covered God in our hearts." Apparently those words or other aspects of their visit in Nain set well with Papunhank, for when he departed on the twenty-ninth, the diarist wrote, "Papunham returned very happy to Wajomik [Wyoming] with his family."[25]

If that description of Papunhank's mood was accurate, it is worth asking why. He certainly would have been encouraged by being in another Native community committed to peace. Here were kindred spirits; their example of peaceable living would have been a pleasant contrast to the warring impulse he had witnessed among most Native bands and whites in the last few years. Being in their midst may have helped him to take heart that better days lay ahead, though he clearly had ongoing fears that warfare might resume. So, too, his spirituality would have resonated with the seriousness of their religious commitments and practice. Papunhank would later explain that he did not yet fully grasp what Moravians had tried to teach him about his sinfulness and need for a savior. But he seems to have been open to what they had to say and the spiritual resources they might offer his preaching and his people. He might also have been pleased to pick up various pointers about how to design a new town. The physical and metaphysical dimensions of life in Nain may have inspired his plans for Wyalusing. Finally, his smile upon leaving Nain may have been prompted by something more domestic. There is a good chance that

Sophia had occasion to meet Joshua Junior (son of the Mahican leader) during their stay.[26] Once reunited six years later, the two would wed. Perhaps a budding romance, and one that could bind peace-loving Munsees and Mahicans together, warmed a father's heart in late August 1758. Even if that is too sentimental a thought, it is noteworthy that Papunhank spent this much time with Moravians and before long, would be back again.

Wyalusing Contacts

Five weeks later the Fourth Easton Treaty convened. The minutes of the conference listed Munsee chief Echgohund present "with Sundry Men, Women, and Children." If Papunhank was among them, he would have heard firsthand the terms of the settlement and observed the power politics of Croghan and the Six Nations. But even if he wasn't, it was certainly not long before news of the treaty arrived. And within another month, he would have learned of the major victory of General John Forbes and the British army in the Ohio Country. As Forbes's troops approached Fort Duquesne, the French blew up the fort and retreated to Fort Niagara in western New York. The war's tide had clearly turned.[27]

With hostilities essentially ended in Pennsylvania, Papunhank and his people moved to Wyalusing and began to construct their new homes and village. No doubt there were many immediate needs to absorb the Munsee prophet's attention. Still, it seems likely that amid their resettlement, he would have been inclined to take stock of the past three years and where things now stood. The British surely had military momentum on their side and increasingly seemed destined to win the war. Was it time for Papunhank to leave neutrality behind and look for ways to aid the British cause? If wider British rule was inevitable, might closer relations with their representatives, including the Pennsylvania government, be necessary to secure their place in the colony? The Six Nations certainly appeared happy to partner with British superintendent Sir William Johnson to advance their mutual interests.[28] Was that a model worth following? At the very least, there was no mistaking the need to defer to Iroquois authority claims over the Susquehanna. Staying on good terms with their headmen would be essential for the Wyalusingites.

At the same time, they could not ignore relations with more local sachems. Teedyuscung had been humiliated at Easton, but he and other Delaware and Munsee chiefs still wielded clout among their own communities. Papunhank would need to make sure that no lasting bitterness over his people's failure to join the fight against the British would threaten their well-being. Could a group like the Friendly Association be instrumental in assisting that effort? They were clearly sympathetic to Teedyuscung's cause, even if they had their own political and economic agendas. Moreover, they shared Papunhank's aversion to war and were willing and able to supply material goods to war-damaged Indian bands. Crown and colonial authorities might not like these Quakers, but they were still a force with which to be reckoned. The same could not be said about the Moravians. Despite rumors to the contrary, they had chosen to stay out of politics and diplomatic intrigues. They wanted to be left alone to carry on peaceful lives within harmonious communities. The Gnadenhütten massacre made clear that wasn't always possible. Yet these people proved resilient. They endured the trial, weathered the storm, and reestablished Native and German towns that offered their inhabitants a sense of solidarity rarely found elsewhere in war-torn Pennsylvania.[29]

Six Nations sovereignty, British ascendancy, Teedyuscung's growing marginality, the Friendly Association's advocacy, Moravian hospitality—all these realities and more pressed in upon Papunhank's mind in early 1759. Like other Native leaders, he desperately wanted a secure, safe place for his people, somewhere they could remain for the longer haul, free to live their lives as they wished. To make that happen, he would need to do his part to cultivate just the right types of relationships both within and beyond his own body. Some would require deference, others tolerance, still others mutual embrace. All would demand great skill. Even with that, though, his followers' fate might very well rest in hands or forces far beyond his control. That was reason enough to keep seeking a sacred power that could overrule all.

Moving to Wyalusing was no obvious choice. Munsees had relinquished all of their remaining homelands in the agreements just made at Easton. Most of them were now resigned to pursue their futures in regions north and west of the Susquehanna. Papunhank might have been expected to follow suit. But instead, ever the independent thinker, he brought his people back down the river in what one historian has called "a last desperate effort to establish an eastern stronghold of the Munsee tribe."[30] Whether Papunhank thought of the move in those terms is unclear. What does seem clear are some of the reasons for their decision. Wyalusing offered fertile land, access to familiar hunting grounds, and ease of transportation. With few or no Indians living in the immediate area, they could move there without disturbing others. Moreover, it was close enough to other Native settlements to stay abreast of important news but far enough removed to create their own type of community. In the prior three years, Papunhank had seen the value in distancing his company from most other Munsees who chose to fight and sided with the French. He apparently saw no reason to join with them now wherever they went. Instead, in Wyalusing, he could preach his nativist message and Delawares, Munsees, Nanticokes, Conoys, and other refugee Indians could freely choose whether to embrace it. Equally important, Wyalusing was sufficiently isolated from white squatters. The town might welcome white visitors of certain sorts but it had no interest in seeing colonists actually settle anywhere close to its domain.

Still, the decision to move to Wyalusing was not theirs alone to make; it was contingent on Six Nations approval. Their claims to that land had just been reestablished at Easton. Though the terms of any agreement with Papunhank's company are not known, the Iroquois presumably would have raised objections to Papunhank's being there if it did not serve their agenda, which in this case was principally to keep whites from infiltrating the area. They likely anticipated that his peaceable company could function as a buffer against white expansion, similar to what they had in mind for Teedyuscung's resettlement at Wyoming.[31]

Papunhank's people situated their new village on the east side of the Susquehanna, employing flatlands, hilltops, and Wyalusing Creek. They built more than three dozen houses and clustered them together. Constructed of wood poles and covered with bark, a typical dwelling measured eighteen by thirty feet, spacious enough to house extended families. Before long, the community grew to between three hundred and four hundred people. The town's appeal resided in its economic sustainability, political quiescence, and religious vibrancy. Its growth must have made Papunhank's leadership more difficult and more contested. He faced an uphill battle to get all newcomers to conform to the rituals and rules he had established, including no liquor and no violence, and to heed his religious teachings, perhaps especially with veterans of the just completed war. It would remain so throughout these years in Wyalusing.[32]

As they built homes, cleared fields, planted crops, hunted for game, performed rituals, and generally settled back into the normal rhythms of Native life, Papunhank renewed his contacts with Moravians and kept track of ongoing broader developments. He went to Nain again with some of his people in the summer of 1759 and spent two more weeks there with the expressed purpose of learning more of the Brethren message. It came to him through word, music, image, and sacrament. Joshua Senior and Delaware Native assistant Anton spent hours "preaching to Papunhank and his people about the Kingdom of God, including the importance of baptism." They also showed them, upon the request of the Wyalusingites, religious paintings including one depicting Christ's deposition from the cross. It had a "profound effect on them," as did witnessing a baptism. Moravian missionary Martin Mack eagerly recorded in the congregational diary the evolution of Papunhank's religious reflections during this visit. On July 3, he noted that the Munsee leader stated "he believed that God was by him sometimes and he sensed it. He said he felt a love from Him, but whether up to now that was indeed from Him has remained a hidden and unclear thing." Two days later Papunhank indicated that he had often spoken with his people about baptism and that they were in favor of it for him. He spent much time listening to the Moravians describe "how their hearts were changed through baptism, and how through it they continue to grow." On the eighth, Mack, Anton, and Joshua spoke at length with him about the central teaching of Moravian Christian faith:

> [We] had a long discussion with Papunhank and one of his people. It had to do with the belief in Jesus as the crucified and how He alone saves us. Papunhank said until now he tried to believe in a God and it felt satisfying from it. But this feeling didn't last. He wondered why it remained a secret for him why this God would die for humans. He felt something was missing in the resolve of his belief. There was much of these material and ideas, which were discussed. Then, in this man's heart a softening became evident, and breaking into tears, he uttered: Oh, God, have mercy on me and make your death clear to my heart.[33]

Emotionally moved and intellectually puzzled, Papunhank returned to Wyalusing and tried to get his head and heart around what he had seen, heard, and felt in Nain. According to another Wyalusingite visitor to the Moravian Indian town, once home, the prophet pronounced to his people, "I've told you many good things to now, and also taught you some good things. But now I find this is not the right path if we are to be saved. We must accept the teachings of the Brethren. I have given great consideration to this and realize there is no other way to attain salvation other than that of the Brethren."[34] However accurate an account of Papunhank's admonitions and convictions at that moment, those words and his interactions with Moravians overall indicate his persistent quest for spiritual insight and peace of mind and his desire to ensure the religious and moral well-being of his followers.

They also reflect his wider strategy to build fruitful alliances. On that score, 1759 brought new possibilities for partnerships. Additional British military victories that year all but sealed the war's outcome in their favor. That prospect convinced the Iroquois to lay aside their neutrality and back a winner. They began to supply warriors for British military expeditions in hopes of gaining material and diplomatic rewards. Meanwhile, with peace secured in Pennsylvania, crown officials and the Pennsylvania government more energetically sought the return of white captives taken during the conflict. Redeeming those prisoners and returning them to their families and communities became a major goal and a persistent demand of colonial authorities and British officers in their interactions with Natives across the frontier. In turn, it became an opportunity for Indians willing to cooperate in that endeavor to win the appreciation and favor of powerful whites. But this was no clear-cut choice. Having Indian families give up the men and women, and the boys and girls they had adopted to replace lost loved ones, was painful work. Emotional distress was often felt on all sides as one family's gain was another family's loss. Over the next two years, more than five hundred white prisoners were returned.[35]

Teedyuscung was enlisted to aid in that work. Perhaps through it, he could regain some of the credibility he had lost at Easton. But some of his supporters were not sure that was possible, and as his politics and personal behavior continued to prove erratic, members of the Friendly Association wondered if he would ever wield the type of influence among other Pennsylvania Indians they had imagined. At that realization, Quaker interest in alternative Indian leadership rose.[36]

A Relationship Begins

Into that void came Papunhank. Details are sketchy on exactly how or when Philadelphia Friends became aware of him. As we have seen, he did not attend the treaty councils in the mid-1750s, and his company lived in places far enough removed to keep him largely out of colonial politics and the Quaker eye—but not forever. Perhaps via Moravian contacts, they learned enough about him and his people by the summer of 1759 to invite them to visit Philadelphia. That face-to-face encounter did not occur until Quakers had learned much more the following spring from sometime Moravian missionary and colonial negotiator Christian Frederick Post, alongside whom they had worked for peace in the previous several years. Post was aware as he set out in April 1760 with Teedyuscung, Moses Tatamy, Isaac Still, and John Hays on a diplomatic mission to Chemung River Natives and Ohio Indians that Quaker patience with Teedyuscung had grown short. In early May Israel Pemberton wrote Post asking him to "tell Teedyuscung that as a great deal depends on him, I desire nothing may hinder his going forward as he promised; if he should fail now . . . he will loose his Credit with the Gov. & the People & with us [Friends] in particular."[37]

By mid-May Post was in Wyalusing writing Friends excitedly about a new prospect. There he found a large, well-laid-out town inhabited by a "religious People" and led by Papunhank, "the beginner of the company & their Minister." He was "a Very Religious Civilized man in his own way, and Shewed us a great Deal of Kindness," Hays noted. This Indian was unlike any they had previously encountered, "civilized" but in his own distinctively Native way. The prophet's dignity, sincerity, and sobriety garnered their admiration. Moreover, the community of Natives as a whole was "very kind & civil to us," Post reported, and "want[ed] to see the Friends chiefly and to show that they really are Friends, they have not joined in the War." Post also observed that they were eager to avoid liquor and to aid efforts to return white captives.[38] Those aims matched precisely the diplomatic message that Post had been commissioned by Pennsylvania's Provincial Council to convey to all the Indians they encountered. He was also to give them strong assurances that no white colonists would be allowed to settle or even hunt on their lands.[39]

Papunhank and his council were eager to hear such messages and inclined to trust the messengers since they weren't strangers. Teedyuscung, Tatamy, and Still had met some of this band before, and Post himself was apparently a known commodity, perhaps through Moravian contacts: "The People here knowing me well desired much that I would keep a Meeting for them, which I comply'd with. My Text was: 'Peace be unto you.' They were all to a Man very Attentive, & I believe what they have heard will not be without a Blessing to them. They afterwards came & thanked me much for my Discourse & staid with me till Midnight. There was about a Hundred of them."[40]

The next morning Papunhank had his turn to speak. He began by declining Post's invitation to "go along . . . to see how the Work of Peace goes." "I am weak & Poor & cannot go," the Munsee said. It was enough "if you go, & whatever you agree upon Let me know, & when I hear of any good Thing I'll lay hold on it and will assist in strengthening it, as far as I am able." Papunhank was willing to partner with Post in peacemaking work, but wanted to do it on his own terms. Physical health may have had something to do with his choice to remain behind. A reluctance to be away from his community for an extended period of time also likely played a role. But the most important reason for staying put may have been his desire to keep his strategic options open in relation to other Munsees and western Indians. He was not ready to be identified as one more Native agent for the colonial government. Papunhank went on to remind Post that when he had visited Wyalusing the prior fall, he had rejoiced at the news of peace Post had brought. That had led the town to return via Post a number of horses belonging to whites. Now they were ready to take the more important step of returning white captives. Post's appeal had seemingly produced some serious soul searching within the community: "We are assured that God knows & sees us as we are," Papunhank declared, "we have not been honest, we have been false & Hypocrites, in so long detaining your Flesh & Blood, & yet at the same Time we thought to please God." Papunhank proceeded to promise to hand over the three prisoners belonging to members of his band, but could not "command others, that are lately come here to live" to do the same. He finished his speech by declaring that he would "freely do what my Brethren the English desire of me; and I wish it was in my Power, I wo.d git back all the Prisoners that are every where scattered about the Woods."[41]

Papunhank's ambitious wish had less to do with wanting to please the English and everything to do with eliminating any sources of ongoing tension or strain that could precipitate further violence. That was now his natural impulse. The war had made it so. The bloody mess had deepened his peace commitments and hardened his aversion to war. Hereafter, he read all circumstances through his pacifism. It shaped his politics and his ethics and guided his decision-making. In this case, he would happily cooperate with "redemption" efforts if they could help to ensure a more peaceful, secure future.

Odds are that Post and his companions took Papunhank at his pacifist word when he proclaimed, "I am great[ly] rejoiced at that good Peace which is so well establish'd, & we all heartily join to it, we like to live in Peace." If they needed any more convincing, they got it from three Assinisinks they met six miles outside of Wyalusing. They brought word of ongoing hostilities and told Post, "We must tell you, we have some bad News amongst us, we would say nothing about it in that Town, because those People do not like to hear of War." Wyalusing had clearly established a reputation as a peace-loving community. It also became rapidly well-known for its adherence to "the ancient Customs & Manners of their Forefathers," something Post and Hays witnessed in full display. By this point Papunhank had long promoted a nativist message as one means of self-preservation and renewal, and it had firmly taken root among his hundreds of followers. Yet given the prophet's substantial contacts with Moravians and reported encouragement to his followers to embrace their teachings, it is not surprising that Post also noted that the town was so anxious to have him preach he did so three times in thirty-six hours. Clearly for Papunhank and some others in the community, their nativism did not preclude listening to what some whites had to offer. In fact, it seems evident that in this moment, Papunhank seized the occasion to try to build bridges with two other powerful white entities outside his company and outside the Moravians. He warmly welcomed these representatives of the Pennsylvania government and let it be known that he was anxious to help diplomatically where he could. And he likewise made sure the visitors knew of the Wyalusingites' strong desire to meet with Friends, whose peaceful and sober ideals matched their own.[42]

Philadelphia Exchanges

Papunhank's impulse to enlarge his community's bonds with other groups took him to Philadelphia in the summer of 1760. His direct outreach to Quakers was something new, but it clearly continued rather than initiated his willingness to approach white Christians. Besides his visits to Nain, he had conversed with Moravians in Philadelphia and Bethlehem and in each case, according to Moravian sources, begun to lobby to have a Moravian teacher sent to his village.[43] At the same time, however, Papunhank clearly wanted to try out other options, so he extended his contacts with Friends whom his community had heard, perhaps via Post, would "be glad to see" them.[44]

Meanwhile, he sought an opportunity to function more actively in concert with the peace work being promoted by the Pennsylvania government. Papunhank and twenty-eight others from Wyalusing came to meet with Governor James Hamilton and the colony's council. Friends Israel Pemberton and Joseph Fox recorded what the Munsees said as they exchanged ideas with the heads of the colonial government. The Quakers quickly learned how Papunhank and his town were already functioning as diplomatic go-betweens, consulted by Indians (including Teedyuscung) and colonial agents alike and entrusted in this moment with returning three white captives and horses to the colonial government. Such news fed Friends' hope that here was a potentially vital political instrument. Even more encouraging, Papunhank asked the governor to prevent liquor sales to Wyalusing Natives. Convinced that "alcohol was a moral corruption that needed purging from Indian bodies and communities," his view squared with reformist Quaker emphases on moral purity and sobriety. The next day, at the urging of the Friendly Association, Fox and Pemberton, now accompanied by ten other Friends, returned to the State House with £30 worth of supplies for the Indian visitors and heard Papunhank lay out nothing less than a new vision of how to carry on intercultural relations in the colony. First, he kindly but sternly declined the gifts offered by the governor, lest their motives in coming to the city be misunderstood by other Natives and become a source of jealousy among those "who transact the publick Business and are wont to receive Presents on such Occasions." Papunhank did not want to give Six Nations representatives or any other politically powerful Indians reason to think he was acting presumptuously. The presents might also "be apt to corrupt my own mind," Papunhank claimed, "and make me proud, and others would think I wanted to be a great Man, which is not the case. [Instead], I think on God, who made us, and want to be instructed in his service and Worship." Gift exchange had long oiled the wheels of diplomacy among Pennsylvania Indians, but Papunhank believed that in the hands of the colonial government, such exchanges had degenerated into a cause of greed, rivalry, and corruption.[45]

The Munsee reformer then declared that he was "a great Lover of Peace." He told those assembled that he had "never been concern'd in War Affairs," fondly remembered the "old Friendship" between Indians and the colony's founders, and would ever be loyal to the British. Still, he was not done calling for change. Standing before the colony's elite, he had an unprecedented opportunity to address sources of injustice that could fuel renewed violence. He was not going to pass up this chance to speak about the things that lay heavy on his heart. So he boldly told the governor and council he wanted to "mention something to you [colonial officials] that I Think wrong in your dealings with the Indians." English traders announced one price for Indian-supplied skins and then paid another: "God can not be pleased to see the prices of one and the same thing so often altered and changed." In turn, Indian suppliers, faced with unreliable prices, resorted to practices that cheated their buyers, such as soaking their furs to add weight to them. Under these conditions, trade relations deteriorated to the point where there was "no Love nor honesty on either side." Gone were the days when economic exchanges were more than a transfer of goods; they had been occasions for mutual respect and dignity. "Therefore, Brother," Papunhank concluded, "we propose to fling This entirely away, for if it remains so we shall never agree and love one another as Brothers do." With the prospect of renewed trade looming ahead and Wyalusing's tangible need for equitable prices, the prophet unflinchingly proclaimed that harmony and peace required a reordering of the economic behavior of whites and Indians alike according to earlier practices and to Christian moral standards, ones plainly understandable to the English.[46]

Hamilton expressed "Great satisfaction" with the religious bent of Papunhank's message and the latter's assurances that Wyalusing's young men "were resolved to regulate their Lives so as to please their Great Creator, and likewise that they would lay aside whatever was bad and displeasing to him." In other words, if Papunhank's sermons could keep potential warriors sober and peaceful, Hamilton was all for it. The governor also gave assurances that the colony's Indian commissioners would address the trading practices issue, urged Papunhank to accept the small gifts being offered, and promised the government's "sincere Friendship and Assistance on all needful Occasions." He also entrusted Papunhank to deliver a message to Achoan (Echgohund), Munsee chief north of Wyalusing, asking him to return all English captives among his people.[47]

As Frederick Post translated the speeches back and forth, Quakers listened in what was likely awed approval as Papunhank espoused principles of peace, sober living, and economic justice—ideals revered by activist Friends. Their delight surely grew when Papunhank finished the day with repeated assertions of his deep religious interest ("I am fixed in my principles, and Shall always abide by them") and "with a solemn Act of Prayer and thanksgiving, which he performed very devoutly." Their delight continued in the days after the conference as Papunhank's band "regularly attended our Meetings during their stay in Town, kept themselves quite free from Drink, & behaved Soberly & orderly." Moreover, the Quakers expressed their "Satisfaction with what they had heard . . . which they said exactly answered to their own Religious Prospect."[48]

That is how Quaker reformer Anthony Benezet characterized Friends' first extended encounter with the Wyalusingites. He likely edited an account of their visit based on government and Quaker sources. Apparently initially intended for private circulation among other Friends and pacifist Christians, it was soon published in London. Suddenly the Munsee prophet was developing an international and interdenominational reputation.[49]

The pamphlet gave highlights of the treaty conference and reported on extended conversations of fellow Quaker Moales Pattison with Papunhank, through Delaware interpreter Job Chillaway, as the Natives headed home.[50] The trip afforded Pattison ample opportunity to observe "the Behaviour of these Indians in General" which he found "commendable . . . particularly the Behaviour of Paponahoal their Chief which afforded me much Satisfaction and Instruction. His deportment was such as manifested his Mind to be quiet & easy, accompanied with a becoming Solidity & Gravity." Moreover, as a group his band appeared to be "very earnest in promoting true Piety, which they apprehend is an inward work, by which the Heart is changed from bad to Good, which they express by the Heart's becoming Soft, & being filled with Good." "An immediate awakening," had been going on for several years in their town, he learned, sparked by Papunhank's own religious enlightenment and preaching. His message had exhorted his community to refuse all participation in the war. They had done so, but now Papunhank was persuaded that was not enough. He confessed to his traveling companions that though he had "ceas'd from War, yet I have not Labour'd to bring about a peace so much as I ought to have done." At the same time, he "often thought it Strange that the Christians are such great Warriors, & I have wondered they are not greater lovers of Peace." The reformer concluded that recent wars had resulted from Indians and whites alike having grown "Proud & Covetous," provoking God's anger and judgment in the form of violence, devastating weather, and disease.[51]

While with Pattison, Papunhank also made a case for civil religious discourse. He noted that too often when people were "Reasoning about Religion . . . they strove to throw each other down or to see which is the wisest." That wouldn't do: "whilst one is speaking the other should hold his Head down till the first has done, & then speak without being in a heat or angry." Respectful listening and gentle responses were the proper means for religious dialogue and another means of ensuring that disagreement did not lead to violence. For Papunhank they constituted an important form of peaceable behavior.[52]

As they parted that July, Pattison asked him for any final words of advice. The Munsee sent him on his way with the assurance that

> there are none that spoke such good words to me as I have heard from the Quakers . . . I have heard a Voice speak to my Heart and say The Quakers are right, it may be a wrong voice but I believe it is the true voice, However if the Goodness, which I feel in my Heart remains with me I shall come again to see the Quakers

> and If I continue to grow Strong I hope the time will come that I shall be joined in Close fellowship with them.[53]

For a people in search of new Indian leadership, the Papunhank of this Quaker narrative could hardly have been more perfect. His performance before the colonial authorities had been appropriately deferential but, at the same time, strikingly prophetic. He wanted the political corruption and economic fraud that had spoiled Indian-white relations to be replaced by integrity and justice. His pacifism seemed genuine, and better yet, he wanted to intensify his peacemaking efforts. His opposition to the sale and use of liquor and his denouncement of greed demonstrated his commitment to simple living. He was active in colonial diplomacy, seemingly trusted by whites and Indians alike, and apparently eager to do more. His willingness to return captives from Indian hands perhaps bespoke a wider opposition to all forms of human bondage. And he revered the old friendship between Natives and the colony's founders and wished to counter the evils that had spoiled it. Finally, his religious faith was real, active, of the "awakened" variety, and perhaps not so tied to ancient Native ways as Post had indicated a few months earlier. It was instead remarkably Quaker-like, a fact that Papunhank himself seemed to realize.[54]

Here, then, was a Native kindred spirit, a man attached to all the ideals activist Quakers held dear. He gave them hope that the darkness of the war was lifting and better political and economic times lay ahead.[55] As Friends met with him that summer, they read Papunhank's every word and deed as more evidence that the type of Indian leader and community they hoped to foster was already forming. In the process, Friends repeated the longstanding pattern of Euro-American Christian bodies to construct, whether in theory or reality, Indian followers (including Native leaders) in their own image.[56]

For his part, Papunhank's interactions with the Provincial Council and with Quakers indicate that by 1760 personal and public trauma pushed him toward seeking additional political and religious allies that could shore up the prospects of his band and relieve some of his own spiritual hunger. He became willing to consider Christianity as one source of potential help—particularly the faith of peace churches such as Moravians and Quakers, which squared with Papunhank's own conclusions, both philosophical and pragmatic, about the ill-advisedness of war and offered a range of other appealing religious ideas and practices. Those bodies might also become useful political friends. He consequently cultivated his contacts with them carefully. For example, Papunhank was apparently willing to tailor what he said to those groups to accord with what they wanted to hear when he met with them. On the heels of his flattering words to Pattison about Quakers, for instance, he spent several days again with Moravians in Bethlehem, where according to their records, he sounded like a good member of the Brethren by speaking of the "Savior's becoming man, His suffering and death" and told his listeners, including Pattison, that "I believe there are many people who know a lot and are able to speak a lot, even finding good words. But if they don't speak of Jesus the crucified one, I can sense it immediately, and I don't wish to listen to it." Such adaptability to his audiences was more a matter of political savvy than intentional duplicity. It helps to explain why several months earlier independent witnesses could give seemingly contradictory reports that in Wyalusing, on the one hand, Papunhank was admonishing his followers to believe Moravian teaching and on the other, overseeing traditional Native rites.[57]

Those testimonies may also point to the "complex way in which Indian religious eclecticism could embrace both customary [Native] practices and Christian beliefs." Papunhank seemed capable of absorbing a range of religious influences and ideas. However, that did not necessarily translate into immediate spiritual clarity. Entertaining Christian ideas and practices ran the risk of intellectual and religious confusion, which in his case could in turn jeopardize the loyalty of his "large following." One Susquehanna Indian described Papunhank as having "his head very full" but not knowing "the correct way. He speaks a lot, but lacks the requisite feeling, and many are dissatisfied." For that Native and perhaps others, Papunhank's preaching and teaching lacked the emotional intensity evangelicalism had helped to associate with true religion by the mid-eighteenth century. From the Moravians' point of view, Quakers confused Papunhank by denying the efficacy of baptism. He himself acknowledged to German and Native Moravians that he had many "questions of faith." He wondered whether his religious feelings were what they were describing when they spoke of "the true feeling of His [Jesus'] suffering," and why his prayers seemed to go unheard. Taking on Christianity was no simple matter of addition. It forced him to deal with matters of both head and heart and left him unsettled in his religious convictions and affections.[58]

Taking on other political allies was also no straightforward matter. His alliance building, as noted before, paralleled many other Delaware and Munsee leaders' efforts and sought to aid his kin and community. But when and how best to do that was tricky business. During the first years of the Seven Years' War he kept his people neutral and as much out of the fray as possible. By the late 1750s, though, with English victory virtually assured, he shifted approaches and looked for ways to be useful to the Pennsylvania government without compromising his credibility among fellow Natives still upset with past colonial policies. Maintaining productive relationships with other Indians was essential, but he also wanted to win the colonial government's favor so his people would have chips to cash in when they needed help. Yet he also wanted to be free to critique the actions of Pennsylvanians, and, if need be, the government. Friendship with Moravians or Quakers might aid in maintaining that delicate balance by giving his community a helpful advocate within colonial political circles and a potential source of economic relief should they need it. Moreover, given the colony's otherwise mostly hostile political environment, they were his only likely allies. He certainly wasn't going to get any help from the Presbyterian-dominated proprietary party and its aggressively anti-Indian constituents. Believing Quakers were eager to explore a relationship, he came to Philadelphia and seemingly fashioned himself and his people as just the sort of Indians Friends would find appealing.[59]

As summer turned to fall in 1760, then, Papunhank may be seen as continuing to pursue the strategies that had kept his people comparatively secure through the prior difficult years: geographic mobility, religious reform, shrewd diplomacy, and alliance-building. What parts the Pennsylvania government and Friends might play in their future remained unclear. So also was Papunhank's role in the Quaker quest to revive the Holy Experiment. But hopes were growing on both sides as they looked forward to meeting again.

Winning Friends and Gaining Influence

That meeting came the following August (1761) at Easton. In the intervening months, Friends continued to show strong interest in Papunhank, and he, in turn, nurtured his contacts with Euro-Americans on his own terms. Papunhank remained connected to Friendly Association members primarily through Nathaniel Holland, a Quaker merchant serving the colony's commissioners for Indian affairs as overseer of the Indian trade at Fort Augusta (Shamokin), located farther south on the Susquehanna River. Papunhank accepted gratefully the tools and other goods the association sent him and, according to Holland, expressed interest in having a white trader set up a store at Wyalusing. Holland was not sure this was a good idea since it might "suffer men of bad practices to come among them as they professed to be a religious people." But Papunhank's concern about the economic plight of his "poor" people overrode that fear, and he saw expanded trade, if carried on justly, as a potential source of help. Holland further reported that Papunhank "spoke very freely in praise of Friends, asserting that he thought they walked nearest to what Jesus Christ had requir'd of us to do." Here again the Indian leader knew the right words to say. In their conversations he also gave Holland sound political intelligence and advice amid rumors of impending renewed conflict. And he left no doubt about his strong pacifism. Holland recounted the prophet's conversation with two military officers in which he told them "that he thought it was unlawful to Warr." When they insisted on the legitimacy of defensive war, the prophet answered:

> He understood the white people had a book which God had ordered to be wrote for them—wherein they were informed that God had made the world & that he had sent his Son Jesus Christ into the world to shew us how we should live to which

> they answer'd that was true, well then says the old man why did not Jesus Christ fight when the people took to kill him. To this I don't understand they made him any satisfactory answer. Then the old man told them he believ'd the white people were very wicked, as they had so great an advantage of that book & liv'd so contrary to it.[60]

Papunhank's critique of the ways of certain white "Christians" didn't end there. When told by Holland that some Senecas, Shawnees, and Delawares had recently stolen a large number of horses and then traded them for rum, Papunhank expressed his sorrow that these Natives "behaved so foolishly." But he went on to explain that "the white peoples seling strong drink to the Indians was the cause of it & if they did not take some measure to prevent it, there would greater Calamities & bloodshed ensue in a few years in this province than has been." The liquor trade had to be opposed and shut down if peace was to endure. Last summer in Philadelphia, he had not felt free "to request a stop might be put to it," but now he felt confident enough in his relations with the powers that be to ask Holland to have the Friendly Association "lay it before the Legislature."[61]

Papunhank likely used Holland to keep powerful Friends interested and they obliged. When the Friendly Association received news in late July 1761 that many Natives were headed to Easton for a treaty, they voted unanimously to send representatives there and quickly spent over £400 on goods to be distributed primarily to Indians attending it.[62] Clearly eager to resume a more active role as advocates for peace and Indian rights, and perhaps also concerned to protect their considerable economic interests, reformist Quakers made the trek from Philadelphia. Once there, they encountered more than four hundred Indians from at least nine nations gathered for ten days of talks with Pennsylvania officials. Papunhank and about eighty of his people were among them, having been strongly urged to attend by a group of Iroquois who wanted them to "hear what they had to say to the Governor." The Munsee leader consented, pleased to report back to the governor that he had completed the small diplomatic task assigned him the prior summer (delivering the message to Munsee chief Echgohund), and ready to explore what more they could gain from the Friends.[63]

As the conference got underway, the two groups wasted no time in getting reacquainted. According to Quaker sources, on the day they arrived, a number of Friends conversed with Papunhank and later that evening found the Munsees gathering for worship. After all were seated, "some time was spent by the Elder Indians in Conversation, after which a short space of Silence ensued, then Papunahung said something, in a deliberate easy manner, in the Way of Preaching." Papunhank proceeded to pause in silence for a few minutes, speak again, pause again, and speak again, each time with greater conviction, animation, and volume. When he concluded with a short prayer, the members of the "congregation" got up and greeted one another with warmth and affection. An interpreter told Quakers that Papunhank's main exhortation was to live lives consistent with the goodness shown to them by their creator, and that these Indians met for worship before sunrise and after sunset each day.[64]

With that reintroduction to the Wyalusing band's piety, Friends' excitement built at the prospect for religious fellowship and more. Over the following week, the treaty council proceeded, but the highlights for the roughly eighty Quakers present and Papunhank's people seemed to be their series of religious conversations and joint worship services. When Quaker preacher Susanna Hatton arrived, for example, about a dozen Munsee women, including Papunhank's wife, and a few men immediately went to greet her, having been told that a "Woman Friend from Europe was coming to see them on a Religious Account." As they met, they grasped hands "without Speaking, at which the Indians were much tendered, & the Tears ran down their Cheeks." They then sat down together in silence and "the Over-shadowing of Ancient Goodness was soon felt, to the tendering of most if not all hearts present, [and] great brokenness appear'd amongst the Indians in the time of Silence." When Hatton finally got up and preached, it produced what another Quaker called "the most melting season I ever saw amongst such a number of people."[65]

Papunhank himself melted amid joint worship a few days later. As Hatton took his hand at the end of a meeting, "he would not Speak for weeping but held his Blanket up to his Face." Earlier that week, he had wondered whether he had made the right decision to come to Easton, so bothered was he by the "drunkenness & noise" of other attendees, some of which interfered with religious services. He told Friends that "when people discoursed about their Maker, they should not be gazing about, hearing & seeing other things, but be steady looking downwards, for these were serious matters." Papunhank indeed took his religion seriously and often gazed downward into the depths of his restless mind and heart. Little wonder the tears sometimes flowed.[66]

Emotions continued to run high in the days that followed for both Natives and Friends, whether in small meetings with Papunhank or in Quaker-led gatherings of several hundred Indians and colonists. Amid the weeping and religious intensity, one Quaker diarist felt it necessary to defend the unusual outpouring of sentiment as something more than folks getting carried away in the moment. He called it instead a genuine "visitation from on high."[67] On the other hand, if these reform-minded Quakers had become carried away, who could blame them? Here they were, worshipping side by side with Indians who seemed genuinely moved by the Christian message. Quaker accounts of the conference took pains to depict Papunhank and his company's spirituality as Quaker-like in its reverence for silence, elder conversation, plain preaching, and the right hand of fellowship, and ignored any alien elements they may have noticed.[68] When added to what Quakers already knew of Papunhank's pacifism, aversion to material gain, and diplomatic trustworthiness, their hopes spiked to new heights. In this very moment under the hot August sun, they thought Pennsylvania colonists and Natives could see for themselves that it was possible to unite for worship across all that divided them and to replace animosity and fear with trust and good will. Perhaps before long, all the obstacles to achieving a lasting peace could be burned away by the light emanating from their model relationship with this ideal Indian.[69]

Quaker optimism certainly did not cool in the two weeks that followed, as Papunhank and some of his community came to Philadelphia and once again, according to Friends' reports, "behaved in an orderly becoming Manner, & attended most of our Meetings of Worship." Based on their interactions, strict pacifist Friends emphasized to other Quakers his heartfelt gratitude for their kindness, deep-seated commitment to being guided by a "Spirit of Love," and unusual sensitivity to the "Workings of Truth." They were also eager to hear him say more about his views on the causes of war, and he obliged. Acknowledging his own moral frailty, Papunhank reiterated his fundamentally spiritual interpretation of conflict: when people failed to keep to that "Love which our Maker had given us in our Hearts, the Evil Spirit gets possession there, and destroys all that is good in us." "This is the Cause," he concluded, "why Men dislike one another; grow angry, and [are] endeavouring to kill one another." In contrast, "whenever they follow the leadings of the good Spirit, it causes our Hearts to be tender to love one another, to look upon all Mankind as one, and so to become as one Family." Such language of good and evil Spirits contesting within human hearts jived well with a Quaker theological vocabulary. More important, Papunhank's words laid out a vision of an "inclusive peace" within which colonists and Indians would be co-participants. By recognizing the "kinship of all people," Natives and whites could unite and counter the temptation to settle their differences violently.[70]

Quaker written accounts from that summer also told of Samuel Curtis, one of a number of Nanticokes who arrived in Philadelphia shortly after the Wyalusing band. He had been a drunk "but having been awakened, to a sense of Religion by Papunahung's Ministry, was become a Sober Man, and after a while apprehended himself called to preach amongst his People." When Curtis unexpectedly rose and spoke for fifteen minutes at a Quaker meeting while in the city, "his delivery was very much like that of Friends, in the like Service." Curtis had been impelled to speak by the "Love which God had put in his Heart." His message was simple: "love one another." His effect was palpable: it "begot a religious awe over the Meeting especially amongst the Younger People."[71]

These Quaker testimonies make clear that if one of Papunhank's goals in coming to Easton and Philadelphia was to make a favorable impression upon influential Friends, he could hardly have been more successful. His performance as preacher, prophet, and diplomat caused Friends—already predisposed to embrace his religion and politics as Quaker-like—to come away with strengthened interest in him and his company. And it was not only what he said but how he said it that drew them to him. As he conversed, "he manifested the sense he was under the necessity & effect of this divine Love as he was speaking by a sweetness of voice often pressing his Hand against his Breast." Predictably, Quakers once again circulated accounts of him to friends near and far. London Quakers expressed some concerns that their colonial brethren not get too carried away. Still, English Friend John Hunt wrote in November back to Pemberton that "thy account of those Religious Indians . . . made deep and humbling impressions upon my Mind. . . . May heaven prosper the world and bring many thousands of them to the saving knowledge of the Truth." Apparently Papunhank and his band could inspire extravagant hopes on both sides of the Atlantic.[72]

At the same time, Papunhank had a prime opportunity at Easton to observe the Friendly Association's political position within Pennsylvanian and imperial affairs. Additionally, he and a large number from his community had multiple chances to sample Quaker spirituality and to experience its power. All of this was vital for his evaluation of potential allies, a strategy whose urgency had increased that August amid his own renewed worries that Pennsylvania's fragile peace would not hold. In private conversations with Friends, he explained why he sought partners. He noted the "abundance of wicked people abroad in the World which made him Sorry, and afraid of his heart being corrupted by them." For that reason, "it was Necessary for those that had good hearts to keep together; that when he heard of any that was Religious he went to see them, in order that they might Strengthen one another." That "was what made him go to & fro." For Papunhank in the early 1760s, moral character rather than race, culture, or theology separated humanity into two camps. Now he wondered what should be done if reports about emerging troubles proved to be true. Should his band accept an invitation to move westward from Ohio Country Indians (in this case, Wyandots)? Was life there likely to be any more secure than it was in Wyalusing?[73]

Papunhank and his people pondered that prospect in the summer of 1761 amid a broader range of strategic possibilities. Aligning with Friends was no clear-cut choice. Quakers had lost considerable political influence in the colony in the past few years and had provoked intense opposition from other settlers, especially for their aid to Indians. Befriending them would almost certainly arouse antagonism from many other whites and Natives alike. Yet Papunhank considered it seriously, given his affinity with Friends' political positions, their history of being advocates for just relations, their economic resources, their moral seriousness, and their spiritual insights that could add to the power of his people's hybrid faith. Nevertheless, he was certainly not ready to rely solely on Quakers. So he continued to navigate carefully Wyalusing relations with other Indians, including Six Nations diplomats determined to realize Iroquois hegemony over the Susquehanna Valley and Munsee warriors still distressed over "lands lost and relatives killed."[74] With other Delawares in the region, he shared the belief that his community's strength depended on building alliances with many groups. But in his case, he wanted them to be people with "good hearts." To that end, in August he once again visited the German and Native American Moravians in Nain and kept his contacts with the United Brethren alive in spite of their less favorable (compared to Friends') assessment of his religion and character.[75]

Prospects for alliance also included the colonial government. Amid the Easton council in 1761, he had been nervous that the governor may have misunderstood something he said about lands. He did not want to be interpreted as complaining about the Wyalusingites' plight; instead, "if he could have peace in himself & get a living it was all he wanted." Such simple but elusive goals prompted him to refuse once more the gifts the governor offered at the end of the conference. Papunhank would take gifts from benevolent Friends; in fact, he had brought gifts of skins to Easton for the Quakers and was dismayed when they initially declined them. He expected to engage in the normal Native patterns of hospitality and knew all too well that his community could benefit from whatever material favors might be provided. But similar to the year before, he did not want to convey an impression of self-importance or political aspiration by accepting the governor's rewards. He was all too familiar with how the government looked upon Indians like Teedyuscung and their pretensions to power. All this was especially crucial at a time when Papunhank may have realized that the colonial government was the body that could be of greatest help to his band. He hoped to keep proving himself to Pennsylvania authorities through peacekeeping work so that when his people most needed it, he would have some political capital.[76]

The Cost of Peacemaking

Such an opportunity for serving the cause of peace arose even sooner than Papunhank might have preferred. As Natives made their way home from Easton, a colonist shot a Munsee in a liquor-fueled encounter. The victim's angry friends and relatives soon set out on a path to take revenge on frontier whites, but as they passed through Wyalusing, Papunhank stopped them and made a passionate plea for giving diplomacy a chance. He "made them presents of large Quantities of Wampum to the value of many pounds, in order to appease their Wrath, & prevailed on them to stop until they sent messengers to the Government of Pennsylvania, in order that the Matter might be accommodated without spilling Blood." Such actions exemplified traditional northeastern Indian means of resolving conflicts and avoiding an escalation of violence. To redress a murder like this, Natives wanted both material and emotional satisfaction. Gifts of wampum provided the former; hoped-for government expressions of condolence would provide the latter. The irate Munsees agreed to wait at Wyoming while several key Wyalusing residents, otherwise needed for the fall hunt, went to see the governor. Papunhank reported through them what his company had done to prevent more bloodshed, and he mentioned as well their efforts to contact other Native groups about returning prisoners and to persuade a group of Mingo Indians to return stolen horses. In response, Governor Hamilton expressed appreciation for their intervention and committed to continue sharing military and diplomatic intelligence. He additionally warned him that any future conflict would be the fault of Indians, assigned him the task of delivering a message of condolence and assurances that justice would be done to the offended Munsees, and promised him that his "kind & friendly behaviour" would always be remembered "to your advantage."[77]

Those mostly encouraging words reached Papunhank at a time when he could sorely use some encouragement. He was seriously wounded after having taken a tomahawk to the neck and arm—his reward for trying to put out other potential fires, or, depending on your point of view, meddling in other Natives' affairs. In Shamokin, where he had gone to wait for the governor's reply, he reproved a group of Indians for some misconduct (perhaps stealing horses). The wrongdoers did not take kindly to his rebuke and tried to shut him up permanently. As Papunhank lay bleeding on the ground, others seized the Indian assailant, but, a Quaker account rapturously recounted, "Papoonhang was endued with so much of a Christian Spirit that he requested he [the Indian] might be loosed & not hurt on his account, Saying, let him go he is a poor Indian."[78]

Papunhank's response to being physically assaulted, at least as it was recorded in the Quaker retelling, confirmed in Friends' minds his thoroughgoing pacifism and endeared him further to their hearts. When Israel Pemberton received news of the attack, he sent a tender note to Wyalusing inquiring "wither our Brother Papunehang is yet alive or not" and assuring his community that "if He is Dead we have no doubt He is gone to everlasting rest, & will recive the reward of welldoing." Pemberton's confidence in Papunhank's salvation bespoke the promise Friends saw in the Munsee reformer and their relationship with him. Just weeks earlier, the Friendly Association had responded enthusiastically to his request to have "some sober religious Persons settled among them capable of instructing their Children to read and write," resolving to send "two or three young Men suitable for such an undertaking" as soon as they could be recruited. Now the association feared that their hopes had been quickly dashed. To their relief, word came from Nathaniel Holland in mid-November that Papunhank was recovering from his wounds. Holland further reported that "the more I see of him the more I admire his patience & forgiving temper." No wonder the merchant decided that because "the old man hath been deprived of his hunt," he was going to supply him for the winter, expenses the Friendly Association ultimately paid.[79]

Friends remained solicitous of the Wyalusingites' security and interested in their efforts on behalf of peace—specifically, their role in helping to return white captives—through the course of 1762. But it was not until June 1763 that they had another firsthand, formative encounter with them. By that point, reformist Quakers had experienced significant disappointments at treaties with Indians at Easton and Lancaster the prior summer. At both conferences, members of the Friendly Association renewed their support for longstanding Delaware charges that the colony's proprietors had defrauded them of their rightful lands. But their voices couldn't compete with the power of Sir William Johnson and proprietor Thomas Penn. When Teedyuscung acquiesced to the proprietary party and joined other Delaware leaders in giving up all claims to Pennsylvania territory, Quaker hopes for a "peace based on justice" sagged.[80]

Papunhank and the Wyalusing community had their own worries about land claims. According to speeches at the Lancaster meeting, town members had gone to the Easton conference "to hear something about the Land Affair, between the Governor and Teedyuscung," but also "to enquire about their own Lands." There, according to a Cayuga speaker representing Wyalusing, they had been told that the colony had bought their lands from the Iroquois. But the Wyalusingites, and apparently the Six Nations, were not sure that had happened. So Papunhank's people reasoned that if their land was to be sold, "they think they ought to be paid for it." Predictably, Governor Hamilton had a different view. He expressed surprise that the Six Nations were bringing the issue to him since the matter had been settled in his opinion at the 1758 Easton Treaty when the government had confirmed Iroquois rights to those lands. If the Wyalusingites had questions or concerns about their right to be there, they and the Six Nations would need to "settle this matter among yourselves."[81]

Amid the grand affairs of state and intercultural relations carried on at Lancaster with over five hundred Indians present, the Wyalusing "matter" was a small affair; unless, of course, you were Papunhank or one of the other sixteen men from Wyalusing at the meeting. Their land rights to the area they had settled in 1758 remained a perennial concern. New fears about their future had likely emerged that spring and summer when they learned that close to 150 white settlers from New England had been allowed to establish the new town of Mill Creek in the Wyoming Valley. Whatever else that portended, it meant new competition for the game they hunted each year. Papunhank and his council likely spent considerable time debating appropriate steps to take in response. Enlisting a Six Nations "uncle" to speak on their behalf at Lancaster in August was apparently one of them.[82]

Historical records are thin for gauging what else was happening within the internal dynamics of Papunhank's community during the remaining months of 1762 and the winter of 1763. One important glimpse, however, comes from the testimony of two Nanticokes, a husband and wife, who lived at Wyalusing. They visited Nain in late October and attended a Moravian service. Afterward, the man told the resident missionary that he had been an "Indian Doctor [shaman], but I am not one any longer, for I cannot help the sick and live in Papunhank's town." Clearly one dynamic going on was the Munsee prophet's efforts to restrict those who exercised sacred power within his community. He did not want traditional shamans practicing in Wyalusing and thereby competing with the message and perhaps the healing remedies he was offering. At least in this case, his efforts to silence alternative religious authorities and to maintain his own dominance succeeded. The Nanticoke went on to contrast Papunhank's message with what he had heard from the Moravians: "There [Wyalusing] they speak of greeting our God and praying as well, but I have never heard anything like this, that our God and Creator receives sinners and wants to be gracious to them and that they can come with their sins just as they are. Praise God that I have come here and have heard the beautiful Word."[83]

Even allowing for missionary exaggeration, the Nanticoke's words are telling. They suggest that Papunhank's preaching remained distinctive. For all the exposure he had had by this point to Moravian (and Quaker) teaching, he continued to sound his own themes.[84] His theology retained a focus on the same creator god he had so dramatically encountered in years past and to whom he still prayed. On the other hand, notions of sin, sacrifice, or atonement were apparently absent, or at least too muted for these Nanticokes to hear. In contrast, with their faith reflective of German Pietism, Moravians in early America emphasized the need for heartfelt repentance and an embrace of the Savior's bloody sacrifice on a sinner's behalf. They accordingly pressed upon Papunhank, in a way Friends like Pemberton did not, his own sinfulness and need for salvation. Their desire was for Moravian Christianity to be an alternative, rather than an additional source of spiritual truth and power for him and his people. As a result, they were distressed by the fact that although Papunhank had repeatedly requested that the Moravians send a missionary to Wyalusing, he made it clear that he "wished to keep his post as a teacher of the people." He apparently imagined himself functioning alongside any pastoral newcomer and retaining the religious authority he had enjoyed for a decade.[85]

A Time to Decide

By May 1763, however, many within Wyalusing were not sure that was a good plan. They were open to having a new teacher among them but were losing interest in hearing from Papunhank. Some combination of strains and tensions had grown large enough over the past months and perhaps years to create a crisis of authority in the community. Ongoing anxieties over land rights, white expansion, hunting territory, and trade possibilities produced mounting stress. So, too, did competing ideas about how much and which variety of Christianity to embrace, or about the efficacy of traditional rituals. Papunhank himself was uncertain; figuring out just the right fusion of old and new ways was perplexing work and may have prompted him to vacillate in the wisdom he offered. His indecision became fodder for critics. Some wanted to connect with one or another Christian denomination more quickly than Papunhank was moving. They, like the two Nanticokes who went to Nain, had apparently decided that Papunhank's message was incomplete. On the other end of the spectrum, some villagers were likely being put off by the prospect of closer ties with whites of whatever beliefs. They had come to Wyalusing less for its religious character than for the security the town provided. Now some of them were leaving. One estimate claimed that Wyalusing had lost as much as 50 percent of its population during the prior year. Community spirits only darkened further when frontier violence resumed in the spring of 1763. In April Teedyuscung's village at Wyoming burned to the ground with him in it, most likely the work of recently arrived settlers from Connecticut. Then in May news came that Pontiac, an Ottawa chief in the West, had launched an attack on the English. Warfare was beginning to move rapidly eastward, with many other Native peoples poised to join in the rebellion.[86]

What should Papunhank and his community do? Was the prophet no longer needed? Had the time come to pass along all of his authority and responsibilities? Was the precious peace he so highly valued to be lost once again not only in community division but in a new wave of violence and bloodshed? Papunhank must have been gripped with a set of conflicting emotions as he sat within Wyalusing's council for the better part of two weeks in early May deliberating their future. No consensus could be reached. Some wanted a Quaker teacher, more wanted a Moravian, and most were ready to stop listening to Papunhank "because they believed that [he] did not preach the correct Word of God." Were they right, he wondered? Was there something more or different that needed to be added to his message of peace and moral duty? Surely he deserved a chance to remain their teacher. After all, where would they have been without him? For more than a decade, he had guided them through one challenge after another with wisdom and care. Were they now trying to humiliate him? How discouraging to be told by former supporters that your words were no longer worth hearing. Did these people truly understand what it took to sustain a community?[87]

Amid a whirl of uncertainty, coincidence or divine providence brought David Zeisberger to Wyalusing at just that moment. Papunhank's repeated appeals to the Moravians to send a missionary to visit his community had finally born fruit. Zeisberger arrived with Anton, a Delaware Native assistant with whom Papunhank had interacted often, to assess the town's interest in hearing the Christian gospel. The visitors went immediately into Papunhank's home where, according to Zeisberger, the Munsee "was very glad and especially excited that we had come to visit them and even before we had eaten anything the entire town had come together in his house that I should preach them a sermon." Warmly welcomed by the prophet and others, Zeisberger seized the moment and spent three plus days and nights preaching and teaching to great effect. He reported that Papunhank himself was among those moved to tears by his message. Council members told Zeisberger that for a "long time" they had doubted that Papunhank "was preaching the pure Word of God to them and thus for some time they had had no services." Clearly the community was having a crisis of confidence and losing trust in both Papunhank and the rituals he had overseen. Zeisberger responded that "Papunhank had told them as much as he knew and had recognized and that they could expect no more of him than that." The German's shrewd graciousness served him well, for that very evening the council made a formal request through him to his superiors in Bethlehem to have a Moravian missionary reside with them.[88]

Papunhank clearly supported Zeisberger's presence and the prospect of a more permanent missionary resident. But why? Would this not inevitably mean a dramatic loss of his religious authority? What place would he have in a community where his would no longer be the dominant voice? On the other hand, might this turn out to be an opportunity for him to retain his leadership role, now in partnership with Moravians, rather than being tossed aside by the Wyalusingites? Might support from the Brethren restore rather than replace his influence? In whatever way the prophet processed those matters, he also saw Zeisberger's arrival as an answer to prayer. At least that is what he said a month later to his community. He told them that "he had considered for several years his and the Indians' condition and had believed that they must lead a different life, otherwise they could not become blessed." Since the prior autumn, "he had prayed to the dear God to show him a people to whom he might join himself, through which they might become blessed and had decided within himself that he would join the first people who would point him to this and he wanted to remain with them. He had always had the Quakers and the Brethren in consideration."[89]

By that point in June, after a brief sojourn to Moravian headquarters in Bethlehem, Zeisberger was back at the invitation of Papunhank and other community leaders, with an appointment from the United Brethren to establish a mission station at Wyalusing. As he arrived, Papunhank was quick to tell him and the community, "Now we want to do well everything that the Brethren tell us to do, so that perhaps they may always stay with us." But as usual, things were not that simple. Hardly had those words been uttered when another option appeared. The next day Quaker social reformer and spiritual leader John Woolman reached Wyalusing, his interest in Papunhank having been sparked by meetings with him in Benezet's parlor in Philadelphia two years earlier. Inclined to expand his ministry beyond fellow Friends, Woolman overcame fears for his own physical safety in hopes of renewing Quaker spiritual contacts with Papunhank's band. Despite the challenges of language barriers, he spent the next five days in religious conversation and worship with Papunhank and sixty or more of the Wyalusing community; he confided to his journal that he "believed that a door remained open for the faithful disciples of Jesus Christ to labour amongst these peoples."[90]

That was a curious comment given Zeisberger's presence. Despite this competition, Woolman apparently remained persuaded that Quakers could make a contribution to the Wyalusingites' well-being. Perhaps he feared that renewed warfare would make Zeisberger's efforts short-lived or retained hope that the warm reception he received in Wyalusing was an indication that Friends might yet play a vital role in the town's spiritual care and development.[91]

No diplomatic envoy, Woolman made a conscious effort not to engage the Indians he encountered in discussions about the resumption of frontier violence lest he arouse suspicions that he was more political agent than evangelist. Nevertheless, he reported back to powerful Friends in Philadelphia that these Indians seemed to have no "Evil disposition towards the English;" they were as concerned as Quakers about present troubles and "would join any Endeavour that could be tho't on to prevent the Spreading this Calamity."[92]

Some members of the Friendly Association wanted to know more and wondered what role, if any, Quakers could now play vis-à-vis Natives. Was the spread of Pontiac's War into Pennsylvania the coup de grace for their cherished experiment? Alternatively, was Woolman's visit a portent of Friends someday overseeing their own Christian Native communities? More immediately, what could they do to provide spiritual care and physical protection for this body of Natives for whom they retained the most "tender Regard"? They decided to lobby the governor to protect the Indians, either by securing them where they were or by recommending to them that they move closer to English settlements. Anthony Benezet went a step higher and wrote to Sir Jeffrey Amherst, commander in chief of British forces in North America, imploring him to keep enraged whites from attacking the "industrious, religiously minded people" in Wyalusing and other settlements of peaceful Natives.[93]

As Woolman had indicated, Papunhank shared Quaker worries about the fate of his company as rumors of Indian attacks and white rage swirled in and out of Wyalusing. As in past times, the Native leader considered how best to ensure the security of his people. But this time he did so amid their growing skepticism that his religious leadership was up to the task. Faced with mounting external pressures, internal community divisions, and a personal dark night of the soul, the Munsee reformer was moved to believe that even closer associations with Euro-American spiritual and political resources were needed. They might literally make the difference between life and death. And he determined with others that it was time for his people to decide which set of white Christian allies to embrace, for "to adhere to two parties [Quakers and Moravians], they would only become more confused than they had previously been." That spring they had been in "much distress for they had seen that they were running around in circles and in this way would never become blessed [saved]." Perhaps not surprisingly, then, almost as soon as Zeisberger returned to his village, Papunhank offered an emotional confession and asked to be baptized. A few days later—and just four days after Woolman had left—the Moravian missionary complied.[94]

Papunhank's spiritual journey had been moving in this more definitively Christian direction for several years. His many conversations with Moravians since at least 1758 and his interchanges with Quakers since at least 1760 had given him substantial exposure to Christian claims and practices. Now in 1763 Zeisberger's preaching, as well as that of his Native assistants, Anton and Nathanael, clearly pushed Papunhank's journey along to the point of eliciting the type of decisive turn to the Savior that Moravians thought necessary for Christian salvation. Throughout May and June, Papunhank's soul had been "disquieted." He was accustomed to internal spiritual struggles and quests, but this seemed almost too much to bear. More and more he felt "in his heart that he is bad . . . and prayed very hard for strength." He couldn't eat or drink. He could only hope for some relief and release, some peace to ease his troubled mind. And finally it came. With the waters of baptism, his self-righteousness was washed away and all things became new.[95]

Like other Indian converts to Moravian Christianity, Papunhank was drawn to this new faith by theological themes and ritual practices that resonated with rather than refuted his Munsee religious heritage. Key among them was the Brethren's commitment to peace. Only a Christian community that shared his pacifist principles had appeal for him. Moravianism provided an acceptable spiritual home where his fight for peace would be welcomed and empowered. Alongside that pacifist theme, his confession following his baptism and later testimony emphasized his giving up a sense of spiritual self-sufficiency and worthiness, a kind of abandoning of himself to the power of the Spirit to bring transformation and direction. In acknowledging his own weakness and spiritual inadequacy, he could become open to an infusion of new spiritual insight and uplift. This was not very far from what he had experienced during and after his adult vision quest. Both were fundamentally about being empowered with a new source of strength, strength needed to endure the daunting individual and collective challenges facing him and his people in the 1750s and 1760s. Historian Rachel Wheeler has persuasively argued that Christian Mahican men, and by extension other Moravian Indians, found in Jesus, and especially in his blood, a reservoir of power that could "help [them] as individuals in their lives as hunters, warriors, and victims of disease . . . [and] in supporting and maintaining their public roles as leaders, as orators, and as diplomats." That analysis seems apt for Papunhank particularly because some of his most important Moravian "instructors" were the very Christian Mahicans Wheeler has studied. Those Indians came to faith in Shekomeko, New York, in the 1740s as the first Native American Moravian converts. By the late 1750s many of them were living in Nain, and men such as Joshua Senior counseled Papunhank on his visits there about the power of Christ's blood. Odds are that Joshua testified to him, as he and other Mahican preachers had done with many others, about the "protection, power, and health that they had found and was available to others through supplication to the Savior." For someone as eager as Papunhank to tap into other sources of power, that message likely became increasingly compelling, especially in the crisis weeks of 1763 when his religious authority and the future direction of his community were up for grabs. As he listened once again to white and Native Moravians teach about the redemptive work accomplished through Christ's bloody sacrifice and as he reflected upon the heartfelt care the Brethren had offered him, his family, and other members of his community whenever they had interacted, the Munsee leader's heart and mind now told him that here was the "one right word of God."[96]

In confessing Christ and receiving baptism, Papunhank stepped out in front of his community and once more took the lead in setting its direction. The Munsee prophet had a transformational spiritual experience that spring. But the timing of his declaration of Moravian Christian faith in retrospect seems to have been shaped by more than the state of his own soul. Amid that summer's growing crisis, Papunhank felt the need to move himself and his band (or at least those who were willing) more fully into the Moravian orbit. Doing so would resolve much of the tension and division that had wracked the community. Moreover, the Brethren could offer through a resident missionary the steady spiritual counsel and comfort required in this difficult time. And they were accustomed to shepherding communities of pacifist Christian Natives. Papunhank had seen firsthand the lives of Moravian Indians at Nain and elsewhere; he may even have had kin among them. Those contacts had steered him down this road. They would be willing and able allies along the path he now had chosen. Furthermore, by June 1763, joining forces with Moravians must have seemed a better option to him than simply having his authority supplanted by them. And yet, almost as soon as that choice was made, Zeisberger was called back to Bethlehem in early July, leaving Wyalusing to carry on once more on its own with Papunhank at the helm. As he left, Zeisberger told Johannes that "now all the Indians were looking to him and that he should ask the Savior for Grace so to walk that they could look at him and recognize what had happened in his heart." Papunhank was to once again function as the spiritual model and head of his people.[97]

He also remained their guiding light politically and diplomatically. For the past five years in Wyalusing, as in years before, the prophet had carefully navigated the community's relations with powers and events largely beyond their control. In that time, he had determined that more than ever, their peace and security depended on building productive alliances. To that end, Papunhank had more fully engaged his people in the wider political, military, and diplomatic affairs of Pennsylvania and colonial America. Nothing in mid-1763 suggested that would not need to continue long into the future. Consequently he remained attuned to what the Six Nations and Ohio Indians were about. And he was not ready to cut off his connections to Friends completely, though he increasingly realized that Quakers could supply few if any of the assets Moravians provided. His request for the Friends to send teachers to his town had yielded no fruit, and Woolman's visit, though cordial, gave no guarantees of future aid. Nor was the Quakers' traditional advantage over Moravians—their political influence—seemingly of much value right now. With war once more at their doorstep, he needed to seek out a stronger political partner. To Philadelphia and Governor Hamilton he therefore went in the fall of 1763.

4

Captives Together

Eighteen months later in March 1765, Papunhank had reason to write to Governor Hamilton's successor, John Penn:

> To the Honourable John Penn Esqr.
> Lieutenant Governor & Commander in Chief
> of the Province of Pennsylvania etc.[,]
>
> Being about to depart in two Days hence with our Wives and Children from the Philada. Barracks where we have Sojourned above a year & intending to go back into the Woods of Wachelusing on Susquehanna to settle there. We think it is our firm Duty to take a friendly leave from You by presenting our hearty Thanks for Your great Goodness to us. We do not come with a String or Belt of Wampum agreeable to the Custom among Indians and as we cannot speak Your Tongue we must endeavor to express our grateful Hearts by this Writing and hoping You will accept of it in Your usual Benevolence from Your poor Indians. We all acknowledge Your great Kindness to us in the late War, we were then in Danger of our Lives from the white people and You have taken us in Your Protection so that we could live in peace & quietness in the Barracks. . . . We thank You for the Liberty we have enjoyed during these times of difficulty to have our Ministers with us & daily attend divine Service. By these means we have been kept in

> the Way of our Salvation & have heard the good Words of our God & Creator that we shall love him & all mankind and be in friendship with the English and we further rejoice & thank You that Mr. Schmick one of our Ministers & David Zeisberger as Brother of Bethl., shall go to live with us on Susquehannah to influence us poor Indians in the knowledge of Truth of the Gospel[.] We have great occasion for such daily influence as there is many of our Indians who are not as they ought be & some of them know nothing at all of our Creator. Your Benevolence & protection towards us are great in our Eyes & have made an impression in our hearts that never can wear out and we will relate all this to the Indians on Susquehanna & testify & declare to them that we are & will ever remain true friends to the English. . . .
>
> *Johannes Papunhang, Joshua Sen., Anton, Sam. Eawens*[1]

With those highly deferential words, Papunhank and the Moravian Indians he had joined thanked the Pennsylvania governor for their physical and spiritual survival. A long nightmare of captivity was finally coming to an end, and they were feeling generous. Events far beyond their control had forced them to become refugees and to depend on a colonial government most other Natives in Pennsylvania were bent on attacking. That hardly made them the friend of many whites, however. Instead they faced more and more provincials fuming with anti-Indian rage and only too ready to wreak vengeance on Natives of any sort.

The wars of colonial North America were never good times for peaceable Natives or for Moravians of any race or ethnicity. Ridiculed as pacifists and suspected of political treachery, they all repeatedly faced physical danger, community disruption, and spiritual crisis amid the recurring armed conflicts of the mid-eighteenth century. Pontiac's War in 1763–64 proved no exception. Coming on the heels of the Seven Years' War, it aroused fears among settlers and Native Americans alike. By its outbreak, Moravian leaders in particular were all too familiar with the havoc war could visit upon their towns. Memories of the 1755 Gnadenhütten massacre rushed through their minds with each new report of Indian raids and white retaliatory strikes. Little wonder, then, that missionaries Johann Jacob Schmick and Bernhard Adam Grube were quick to send an appeal to Pennsylvania's government in July 1763 for protection of their Indian congregations at Nain and Wechquetank. Those two communities represented virtually all the fruit of Moravian evangelistic efforts among Indians in the northern colonies during the prior quarter century. Schmick, Grube, and their fellow Native petitioners knew that all their lives were at risk. They also knew that the future of Moravian Indian towns and United Brethren mission work among Native peoples hung in the balance. Twenty-five years of missionary labor could come to naught if these peace-loving Natives became casualties of war.[2]

The newly baptized Papunhank and his mixed community of Munsees, Delawares, Nanticokes, and Conoys at Wyalusing had similar worries. As summer turned to fall in 1763, events only degenerated, leaving Papunhank's band feeling increasingly vulnerable. They, too, were pacifists, or at least that was the message that Papunhank had been preaching for the past decade and to which some of them adhered. He wanted no part in the hostilities except to contribute if possible to their cessation. But neighboring whites and Natives gave no signs that the Wyalusingites would be left alone. Somehow they, like the Nain and Wechquetank Moravians, needed to find a place of refuge.

For better or worse, Philadelphia became that place for all of the Moravian Indians and some of Papunhank's community. Together they spent the sixteen months from November 1763 through March 1765 as war refugees there. Within the confines of the city and more precisely, the walls of the British army barracks, their stories rapidly merged. Papunhank soon exercised key leadership for all of the captive Natives, and the larger Moravian community reciprocally embraced the twenty-two exiles from Wyalusing. In total, the refugees numbered 149 women, men, and children when their urban sojourn began. At that point none of them knew how long nor how difficult their stay in the city might be. If they had, few of them would likely have come. Nor did they know where their future home would be. Like refugees before and since, they spent much of their time wondering if they could ever return to their former homes and imagining what life might be like somewhere else. In the end a remnant left Philadelphia headed for lands familiar only to a few. German missionaries would ostensibly lead them. But in fact Native brothers largely showed the way. And Papunhank was chief among them since it was to Wyalusing they went to start over in March 1765.

As captives together, Papunhank and Moravians developed a relationship of mutual dependence that proved critical for the survival of the Moravians' missionary enterprise and the viability of Moravian Indian towns. It also brought about the reinvention of Papunhank's authority and community. His story now became inextricably linked to the wider Moravian story. Together their experiences reveal the challenging and often tragic results of being displaced persons amid violence in the eighteenth century. It reveals as well Papunhank's persistent quest to secure a peaceable place for his people.

Removing to Philadelphia

The summer and fall of 1763 became increasingly frightful for the Wyalusingites and for Moravian Indians at Nain and Wechquetank. Various grievances prompted Natives from many tribes to join forces and engage in attacks upon British forts and raids upon colonial settlements. At least part of their inspiration came from the Delaware Prophet, Neolin, who endorsed armed resistance against whites. The pace of retaliatory violence quickened in September and October. By that point blood flowed ever more freely in the Pennsylvania interior. Shawnee and Delaware war parties and the militia units raised to combat them took turns killing and scalping whatever whites or Indians were handy. As before, peaceful Natives scrambled to reassure hostiles on both sides that they were neither aiding nor abetting the enemy. But amid deepening suspicions of Christian Indians and a growing hatred of Native persons in general, their pleas fell on mostly deaf ears. The flow of events left no doubt about the danger they were in: Cumberland County militia shot three Wyalusing Nanticoke Indians in the back; Northampton County militia murdered Zacharias, a baptized Delaware, along with his wife and child, following a visit to their Indian kin at Wechquetank; Renatus, a member of the Nain community, was arrested erroneously for the murder of tavern owner John Stenton and other militia men thought responsible for Zacharias's death; and a militia unit marched ominously toward Wyalusing to wreak vengeance on any Natives they found there until they decided to turn back after coming upon the gruesome remains of an Indian raid at Wyoming.[3]

Under such circumstances, German and Native leaders at Nain, Wechquetank, and Wyalusing made increasingly desperate appeals for protection to the Pennsylvania government. Governor James Hamilton provided some assurances of help in August, but only on the condition that the Moravians remained friendly and with the caveat that it was difficult to distinguish between friendly and nonfriendly Indians.[4] Companies of armed whites shared the latter opinion, or perhaps more precisely, had little interest in making that distinction. More than once they showed up in Wechquetank and told missionary Grube that if any of his Indians were found in the woods, they would be killed. Grube responded that all the Indians of his town were under the governor's protection but "they said, nobody would regard it." No wonder he noted on October 6 that "our Indians were very much afraid of the Soldiers and Enemy Indians." He decided three days later to move the whole community to the white Moravian settlement at Nazareth because they were "in Danger of our Lives ... [and] fear[ed] to be kill'd by white people and savages."[5] That same week Moravian leader Peter Boehler wrote to Hamilton imploring him to protect "these friendly and innocent Indians" and warning that if instead they were destroyed, "this would not only bring a Blood Guilt upon our Country" but other Indians, knowing of the Moravian Indians' innocence, "would be so enraged that they might come down in such numbers, that neither Bethlehem nor perhaps any other Place between this & Germantown might be able to make a stand against them."[6]

Once in Nazareth, appeals for help continued. Grube likely worked with Boehler and other German Moravian leaders to put together a "Plan for Protecting and Supporting the Christian Indians" to be presented to Hamilton. They were clearly eager to toe the line and gain whatever provincial approval was possible. The plan called for the Indians to be restricted to the lands of Bethlehem and Nazareth, to muster daily for attendance, and to be subject to white overseers who would report any Indians that misbehaved. The government's part would be to pay a small daily stipend for each Native since they were going to be kept from hunting, their main means of sustenance.[7]

Whatever appeal the plan might have had, it became a moot point when in early November Hamilton and the Provincial Council ordered all of the Nain and Wechquetank Indians to remove to Philadelphia. There they could be protected and watched more closely, for more than a few government officials were persuaded that these "friendly" Natives were secretly helping hostile Indians with guns, ammunition, and other trade goods.[8] Amid war, racist attitudes hardened; no Indian could be trusted. The Moravian Natives were not sure that was the best plan or where they wanted to go. In the city they might be forced to mix with other interned Indians who were "not of the same Way & Principles as they" and that "their Youths would be corrupted, as sad Experience hath taught them already" if they were located too close to whites.[9] Yet despite those fears, they complied, handing over their weapons and tearfully leaving much of what was familiar behind. Their dire situation had left them little choice but to submit to colonial authorities dutifully for what they no doubt hoped would be a brief season.[10] They arrived in Philadelphia on November 12 and immediately encountered an angry mob in no mood to protect any Indians: "The fury of the people in Philadelphia was indescribable, and we had to stand in front of the barracks for fully three hours and take all kinds of disgrace and scorn." Rebuffed by soldiers unwilling to give up their quarters, the Moravians had to make their way through the city, accompanied by "many thousands," and then travel by boat five miles south on the Schuylkill River to Province Island. It became their new place of refuge in a hostile world.[11]

Papunhank and other key Wyalusingites including translator Job Chillaway and brothers John and Samuel Curtis kept close tabs that fall on the fate of the Moravian Indians. They also worked hard to avoid riled-up militia, maintain fruitful contacts with Quaker and Moravian leaders, and reassure the Pennsylvania government of their loyalty and dependability at every turn. In late July Papunhank and Chillaway passed along military intelligence to Colonel James Burd at Fort Augusta regarding raiding parties of both whites and Indians. Then in a September message, the prophet told the governor and Provincial Council, twice for good measure, that apart from completing the diplomatic tasks assigned to them and acting on behalf of peace, the Wyalusingites had "minded nothing else but the religious worship of God." In response to their overtures, the Friendly Association promised to support them in this critical time while Governor Hamilton was willing to call them "Friends," thank them for past services, and enlist them to carry peace messages back to the assorted Natives living above them on the Susquehanna and Chemung Rivers. But he was also quick to absolve his government of responsibility should angry whites take revenge on any Natives (friend or enemy) for the "Barbarous" acts perpetrated by raiding Indian parties. If any more Indian blood was shed, Hamilton pronounced, "you must blame those Indians who have so unjustly struck us, as People who have been so much hurt, cannot be restrained from taking Revenge."[12] Such words directed at Papunhank hardly helped him sleep better at night.

Yet at the time it was probably the best he could hope for. With tensions rising, fears spreading, whites increasingly disinclined to trust any Native, and the whole region poised to explode with even greater bloodshed, Papunhank concluded that nothing less than direct government protection for him, his family, and his community would ensure their survival. He was encouraged, then, when more promising news arrived in early November. Word came, supposedly from new governor John Penn, that the Wyalusingites should either head north to New York to find refuge under the watchful eye of Sir William Johnson or come to Philadelphia to join other Moravian Indian refugees. Having options was good, but neither solution was perfect for both entailed significant risks and costs, including the likely loss of most if not all of the autonomy they had enjoyed in Wyalusing. Community members had little time to deliberate over what to do and even less clarity about what their decisions might mean for the long run. The fact that in the end, they chose at least three different paths reveals division in that moment about what should be done.[13]

For his part Papunhank sent word that "our hearts inclineth towards you, the Governor of Philadelphia."[14] His decision may have been influenced by his earlier positive encounters in the city in 1760 and 1761 with Quakers or by the fact he was going to be a prime witness for the defense in the trial of Renatus, the Christian Indian accused of murder. He may also have seen it as a way to solidify his band's attachment to Moravians or to maintain his visibility and utility in the eyes of the Pennsylvania government. Yet it was by no means a straightforward choice. Papunhank could not guarantee what might befall them in the very center of white power. They wanted and needed protection. But was removal to Philadelphia the wisest course of action? Most of the community didn't think so. Only twenty-one other Wyalusingites went with him south to the city. Another small contingent, including one of his daughters, opted to stay in or near Wyalusing, hoping to hold onto something of the life they had enjoyed there. A larger group numbering between 100 and 150 Indians and including his brother, Tschechquoapesek, migrated north into southern New York and entrusted their futures to Sir William Johnson and the Six Nations. For them, remaining in Indian country apparently held more promise, even if it meant foregoing the leadership Papunhank had long provided. Finally, it is possible that some Wyalusingites joined Pontiac's rebellion. They were at least accused of doing so by the Paxton Boys less than three months later.[15]

Unsure of what lay ahead, Papunhank and his small enclave rolled their wagon of belongings into Philadelphia on November 25.[16] The resumption of warfare had necessitated them making a hard choice among several less than desirable options. Each day of the past few months had seemingly brought new reductions in the Wyalusingites' autonomy. It had also brought them to the point of breaking apart. No one knew how long their separation might last or if they would ever come together again. More immediate concerns about sheer survival had taken precedence over preserving intact the community Papunhank had first formed more than a decade before. War had not yet literally killed most of them, but it had destroyed their village bonds.

Papunhank must have wondered if there was any viable future for those whom he had led. Surely he was disappointed that so few followed his lead now. Whatever his thoughts and feelings, they arrived in the city having to bank on little more than the mercy of whites in and out of government to keep them alive. Much the same was true for the Moravian Indians from Wechquetank and Nain. Soon new violence would link the fates of these various groups of peaceable Natives even more closely.

Peace Advocate

Papunhank entered Philadelphia determined to remain an advocate for his community, near and far. Even if most of them were no longer present with him physically, he was ready to devise whatever means he could to promote their cause and the cause of peace. That meant drawing on whatever diplomatic ability and political capital he could muster. On December 1 he appeared before the colony's Provincial Council and delivered through John Curtis and Job Chillaway bold speeches that first conveyed important diplomatic messages from the Six Nations and from fellow Munsee headman Newollike, and then went on to appeal for renewed endeavors toward friendship between whites and Indians. Papunhank acknowledged the encouragement of the Pennsylvania government to recall the legacy of harmony established by their ancestors. But then he upped the ante and proclaimed, "You look but a little way [into the past], but I don't; I look as far back as the Creation, when God Almighty first made us & placed the good Spirit in our Hearts." Whether that conviction stemmed from Moravian teaching, a Quaker theology of the Inner Light, or traditional Munsee cosmology, it reflected Papunhank's fundamentally religious understanding of human behavior. Even after his Moravian baptism, he retained the language of a "good Spirit" in describing what was necessary to guide people's actions. For the moment his "good Spirit" was keeping him from deciding that the recent murders of the three Wyalusing Nanticokes by whites was reason enough to end his "Endeavours to preserve our Friendship."[17]

Of course, did he really have another option? Turning against or alienating the Pennsylvania government at this point would have spelled almost certain doom. He could ill afford to add another enemy to his list of foes. For their part colonial officials wanted to get as much value and intelligence out of Papunhank as they could. So ten days later he was back in front of the Provincial Council being asked by Governor Penn how best to protect the Wyalusingites and "all other Indians as are against the War" and to explain why "Enemy Indians" were "committing the present Ravages and Murders upon the Frontiers." Penn also wanted to know who specifically those enemy Indians were. Papunhank took thirty minutes to ponder a response to those delicate questions. Once ready to speak, he began by declaring, "I can scarcely find what to say in answer to my Brother." But in fact he seemed to know exactly what to say as he employed all his well-honed oratorical and diplomatic skills in the speech that followed. He quickly proceeded to tell the Pennsylvania government that he could not "answer to the Behaviour of any of the Indians who live to the Westward" but did know the minds of Delawares and Munsees living in "my Neighborhood." Those Indians had found it difficult to understand why English forts had remained garrisoned following the end of the Seven Years' War and why soldiers had attacked peaceful Natives when the latter had merely ventured westward toward the Allegheny to trade and hunt. The results were retaliatory raids first by Indians and then by soldiers. What might happen next in the Susquehanna Valley, Papunhank shrewdly suggested, could very well depend on how his people were treated in Philadelphia. For as he left Wyalusing for the city, he had met with a group of Munsees responsible for some of the raids who told him "all the Warriors should be very glad to know whether they [the English] treat you kindly or not, and how you are used." With that turn of phrase, Papunhank managed to present the fate of his people in the hands of the Pennsylvania government as a kind of barometer other Natives would use to determine whether frontier violence should continue. Peace, in other words, would directly depend on the

Wyalusingites getting the protection they needed. And, he continued, on his being able to return to Indian country to "let the Indians there know how friendly I have been received." With that appeal, the first of many he would make over the next year to get government approval for a journey back into the woods, Papunhank fashioned himself as a still essential go-between for colonial authorities.[18]

In a few well-chosen words, the Munsee reformer had subtly insinuated to the governor the critical value of his people and himself for the future of Pennsylvania. But Papunhank was not quite done. He sought to seal the deal regarding government favor for his community by stroking Penn's ego through assuring him "that we have not any better method to take for the security of all such Indians as are friendly disposed to you, than to invite them in as you have done us." Whatever doubts the prophet had about the wisdom of coming to Philadelphia, he was not about to share with the Provincial Council. Instead he confirmed their plan and concluded with one final brilliant rhetorical move. He implored them to "take pity on me, and not confine me in your Gaol on account of any false Reports or Stories that you may hear, as you have done one of our Brethren, who is now confined here." Papunhank may have had some genuine concern about being falsely imprisoned. But in this passing moment, he seized the opportunity to play on the government's good will toward him to make an appeal for justice for his fellow Christian Indian, Renatus.[19]

Papunhank's impressive public performances before the governor and Provincial Council reveal his leadership talents but mask the intense stress he was under. More private moments during the first ten days of December show a man resorting at least once to excessive drink, a vice from his preprophetic days, and to verbal complaints, even to his Moravian "overseers." Zeisberger reported that he had "spoken much with Johannes Papunham and Job Challowag [Chillaway] and heard more from them than I wanted to." One immediate concern was whether the Wyalusingites would join the other refugee Indians on Province Island. Chillaway favored that plan, but Papunhank seems to have been less sure. Zeisberger himself worried that if brought together, the Wyalusingites might continue some unruly behavior they had shown en route to the city and the Moravian Indians would get the blame from Philadelphia residents.[20]

Initially, then, whether the two groups of Natives would join forces or even share facilities was uncertain. But on December 13 Papunhank and his band left their temporary quarters within the Pennsylvania State House and moved to Province Island. There the Nain and Wechquetank communities were beginning to settle into their new surroundings under the oversight of Grube and Schmick and their wives. On their collective minds were questions about what the Natives would do with all of their idle time and whether they were really secure.[21]

The Paxton Crisis

Events within the next twenty-four hours raised even graver doubts about the latter. Dozens of disgruntled whites, soon to be known as the "Paxton Boys," descended on a group of peaceful Conestoga Indians in Lancaster County, killing and scalping six Natives and burning their town. The attack sent shock waves across the colony and prompted Penn to issue invitations to the surviving Conestogas, as well as to any friendly Indians still at Wyalusing, to come to the city for protection. Before the former group could oblige, however, the Paxtonians returned and finished their bloody work on December 27, killing all of them and soon after announcing plans that their next targets were the refugee Indians in Philadelphia.[22]

The armed frontier inhabitants voiced numerous grievances but none more essential than the claim that the colonial government had no business protecting and supplying Indians. How could it, they insisted, in the wake of its failure to provide adequate defenses for whites against raiding Indians? Stirred by religious convictions about the responsibility of government to serve the welfare of all, they convinced themselves and much of the rest of the colony that their extralegal violence was legitimate in light of their government's inaction. Mostly Presbyterians, they thought unduly influential Friends were particularly to blame for the miseries other Pennsylvanians had suffered, and now they would need to pay the price. As for the refugee Indians, they were no different from all other Natives—enemies to be removed through one means or another from the colony. Those views were unsettling, to say the least, to officials, Native Americans, and Quakers alike in Philadelphia. Their fears only intensified when reports came that the Paxton Boys were already marching toward the city to wreak their vengeance on both the perpetrators and the beneficiaries of such ill-advised policies.[23]

Members of the Friendly Association had responded to the news of the Wyalusing Indian arrival in Philadelphia in late November with quick offers of material assistance. But they also wanted the Natives to be sure they understood that it was the government's responsibility and not the association's to provide for them. They were clearly excited to have Papunhank back in their midst, yet they did not want him to have false expectations of them based on his prior visits to the city.[24] Such a worry now proved trivial in the face of the Paxton Boys threat.

With an attack seemingly imminent, government officials, Moravian missionaries, local Friends, and the Natives themselves scrambled to devise an escape plan. The interred Indians were told on December 29 that they had to leave Province Island, but where would they go? Various possibilities emerged in the next few days, including an offer from Israel Pemberton and other Philadelphia Friends to transport them to the care of Quakers on Nantucket Island in New England. However generous, the Moravian Indians and their white missionaries quickly declined that proposal "in the hope that our dear Father will show us another means by which we can be in security."[25] By January 4 Schmick and Grube were desperate enough to tell their superior in Bethlehem that they would support the governor giving "our Indians weapons again in order to defend themselves against the murderers, for we believe that otherwise not much will be done against them."[26] The prospect of another massacre of the innocents was too much for them to bear. In the end, the means settled upon was a middle-of-the-night departure from Philadelphia and a scheme to travel north through New Jersey, then cross to New York, make their way up the Hudson, and finally to head west into Six Nations country where they might come under the general protection of Sir William Johnson. There was even some hope that they could eventually find refuge back along the upper Susquehanna and there reunite with other Wyalusingites in southern New York.

Governor Penn wrote to Johnson on the day of their departure claiming that "tho' I could easily have afforded them a sufficient Protection, yet I [have] chosen to gratify them in their desire to be sent to you . . . [so] that they might be rendered easy in their minds, & the Wighalousin [Wyalusing] Indians get home to their Families, who will imagine them put to death as they will hear what has been done at Lancaster."[27] Penn's bravado aside, his remarks suggest that Papunhank likely influenced this plan. Though its formal architects were the governor, the Provincial Council, and the commissioners assigned to oversee the refugee Indians, its design squared so well with the prophet's interests that his input seems probable. He had reasonably strong diplomatic connections to the Six Nations, had won a favorable reputation with Johnson, knew that most of his Wyalusing brethren had already removed to southern New York, would not have favored arming refugee Indians, and was unsure from the start about being in Philadelphia.[28] Surprisingly, however, on the very first night of the group's departure (January 5) "our dear Joh. Papunhang, with his family, was called back by the Governor which made us very sorry." It also reportedly made Papunhank very unhappy. Penn explained two days later that Papunhank and other refugees from Wyalusing had "now gone to live with their Friends in Jersey below Burlington, Where I make no doubt they will live very happy, as the Governor of the Jerseys has promised them his Protection."[29]

Why Penn and Papunhank acted in this fashion is not clear. On the surface it made no sense since the ultimate destination of the refugees—reunification with other Wyalusingites—would have meant more to Papunhank's group than to the larger Moravian body. It is possible that Penn had received some intelligence that the Wyalusingites and perhaps Papunhank in particular were especially dangerous commodities to transport. Their ties to Quakers made them special targets for the Paxton Boys, and their occasional diplomatic assistance to the Pennsylvania government in the past bred ill will from disgruntled Natives. Penn may not have wanted to jeopardize the whole convoy by allowing

Papunhank to be part of it. Alternatively he may have decided that Papunhank might still prove to have value as a government instrument and therefore keeping him closer at hand had some merit. Even more likely is the possibility that influential Friends persuaded Penn that Papunhank would be better off under their care in the home of prominent Quaker Abel James in Frankfurt, New Jersey. Maybe this was the moment when they could reestablish more substantial links to the Munsee leader.

Whatever its motives, the plan proved ephemeral as Papunhank and his family stayed in New Jersey only three weeks. By that point the main body of Moravian refugees had already returned to Philadelphia, having been rebuffed at the New York border on orders from its governor, Cadwallader Colden.[30] Hearing that news, Papunhank sent word that he wanted to rejoin his fellow Moravians, much to the disappointment of Abel James, who tearfully wondered "what must the Brethren have indeed that their people are like this?" James himself may have been partly responsible for the Munsee's decision; he had invited Moravian missionary Schmick to visit Papunhank and his family on January 12 at Frankfurt. Schmick obliged and made three visits there within the next nine days. Papunhank and his family arrived back in Philadelphia on the twenty-ninth and "were extraordinarily pleased to see us," according to Grube and Schmick. Bonds of affection for his Moravian brethren had no doubt pulled Papunhank back to Philadelphia and indicate the level of commitment that had already grown up between them. But so too did his feelings of vulnerability and dependence. Quakers in New Jersey could not offer the type of armed protection available in the city. And the threat was real. Within ten days of his return, Friends told him that "enemies" had wanted to attack him and his family in New Jersey but fortunately, they had already left for Philadelphia.[31]

Philadelphia could hardly be described as a safe haven, however. Events now climaxed as several hundred Paxton Rangers reached the city's edge on February 4. For the next four days, tensions ran high as opposing forces poised to do battle. Royal troops and local militia, including as many as two hundred armed Quakers, stood ready to defend the refugee Indians housed once again in the city's army barracks. Perhaps fearing the willingness of his soldiers to fight for Natives, the British commander, Captain Schlosser, even "put weapons into their [the refugee Indians] hands." Fortunately, diplomacy prevailed; grievances were submitted, the Paxton Boys headed home, and a pamphlet rather than a literal war ensued. Over the next year, powerful Quakers were excoriated repeatedly for their sins of commission (aiding Indians of any variety) and omission (failing to protect white frontier settlers adequately and then failing to provide adequate relief to war victims after the fact). Friends' rejoinders could not prevent a further erosion of their political influence.[32]

To Wyalusing and Back

Papunhank and the other hundred-plus Natives in the barracks had spent those early February days, in the words of Moravian missionary and chronicler John Heckewelder, "in terror, and hourly expectation of the rioters." All of them were frightful about their own survival. Yet before, during, and after the Paxtonians' "visit," Papunhank had managed to keep his eye on the bigger picture. In particular, he feared the potential resumption of wider warfare and its likely impact on other Indians—perhaps especially those Wyalusingites who had not come to Philadelphia with him—as well as on whites. Specifically, he was anxious for the government to get a message out that the Christian Indian refugees in the city were still alive "so that hostilely-disposed Indians will not come to the idea that we had all already been killed." Papunhank had promised to send word back to Indian country about his fate since when they left Wyalusing "some of his friends apprehended that he and his company would by killed by the White People." Ever the peacemaker, he worked with Moravian missionaries to draft a letter with that message to the governor in his name to be sent to interior Indians, and then met with military officials on the sixteenth and seventeenth to discuss his concerns further. Four days later, Governor Penn showed up incognito at the barracks and talked directly with Papunhank. Penn was reluctant to have any official message sent to the Wyalusingites but "had no objection to Papounan's Journey to the Indian Country, to acquaint his Friends of the kind treatment" Penn's government had provided. So later that day, the Munsee leader headed out of Philadelphia, tears in his eyes, with his colleague and interpreter, Job Chillaway, bound for the Pennsylvania frontier.[33]

The prayers of their Moravian brethren in the city went with them. Missionaries and Natives alike were only too glad to support the leadership that Papunhank now seemed to exert naturally. His experience in negotiating with the colonial government, knowledge of the Pennsylvania interior, connections with various Indian peoples, and reputation for peace set him apart from anyone else in the community. Penn recognized that as well, and he was prepared to employ Papunhank once again as a diplomatic envoy, even if he was now telling the Pennsylvania Council that the invitation to the Wyalusingites to come to Philadelphia in the first place had not come from him. It had actually come from "some private people [presumably members of the Friendly Association], who took every opportunity in their power to interfere & meddle in Indian Affairs." At that moment with the Paxton Boys crisis still pending, Penn had good reason to be distancing himself from that decision.[34]

The two Natives had a small military escort to Fort Allen, northwest of the city. Then at great personal risk from vengeful whites and warring Natives, they continued northward on their own ostensibly as "messengers of peace to the hostile Indians, [sent] to inform them that they were all alive and to desire them to lay down the hatchet."[35] Papunhank had no trouble endorsing that unofficial mission, and in that way, carrying the hopes he shared with the Pennsylvania government and the British army for an end to the violence. He knew that renewed peace was the only path to his community's long-term survival and its more immediate re-formation. He also knew that there was no future for them in Philadelphia. Internment there should only be endured for as long as was absolutely necessary.

The other refugee Indians agreed. They were all anxious to figure out where they could go. Grube assumed that some version of the original plan to get them to New York and William Johnson's oversight would eventually be implemented. But for the moment the government, according to Schmick, had "no idea where to place our Indians or send them. For to let them settle again on their previous places or to send them into the Indian Lands, the former places them in danger of their lives at this time and the latter exposes them to the temptations of wicked Indians to force them to join them in murdering." Schmick noted that his flock of Moravian Indians from Nain wanted to move back to their former homes "because they are afraid to live in the woods and to see the wild nature of the Indians and to be treated in a hostile manner there." They hoped that Papunhank's mission would show the government what could be done "for them to return to freedom." For that reason, Schmick said, "the present journey of Johannes Papunhank is very dear to us and to the Quakers as well."[36] Like the Natives from Nain, the Munsee prophet likewise didn't know whether it was possible to move his band back to their homeland on the upper Susquehanna. Nor did he know the fate of those who had stayed there three months earlier. Gaining answers to those questions surely motivated his willingness to take this life-threatening journey.

When he and Chillaway arrived back in Philadelphia on March 25, Papunhank's daughter was with them. That was a clear sign of what they had found in Wyalusing. They reported that "the Indians up there . . . live in much uneasiness and have to suffer much hunger." Scattered by threats from other Natives, the Wyalusingites they encountered in northern Pennsylvania were struggling to sustain themselves through the winter on handfuls of maize. Furthermore, Papunhank was worried that a wider war was about to break out between the Six Nations and the Delawares. No wonder he brought his daughter back with him. Even the grim realities of life in Philadelphia were a better option. According to Zeisberger, "Johannes said it is much better here in the barracks than up there in the woods where they would have to live in constant fear, for there were still good people here who loved the Indians."[37]

Things in Wyalusing only grew worse the next month. Many of its former villagers had moved to the towns of Otseningo (also known as Zeninge or Chenango; present-day Binghamton, New York) and

Chugnot within Onondaga territory the prior fall when Papunhank had left for Philadelphia. Nanticokes and Conoys had invited them there and told them that Wyalusing was in harm's way. But their new locale brought its own challenges. At the same moment Papunhank was back in Wyalusing in March, many of them were at Johnson Hall near Albany to ask William Johnson for food and clothing supplies. He agreed but said that in return they would need to supply him with as many able-bodied warriors as they could muster to join his army to take on enemy Indians. For the pacifist prophet, that would have been a hard bargain to swallow. But these Wyalusingites did not have much negotiating space. They described themselves to Johnson as "being a little enlightened by the Christian Religion," presumably to gain his favor, and then pledged to supply sixty warriors. Two months later they explained to Johnson that their men had not joined the army of Captain Andrew Montour in April for its search-and-destroy mission along the upper Susquehanna because a group of Mingos had told them to stay put. Johnson was not pleased, told them to listen only to him, and warned them that unless they complied, "your People now in Philadelphia . . . will [not] be well treated." However idle that threat may have been, by late June, their ranks had joined up with Johnson's army en route to Niagara. Perhaps Papunhank's persistent peace message had made them reluctant warriors, especially if it meant, as it would have, participating in the destruction of their former town alongside Montour's forces. His army laid waste to Wyalusing and other Indian settlements along the Susquehanna and Chemung Rivers. There were no Wyalusingites left in Wyalusing after that.[38]

Barracks Life and Death

Sobered by what he had seen in Wyalusing, Papunhank and other community leaders nevertheless remained determined to find a way out of the city. Within days of his return, they were back lobbying various government officials to approve the original plan to move them to upper New York and to the care of Johnson. The Natives proposed that if the governor could get them safely to the New York border, they could make the rest of the trip through the woods on their own.

Penn and members of the Provincial Council were not wholly unsympathetic to what the refugees wanted since they were anxious to have the Natives become someone else's headache. But ongoing frontier warfare made the plan too risky. Pennsylvania didn't want to shoulder the blame if some of these Indians were harmed en route or worse yet, chose to join Pontiac's rebels. Instead, the governor sent word through Joseph Fox, commissary in charge of supplying the refugees, that all of them would be moved back to Province Island where their stay would not be "long because the Lord General promises soon to have peace with the Indians." Three days later, David Zeisberger more accurately predicted that they would be there "this whole Summer or probably remain a whole year."[39]

Remain they did, and in the barracks rather than on Province Island. By mid-May the governor had decided the island would be too unhealthy for them. Better to stay in the barracks, which now had more room thanks to the redeployment to the west of most of the British troops who had been guarding them.[40] That was one sign that some greater measure of calm had descended upon Philadelphia by late spring.

The refugee Indians surely needed some calm. The first part of 1764 had been tumultuous to say the least. Yet amid all the upheavals of their first five or six months in captivity, they managed to establish, especially after their aborted sojourn to New York, some daily routines that provided a modicum of normalcy and stability. Prominent among them was a pattern of Moravian religious services that filled numerous hours throughout the week. Each morning and evening the community gathered in the barracks' kitchen for worship to sing God's praises, pray for his mercy, and listen to missionaries Grube, Schmick, and Zeisberger preach from the texts assigned for that day. Other familiar practices including love feasts (a worship service during which the community shared a simple meal), *Singstude* (song services), foot washings, and *Abendmahl* (communicant preparation) were held. Familiar that is to the Moravian Indians from Nain and Wechquetank. For Papunhank and other Wyalusingites, much of that was relatively new. Papunhank's prior exposures to Moravian piety had never lasted more than several consecutive weeks. Now he and his family and other Wyalusing migrants were being fully immersed into Brethren spirituality over the course of many months. Indications are that they were receptive to being brought into the Moravian fold. By early June three Wyalusingites, including Papunhank's twenty-two-year-old daughter (Sophia), had asked for and received baptism. Two months earlier, her father had been especially moved during Holy Week services. On Good Friday, when the story of Jesus's suffering was read in the Mahican language, "many tears were spilt in the process, our Johannes Pepunhang, who heard it for the first time, was particularly taken by it." That evening, forty-two took Communion and "Joh. Pepunhang had the blessing of watching."[41]

To be invited to observe the private Holy Communion service was a key step within Moravian theology and practice toward a person attaining full communicant membership. It indicates that the Munsee prophet was becoming increasingly bound to Moravianism and to the larger body of Moravian refugees, and they to him. Living, working, and worshipping together, deeper connections developed in the face of common foes and struggles. When daughter Sophia was baptized and then married two weeks later to Joshua Junior, son of key Mahican Brethren leader Joshua Senior, even stronger religious and kinship attachments were formed. At the same time, though no longer in a position to exercise the same level of religious authority he had enjoyed for the past decade, Papunhank emerged as the most important political and diplomatic leader for the whole Native refugee community, not just for the Wyalusingites. He consistently took the most initiative with the government in trying to devise a solution for all the captives, and Moravian and non-Moravian Indians alike were ready to follow. The German missionaries recognized and usually supported his leadership; no Native figures more prominently in the congregational diary they kept or the letters they wrote to their supervisors in Bethlehem. They urged Papunhank "to keep himself very close to the Savior every day and to have the feeling of His blessing palpably near." He obliged and remained attentive to their spiritual admonitions during the first half of 1764.[42]

The Moravian pastors had plenty of other attentive listeners, or at least curiosity seekers. One hundred and fifty Indians residing in the city was a novelty. Urban and rural, young and old came in droves to the barracks, especially in the first months of the year, to take a look at these Natives. If a document prepared the prior fall describing physical differences between Moravian and "wild" Indians can be trusted, the visitors would have seen men and women who were fully clothed, wearing hats or caps but no feathers, with long hair and unpainted bodies. Those distinguishing characteristics made no difference to the mockers and scorners who came simply to vent their anger and frustration at Natives of any variety. But other whites came with more benevolent agendas. Philadelphia Friends, both prominent and not so prominent, visited regularly and usually brought some form of charity. White Moravians from the city and surrounding area likewise came often to worship alongside the captives. They were joined by members of other denominations, or none at all, interested to see and hear these Christian Indians. In late February Schmick noted that "there were so many white people that half the audience had to stand outside the door. . . . Nothing charmed the people more than to hear the Indians sing, and if we had a larger gathering space we could have several hundred in attendance daily." On Sunday, May 6, the Moravian diary reported that more than a thousand people were there to see the Indians.[43]

Some in the visiting crowd usually heard the sermon, but others were more interested in buying "many baskets and arrows and bows from the Indians." Those products were the fruit of the all-too-insufficient labor Natives performed during their captivity. From the moment the decision had been made to remove to Philadelphia, Moravian leaders worried about the prospect of Indian idleness in the city. What would their charges do to fill their days when their normal work routines were not possible? Occasional donations of wood allowed their men to carve spoons, their women to weave baskets, and their young people to craft bows and arrows. All were sold to white visitors "so that they could buy some bread for their children." That was hardly enough income to subsist upon or enough activity to occupy their time.[44]

Tragically, beginning in May, too much of their time was devoted to caring for their sick and dying. Isolated cases of smallpox and other diseases afflicted and even killed a few community members early in the year. That was a small harbinger of things to come. "Our Indians are beginning to get ill," Schmick wrote on May 21, "Joshua Senior is not quite recovered, Johannes, Little Lore's husband, has been ill for 5 days today and will probably be called Home . . . Little Sophia, the third daughter is also sick in bed and Tabea has the same illness, namely Yellow Fever. . . . Where the illness rages the Savior will doubtless take many home and save them from all distress." Similar heartbreaking reports became all too common in the missionary letters and congregational diary during the next few months as a smallpox epidemic, "supplemented" by cases of dysentery, besieged the community from May through August. The pox proved no respecter of persons, taking male and female, young and old, Mahican and Delaware, Indian and white. The death toll was ten in June. July was worse; Schmick reported on the twenty-fifth that there was "no appearance that the Illnesses will cease any time soon. Since the 20th of this month 20 of them have been taken from this mortal life." Eleven more succumbed in August, including Johanna Maria Schmick, the fourteen-month-old daughter of the missionary couple. By year's end disease had claimed the lives of fifty-six Native men, women, and children.[45]

Under those circumstances the refugee community was strained to the breaking point. Sickness and sorrow were everywhere. Something dramatic needed to be done. Papunhank and other Indian leaders became increasingly desperate for another option besides remaining in the city and watching helplessly as loved ones passed. Everyone grew restless; in early July, Grube wrote that "most of them [the Indians] want to leave for the woods because they believe that they will all die here." Papunhank didn't know what to do except to resume his search for a way out of Philadelphia. By midsummer he was prepared to go back to Indian country whatever the consequences. In August Schmick told Governor Penn that Papunhank and many of the younger males wanted "to be in the wilderness again because they are so sick here." When Penn responded that ongoing war made that plan impossible,

Papunhank insisted that he speak to Penn himself, to which the governor expressed amazement and reiterated that if the Munsee's point was simply to ask again to return to the Susquehanna, "then it would be futile that he speak with him." In October Papunhank led a delegation to the colony's chief justice asking for permission to depart the city. Grube and Schmick noted that by that point "almost all our poor people have the intention of leaving, and therefore they work hard to bring it about yet this fall." The missionaries' advice to their Indian charges "to have patience and leave it to the direction of the Savior" was now having "little effect." Papunhank had persuaded most of the refugees that their individual and collective survival depended on them taking action now before it was too late and even if it went against the counsel of their Moravian overseers. Finally in November, he and three associates, without Grube and Schmick's knowledge, acquired a pass from the governor to travel to the Susquehanna to scout for a future settlement site, and in the opinion of the white missionaries, to engage in the hunt.[46] Papunhank perhaps believed that participating in the longstanding rhythms of the Munsee year might provide a salve for the wounds of the past twelve months and better provisions for the winter ahead.

He also went to discover the fate of the rest of his Wyalusing band, or at least those who had remained within Pennsylvania. What he found confirmed his worst fears. When he and traveling companion Joshua Senior reached Wyalusing,

> they met no more Indians, rather, most everything . . . [was] destroyed. The Indians from the six nations [had] wreaked havoc on the Susquehanna last summer, mowed down the corn, and spoiled things: shot the cattle and burned many small towns of Delaware and Mennisingen [Minisink or Munsee] Indians. A few they killed and cut into pieces. The Indians up there are said to have spent the summer in the greatest confusion and fear.

No doubt heartbroken at the loss of the town he had built, Papunhank must have pondered whether the choice to bring some of his people to Philadelphia, despite the danger, disease, and death they had encountered there, was the right one after all. Joshua thought so: "We had thought that we had it very hard during the time here in the barracks, only it is no comparison with that with [*sic*] the Indians in the wilderness have suffered, and we recognize now that the Savior himself directed our circumstances, as the Brethren often said."[47]

Restless Souls and Community Divisions

Those pious words from Joshua belied the spiritual struggles that he and much of the rest of the refugee community had experienced in the prior six months. The onset of epidemic disease and death multiplied the considerable frustrations and anxieties the exiles were already feeling in the spring of 1764. Their restlessness was not only physical but spiritual. By the end of June, the missionaries reported that they had "explained various matters to our people in a special service, particularly about going home [dying], because various of them have let themselves come into reasoning about it. Anton said at last: It is true what our wise brothers say, I know their hearts, and whoever says or thinks something against them, he speaks or thinks against the Savior, and I will have no part of it." Those pronouncements revealed growing unrest with the missionaries' teaching and hardly settled the matter. "Joshua is confused," wrote Grube in mid-July, "[as are] most of the others on account of the illness especially the smallpox. Joshua has probably reasoned a lot during the illness and has lost his heart and will not let himself be corrected." Schmick concurred a week later: "Each and every day occasions us new distress and misery. . . . Our Indians . . . have been thrown into confusion because of the illness." What were they to think amid so much loss? Had the Christian God abandoned them? Why were their prayers and medicine so ineffectual? What was the meaning of their suffering?[48]

Even Papunhank succumbed to doubts by late August. "The poor man is weak in his heart," Grube observed. A week later he described him as "very confused." The prophet's spirits had sunk to new depths. He was getting nowhere in his efforts to get himself or anyone else out of the killing fields the barracks had become. It was harder and harder for him to feel any comfort from the "blessed Savior" when death kept snuffing out hope. Native brothers and sisters with whom he had grown close during the past nine months were either dying or questioning their Christian commitments. No one seemed able to ease his discouragement. Grube's own frustrations over that fact boiled over in a letter to his supervisor: "It would have been well if his [Papunhank's spiritual] caretaker, Father David [Zeisberger], had visited him once, only I hear that he has found his heaven in Christiansbrunn and he doesn't want to leave it ever again."[49]

"Everyone was glad to see him" when Zeisberger showed up in the city two weeks later, "preached with blessing . . . [and] also spoke with John Pepunhang."[50] If in that way, Grube's frustration and Papunhank's confusion were largely or at least partially dissipated, other antagonisms large and small surfaced during the captivity that were not so easily abated. Fear of attack, uncertainty about the future, physical confinement, meager food and accommodations, boredom, and most especially, deadly disease were a toxic recipe. Under the best of circumstances and with the fullest of resources, any Native community would have been hard-pressed to hold up under such an assault. The Indian refugees had no such luxuries. They were living in a hostile, alien space where few familiar elements of their former lives, whether in the Moravian Indian towns (Wechquetank and Nain) or Wyalusing, could be reproduced.

Little wonder, then, that relationships of all sorts became frayed. Joshua Senior and his wife, Bathsheba, had a long but volatile marriage. The pressures of captivity sparked several rounds of bickering and estrangement.[51] Renatus, the Nain Native accused of murder, not only wallowed in jail for eight months awaiting trial, but while there, endured the news that his father, wife, and son had all died. Then within four days of his acquittal in June, his fourteen-year-old sister passed away. The community rallied around him and worked hard to find him a new marriage partner. He complied with others' wishes and wed Marie in November, but within a couple of weeks, the two were separated and he was ready to run off (at least figuratively) with another single woman, Christina.[52] Just at that same time, most of the young males among the refugees were upset that Papunhank, Joshua Senior, Joshua Junior, and Bartholomew had run off into the woods without them. It didn't matter that they were the only ones given permission to leave the city. The young people felt deceived by the elder leaders. From their perspective, Papunhank and Joshua Senior had "always pretended that they took so much trouble for the sake of the young people and now . . . [we] see that they meant themselves."[53]

Generational tensions were a predictable by-product of widespread frustration. Likewise, ethnic tensions emerged within the community. Historian Amy Schutt has proposed that by this era, Natives had developed stronger national identities. Among the mixed refugee ranks of Munsees, Mahicans, and Unami-speaking Delawares, she finds cracks in communal cohesion developing along tribal lines. In particular, higher death tolls from disease for Mahicans compared to Munsees and Delawares strained relations among the groups, and in her view, became a long-term source of resentment. Even more specifically, because Papunhank and his family all survived, they became special targets of a latent animosity that surfaced in later years.[54]

Marital breakdowns, generational conflict, and ethnic tensions arose alongside a growing, though ultimately temporary, rift between the German missionaries and their Native charges. Two overlapping or interconnected issues contributed to the strain: missionary efforts to control the moral behavior and spiritual inclinations of the refugee Indians, and missionary reluctance to engage in the politics of the Natives' plight. Coming from Wechquetank and Nain, as well as earlier missionary assignments, Grube and Schmick were accustomed to upholding high standards of behavior within their Indian communities. In their view, the credibility of the communities' Christian witness and reputation for moral uprightness were at stake, as were Moravian claims that "their" Indians were different from "wild" Indians. They brought those expectations to Philadelphia and layered them on top of concerns about the physical safety of their Native brothers and sisters. The city presented all kinds of dangers to life and limb—and to souls. Best, then, to keep a tight rein on where and what the Indians were up to. Pennsylvania authorities agreed. They didn't want Natives roaming about precipitating incidents of one type or another. So the missionaries devoted considerable energy to corralling their charges within the barracks lest they fall sway to the corrupting influences surrounding them or antagonize political officials whose help they needed.

The first few months of captivity went well with only a handful of cases of Indians acting "badly." Then the epidemic hit and with it, rising rates of misbehavior. When the missionaries declared "our young people gave us much distress today," that was their way of saying that some had gone off drinking or otherwise caused a disturbance. It also conveyed their anxiety about the young sharing in the spiritual confusion and disaffection brought on by so much death around them. By late November Grube simply confessed that "here in the barracks I am getting more grey hairs, for one can do nothing but worry." He, more than Schmick, came to interpret negatively any Native impulse to want to get outside the confines of the barracks and even the city. For him, it was a sign that they wished to escape Moravian oversight and authority. For them, it was a natural reaction to what felt like overly paternalistic and protectionist policies. After a year in captivity, Grube told a Bethlehem official, "I don't trust any of our young people. Now everyone is going out where ever they want to." In his mind, such Indian "freedom" equaled a loss of his control and portended a highly uncertain future for Moravian Native missions.[55]

It also complicated the missionaries' role in any political resolution of the refugees' predicament. Moravian leaders in Philadelphia and Bethlehem were extremely empathetic to the Natives' plight when they were removed to the city and worked diligently with government officials to find alternative arrangements. When the first plan stalled at the New York border, they remained willing in February, March, and April to serve as go-betweens for Papunhank and the whole community with Governor Penn in advocating that they be moved. But when those efforts came to naught and ended any prospect of an imminent departure from the city, the missionaries became increasingly resigned to the status quo even while many of the refugee Indians grew ever more restless and discontent. Hence, as noted earlier, their encouragement to their charges "to have patience and leave it to the direction of the Savior" fell mostly on deaf ears as the year went on. From Schmick and Grube's standpoint, as difficult as life was in Philadelphia, they and their wives were at least able to carry on their regular pastoral duties and care for their Indian congregants. If the Natives began leaving the city piecemeal and started scattering about in Indian country, there was no telling whether a Moravian Indian town could be regathered or what would become of the Natives' spiritual condition. Moreover, as refugee frustration with not being able to leave the city grew, the missionaries did not want to be blamed for government intransigence. So they withdrew more and more from the process of finding a political solution to the refugee problem, even while repeatedly conveying to Papunhank and others their concerns about any of them going to the "wilderness again." That explains why in November Papunhank and his three associates bypassed Grube and Schmick and went directly to government officials for a travel pass to the Susquehanna. When informed of this plan by Joshua Senior, Schmick, "in order to prevent more hostility" over the issue, simply told him "you all are doing this for yourselves and we have nothing to do with the matter, you are all just risking your lives." He went on to report to his superiors in Bethlehem that "we have been quite passive in all this and have not tried to meddle in government affairs."[56]

Going Home

Community tensions began to subside in early December with the news that a peace accord had been secured with most of the rebellious Indians. The refugees rejoiced and now had some hope that their captivity would finally be coming to an end. Then Papunhank's party of four returned after five weeks away and expressed great appreciation for the advantages of life in the city with the Moravian brethren compared to what their compatriots had endured in northern Pennsylvania. Those words no doubt soothed relations with Schmick and Grube. Joshua Senior went on to report that while in Wyalusing, they had been told that during raids on Delaware and Munsee towns, Six Nations warriors had declared to their Native enemies, "now you can imagine how it felt to the white people when you perpetrated the same thing upon them, we want to give you the same feeling, so that you might have the right understanding of it." Escaping that type of destruction was just one reason to celebrate on Christmas when "Br. Schmick held a blessed festival sermon . . . [and there was] an especially blessed peace to be felt among our people." Four days later a Communion service was held, and Joshua Senior and Bathsheba participated for the first time in many months.[57]

Whatever pain Papunhank now associated with Wyalusing was not great enough to keep him from believing it was nevertheless the best place for him and all the Moravian Indian refugees to start over. Upon his return to the city, he began to lobby the relevant parties toward that goal. With peace achieved, the Pennsylvania government could endorse a plan to resettle the Christian Indians in a place comparatively far removed from white settlers and most other Natives. But the governor told Papunhank and Joshua Senior on January 24 that he would first need to write on their behalf to Sir William Johnson and get his opinion on the matter. Such a delay was distressing at a moment when urgent action was needed. Rumors were circulating that a new outbreak of smallpox had occurred near the barracks. Natives pleaded to be released from the city before it was too late. Many of them supported a proposal to let them move back to Nain for the winter. White Moravians in Bethlehem and government authorities in Philadelphia considered it but in early February decided that it was not feasible because non-Moravian whites in the Lehigh Valley remained too hostile toward all Natives. Bethlehem leaders concluded that a more remote location was needed and came round to supporting Papunhank's proposal to bring the refugees to the upper Susquehanna. The refugee Indians themselves concurred. They were more than eager to begin again in a place where they could live freely according to the blended ways of their Native mothers and fathers and their white Moravian brothers and sisters.[58]

For their part, Schmick and Grube remained "totally passive" during January and most of February about when and where the Moravian Indians should go. They were content "to leave it to our dear Father, who will direct everything according to his will." But the Indians couldn't be that patient. It was their "constant desire . . . to get away from here into the woods." They kept sending Papunhank and Joshua Junior back to the government asking when they could leave and always got the same answer, "Soon, soon." Frustrated in their appeals, Joshua Junior "finally turned to us," Schmick reported in early March, "and asked that we concern ourselves with them and do something in this matter, otherwise the young people will set out, leave there and nothing good would come out of it for the rest of them." Faced with that prospect, Schmick relented and went to speak with commissary Joseph Fox about a departure date and provisions for the group for their journey and their first few months in Wyalusing. Fox agreed to help and in the end secured both public and private funding to aid the refugees.[59]

With formal government approval of their moving plans achieved on February 26, the Moravian Indians set March 20 as their "liberation" day. Yet there were still plenty of details to work out. They would all move initially to Wyalusing "because they will have it good there and find well-cared for land for planting." But there seems to have been some question whether the Mahicans in the group might eventually form their own town. At the very least, due to that people's having not lived along the Susquehanna before and separate relationship with the Six Nations, they would need to inform the Iroquois of what they were doing and get their approval for settling there. There was also some question about the wisdom of bringing white Moravian missionaries with them prior to hearing back from the Six Nations. Joshua Senior didn't "know if it is a good thing" but "Johannes Papunhank was of the opinion that a [Moravian] Brother might well go on with them." As usual, the prophet's view won out and the stage was set for Bethlehem to appoint Zeisberger and Schmick as the ones to "bring the little Indian congregation to the Susquehanna." Schmick accepted the call "with his full heart," a heart nevertheless afraid that once there, the Indians "might easily be led astray through the power of the evil enemy who has his reserves on the Susquehanna; how easily it might come to pass through the temptations of the wild Indians and they fall as sheep among the ravening wolves and could be scattered God knows where."[60]

Papunhank probably did not share those fears. He was too excited to be going home and too grateful to be melancholic in this moment. His final few days in the city were spent packing wagons and co-writing a letter of thanks on behalf of the Christian Indians to Governor Penn. As quoted at the beginning of this chapter, the address expressed gratitude for the government's protection and provision, cited the benefits of having been accorded the "Liberty . . . to have our Ministers with us," and pledged "that we are & will for ever remain true friends to the English." Papunhank knew better than any that continuing to navigate relations skillfully with Pennsylvania's government would be a key for their security.[61] The Indians also expressed great thanks to Joseph Fox and to other benevolent Friends who had come to their aid. A number of Quakers, including Pemberton and Benezet, had regularly visited the refugees, especially in the early weeks and months of their internment. They had come with words of encouragement, offers of assistance, and even, among some, a willingness to go against their own peace testimony and take up arms.[62]

Men like Fox, Benezet, and Pemberton no doubt relished the opportunity to reconnect with their friend Papunhank during his time of captivity. Yet, as the months passed it must have become clear to all four men that their previously cherished hopes for one another were not going to materialize. Neither Papunhank nor the Friends could supply the other what had seemed possible a few years earlier. By 1764–65 activist Quakers, including members of the now disbanded Friendly Association, were reeling from a decade of war, a bloody pamphlet fight, and the loss of much of their political clout. Strengthening ties to any Indians at that moment would only make their situation worse. Moreover, Philadelphia Friends' attention had turned to determining how to discipline those members who had taken up weapons in February, a discussion that lasted into 1767. They also became preoccupied with and divided over efforts to make Pennsylvania a royal colony.[63] Activist Friends remained fond of Papunhank, but it was clear that he was in no position to help revive their political fortunes or resurrect their Holy Experiment. Nor could they be of much help to him. During his months in Philadelphia, he had seen firsthand how much Quakers—

especially those Friends with whom he had interacted most—were hated by other Pennsylvanians. To be linked with them eventually did nothing less than put a target on Papunhank's back. In addition, they offered no alternative prospect for what to do or where to go in early 1765. Friends had no plan or means to have a Quaker Indian town, and he certainly did not want to stay in the city.

Papunhank's choice that spring to continue his attachment to Moravians, then, was the only choice he really had and came as no surprise. He had arrived in Philadelphia following a substantial loss of influence and with only a small portion of the community he had led for more than a decade. He now left with a reconstituted company. This alliance gave him the means to leave Philadelphia, resume life in Wyalusing with a critical mass of like-minded Natives, and gain wider Moravian religious, moral, and financial support. The Moravians had in essence helped to save Papunhank by restoring to him political and religious authority, spiritual satisfaction, community bonds, and a more secure future.

But he had also helped to save them. He provided the means for Moravian Native missions in the northern colonies to continue. The future of the Brethren's missionary enterprise hung in the balance as the period of captivity came to a close. No one among the church's white leadership in Bethlehem or Philadelphia knew what would become of the refugee Indians or whether German pastors would remain with them. That spring they were forced to reassess their entire missionary program. As they dreamed of reestablishing a Moravian Indian town, they knew that that possibility depended on the decisions of many others: the Pennsylvania government, the Six Nations, colonial settlers, Sir William Johnson, and the refugees themselves. Far more than anyone else, Johannes Papunhank helped them realize that dream. Though an "outsider" when he and the other Wyalusingites joined the much larger body of Moravian Indians in Philadelphia, he quickly emerged as the most important leader there and played a crucial role in helping the refugees, despite their differences and occasional divisions, meld into a single community. From February 1764 on, he took the greatest initiative in lobbying government officials, listening to the heartfelt longings of fellow Natives, and seeking out a long-term solution to their plight, even at great personal risk. By this point in his life, he was long habituated to such work. Caring for the security and well-being of his community—in this case, a reconstituted community—came naturally. Or perhaps it is more accurate to say, he was driven to it ever since becoming a prophet by his passion to have his people, and all peoples, live peaceable lives in accord with the Creator's intent. Observing and sharing in their suffering in the city only intensified his will to find a way out. Moravian leadership eventually supported his plan because he offered the only viable means to save their evangelistic enterprise. They would send German missionary pastors to the new town, but they would rely on Papunhank to clear the physical, political, and diplomatic path for them.

And so on March 20, 1765, after sixteen months of exile, Papunhank headed home, now in the company of eighty-two fellow Moravian Indians who had become his new band. That day they moved quietly through the city streets in their wagons loaded with women, children, and baggage. Few took note, a far cry from the mobs of Philadelphians who had angrily greeted their first arrival. In the relative silence, they bade one last farewell to the husbands and wives, sons and daughters whose journeys had ended in that alien place. And they began to ponder what lay ahead. Thanks to a combination of skill and persistence, Papunhank had secured for them a physical and political space to begin anew. In the process he made possible the continuation of Moravian outreach to Native peoples. Existing accounts of Moravian history that credit German missionaries as almost wholly responsible for sustaining and renewing Moravian evangelism of Indians in 1765 are therefore simply incomplete. As in many other instances in early America where Natives were the key players in the Christian evangelism of their own peoples, here Papunhank was indispensable in making that possible.[64]

5

From Prophet to Guardian

Two months after leaving Philadelphia, Papunhank and the other survivors of the long captivity began to settle into Wyalusing. They were relieved to be there and ready to construct a new physical and spiritual home, no one more than Papunhank.

> Saturday the 18th [May 1765] After that we had a little conference with Anton, Josua, Johannes Papunhank and Nicodemus and looked around our cabin for a good place to build new dwelling houses and one for services. For the latter Johannes offered to move his large, shingled cabin down here because he wants to build another [house] down here.... Sunday the 19th in the morning and found Sinner Hearts yearning for Grace, who testified with feeling how much they need the Savior and the Holy Communion for strengthening and life.... Johannes Papunhank also recalled himself to remembrance, testifying of his frequent longing for the Holy Communion and thus to be united with the Savior and that his heart is the same, even today. Br. David preached the sermon on the Watchword and the Savior Himself acknowledged this. In the afternoon, we considered Johannes' situation before the Savior and he received the Grace of going also to the Holy Communion and when he was told of this it occasioned tears of joy and [joy] in his heart. After the evening service the Communicant Brothers and Sisters, 21 of them all

> together, came together into our cabin, which was hung inside with blankets. We let ourselves receive the gracious Absolution from the Friend of Sinners [Jesus] and thereafter had an altogether blessed Holy Communion, to which Johannes was graciously admitted for the first time. All the Brothers and Sisters rejoiced at this, especially since he was baptized here and was here admitted to the enjoyment of the Body and Blood of our Lord. They were all very heartily glad for him.[1]

Finally home in Wyalusing, Papunhank was now also home in the inner circle of Moravian believers devout enough to be admitted to the holiest of acts, the taking of Communion. Another critical milestone in his religious journey, it further sealed him to Moravians and them to his authority. Brothers and sisters, Indian and European, welcomed him into their fellowship just as he was welcoming them into his former homeland. Perhaps that was no coincidence. Both parties seemed to realize that the mutual dependence they had developed in Philadelphia would need to continue if they were to prosper. Establishing a Moravian Indian community in Indian country was a new enterprise for the United Brethren and a turning point in their missions' history. Previously, their Native congregations in Pennsylvania had been situated near white settlements where immigrant Moravians frequently interacted with Native residents and provided much-needed support. The growth of anti-Indian racism among white colonists by the 1760s, however, eliminated that option. White hate and hostility forced the Philadelphia exiles into a more distant removal than most of them would have preferred and necessitated the creation of a new type of Moravian Indian village, one more dependent on Native leadership. Exactly two years earlier Papunhank had excitedly welcomed David Zeisberger into his home and had him preach to the community even before feeding him.[2] Now he was offering that same home to be the meeting house for the newly arrived refugees. There they could worship together the god Papunhank had embraced and in this first Communion, tasted. Song, word, and sacrament brought something familiar to this new and unfamiliar land. They needed someone literally to show them the way there and to supply a long absent peace, freedom, and stability. Papunhank was eager to fill those roles, and they were ready and willing to follow.

With natural aplomb, he asserted a community leadership reminiscent of earlier days. From the moment they left the city, and in many ways even before, Papunhank took the lead—navigationally, politically, diplomatically, and economically. Others were ready to defer, including missionaries Schmick and Zeisberger.[3] They recognized this was Papunhank's territory and willingly endorsed his authority. He knew the ins and outs of the land. More important, he knew the ins and outs of Native relations. Any hopes they harbored of staying put in Wyalusing and truly making it their home depended largely on his negotiating skills. Much of his time and energy during the next four years would be devoted to securing the community's right to be there and some measure of autonomy within the umbrella of Iroquois sovereignty. His efforts occurred within the larger context of a fragile peace. Though Pontiac's War was over, the Pennsylvania interior, including the Susquehanna Valley, remained unstable and periodically violent.[4] Papunhank would have fewer occasions in these years to sound his pacifist message publicly, but he retained his deep commitment to nonviolence. Rising imperial tensions, ongoing white expansion, widespread anti-Indian racism, renewed assertions of Iroquois power, and persistent fears of new warfare regularly imperiled the Wyalusingites. Substantial challenges were nothing new, however, for the Munsee leader or for Moravian Indians in general. He was long accustomed to navigating tricky diplomatic waters with the Six Nations and the Pennsylvania government. His experience in those domains proved invaluable. Still, he couldn't guarantee results. He would have to keep insisting that these peace-loving refugee Indians in eastern Pennsylvania deserved to remain and be allowed to live, work, and worship as they wished.

Papunhank would also have to make his own adjustments to life back in Wyalusing. The upper Susquehanna Valley was not new for him as it was for many of the other refugees, but still much had changed in his own circumstances. Most dramatically, he no longer wielded the same type of religious authority he had exercised in years past. His days of being the principal spiritual voice and prophetic leader of his town were over. Joining the Moravians had made sure of that. Yet there was still much he could do. Or at least there was still much that he wanted to do to regain more autonomy for his community, share the Christian hope he had found, and work on behalf of a longer-lasting peace. Between 1765 and 1768 those goals dominated Papunhank's life and the strategies he pursued. They kept him frequently on the move even as he settled once more into Wyalusing and oversaw its construction and growth as a viable Moravian Indian town. Hunting trips, diplomatic forays, sojourns to Bethlehem, and even an evangelistic expedition to Indians on the Allegheny River brought the "old man" numerous challenges and frustrations. But also much contentment. He was finally back in Indian country, resuming the rhythms of life he cherished and guarding the community he was now helping to re-form.

Journey to Wyalusing

Getting to Wyalusing proved no easy task (see figure 7). The tiresome months of lobbying to leave Philadelphia and going stir crazy in the barracks were finally over, but they were hardly the end of the refugees' troubles. As they began their trek, they shed new tears for those loved ones left behind in city graves. Two days after departing the city they were in Nain. Good memories flooded the minds of those Natives who had lived there previously, some for as long as five years between the late 1750s and their flight in October 1763. Many of them had expressed a desire within the past few weeks to go back permanently to their former village. But they had been told that was impossible because the attitudes of neighboring whites toward them still matched the cold March wind that swept through the deserted town. So they were now there instead to say a final farewell to Nain and to rest up for the arduous journey ahead. For eleven days they huddled into their old houses, trying to stay warm amid heavy snows, and pondering both what had been and what was to be. Many white Moravians came from nearby Bethlehem to offer encouragement and solace, to sing songs and pray prayers, and in some cases, to buy their

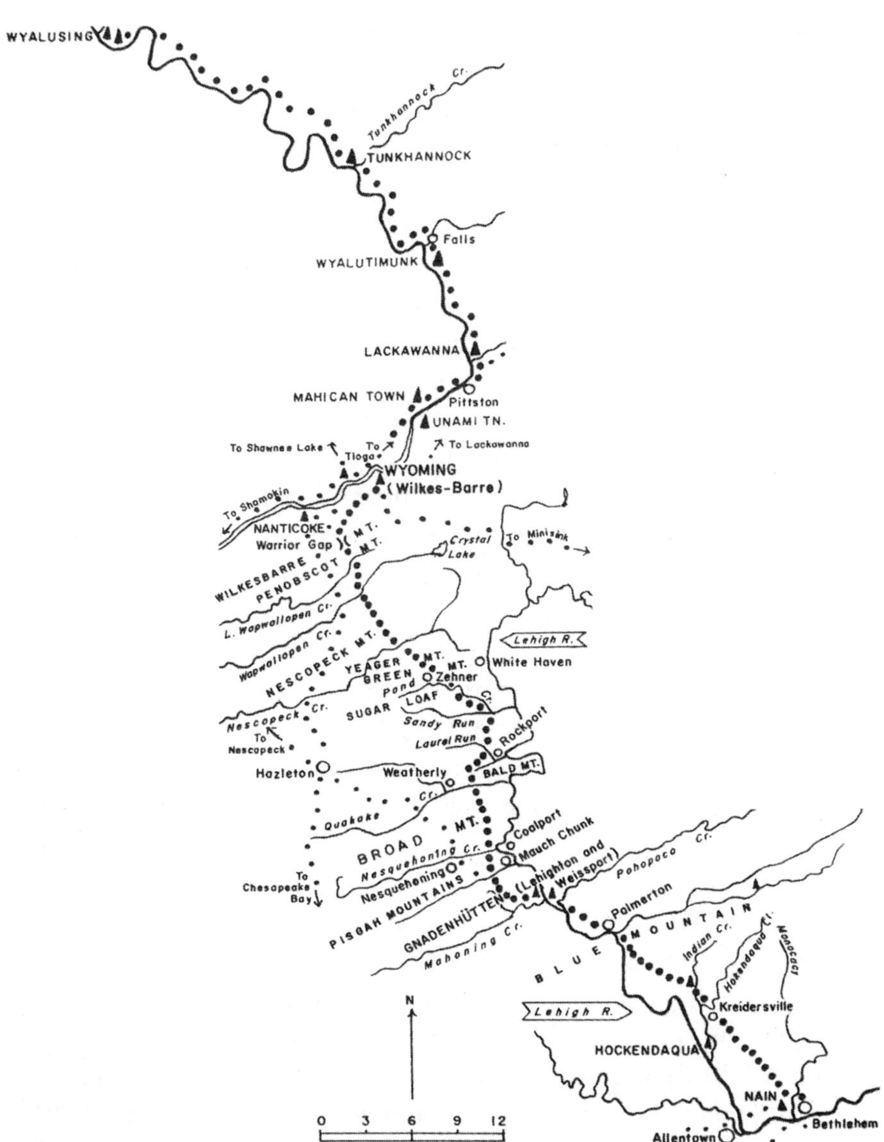

Fig. 7. The Bethlehem to Wyalusing Trail.
From Earl P. Olmstead, *David Zeisberger: A Life among the Indians* (Kent OH: Kent State University Press, 1997).
Courtesy of Kent State University Press.

homes. On April 2, the eve of their departure, missionary Bernhard Grube gathered the Natives one last time and according to his pastoral colleagues, had "a heartfelt farewell *band* with his dear Indians, recommended them together to Jesus' bloody wounds, and closed his thirteen-year work among them for the time being."[5]

Over the next thirty-eight days, Papunhank took the lead in guiding the company at every turn as they trudged their way across the Blue Mountains and through the "Great Swamp" toward Wyalusing. The Munsee leader clearly felt great responsibility to get them there in one piece. He should have; he was the one who had pushed his old town as the best place for them to go and convinced government and Moravian authorities to support his plan. Papunhank knew the way—in fact, multiple ways—to get from Bethlehem to Wyalusing, having traversed it many times. But this trip was different. For one thing, they had to make sure they avoided frontier whites still fuming with anti-Native rage. It did not matter that they were *Christian* Indians committed to peace. They were *Indians* and that made them the enemy. So Papunhank needed to carve out a more circuitous route to ensure their safety. Moreover, there were dozens of persons of all ages in their party, not just a few men, and they had all their earthly belongings to haul. Winter was just ending, and early spring rains and melting snow kept rivers and creeks high, mud thick, and trails tangled with fallen tree limbs and thick laurels. Ascending hills and mountains presented even worse problems. Steep, rocky climbs were treacherous, and higher elevations still had several feet of snow impeding every step. Perhaps worst of all, the refugees had too little food with them from the time they left Nain. Government, Quaker, and Moravian officials had all provided some items or promised future supplies; for example, on April 5 Thomas Apty, the commissary of the Pennsylvania government, told them to come back to Bethlehem in six weeks and collect an additional seventy-two tons of flour. But that wasn't going to solve their immediate shortage. They would have to fend for themselves. By April 8 and 9, they were already out hunting because they had no meat. On that occasion their men "returned in the evening very tired, hungry, and empty." Fortunately, Papunhank showed up a short time later "not only with our [runaway] horses [he had gone out the day before to retrieve them, knowing how much they would be needed], which they had found, but also happily with letters from Br. Grube in Bethlehem and from Br. Dencke in Christiansbrunn together with some oats for the horses and 2 loaves of bread for our future refreshment."[6]

That was just one small case of Johannes coming to the rescue. During the next month he would do it over and over. On the eleventh he rejoined the group after scouting five miles ahead through difficult and sometimes dangerous terrain and wisely advised them to remain where they were because high water and deep snow meant that the creek could "be crossed neither with the horses nor on foot." On the thirteenth "Josua, Senior, and Johannes Papunhank took upon themselves with some other Brethren to chop open the way to the large creek 5 miles away and to mark the trees." The next day the two of them and fellow Native Moravian leader Anton talked with Schmick and Zeisberger about whether "one of them [should] go on ahead to Machelusing [Wyalusing] and let the 6 Nations know by means of a messenger that they are on the way to the Susquehanna with their wives and children." The group decided to wait to send the message until they arrived, but their conversation makes plain their concern to follow proper Indian diplomatic procedures and to acknowledge Iroquois sovereignty. There is little question that Papunhank would have been at the forefront of that discussion and the likeliest one to go ahead of the group. He was the experienced diplomat (alongside Zeisberger) and most familiar with Iroquois protocols. Their choice to wait may even have been dictated by their need for him to remain with the pilgrims. On the seventeenth he "shot 1 old and 3 young bears . . . which the weary Brethren . . . enjoyed with thanksgiving." On the nineteenth he traversed six miles ahead with several men to cut another path through the woods, and on the twentieth he and Joshua Senior chopped down two trees to serve as a bridge over another large creek.[7]

As these examples illustrate, the company's slow but steady progress toward Wyalusing relied on Papunhank and a few others for virtually every step they took. Almost every morning and evening the community gathered for worship and drew spiritual sustenance from the words Zeisberger and Schmick offered. Many sang hymns in camp or as they walked along each day. But practical sustenance on the trip depended largely on Papunhank. His family also proved instrumental. As the hungry and tired migrants approached the Susquehanna River in late April, his wife took advantage of knowing the area to scrounge for wild potatoes. Then once in Wyalusing, knowing the community's short- and long-term food needs, she left within forty-eight hours of their initial arrival with a friend on a trade mission; they traveled three days by canoe to purchase bread to eat and maize to plant. Meanwhile, back on April 30, "friends of Josua Junior's wife [Papunhank's daughter Sophia] came from Lechawachneck [Lechaweke], 15 of them. They offered their two canoes right away to help us move to Machilusing." Sophia's years of living along the North Branch of the Susquehanna were now paying dividends for the whole group. Others must have been encouraged at the prospect of being led by a family familiar with the natural environment and well-known to their new neighbors.[8]

Far less encouraging, reports began to circulate that violent whites might once again attack area Indians. The Pennsylvania frontier remained unstable and disorderly in the aftermath of Pontiac's War. The travelers' fears of being attacked deepened after Delaware interpreter Job Chillaway, along with his wife, children, and several other families, joined the company en route. They were fresh from being in Shamokin, where they had been unable to secure supplies and "had left hurriedly and came here when they were told by the soldiers that the Paxton [Boys] wanted to come there in two days and seek out all the Indians and murder them." Fourteen months after the Paxton Boys crisis had been "settled," they were still striking fear into Pennsylvania Indian hearts. Governor Penn and the colonial government had made no concerted effort to bring the perpetrators of the Conestoga murders to justice. That remained a sore point for the Provincial Assembly and Pennsylvania Indians for the rest of the decade. No wonder that when another area Native encountered the newcomers, Schmick noted that the man "was very glad to see Josua and us and that no hostile white people had arrived, of whom the Indians hereabouts are very afraid."[9]

With sore feet, hungry bellies, and a mix of hopes and fears, the refugees from Philadelphia, plus a number of joiners-on, arrived in Wyalusing on May 9. Papunhank greeted them there, having gone ahead a day earlier "in order to arrive before us in Machilusing and to arrange our sojourn [there]." Those were fitting words, for the Munsee prophet had indeed arranged their sojourn, almost from the time he himself had left the banks of the Susquehanna eighteen months earlier. Seeing a large contingent of Brethren arriving in canoes or on horseback must have brought back memories of the November day he had left most Wyalusingites behind. Now he was at the helm to fill the town again.[10]

Building the New Wyalusing

The first hours, days, and weeks at Wyalusing offered a preview of the new town's life over the next few years and Papunhank's prominent place in it. The most immediate tasks were to provide for everyone's basic necessities—food and shelter. Hardly had Johann Schmick dismounted from his horse on the ninth when he "went right away with Johannes Papunhank around to view the devastated cabins, some of which stand very near the Susquehanna and are scattered irregularly far from each other, one here another there." Schmick observed, apparently with a certain disdain, both the destruction wrought by Andrew Montour's forces the prior spring on Munsee and Delaware towns and the typical, more dispersed layout of houses within Indian villages. Moravians preferred to cluster their dwellings together, a Euro-American pattern the missionary now wished to extend into Indian country and to which Papunhank accommodated as he set about assigning homes and farm plots. Everyone seemed to presume that he would or should be in charge of such civic duties. That first night he housed the two missionaries, along with several Native families, in his large cabin (apparently a survivor of Montour's destruction), another early indication of their dependence on him. The next afternoon Schmick "applied to him for a separate cabin for me and my dear David [Zeisberger] and he indicated to us a small one without a roof, but it was near the Brethren and Sisters and we liked it."

A few days later, "Papunhank went with the Brethren and Sisters to assign them their farms. . . . During the day each cleared their parcel and burned the old grass and straw that stood there. . . . Some of the Sisters began to sow garden things and everyone was busy on the farms." The next day they planted maize. Familiar Native agricultural routines, dominated by women, began to be reestablished after the long hiatus in Philadelphia, along with customary hunting patterns. Within twenty-four hours of arrival, the community resolved to send "all the male persons" north on a hunt "because of the lack of provision." They returned three days later with "one large bear and nine deer." The community also went fishing. On May 20 "more than 1400 shad were caught, which were large and fat."[11]

Still, it wasn't enough. Having adequate food supplies remained a problem at least until they harvested their corn in late October. Insects and grasshoppers ate other crops. Zeisberger called it a "plague" and reported in late June that the "famine" was "oppressing the poor Brothers and Sisters and everyone is looking for ways to survive." At that point most of them were out hunting or away at other settlements buying flour. Since their arrival, Papunhank and other community leaders had wrestled with what to do. With nearby Indian towns also hurting for food, their best option early on was to return to Bethlehem for additional provisions. Between thirty and forty of them made the trek back in late May and returned ten days later with much-needed supplies including four purchased cows. Looking to Moravian headquarters, whether for economic or spiritual support, became a standard feature of life in Wyalusing. Frequent interchange between the two locales occurred. Brethren officials were ready and willing to assist their new missionary outpost since it constituted the future of their evangelistic efforts. But given their distant locale, those officials could not provide anything more than stopgap measures when it came to Wyalusing's physical needs. The town had to become largely self-sufficient and resume traditional Native subsistence practices.[12]

Feeding themselves was of course only part of the work to be done. With "most of the cabins fallen in or torn down or burnt," the tem-

Fig. 8. Artist sketch of Friedenshütten settlement on Moravian Historical Society monument, Wyalusing, Pennsylvania. Photo by author.

porary shelter they had found in existing structures needed to be upgraded. During June the Indians constructed thirty-four houses, thirty of them in the Native style of bark-covered huts and four as more substantial log cabins. Most likely the buildings were concentrated together in accord with Moravian wishes. Certainly that was the case a year later after the community relocated to a nearby spot (a mile or two from where Papunhank's earlier town had been) more advantageously situated near the river's edge on a flat piece of land. Residents moved buildings while Papunhank and Anton once again assigned farmlands. By January 1767 the town completed a larger meeting house positioned squarely in the middle of the one street of houses. Papunhank's cabin sat kitty-corner to it, right next to the resident missionary's home, a material reminder of both men's authority (see figure 8).[13] Within another year or two, there were twenty-six log cabins with shingled roofs, windows, and chimneys, and ten bark-covered huts, a sign of the town's growing solidity and embrace of Euro-American building styles.[14]

Adopting elements of European culture was not new for these Natives. Moravian Indians were accustomed to blending Native and European ways. While at Nain and Wechquetank, they had apparently set themselves apart from other Indians through their hair and clothing styles and lack of body paint. They kept up those practices in Wyalusing. But there was still no mistaking them for whites. They were Indians. That did not mean, however, that they shared nativist aversions to European goods and customs. Many saw value in aspects of European culture even while rejecting other elements. Papunhank's critique of white trading practices did not keep him from acquiring certain items; he wanted fair trade rather than no trade with whites. He and many others from Wyalusing made the Moravian store at Rose Tavern, located eleven miles outside of Bethlehem, one of their main trading posts. They also welcomed Quaker trader John Anderson once or twice a year to their community between 1765 and 1769. On the other hand, traders from Paxton en route to Wyalusing were told "that they needed to go no further for they would sell no rum [there]." They turned around in disgust, only to return six months later to be told again that they were not welcome in the town.[15]

Responsibility for determining who would live at Wyalusing rested squarely in Indian hands, especially Papunhank's. Shortly after the refugees' arrival in May 1765, a few Native women complained to the missionaries about a white man staying with Job Chillaway. He had made threatening remarks including the claim that "he would not go away until he had 2 Indian scalps." Schmick and Zeisberger told the Sisters "that they should talk to Johannes Papunhank about it, [for] we cannot become involved in it, much less forbid him to be here." The white pastors recognized the pitfalls in exercising a political power they had no right to claim. They understood that this was Six Nations "turf" and Papunhank was the only one among them who might have some rightful authority there. Additionally, as before in Philadelphia with the issue of when the captives would be allowed to leave, they did not want to be blamed by one party or another for unpopular decisions.

Therefore, they were quick to pass the political reins to Papunhank and to rely upon his judgment.[16]

In this case and others, he, Anton, and other Native leaders of Wyalusing recognized the importance of monitoring the social, religious, and economic bounds of their community. They needed to be effective gatekeepers if it was going to be the type of town they wanted. Papunhank had persuaded other Moravians that Wyalusing was the right place for them to go partly on the basis of its comparative geographical isolation from both whites and large clusters of non-Christian Indians. That promise proved in practice only partially true. As soon as it was reestablished, Wyalusing drew many visitors, and newcomers kept coming throughout its seven-year history. On the one hand, that was good news since it provided ready opportunities for evangelism. However, community leaders quickly realized that allowing outsiders to have free reign in the town threatened to subvert its Moravian aspirations. Hence, they had limited tolerance for groups like the Paxton traders. On their return visit, Anton was chosen to tell them to leave. At that point, some of the traders had been hanging around the town for several weeks "by which means much frivolity"—in other words, much drinking—ensued among the young people. They and the rum they trafficked were simply bad news. Some Native "strangers" could also be cause for concern, as when Anton and Johannes expressed reservations about Nanticokes and their practice of digging up buried loved ones, cutting the flesh from their bones, and taking the bones with them. To preclude such behaviors and others deemed inappropriate, Wyalusing's Native leaders held interviews with "all strange Indians, especially with those, who wished to become inhabitants of Friedenshuetten, to examine into their views, and to declare to them with kindness and firmness, that all who were not truly desirous to turn unto their Creator and Redeemer, should positively not dwell in the place, nor even stay in it for any considerable time."[17]

Planting the Faith

Some Indian visitors were no doubt perplexed by what they heard and saw in Wyalusing. The very concept of a Christian Indian town was strange and disturbing. Christianity, in their minds, was an alien weapon employed by European colonizers. It would destroy Natives, not save them. But as with their adoption of certain European goods and customs, Papunhank and other Moravian Indians saw things differently and took a similar, selective approach to "European" religion. The Munsee prophet's critique of certain white Christians' sins, such as war-making and fraud, did not keep him from embracing Christianity. Nor did he see his new faith as a "European" entity. It was instead the "one right word" for all peoples, not the possession of a particular nation or culture. Accepting it and trying to live by its precepts did not make him or other Native Moravians into Europeans, or into whites, or any less Munsee, Mahican, or Delaware. They remained thoroughly Native. But now they were Native *and* Christian. Both identities were essential to their sense of self, at least among those most committed to following Jesus the Savior. Papunhank saw himself as one of that body, eager to partner with Indian and white believers in establishing Wyalusing as a Moravian community.[18]

To that end, little time elapsed before typical patterns of Brethren spiritual practice were put in play. They instituted daily morning and evening services and, as noted earlier, celebrated Communion within ten days of their arrival. By year's end they had offered the sacrament four additional times, baptized three adults and two children, held children's services, song services, and love feasts, adopted the same set of statutes that had governed Nain and Wechquetank, and welcomed John Roth as a resident missionary alongside David Zeisberger. (Schmick had stayed in Bethlehem following his return there in May; he replaced Roth in Wyalusing in July 1766 and Zeisberger left in September 1766.) They also depended on Johannes Papunhank, Anton, and Joshua Senior as key Native assistants. As with past Moravian mission congregations but even more so, Wyalusing was ostensibly directed spiritually by the missionaries but relied heavily upon Indian Helpers recruited from Native communicant members. Living in Indian country rather than near Bethlehem, missionaries could no longer count on regular aid from nearby colonial brothers and sisters. They had to turn more frequently to Indian Helpers to assist in "visiting from house to house, comfort and care of the sick, settling quarrels, enforcing all spiritual and civil ordinances of the congregation, assisting with worship and conducting some meetings for the Indian members, and occasional emissary duties in relationships with the Indian councils." A full year before they had left Philadelphia, Zeisberger had identified Papunhank, Joshua, and Anton as key "Laborers" in any future Moravian Indian congregation. Little wonder, then, that they emerged, or rather continued, as the most important Native leaders in the community. In August 1766 that became more official when Johannes and Joshua "were named as *Vorsteher*" (presiding officers or wardens) of the congregation, appointments "they gladly accepted."[19]

By that point, the new Moravian town had been christened *Friedenshütten*, "huts of peace," an apt name for the haven they wanted it to be. In practice it proved to be a refuge not only for the Philadelphia migrants but for many area Indians anxious for some greater measure of communal stability and economic sustenance after years of disruptive warfare. Native visitors of various tribes streamed through on a regular basis, attracted by the prospect of food and security and as a result of Papunhank's "large acquaintance." His reputation drew newcomers familiar with the old Wyalusing and often curious about the Moravians' message. "Our services are well attended by the *Fremden*, many of whom live here," noted Zeisberger in June 1765, and those patterns continued. The community grew by 30 or 40 persons to 146 by the end of 1765, to 172 by the end of 1766, and to 185 by the end of 1767. Of those, anywhere from a third to nearly a half were unbaptized adults and children. Clearly, there were opportunities to spread the Christian gospel to other Natives right in Friedenshütten.[20]

The community's believers did not waste that chance to share their Christian beliefs. Moravian evangelism reaped especially notable results from the fall of 1765 to the spring of 1766. From Papunhank's perspective, the spiritual blessings began even sooner. On August 2 his daughter Sophia had a baby girl. The newborn was baptized two days later as Anna, an event that seemingly triggered deep religious feelings in her grandmother. Papunhank's wife sought out Esther, a well-respected Native Moravian widow in the community, for spiritual counsel. She told Esther "that she felt it very necessary to be washed from her sins in the Savior's Blood." During their time in Philadelphia, she had been surprised that baptism had not seemingly improved the behavior of other Indians. "But now she felt so poor and miserable that she could see that she needed it most urgently and hoped that the Savior would soon grant her this Grace." Three days later Zeisberger met with her and found her to have a "soft heart . . . weeping for the Savior." Chances are Papunhank shed some tears that week as well.[21]

Lots of other crying accompanied the spiritual revival that began in earnest the next month. "Recently there has been a special emotion among the *Fremde*," Zeisberger wrote in late September, "the Savior is working powerfully among them and also among Brothers and Sisters, with whom things had been a little lukewarm. Many have been touched and uplifted." A month later he noted that "everyone here is being touched by the Savior," and a month after that he (or Roth) described the compelling evangelism of Native apostle Anton:

> [During the evening service] there was an amazing weeping. I wanted to go visiting this evening, but as soon as I got to Anton's house I heard an excessive weeping. Anton had to repeat the whole sermon and text, and added a lot. He began with the promise of Paradise, went through all the Prophets, how the Patriarchs had all waited on Him [Jesus] and it was now fulfilled in this time. Continued on concerning His life from His Baptism, what His father had said from Heaven "Hear ye Him," from His blood-filled Sweat on the Mount of Olives, from all his Suffering, Death, Rising from the Dead and Ascension. Now He sits there in Heaven with all His Wounds, which were given Him for our Salvation. "If you believe this, you are blessed [saved]." . . . I had never heard a sermon like it in my life. He had the Bible down pat.[22]

Anton's witness testifies to the extensive biblical knowledge and theological understanding some Native Moravians acquired. While he had been among the Brethren much longer than Papunhank (baptized in 1750), his example suggests the trajectory of religious learning the

Munsee reformer was likely on. Papunhank's daily contact with Indian believers and missionaries for the past two years enmeshed him in Moravian teaching and made him increasingly well prepared to share his faith. Before long he, too, was proclaiming "the love of the Savior" to "unknown Indians" and would later join Zeisberger in preaching to Natives outside of Wyalusing.[23]

For now, though, he was likely content marveling at the spiritual interest the non-Christian and Christian Indians alike continued to display. According to Zeisberger in January 1766, they could not "hear enough about Him [the Savior]" and literally felt the power of the Gospel in bodily exercises reminiscent of the Great Awakening two decades earlier: "everyone shivered and quaked until we thought they would fall unconscious; during this they cried a lot." To the missionary, it was as if there was "an evil spirit within the people who fights against the word of Jesus' death."[24] Alternatively, Natives may have understood what was happening as a normal part of spiritual questing. Either way, a contest for souls was underway in Wyalusing. Alongside the Moravian Christian witness, residents periodically encountered traditionalist religious voices. That same month, for example, several "disciples" of Munsee chief Newollike's preaching in Otseningo "tried in vain to persuade some of the [Indians] here to come to their festival or *Gindegey*." Then the next month, an "Indian Preacher" arrived and spent several days going from house to house "saying that he knew the right way to God, they should only follow him, for everything else that they heard here were lies." Some laughed at his preaching, Anton rebutted it. The preacher "soon got up and left," but the spiritual questions and strivings in the community persisted.[25]

For Papunhank, such visitors may well have drawn his mind back to the days of his own preaching and the ancient festivals he had helped revive. Becoming Moravian meant leaving most of that behind and replacing it with a different set of rites and rituals. As far as is known, he made that transition smoothly and wholeheartedly. He neither objected to the new ways nor reverted to the old. Perhaps that was possible because he, like other Moravian Indians, may have infused Christian ceremonies with meanings rooted in older Native traditions.[26]

Papunhank had more angst about the spiritual choices of other family members. That drama lasted at least until July–August 1766 when his wife once again felt drawn to Christian baptism yet hesitated. Finally, on August 10, Schmick baptized her as Anna Johanna "amid the shedding of many tears from those being baptized as well as from those who were present." Her step of faith may have eased one source of anxiety for Papunhank three years after his own baptism and exactly fifteen months after the struggle to construct Friedenshütten had begun.[27]

Six Nations Diplomacy, Phase One

Arguably the most important, and stressful, part of getting Wyalusing established was winning the right to be there. Unless and until the Six Nations approved of the Moravian Indians settling at Wyalusing, the new town could be there today and gone tomorrow. Papunhank knew that full well. His past experience in the Susquehanna Valley familiarized him with the challenges of navigating relations with the Iroquois Confederacy and its subordinates. He and other community leaders would need all the diplomatic skill they could muster if their company was going to be allowed to stay. Rehearsing their efforts in detail is necessary to reveal the complexity of their task.

Uncertainty about their future was hardly new for these Natives. Despite their various backgrounds and tribal identities, all of them had experienced frequent migrations. It was an almost inevitable part of being an Indian within British colonial America in the eighteenth century. But that didn't mean they liked it or were anxious to move again. If necessary, they would comply with orders to do so, but their clear preference was to remain in Wyalusing, and they looked to Papunhank more than anyone else to make that possible.

For the Munsee prophet, their reliance on him was both worrisome and gratifying. While appreciating the trust and confidence the community repeatedly showed in his leadership, he did not want to disappoint them. For the past fifteen years he had endeavored to protect and preserve Native communities gathered around him. It had never been easy. War, raiding militiamen, forced migrations, epidemic disease, and urban captivity were only the most dramatic obstacles he and his people had had to overcome. Now with renewed hope and promise, his reconstituted company had come to Wyalusing at his initiation. The last thing he wanted was for its new life to be aborted. The town's relative isolation, opposition to the liquor trade, watchful eye over white and Native visitors, and vibrant religious practices were all valuable strategies for communal health, and ones both highly familiar to Papunhank and consonant with Moravian values. Yet right from the start, everyone realized that more would be necessary to achieve the stability and security they sought.

The place to begin was to notify the Six Nations of their arrival. On May 15, 1765, leaders in Wyalusing sent a Native messenger to Oswego near Lake Ontario "with the words he has heard from our Indians and the string of wampum." He was to tell the Iroquois that the Wyalusingites were the Natives who had been removed to Philadelphia and protected from hostile whites by the Pennsylvania government. That body had now sent them to Wyalusing where they planned "to live in peace and quiet, until they receive answer from the Six Nations as their Uncles about whether they should remain here or build on another place on the Susquehanna where they can continue to live and dwell in undisturbed quiet." They also requested permission to have a Moravian minister live among them "so that they and their wives and children can live in peace and quiet with all people." That was not an uncomplicated request. Asking for whites of any sort to be allowed to live in Six Nations territory was tricky business at a time when the Confederacy was intent on halting the flow of white squatters onto Indian lands. To that end, they were in the midst of negotiating a treaty with Sir William Johnson that set down a firmer boundary line between colonial and Indian territories. It ran from the "upper Susquehanna River through western Pennsylvania to the Ohio River." Lands east of it belonged to the colonies, all the lands west to Indians. Wisely, then, the Wyalusingites' words readily acknowledged Iroquois sovereignty and expressed their almost desperate desire to find somewhere (preferably on the Susquehanna) they could be left alone to live quietly and peaceably.[28]

Soon though they learned that the Six Nations had their own ideas about what would be best for the Moravian Indians. Togahaju, the Cayuga authority over the upper Susquehanna Valley, summoned Papunhank, Anton, and Joshua Senior to his village on Cayuga Lake in Iroquois territory. He singled them out because each of them had sent separate messages to the Six Nations and represented the three principal ethnic groups at Wyalusing—Munsee, Delaware, and Mahican, respectively. Iroquois diplomacy was accustomed to paying attention to such distinctions and likely aware that even then, Johnson was considering a plan to cluster the Delawares on the Susquehanna River at the Great Island on its West Branch, and the Mahicans somewhere north of Tioga on its North Branch. Centralizing them in large towns would allow for tighter supervision. Few if any of the Moravians were enthused by that scheme since as Zeisberger put it, "it would really be bad if our Indians had to live among the heathen. Not much good would come of that." Furthermore, it would split their community. Zeisberger urged the three Natives (another Indian, Andreas, went in place of Joshua) to tell Togahaju that "there are 2 kinds of nation here, namely Mahicans and Delawares, but that they were 1 people . . . and no longer wanted to live as the other Indians do." The Cayuga chief honored their request to stay together and granted them permission to worship as they pleased with a Moravian minister. Those were important concessions, but he was not done. He wanted them to move to "another place that is close to me, namely on the upper end of Cayuga Lake, that will be a better place for you than the other." Wyalusing was unsuitable, he told them, because "the whole area is stained with blood," a reference either to the seventeenth-century conflict there between the Iroquois and Andastes, or the more recent Pontiac's War. The unspoken reason to have them move, however, was the likely sale of those lands to whites. Clearing Wyalusing of Natives would facilitate that transaction.[29]

Once home, Papunhank and the community considered their options. The locale Togahaju offered had "good land, [and] enough wood, water, fish and salt," but the hunting was poor due to a lack of game. In addition, a group of non-Christian, and presumably troublesome,

Tutelos lived very nearby. Moreover, the Finger Lakes region was a long distance away. Moving there seemed too extreme, yet remaining in Wyalusing seemed less and less likely. Papunhank hoped to buy some time before answering the Cayuga sachem. He told him that a response would be forthcoming when their corn had ripened. That seemingly meant late summer or early fall, but Togahaju was still waiting for their reply in the spring of 1766. In the meantime, Papunhank and Zeisberger independently explored other diplomatic channels in quest of a more favorable outcome. While the missionary lobbied another Cayuga chief, Tajanoge, when he visited Wyalusing in July, Papunhank solicited help from a sachem in Otseningo. Neither effort brought any immediate results.[30]

By the fall stress over the community's fate had its Native leaders at odds with one another and ready to appeal to the Pennsylvania government for help. Mahican Joshua Senior was already troubled by a near-broken marriage and a sense that his people were being slighted by the town's Delaware-Munsee majority and the Moravian missionaries (he missed the Mahican-speaking Schmicks). Now Papunhank and Anton told him that the response to the Cayuga should really come from him. They claimed that the Delawares and Munsees "already had their place where they had lived previously [on the Susquehanna]. It was therefore really [only] the concern of the Mahicans." Papunhank and Anton were presumably trying to convince themselves and others that their peoples had solid historical claims for their right to live in Wyalusing whereas the Mahicans did not. Though silent in reply, Joshua clearly resented having the buck passed to him. In this case, Zeisberger agreed with the Mahican and urged all of them to consider themselves "*one* people and not two." Then, at Joshua's initiation, the three Indians proposed using Newollike, the Munsee chief at the "Great Island" on the West Branch who happened to be Anton's brother-in-law, to present their case to the Six Nations since he was the key sachem in the area and "they could not very well pass him over without drawing hatred and enmity upon themselves." But Zeisberger dissented from that plan because in his view, Newollike had limited understanding of the Moravians. Finally, they concurred on a suggestion to send a petition to the governor asking him to intervene on their behalf with Johnson "that he should put in a good word for us with the 6 Nations, that we should be allowed to live on the Susquehanna or best of all in Wajomick [Wyoming]." But Joshua remained unhappy with that plan and sent a secret message to Newollike staking out his own position.[31]

For whatever reasons, nothing apparently came of those actions apart from ongoing friction, so by spring 1766 Wyalusing's leaders ventured forth on two other diplomatic forays. One proved a failure, the other a success. In March Papunhank and Anton reverted to asking Newollike for help. By that point, Togahaju was impatient for an answer, his corn having long since been harvested and now mostly eaten. Newollike refused to aid them, however, saying he "wanted nothing to do with them," perhaps because he was aware of the divisions among them and didn't want to jeopardize his own relationship with the Six Nations. Though urged a few weeks later by fellow Munsee chief Echgohund to go back to Newollike one more time, the community opted instead to gird its loins and send four Native representatives (Papunhank, Anton, and two others) along with Zeisberger directly back to the Cayuga.[32]

By that point the missionary better understood how crucial all these diplomatic dealings were to the future of the Moravian Indian community and how important Papunhank was to those negotiations. Zeisberger and others in Bethlehem had "always thought the matter was not so significant; the Indians could live where they wanted to and did not need to make such a fuss about where they lived but could just remain quiet and peaceful, and stay where they were. But I have found that the matter is really different. None of the Indians can or may establish a *Town* without first having the permission of the 6 *Nations*." Moreover, he was now aware that "Johannes is actually a *Chief* and was made this by the 6 Nations before he was baptized, and therefore they will also see him as such."[33]

So on May 1 they met with Togahaju and his council and Papunhank made their main appeal:

> Uncle! You made known to us last year that you wanted to remove us from Wihilusing and place us at the upper end of this lake.

> Now, however, it is our desire that you would permit us to remain at Wihilusing. We have already built us homes, and the place which you cleansed for us a year ago is agreeable, and we like to live there, as we can live there quietly and undisturbed.

After Zeisberger reinforced the distinctiveness of Moravian Indians and their towns, including their aversion to war, Togahaju issued the decree the Wyalusingites wanted to hear: "Up to this time you have had no abiding place, but now I will take you and seat you permanently. You can therefore remain there, and the land shall be yours . . . all the land from Wihilusing up to some distance beyond Tioga. . . . There you may build, plant, hunt, fish, and make use of the place as you wish."[34]

Six Nations Diplomacy, Phase Two

Buoyed by their success in Cayuga, which included the promise that their land tract "was only reserved for Christian Indians," Papunhank, Zeisberger, and the rest of the community went forward with relocating the village and building many new structures.[35] They assumed or at least hoped that their right to be there was now secure and they could confidently proceed with settling in more permanently during the summer of 1766. Yet the two leaders' past experience with the vicissitudes and complexities of relations within Indian country and along the Euro-American-Native frontier likely alerted them to the possibility that the matter was not as resolved as it seemed. In this instance, it took only a couple of months for that to become clear. More diplomacy was required to gain full Six Nations assent to their staying in Wyalusing, and even then, there was no telling how long that would remain the case.

Papunhank was accustomed to the rumors, misinformation, and purposeful lies employed by whites and Natives alike in their dealings in early America. Such diplomatic "tools" had long been used in hopes of gaining strategic advantages within intra-Indian or intercultural relations.[36] The Munsee prophet was no fan of that approach. His moral compass pointed him toward straightforward declarations of his people's needs and desires. Deception or duplicity of whatever form in the end would produce distrust, and distrust almost always resulted in violence. That was reason enough to put little stock in troubling reports of one sort or another that circulated in and out of Indian towns. Hence, when Papunhank and Zeisberger returned in late June from attending an important synod in Bethlehem and were informed by worried residents that the Cayuga chief had died and a messenger from Otseningo was arriving with bad news, Johannes's response was "it does not mean anything."[37]

Still, dispelling rumors was one thing, and knowing how best to carry on effective relations with area sachems and the Six Nations another. There was no simple road map to follow and plenty of room for disagreement, as became evident over the next few months among both the Natives and missionaries of Friedenshütten. A messenger from Otseningo did in fact arrive in mid-July and brought disturbing news: other Iroquois were displeased with Togahaju's unilateral decision to issue the land grant to the Moravians because that territory had already been given to other Indians who had been scattered in the war but might someday return to claim their lands. Togahaju defended his action at a Six Nations council but left it in that body's hands to determine whether they would "take the people [the Moravian Indians] away from there and put them somewhere else." If that word wasn't worrisome enough, Newollike and Echgohund soon showed up and made it clear that the former wanted to function more directly as the sachem of Friedenshütten. Three weeks later Newollike was back in town claiming to have a message from Togahaju that reprimanded the Moravians: "you have opened your mouths too wide; as soon as you departed from me you said that I had given you the land Machalusing, which is actually not true, because I cannot do this without the agreement of the 6 Nations." Reeling from that rebuke, Papunhank and Anton favored sending a reply to the Cayuga chief through Newollike with the appropriate belts and strings of wampum "to make everything good." But Joshua Senior dissented insisting that "if we get involved with this, then we will live a tortured existence; where are we supposed to get the Wampum for the Belts and Strings to give if messengers always come to us and want us to take the messages further on to the Cajuga Chief?" Joshua was apparently not only questioning the financial burden of the other Natives' approach but whether Moravian Indians should engage at all in this type of diplomatic protocol. For the moment, however, his arguments proved unpersuasive. His community was not ready to opt out of those traditional practices and chose to enlist Newollike's aid instead. Not surprisingly, "as soon as they charged him with the matter, he accepted this and asked that they might sometimes provide some assistance"; in other words, a tribute payment or diplomatic favor. The community also discussed selecting "a Chief of the Nations, because there is always one in Town looking out for order and the good of the people. However, no one was willing to do this and Joshua said, 'I will not get involved in this at all; I cannot serve 2 masters either. If I do something for the Savior and can translate, that is enough [ink smudge] for my heart.'" Papunhank and Anton apparently concurred that a single sachem for Friedenshütten drawn from their ranks would not be wise. They probably thought that it would only exacerbate current tribal tensions in the community.[38]

Missionaries Johann Schmick and David Zeisberger similarly disagreed on how to proceed diplomatically. Schmick and his wife had been assigned at the June synod meeting to return to Wyalusing in July to replace Zeisberger and Roth. In some ways, the couple's presence helped to harmonize the community. His preaching in Mahican—Zeisberger and Roth used Unami Delaware—and their familiarity with many of the Mahican believers brought comfort to those in that group who had felt at least partially ostracized or neglected by the Delaware-Munsee majority. On the other hand, some of Schmick's policies clearly irritated Zeisberger, who remained at Friedenshütten until September 1. Once back in Bethlehem, he leveled a number of criticisms to the overseeing board, the Oeconomats-Conferenz, which in turn sent Schmick an accusatory letter. While the precise nature of all of Zeisberger's claims is unclear, Schmick's response in October to the Conferenz indicates that some of the complaints concerned the way Schmick had handled communications with the Six Nations. Zeisberger may have rightly considered Schmick a novice in such affairs compared to his long history of interactions with the Iroquois. He had actually raised questions about his colleague's diplomatic actions as far back as June 1765. But he hadn't said anything directly to Schmick then or during the summer of 1766 when they were together, a silence Schmick in retrospect found "very troubling" and evidence of Brother David having not acted "as a faithful and honest colleague." Schmick defended his actions, leveled counter accusations, such as rehearsing Roth's statement upon leaving Wyalusing that "it was like Sodom and Gomorrha here," a slight on Zeisberger's oversight of the community, and insisted that the town's Indians were unsure about Zeisberger's purposes in pursuing another trip to Onondaga.[39]

Strained relationships were perhaps bound to happen amid the stresses of life in Friedenshütten, especially after the distressing messages from Otseningo and Newollike. With or without support from the Moravian village, the Oeconomats-Conferenz decided that Zeisberger and a young colleague, Gottlob Senseman, should be sent to the Six Nations to ascertain Iroquois sentiments about Togahaju's actions and "to renew old friendships." The veteran missionary's earlier sojourns among the Onondagas paid dividends, as they welcomed him back after an eleven-year absence and listened attentively to his long speech about the fortunes and misfortunes of the Friedenshütten Indians. In the end, he wanted to know whether "the land along the Susquehanna, below Tiaoga, belonged under the direction of the Chief in Cajuga" and if the Six Nations Council endorsed the land grant made to them by him. They quickly answered that the Cayuga chief was the rightful authority over that land and to him the missionaries should go for further clarification about living on it. Consequently, Zeisberger and Senseman headed to Cayuga where Togahaju corrected the information they had received from the Otseningo messenger and Newollike. Togahaju had wanted them to know primarily of his concern about reports that they were allowing white traders to establish a post at Friedenshütten. They assured him they were not, and he in turn assured them that "he was the man" with whom they should deal directly about their land, rather than any of the local sachems including Newollike. Pleased with that word and with growing confidence that things were going their way, the two missionaries returned to Onondaga and heard the Six Nations speaker, Tianoronto, pronounce that "the matter which the Chief Togahaju, in Cayuga, treated and concluded with you, meets with our and the whole house's consent. . . . It pleases us very much that you live in Friedenshuetten, and that you shall have a council fire there, which is intrusted to you, and which is no small matter."[40]

One would have thought those words sealed the deal for the Friedenshütten Indians, but within the malleable world of Six Nations diplomacy, it would take one more encounter with Togahaju before Schmick was prepared to write that they had "a *Confirmation* that we have permission to live here." In January 1767 the Cayuga sachem summoned the town to send representatives to meet him for talks. Papunhank was one of two men chosen to go; a month later, they had still not returned. Schmick waited impatiently, echoing the concerns of Joshua Senior about the costs of operating according to Native protocols: "Where are we supposed to get the Wampums for this and who can always undertake such long journeys?" Finally, the men arrived, carrying clear messages from the Cayuga for their community. They were to "remain living where you are," communicate with the Six Nations through the chief at Hallobank (a relative or subordinate of Togahaju who was located in a town on the North Branch of the Susquehanna River in what is now southern New York), and most importantly, inform any white settlers moving into the lands between Wyalusing and Wyoming that they were forbidden to do so. Togahaju, and by implication the Iroquois, wanted to keep those lands "for my friends the Indians, for their hunting, so that they find something on it and can have something from it, which they need for the nourishment of their bodies. I do not want to sell this land." That was just what Papunhank and the other brothers and sisters in Friedenshütten wanted to hear. With Schmick they exclaimed, "Praise be to the Savior for this . . . we have permission to stay here and can stay put."[41]

Papunhank the Evangelist

With that good news, Papunhank's attention turned to more eternal matters. In the months that followed, his Christian faith flourished amid a rare spell of peace and stability for his Moravian community. Freed for the moment from political and diplomatic worry about where they would live, he became more and more fervent in his devotion to Brethren teaching and in his desire to share the Christian message with other indigenous peoples. He had now spent considerable time with Moravian brothers and sisters, absorbing their wisdom and observing their piety. His understanding of Scripture and the particular emphases of Brethren theology, including the focus upon Jesus's suffering and sacrifice, grew while listening to Grube, Schmick, and Zeisberger explicate the Watchword, as well as when he was singing hymns in Mahican, Delaware, English, and German, or praying and conversing with Anton, Joshua Senior, and other Native believers.[42] In 1765 and 1766 he had become a communicant and then a church official, and now was poised, even eager, to deepen his commitments and service to the Savior.

The Friedenshütten diary for 1767 testifies repeatedly to this type of spiritual interest on Papunhank's part. The entry for January 1 provided a foretaste of what was to come: "Johannes was very glad and thankful to the Savior that he had made and preserved him so happy and blessed, especially in these great festival days [Christmas and New Year's] and had let him experience the new year. During this he said, 'For several years I have experienced these festival days as a baptized person, but God knows, never as blessedly as now.'" The next five months brought a host of other spiritual encouragements for Papunhank: a widow friend expressed her longing "to love the Savior and to be washed with His Blood," and was soon baptized; a larger, warmer, and more aesthetically pleasing meeting house was constructed and dedicated; son-in-law Joshua Junior ended a period of estrangement from the communion table and participated in February alongside his wife Sophia, she for the first time; Papunhank's wife, Anna Johanna, and their younger daughter narrowly escaped drowning in a Wyalusing Creek at flood stage; and a few weeks later, Anna Johanna took Communion for the first time, and shortly thereafter daughter Sophia gave birth to another baby girl.[43]

Amid these blessings Papunhank was ready and willing to share a spiritual word or lend a helping hand wherever he could. For several nights in early April, he and two other Native believers spent hours following the evening service meeting in their cabins with interested Indians and counseling them on "what the Blood from the Savior's Wounds does for sinners." All eastern woodland Native American peoples believed that blood was powerful; telling them that Christ's blood, stoically shed on a cross as he was tortured by his enemies, had the power to heal them was not such a strange or preposterous claim. Ten days later Papunhank opened his home to a spiritually seeking Native couple. When smallpox invaded Friedenshütten in May, he quickly offered another cabin he had built across the Susquehanna as an isolation ward for the ill and then cared for the sick himself along with fellow Moravian Indian, Philip. As the two men returned to the town, they said that "the mercy the Savior had shown them and those who were ill was beyond their powers of description and how happy they had been each day in His dear Presence, and still are and how well they had felt in their hearts near to Him and His Wounds, and thus had blessed days and hours." Riding that spiritual high in June, Papunhank helped rebuild a cabin for the recently widowed Helen, and in July he served, as he did on many occasions, as the town's messenger to Bethlehem.[44]

During these spiritually prosperous days Papunhank functioned more frequently as an informal preacher and teacher. For almost a decade, numerous Moravian Indians had been witnessing to him of his constant need for the Savior, and in the process, provided models of how to evangelize fellow Natives. Now he followed suit and took advantage of opportunities to share his strong religious convictions and feelings and to recapture some of the prophetic power he had earlier exercised. On July 22 the diary recorded, "Br. Johannes spoke on this subject ["the Little Lamb's Death and Suffering"] to the hearts of Job [Chillaway] and his family and the son of Paulus, that they should seek life and happiness for their hearts with the Savior and in His blood-filled Wounds." Then in early August, "when the unknown [i.e., outsider] Indians visited the Brethren Anton and Johannes spoke to them of the Savior's great Love and Mercy for the poor Indians, which they heard gladly." Such passages indicate Papunhank's willingness and ability to evangelize. They also reveal Schmick's confidence in him to do it well. Papunhank's words, deeds, and emotions in the eyes of the German missionaries bespoke a man of authentic Christian faith, someone who could be trusted with the weighty responsibility of proclaiming the truth.[45]

Papunhank became eager to do even more to share the "Savior's great Love and Mercy" with other Indians. A chance to fulfill those longings emerged when David Zeisberger arrived back in Friedenshütten on September 24 and announced that he had been commissioned by Bethlehem to go to Indians along the Allegheny River to investigate their interest in hosting a Moravian missionary. Western Delawares and Munsees had apparently sent word earlier in the year that they would welcome a white Christian teacher. Zeisberger wanted two Native assistants from the village to accompany him. He predictably asked Anton given their past joint labors and "since he had previously intimated that he would be glad to accompany me on a trip in that direction." Anton quickly and enthusiastically accepted and then immediately proposed Papunhank as the third member of their team. Based on seeing how his friend had interacted with non-Christian Indians in recent months and hearing his heart for evangelism, he believed "Johannes would also gladly go there. He has often thought about that." Anton's instincts proved right; when invited to join them, Papunhank "was heartily willing to go" and "declared that he had long cherished the desire to do something for the Savior, if only the Brethren would send him."[46] Such remarks illustrate his religious passion, but they also hint at a pent-up frustration at not being afforded greater spiritual responsibility or religious authority. Moravians had been leery of Papunhank's desire to continue as a religious teacher in the years prior to his conversion and baptism. Since then, they had gradually afforded him more elbow room to witness to his faith. Now he had an unprecedented chance to be in the vanguard of their first outreach efforts to the Ohio Country. He wasn't about to miss it.

Zeisberger's destination was Goschgoschunk, a mostly Munsee enclave of three small towns along the Allegheny River in what is today Forest County, Pennsylvania. The trek there was formidable through difficult and unfamiliar terrain. "Anton and John did not know this region," Zeisberger noted, an understatement about the challenge they faced in making their way. But as in prior trips, Papunhank did whatever it took to blaze or find a trail. After seventeen long, hard days of travel, much of it through Seneca country along the future New York-Pennsylvania border, they arrived and "were heartily welcomed in the town and given a lodging in the house of one who was a close friend of John [Papunhank]." Goschgoschunk turned out to have lots of people Papunhank knew, including in all likelihood his brother, Tschechquoapesek; they were former Wyalusingites who after parting company with him in November 1763 had at various points in the past two years moved to this region (Goschgoschunk was founded in 1765). Many of them had attended Zeisberger's preaching back in May and June 1763 in Wyalusing and remembered enough of Moravian worship practices to seat "the men on one side and the women on the other."[47]

Did Papunhank know that he would encounter old friends and followers on the Allegheny, and perhaps even a close relative? Had his longstanding contacts in Indian country made him aware that Natives from several former Munsee towns, including his own, had moved to western Pennsylvania? Was that part of why he was so anxious to travel with Zeisberger and Anton? Had he long cherished a desire to be reunited with some of these folk and preach to them again? Available sources are frustratingly silent on those intriguing questions, but it seems reasonable to suppose that he had at least an inkling that he might run into some persons he knew. Those may have included not only his brother but his wife's mother and sister, who, according to the Friedenshütten diary, arrived at the Moravian town on November 10, 1767, having come "from Coschcoschink [Goschgoschunk] to visit and to hear words about the Savior." Others of his own kin, as well as that of other Friedenshütten residents, were also scattered across western Pennsylvania and southern New York. He may have harbored hopes of meeting them in one town or another.[48]

Whomever he anticipated seeing, actually finding familiar faces in these unfamiliar woods must have been a dramatic moment for Papunhank—and for the former Wyalusingites. Much had happened to all of them since the dangers created by Pontiac's War had forced them to scatter four years earlier. They had taken different paths to survival but now their roads met again, at least for this one week. Stories were likely shared about the harrowing times they had experienced before and after their separation. Warfare, disease, food shortages, displacement, migrations—those challenges and more had been their common lot. They probably spoke as well of families and kin, of babies born and loved ones lost. And they talked of futures, earthly and eternal. Some must have felt a certain déjà vu as they listened to Zeisberger preach but even more when Papunhank addressed them. Here was their old prophet earnestly appealing to them once again to heed his words. As Zeisberger described it, after each time he completed a sermon, "my companions [Anton and Papunhank] began, explaining further the meaning of the words. They spoke out of full hearts and boldly witnessed for the Savior, until late at night." Papunhank must have indeed had a "full heart" spilling over with emotion as he endeavored to make the Christian message plainer for other Indians and seized chances to teach and counsel those he had once led. He likely harbored a special hope that his kin would follow his lead once more, this time into the Moravian fold.[49]

The week's drama continued for Papunhank as he engaged further with Ohio Country Native beliefs and behavior. Certain moments must have brought back vivid memories of Munsee communities to which he had earlier belonged. As was typical of Native audiences, those in Goschgoschunk "were attentive and conducted themselves in a quiet and orderly manner" as Zeisberger and his Indian assistants sermonized. Whether that indicated any real interest in what they were hearing was another matter. Some, like the blind chief, Allemewi, and his wife seemed very receptive, perhaps in their case because their daughter, Rebecca, was already a baptized member of the Friedenshütten congregation. Their responses made it appear that "the people are very eager to hear about the Savior. They relish the message concerning the death and sacrifice of the Redeemer, though it is a new teaching to them." Yet each evening many of them, especially the young people, danced the night away, maintaining traditional practices that brought joy, release, and sacred power. At least that is what they had been told by their religious leaders. One of them, an Indian preacher named Wangomen, listened closely all week to the Moravians but was far from ready to accept the evangelists' message as truth. On the contrary, he disputed their theology, promoting instead a strongly nativist message, complete with claims for separate creations and afterlives and multiple (white and Indian) ways to salvation. His sparring with the Moravians climaxed in a no-holds-barred exchange in front of a large Native gathering in which Zeisberger took over after he "noticed that Anton did not know exactly how to answer him." Whether that was an accurate read of the situation or an instance of his paternalism and prejudice, the missionary then claimed that "during the whole time of our stay here I had dealt tactfully with the man, thinking it would mean a good deal for this region if I should succeed in winning him. But when I saw he denied the merit of the Savior and His blood and wished to rob Him of His honor, I could no longer bear it." So he let Wangomen have it with full force, dismissing him as Satan-possessed and a devil-worshipper. "Do not imagine that you have any part or communion with God, for you must not think that He has any pleasure in your pretended worship, since this is an abomination before Him." Such "words were indeed hard," Zeisberger admitted afterward, "yet I felt that I dared not speak otherwise." Not surprisingly, after he had delivered them, "for some time there was silence."[50]

There is every reason to imagine that Papunhank was among those keeping quiet, surely sobered by what he had just heard, maybe even stunned by it. For one thing, he had likely not heard Zeisberger or any other white Moravian speak quite so harshly to an Indian, especially when trying to evangelize him. His sympathies certainly lay on the missionary's side as far as what he believed about God and salvation. Yet here was an Indian prophet, not wholly unlike the man he had been, being castigated as knowing nothing about the true God. Papunhank likely felt some empathy for him as he recalled his own long conversations with German and Native American Moravians before his conversion in which they critiqued his message and the state of his soul. Somehow they had always done it in a way that brought him back for more contact. He may very well have wondered if Wangomen would be similarly inclined.

The Indian preacher got his chance to hear more from the Moravians, whether he wanted to or not, the following spring when at Bethlehem's urging, Zeisberger returned to Goschgoschunk, this time with fellow missionary Senseman and three Native Christian families from Friedenshütten. Their intent was to plant a new mission congregation there. The party included Anton, his wife Johanna, and their grandson Christian, but not Papunhank. He apparently wasn't considered by those making the decision; at least he wasn't asked to go. Perhaps they knew that the community believed it could not afford to lose two key Native leaders, Anton *and* Johannes. Schmick admitted that the loss of Anton was "very painful to me," and expressed "hope that the Savior will fill Brother Anton's place here and one of the Delaware Brothers will be chosen and given the necessary courage to witness." Having Papunhank depart as well would have been too much. He was too valuable a member to part with, especially now that violence had resumed on the Pennsylvania frontier with the murder of ten Indians, including four women and two children, and new uncertainties had emerged about the potential sale of their lands. For his part, Papunhank himself may not have been eager to go. He had invested too much, psychologically and otherwise, into the re-creation of Wyalusing to leave it behind until he had to. That day might eventually come, but for now, its needs and problems were what he would continue to address. He had had his taste of life and evangelistic work in the Allegheny region, and while it afforded him moments of exhilaration as he declared his Christian faith, it may also have been disturbing. He had grown accustomed to living within a majority-Christian community. Seeing painted Natives dance and drink till dawn and hearing Indian preachers proclaim an antagonistic nativist gospel likely disquieted Papunhank and persuaded him that his proper place was in Friedenshütten.[51]

Six Nations Diplomacy, Phase Three

There was always plenty of work to do there, even in the good times. In many respects the town was flourishing. During its first three years, it developed a strong agricultural base and enjoyed bountiful harvests. It also kept a growing number of cattle, horses, and pigs. As a result, the community after its first few months avoided the severe food shortages that afflicted other area Indian villages and could comply with the Six Nations dictate that they help feed sizeable groups of Tuscaroras and Nanticokes when they passed through. It may have also helped them to ward off disease more successfully than other Native towns. Living in sturdy log cabins likely aided the Friedenshütteners' physical health. With each passing year, more and more of the town's residents had dwellings that provided better protection from the elements. Visitors were consistently impressed by the size, orderliness, and solidity of the town's physical plant, which in 1768 saw the meeting house roof raised and shingled and the addition of a belfry. The new bell brought worshippers to the chapel where they could view two new paintings adorning its walls, one of Christ's nativity and the other of his agony in the Garden of Gethsemane on the eve of his crucifixion. Native believers had requested the religious art. As elsewhere among other Native peoples in early America when they encountered Christian art, these visual representations proved to have an especially moving effect upon Indian religious sensibilities in Friedenshütten. Schmick repeatedly noted in the mission diary how the artwork captured the attention and spurred the spiritual interest of residents and visitors alike. That was just one indication among many in the diary's pages of the community's robust religious life. Almost daily the missionary and his Native assistants conversed with men and women wrestling with their spiritual condition, searching for some greater peace.[52]

All those signs of prosperity occurred against a backdrop of gathering clouds, however. When in January 1768 Frederick Stump and John Ironcutter brutally killed and scalped six Indians near Shamokin, and then murdered four more the next day to keep them from reporting the crime, they set off a wave of new worry among whites and Natives that blood-spilling combatants would once again terrorize the Pennsylvania frontier. Fears only worsened when a group of armed colonists liberated the two suspects from their jailers and in the process communicated loud and clear their Indian hatred and disdain for provincial justice.

Schmick urged his congregants to pray for peace and then resorted to a tactic used in earlier, more violent times—he wrote a pass for Papunhank and other Natives traveling to Bethlehem "to shew the white people" en route. Then, perhaps at Papunhank's urging, Bethlehem officials sent a letter to the Pennsylvania government asking them to take "kind Notice & Protection" of the Indian settlement at Wyalusing. Those were two ways of trying to ensure Native Moravians' safety. In March Governor John Penn and Sir William Johnson proposed other means. Penn turned to his old diplomatic partner, Papunhank, to deliver two proclamations establishing a £200 bounty on Stump's head and two belts of wampum which the government wanted the Moravians to pass along to other Susquehanna Valley Indians. Apparently they hoped that the pacifists could protect themselves and others by convincing other Natives to stay peaceful. Penn knew well Papunhank's past record of peacemaking and looked once more to him and his community to pacify any revenge-minded Indians.[53]

Alternatively, after expressing his regret for the Stump murders, promising to see justice done, and offering assistance to the victims' families, Johnson presented a removal plan for some of the Friedenshütteners: "I think you Mohicans [Mahicans] live too scattered from the rest of your friends, it would be best that you lived in a Body at Oghquago [Oquaga], Otseningo, or some where in that Quarter, You would be more under my Eye and Care. Consider what I say it being for your Interest." Johnson's design to bring all the Mahicans together echoed a "concentration" plan he had floated the prior summer in which any remaining New Jersey Indians and all Delawares on the Susquehanna were to move to the Allegheny to live in ethnically homogenous towns. It also squared with emerging Native strategies in the west. Delaware sachem Netawatwees (also known as Newcomer) and Munsee chief Packanke (also known as Custaloga) wanted their respective peoples to congregate under their leadership in the Ohio Country. Both chiefs wanted to enhance their nations' (and their own) power through augmented numbers and concentrated settlements.[54]

While formal invitations to the Friedenshütteners to move west wouldn't come until 1771, Johnson's appeal to the Mahicans presented Papunhank and the rest of the community with the immediate prospect of losing many of their spiritual brothers and sisters. Odds are that was a disconcerting possibility for Johannes. He was used to living within ethnically diverse towns. Though he and Joshua Senior had had their differences, for the most part the two had worked well together, bonded by their marriage ties and shared concern for the welfare of all. Losing Joshua's leadership, especially on the heels of Anton's departure in May, would severely weaken Friedenshütten and likely place an even greater burden on Papunhank. Losing all the Mahicans would diminish their numbers and make them more vulnerable to displacement. For the Mahican Moravians themselves, they had to consider the pros and cons of moving. Many of them had now spent decades living within Moravian communities, yet the first year or two in Wyalusing had been stressful. Antagonisms of various sorts along ethnic lines had emerged, prompting thoughts of having their own separate town. That was reason enough to take some time to deliberate on Johnson's invitation. A few months passed before the Mahicans in mid-July announced they would stay in Friedenshütten, though a month earlier Schmick privately reported that Joshua and the others had concluded that they did not want to live among non-Christian Mahicans. It would be too difficult there to fulfill "their hearts desire . . . to live in peace, to love the Savior and . . . to live as children of God and not like the wild Indians."[55]

Just as that Johnson-initiated proposal was being decided, another one presented itself to the community: whether to attend a large treaty being organized for the fall. In April, on the heels of an Iroquois peace settlement with the Cherokees, Johnson announced plans for a congress to be held near Albany with the Six Nations and their "dependent" Indians. Since at least the prior fall, the Iroquois Confederacy as well as Ohio Country tribes had been expressing a desire to reach an agreement with the British on a more permanent boundary line delineating a western limit to white expansion. The Proclamation Line of 1763 had quickly proved ineffective. The Stump murders only enhanced the conviction that more violence would follow unless settlers and Natives had a clearer sense of where colonial territory ended and Indian lands began. London officials agreed and pushed Johnson and his counterpart in the southern colonies, John Stuart, to craft agreements. But that was no easy matter to handle amid many competing interests and claims and unchecked colonial migration.[56]

Papunhank and the other Moravians at Friedenshütten likely understood that they had much at stake in this affair but imagined that they would have little or no influence over how it would be resolved given their small numbers and dependent status. They also claimed that attending the treaty would be a distraction to their spiritual work. So Papunhank told the town's Cayuga overseer, Gagohunt, in July that

> we do not think that it would be good for us and for our hearts [to attend]. We have great things before us and together here are daily getting to know our Creator and Lord and to come to love Him in our hearts and in this we feel well. Now, if we should go there where many other things will be spoken of, we could suffer damage to our hearts, lose what is good and be very sad about that. Nor do we have anything to do with war matters, for we love our Peace. Uncle! It is thus better for us to stay here at home and to remember you all before the Savior so that you make good Peace and Rest for all Indians.

The community preferred to have the Cayuga chief represent them. To their great relief, he agreed to let them "know everything that is said and arranged at Johnson's." That added to the community's already good feelings about Gagohunt's oversight. The prior day he had repudiated a report from Echgohund, the Munsee sachem from nearby Schechschiquanünk, that he was upset with them for sending Zeisberger and others to Goschgoschunk without informing him first. On the contrary, the Cayuga said, he had no objections to the Zeisberger mission, but he did want the rest of them to stay put in Friedenshütten. Lands "over the Allegheny Mountains" were "not good, for there it is very windy and so stormy that great trees fall over, that it is not good to live there and my Uncles can be harmed." In other words, the Six Nations didn't want their authority over the

Wyalusingites weakened by them moving west to lands less securely under Iroquois control. So he told them to "stay here in Wichelusing, sit by the fire that I have made here, so that I can stop here as I go by and smoke my pipe. Remain with the good thing that you have, to know God. Do not leave it." Delighted that "he left us with assurances of his good will," the community still offered an apology for failing to notify him of Zeisberger's journey and treated him to a special meal.[57]

Staying within the good graces of Gagohunt was a definite diplomatic plus. But it was insufficient in the long run to ensure a favorable outcome in the Treaty of Fort Stanwix, or in the short run to prevent more drama in Friedenshütten over attending the conference. In mid-September a Six Nations messenger informed them and other Indian towns along the Susquehanna that they were each to send two representatives to the treaty. More particularly, the messenger delivered a string of wampum from Abraham, a New York non-Moravian Mahican, asking Joshua Senior and a few other Mahicans in Friedenshütten to attend. Within twenty-four hours the community declined both invitations, indicating that the Cayuga chief would represent them. That was not the right answer from Abraham's perspective, however, so five days later new messages arrived, this time insisting that Joshua attend. Joshua begged off once again, though, claiming he had too much work to do and that for twenty years he had lived "without the Indians' gifts" and didn't intend to take them now. However principled his aversion to getting caught up in the intrigues of Indian diplomacy may have been, others in the community were not sure it was the right strategy in the present moment. Rumors were swirling that their lives might be in danger if they refused to attend the treaty. Consequently, they gathered for a meeting and expressed support for sending Papunhank, Joshua, and two others to Fort Stanwix to listen "to everything at the Treaty. Otherwise something difficult might happen to us." They recognized the potential damage that could be done to them not only in the treaty itself but through alienating those Natives pressuring them to attend. After considerable discussion, they won the day and Joshua and Johannes agreed to go.[58]

Two days later they changed their minds again. Schmick had grave doubts about the merits of participating in a treaty conference. His worries included the potential ill effects of consorting with non-Christian kin and other "wild" Indians. He seemingly possessed remarkably little confidence in the ability of men as stalwart as Joshua and Papunhank to withstand the temptations of treaty gatherings. Schmick wanted to be sure that the Savior was on board with the idea of them going to the council so he sought to know "His will [almost certainly through casting a lot], and it was this: he was against the Indian Brothers going there." Schmick promptly informed the two Native assistants of what he had learned about God's preference, and they deferred to that wisdom. When they told the Six Nations messenger of their final decision not to attend, he warned them that in all likelihood, another messenger would soon arrive with even harsher words.[59]

In the end that did not happen, and the treaty went forward without any official representation from Friedenshütten, though one community member, Billy Chillaway (Job's brother) attended.[60] Why Papunhank chose to remain at home is worth considering. Schmick's probable use of the lot gave added clout to the decision not to go, and Papunhank apparently did not want to disobey that Moravian means of determining God's will in the matter. Yet even before that point, he seemed disinclined to attend, though willing once the opinions of the broader community were sampled. Perhaps he too was leery about mixing with many nonbelieving Indians after his experiences at Goschgoschunk the prior fall, or saw local responsibilities to his family and town as more important. He may also have been influenced by the fact that the messengers were mostly interested in getting a Mahican to come to the treaty, so he saw it as less important for him, a Munsee, to attend. Another possibility is that he rightly intuited that the real pressure for some of them to attend was coming not from Johnson but from more local sachems who wanted to exert power over their community. But his choice here went against the impulse he had shown since 1760 to want to be at important councils and to have some type of voice in their proceedings. In this instance, he reverted to the more isolationist strategy he had employed in the 1750s when he stayed away from major treaties at Easton, either to keep a low profile or to avoid compromising situations or pressures. When trying to dissuade them from going, Schmick reinforced the latter concern by insisting that "the Enemy was looking for opportunity to lead them into temptation and to entangle them in Indian concerns and alliances that were unfitting for children of God."[61] Whatever Papunhank's motives, he no doubt held out hope that any agreements reached at Fort Stanwix would not adversely affect his Moravian community.

That proved to be wishful thinking. Chillaway brought back reports that Johnson and others at the huge gathering—there were about three thousand Indians there along with government leaders from New Jersey, Pennsylvania, and Virginia—thought highly of the Friedenshütten community: "You and your Indians in Wichlusing are my good friends. If only there were many Indian sites like this, I am sure that they love peace." But the terms of the treaty itself were less than favorable. The new boundary line agreed to by Johnson (acting on behalf of the British crown and its colonies) and the Six Nations ceded vast tracts of Iroquois Confederacy lands, including territory along the North and West Branches of the Susquehanna River, to colonial authorities. Suddenly the homes, fields, and hunting grounds of the Friedenshütteners were in the hands of the Pennsylvania government and no longer controlled by their Six Nations uncles.[62]

That was "disagreeable news" to say the least for Papunhank and the rest of the town. They had worked diligently—no one more than him—to secure their place ever since their arrival in Wyalusing in May 1765. Their efforts to persuade the powers that be, particularly their Six Nations overseers, that they should be allowed to stay there had been successful, and they had rewarded Iroquois trust with constructing a model community. Healthy, prosperous, and peaceable, it fed and housed sojourners, preached against revenge and retaliation, prohibited the liquor trade, and its few whites were nonthreatening missionaries. Now all of that was once more in jeopardy. The treaty accommodated the ambitions of Governor John Penn and other Pennsylvanians to expand the bounds of white sovereignty and settlement westward.[63] What that meant in practice for Friedenshütten remained to be seen. Would some accommodation for them be made or was their cause already lost? Was another removal going to be necessary if they hoped to have sufficient independence and autonomy to maintain their Moravian identity and commitments?

Those questions surely troubled Papunhank as 1768 came to a close. He must have been disappointed in and perhaps even felt betrayed by the Iroquois choice to relinquish the Susquehanna Valley, even if that prospect had been growing increasingly likely in the past few years. He may have also had some second thoughts about whether he should have been at Fort Stanwix to plead his case. In retrospect, his failure to go was probably a serious miscalculation. His presence wouldn't have changed the outcome but at least he could have said his piece and brought a greater awareness of his community's circumstance. An influx of white settlers now seemed bound to happen and little good could come from that. No one in Friedenshütten would blame him if such a prospect brought on a new wave of melancholy. Yet their impulse to care for one another would have also inclined them to remind him of how far they had come and how blessed they had been since their long days in Philadelphia. Papunhank had led them into the wilderness—which of course was no wilderness at all for him—and been one of their chief guardians as they made a new home in his old home. As always, challenges of various sorts had beset them, including just getting along with one another. Nevertheless, they had persevered, generally held their own diplomatically, and even flourished economically and spiritually. As Zeisberger described it in August 1768, "Oh how happy our Indian Brothers and Sisters in Friedenshütten can be that they have such a little place where they are closed away from all the noise of Satan."[64] Papunhank had had a major hand in making possible all those signs of well-being. His prophetic leadership looked different from what it had been in the 1750s and early 1760s. But its central goal had essentially remained unchanged: to secure a peaceful home for his people where they could serve God according to their best understanding in relative freedom. No need, then, to lose all hope just because of a disappointing treaty. Instead, they went back to work and worship and whatever else might enable them to fulfill Papunhank's deep longing for a peaceable kingdom.

6

New Trials

For the next three years, Friedenshütten's future remained in doubt. No one knew for sure what the Treaty of Fort Stanwix would require. Amid that uncertainty, in May 1770 Papunhank stated as plainly as he could to Cayuga chief Gagohunt the hopes and dreams of his people:

> If you are considering where the Indians in Schommunk [Chemung] and Hallobank will move in the future, please consider that we in Wichlusing have no strong connection to them and are not able to live among them in their Towns. We are different. We need peace and quiet to live as we worship God and lead good lives. Should we be forced to live with Indians in our midst who are not like-minded, there will certainly be no peace and quiet. And when we are near to their Towns we will also find no comfort. They go to the Whites, procure rum, and return to us and want to be fed. They also tempt our young people to drink alcohol. We would be forced to confiscate their rum until they leave. We don't want to do that nor do we like that idea, but we don't want our young folk to become accustomed to drinking, and become weak in body and soul. Uncle, consider this! And relay this to other Chiefs, who are also our uncles, and that we do not want any land of this type. We want to live in peace and quiet for not just 4 or 5 years at a place, rather for many years.[1]

If somehow that message wasn't clear, Papunhank went a few weeks later to Hallobank to reinforce it to Gagohunt one more time:

> We cannot be involved in any of the Indian treaties, land affairs, nor any other such future matters or dealings. We love peace and all things virtuous. Whatever the Chiefs of the 6 Nations determine and act upon in the best interest of all Indians, we support this and are grateful for. We plead with the Chiefs of the 6 Nations to allow us to remain here in Wichlusing in peace, and that we be exempted from the aforementioned dealings. We want to love God, to learn to know Him and avoid damage to our hearts.[2]

Five years removed from their Philadelphia captivity and enjoying relative calm and stability, Papunhank and other Friedenshütteners wanted nothing so much as to be left alone. They envisioned a kind of splendid isolation in Wyalusing. Their town could be an island of security and an oasis of piety, a place to live long-term and plant deep roots. They were tired of moving about and frustrated with the twists and turns of diplomatic deals and political intrigues beyond their control. They hoped that the regnant powers would reward their fealty with assurances that they could stay put. Surely the Six Nations could understand that Friedenshütten was different from other towns.

Above all, the community loved peace. It couldn't help but keep mentioning it. And who better to proclaim that message than Papunhank? He had been sounding that note for two decades. His peace discourse had echoed across Pennsylvania's hills and valleys even when the clamor of war made it hard to hear. As a result, no one in the entire region from the Six Nations in the north to Philadelphia in the south was better known as a peace advocate. His pacifism had found a receptive home within Native Moravianism, and together they had crafted a town that lived up to its name—"huts of peace." So here he was again explaining to their Cayuga overseers his community's deepest values and pointing out why the proposed move would threaten them. They abhorred the damage white liquor traders did to Native young people and whole communities. To be forced to live near or in Indian towns that tolerated or even fostered such behavior would breed unwanted but inevitable conflicts and by implication, violence. The peace and quiet they cherished would be impossible.

At that same moment, David Zeisberger said the identical thing to Munsee and Delaware chiefs in the west. He, too, insisted that Moravians simply wanted to live in peace and quiet and had no vested interest in wider political affairs. That required that they have a piece of land separate from nonbelieving Natives where they could build homes, grow food, worship the Savior, and offer Christian salvation to all those who would listen.

This Moravian vision, now fully shared by Papunhank, was eminently reasonable and tragically impossible in late colonial America. Visitors to Friedenshütten, especially white ones, regularly marveled at the impressive Indian town. They had never seen anything like it in Indian country with its well-built houses, flourishing fields, chapel and schoolhouse, and hymn-singing Natives.[3] For such a place to want to continue unimpeded by the distractions and disturbances of the outside world was quite natural. After everything many of the residents had experienced in the prior fifteen years, who could blame them for wanting to see their current, far happier circumstances persist? Yet to the extent that they imagined that they could stay immune or set apart from larger developments within Pennsylvania and early America, they were fooling themselves. Neither whites nor other Indians could or would give them that much independence. Papunhank knew that, but even he wished that somehow their unique community could be left to flourish on its own.

As the town's key diplomat, Papunhank remained acutely aware of Friedenshütten's tenuous position and its need to keep navigating strategically its relations with a host of Native and white outsiders. None of that was new; the Treaty of Fort Stanwix only made it more necessary, as did renewed fighting in the region, this time between New England newcomers and white Pennsylvanians in the Wyoming Valley. During the next three years, Papunhank felt the stresses and strains of trying to protect the town's interests when it had little clout apart from the power of its own good example. Yet ironically that too proved to be a source of its undoing, as it attracted more visitors who wanted to stay long-term than it could sustain, and made both the people and land of Friedenshütten prized commodities.[4]

If all that weren't enough to worry about, events in the fall of 1771 threatened to tear the community apart from within. As usual, Papunhank was at the center of the action. Seemingly out of the blue, old friends accused the Munsee leader of practicing witchcraft. Everyone knew that Papunhank had long possessed special spiritual powers. But now some believed that they were powers of darkness, a literal and figurative poison killing community members. What prompted such damning claims? How could the apparently harmonious Moravian enclave come to such a point? And what did it mean for Papunhank, Friedenshütten, and the future of Moravian missions?

New trials like these eventually precipitated the need for new beginnings by the summer of 1772. The elusive hope of finding a more permanent homeland took Papunhank, his family, and the rest of their Moravian brothers and sisters westward into the Ohio Country. Indians there had been lobbying for the Brethren to join them ever since Zeisberger had established a foothold in the Alleghenies in 1768. Friedenshütteners kept close track of developments in that mission outpost during its first months and years and rejoiced whenever news trickled back that more Indians had placed their trust in the Savior's wounds. Papunhank and his wife, Anna Johanna, had special reasons to shed tears when word came that Zeisberger had baptized siblings of theirs. Such joys mixed with the frustrations and tensions that beset Papunhank and Friedenshütten in its final three and a half years.

Lobbyist Once More

The year 1769 opened with events that portended much of what lay ahead for Papunhank's people. On the first of January, western Delaware leader Killbuck spoke with missionary Johann Schmick about his three-week stay at Friedenshütten. He had traveled there after attending the huge gathering at Fort Stanwix and reported that he was "happy that I came here, where I have personally seen many good things in 20 days; I also heard good words about God daily. I will not forget this, but will remember it well and when I get home I will tell my friends everything, because we also have a lot of good people in our town who will be happy to hear words about God." Home was Gekelemukpechünk or Newcomer's Town in the Ohio Country, about one hundred miles west of Pittsburgh. Newcomer, or Netawatwees, was the Delaware "king" interested in bringing all Delawares together into a single nation. Knowing what his headman wanted and what the Treaty of Fort Stanwix likely meant for Friedenshütteners, Killbuck was not so subtly selling his community as a new place of refuge, even playing up the spiritual interest of his neighbors. Similar friendly overtures to Christians had been made earlier to Quakers formerly connected to the Friendly Association. On the other hand, the same western Delawares had flatly refused to allow visiting Presbyterian missionary Charles Beatty to stick around in 1766. Netawatwees apparently knew which types of Christians he wished to recruit to his town—pacifist-inclined ones—though his council would keep debating the wisdom of admitting any of them, Native or white, for the next decade.[5]

For the moment, Friedenshütteners were thinking more about how to stay put than where to go next. Schmick met with Papunhank and other Native assistants to discuss a response to the new treaty. They reviewed a letter sent on their behalf to Governor John Penn back in November by Moravian legal counsel, Lewis Weiss, in which he reminded Penn that the Moravian Indians had settled at Wyalusing following their departure from Philadelphia "with the knowledge and approbation" of the colony's government. The letter requested that the governor not consider any applications or make any grants "for Lands interfering with their said Settlement" until Penn considered forthcoming petitions from the Native Brethren at Friedenshütten. Papunhank spent the next month crafting the petition, and by early February it was ready to be delivered.[6]

No doubt influenced by Weiss's legal advice and input from Bethlehem leaders, the document aimed to convince Penn to set aside the territory the Wyalusingites had been using since 1765 so that the Natives could remain there. It proposed that the lands be entrusted to a group of men who would make the lands available to the Indians and presumably oversee their use. When the time came in some distant future that the town's Native residents "for the good of the state must remove," these trustees would sell the improvements on it "for the benefit of the Indians" within whatever restrictions the governor and proprietors might establish. As for why the governor should consider taking such steps, the petition set forth several arguments. First, these were the lands that were originally Papunhank's "plantation." By implication, that gave him some sort of historic claim. Moreover, in 1765 he had gained Iroquois approval for resettling there with the other Philadelphia refugees. Since arriving, they had made numerous improvements upon the land (houses, meeting house, school, cleared lands) and "by their connection and intercourse with Christians become in some degree civilized." To live well, they would need the lands in and around Wyalusing, perhaps as far as six miles to the north and south, to have sufficient hay, wood, and space from encroaching settlers who might give Indians "opportunities to buy rum, which must tend to the utter ruin of their young people."[7]

Whatever its outcome, the petition revealed much about Friedenshütten. It began, "The Petition of John Papunhan and Joshua the Mohican, in behalf of themselves and their friends—the Indians that live at Wialusing." In other words the request came from Indians, not white Moravian missionaries. In addition, naming Papunhank and Joshua showed their ongoing civic leadership and would have reminded Penn of his substantial interactions with Papunhank five years earlier during their captivity. It also reflected the need to recognize the separate ethnic identities of the town's Natives. Mahicans, Delawares, and Munsees would need to work together in this moment if Friedenshütten was to survive. In the wake of the treaty, any legal rights to their lands were increasingly dubious, but the petitioners nevertheless appealed to Papunhank's historic presence in Wyalusing and his obtaining Six Nations approval for returning there in 1765 as grounds for affording the Wyalusingites special treatment. The character of this Indian community—economically productive, agriculturally based, largely Christian, averse to alcohol, and by implication peaceable—also demanded notice. None of those purported virtues made them any less *Native* but they did set them apart from other Indians. Why wouldn't the Pennsylvania government want them around, and wasn't such behavior worthy of some accommodation the petition seemed to say. It made plain that the town was not well-off enough to purchase or rent the lands it wanted to retain. If and when they had to move, they expected or at least hoped for some payment for the improvements on the land and some provision of new lands upon which to settle through the "wonted goodness" of colonial authorities. That had been the practice in Pennsylvania when earlier groups of Natives had been removed to new homelands. They wished to be treated in the same way.[8]

With petition in hand, and an accompanying letter of support from Schmick, Joshua and Johannes set off in mid-February to meet with Governor Penn and initiated a series of exchanges that over the next six months provided some reason for hope. In March Penn sent back word that because "you were a peaceable and a quiet people and behaved very well, you should not be disturbed in your possessions at Wyaloosing." But having heard that they remained fearful that their lands were to be taken away, he sent another letter in June that more forcefully laid out his position in a series of four points: they could count on his promise that they could stay in Wyalusing; he had instructed surveyors to stay away from their lands; they were to avoid giving any encouragement to "the New England people who have taken possession of the Proprietaries' lands" at Wyoming; and they were to get along with Job Chillaway who "took up his land to secure it for himself and the rest of you."[9]

Papunhank and others in Friedenshütten found Penn's response both encouraging and perplexing. When they wrote back in August, they addressed the governor's letter by first expressing thanks for the "good words" about not being "disturbed" in their possessions. They were also glad not to have to worry about a return visit from the same land surveyors who had shown up in early June claiming to have orders to survey Wyalusing. On that occasion, the Moravian Indians had refused to allow Charles Stewart to do his work based on what Penn had sent them in March. Those issues and the fate of Wyalusing in general were minor distractions for the governor compared to his far greater concern about a new incursion of Connecticut settlers into the Wyoming Valley. Armed conflict in the region between white Pennsylvanians and Yankees seemed increasingly likely, and the last thing he wanted was for any Indians to help the New Englanders. The Friedenshütteners had no problem reassuring him that any rumored connections they had with the newcomers were false and to urge the governor "not to believe every report of us. There are many bad Indians, and all say they come from Wialusing, as they pass through here." Then they came to his final point. What he had written about Job Chillaway was curious. Town members told Penn that they were happy to get along with Chillaway. But they were unclear why he was apparently negotiating with the governor to get legal title to Wyalusing lands when they had "never desired him to take up any land for us, and upon what account he could call Wyalusing his land, we do not know." His actions were "to our prejudice, for our worthy Brother John Papunhank, was settled here two years before him, and Job has but this year begun to clear some new land, and has the least judgment of us all." Papunhank and other leaders were clearly leery of Chillaway's designs. They were likely aware that he had filed an application for these lands with the Pennsylvania government back on November 26, 1768, perhaps acting on news from his brother Billy who had attended the treaty at Fort Stanwix. Schmick had informed Moravian missions overseer John Ettwein back in January that the community opposed having their land entrusted to Chillaway because "they don't want to be dependent on him." If he owned the land, he could admit unwanted whites or Indians. Worse yet, he might sell all the land to whites, forcing the Moravians to move away. Figuring out Chillaway's motives and navigating relations with him would prove increasingly difficult for Friedenshütten and especially for Papunhank.[10]

If all that wasn't complicated enough, the town in these same months had to sort through conflicting reports from Indian sources about the terms of the Fort Stanwix Treaty. Cayuga chiefs, jealous to retain oversight of the Wyalusing Indians, sent word in late March that they should not believe everything western Delaware emissary Killbuck had told them or be tempted by his offers to move to the Ohio Country. Instead, they should stay put and develop stronger ties to the Six Nations:

> 4 years ago you returned and we established you here. We made a new fire together, so that by moving beyond the past [Six Nations' destruction of the town during Pontiac's War] we could relight our peace-pipe, rest together and warm ourselves by the fire. Uncles! Now you are more secure here. May the logs burn closer together and let's add a piece of good wood to the fire, so that it burns better and brighter. And if . . . white people come too close and want to pressure us, and [you] don't want to or [are not] able to live here any longer, we will search out another beautiful, acceptable piece of land for you. This I and my brothers want to assure you.

Such claims of Iroquois benevolence seemed disingenuous or at least confusing at a time when the Wyalusingites were pretty sure the Six Nations had just sold the lands they were living on to whites without consulting them.[11]

Even that point became blurry a month later. An elderly associate of Gagohunt informed them that while the Iroquois had sold Cayuga lands at Wyoming and Shamokin, "this did not include the land where the Brothers live." He insisted that the final boundary line established by the treaty had not yet been firmly set. According to him, the Six Nations had made plain to Johnson that any whites settling in the newly purchased areas should not infringe on Native hunting areas nor assume they had mineral rights on the land. Ten days later the community heard much the same message from Gagohunt himself. He insisted that "Wichlusing was not sold and remains in the possession of our Uncles [the Six Nations]." All these Cayuga words encouraged the Wyalusingites, but they wondered if they were reliable or enforceable. Neither the British nor the Iroquois seemed especially able by that point to control the actions of incoming settlers. Schmick expressed to Bethlehem the town's frustration:

> We hear all kinds of things and do not know what we should believe. Once we hear that it [Wyalusing lands] has been sold, on the other hand that it is not. Now we hear again that it is probably given to the Indians by the Governor and that it was in the newspapers, but now it is otherwise. A gentleman in Philadelphia has it, it belongs to him. Thus let us know how it is, and what is concerned, and why our people still haven't gotten an answer.[12]

As 1769 progressed, then, the Pennsylvania government, the Six Nations, local Cayuga chiefs, the British, Ohio Delawares, land speculators, and eager white settlers all kept Papunhank and his community unsure about their future. Offers of aid had come from several of these sources. Yet in each case the self-interested agendas of the competing parties were barely hidden. They wanted more people or more land or both. Friedenshütteners weren't ready to provide either.

Many Talents, Many Roles

While the waiting game proceeded, Papunhank gave no signs of wanting to move. He had spent most of the last decade in and around Wyalusing. It was familiar territory; it was his town. He had formed it twice and in both instances made it a success. His family was there, and although he had also found family in Goschgoschunk in the Alleghenies, that place felt alien and too full of Native religious practices he had left behind. His strong sense of divine calling, before and after his Christian conversion, led him to bring a people to *this* place. He was determined to keep them there and to help them flourish as much and as long as possible.

All of this explains why Papunhank continued to throw himself into every aspect of Friedenshütten life during his final years in Pennsylvania. Moravian diaries and letters portray him as peripatetic, constantly moving about perhaps for the sake of not having to move. Activity was an antidote to anxiety for him. It likely helped combat bouts of discouragement and depression. It also enabled him to fulfill a wide range of responsibilities and as a result, to retain a sense of self-importance. In that, he was not deluded. It is easy in retrospect to fall into the trap of imagining, due to reliance upon Euro-American sources and racial assumptions, that the German missionaries in Friedenshütten or Moravian leaders back in Bethlehem called all the shots for the community there, that it was *their* town. But no one in the village at the time saw it that way, not even the missionaries. They were there at the request of the Christian Mahicans, Munsees, and Delawares and with the approval of the Six Nations. The missionaries exercised important leadership, most obviously over religious matters. But the overall direction and character of the community rested in Indian hands. Their families, their strategies, their choices, their hard work, their spiritual interest, and their rhythms of life gave shape and tone to Wyalusing.

And no one was more central to its operation or ethos than Papunhank. As the town matured, he continued to play many vital roles. Much of his time and physical energy went into hunting as it had for decades. It remained one of the great pleasures and necessities of his life. Hunting took him away from the village for days or weeks at a time in all four seasons of the year. He spent long hours with one or two Native brothers, or all alone, soaking in the sights, sounds, and smells of the Pennsylvania woods he knew so well. He typically went south from Wyalusing following well-worn paths, often into the Wyoming Valley, though now some of those hunting grounds were off limits. In the woods he likely found much of the peace and quiet he desired for his community and himself but which outside pressures too often made elusive. Papunhank enjoyed using skills taught to him many decades before and honed over a lifetime. They were a reminder that not everything had changed for Munsees in the eighteenth century. Going on "the chase" kept him connected to the ways of his fathers, to the traditional practices of Munsee men, and to the historic role of providing for the basic needs of his band. Supplying them with meat was one part of keeping them well fed. So on July 1, 1769, when "Brothers Johannes and Cornelius returned from the hunt with a deer and bear, they divided this up among the Members, who were very pleased."[13]

Regular hunting expeditions complemented the town's other economic activities. After four years of settlement, Friedenshütten boasted hundreds of acres of corn and grain and substantial herds of cattle, pigs, horses, and sheep. It carried on sugar camps in the spring and gathered berries and cut hay in the summer. Town members especially appreciated having adequate food in the summer of 1769 when most other Indian towns in the region faced great want. In early May Gagohunt had described a "great hunger and lack of food among the Indians up in Anahochquega [Oquaga], Hallobank, Owego, and Zeninga." Conditions only grew worse as the summer wore on. By late July he reported that there was "famine among his people." Combinations of severe weather, insect infestations, crop failures, and reduced numbers of game likely account for their hunger. Waves of disease in the spring and fall may also have been causes and effects of their subsistence crisis. Meanwhile, Friedenshütteners were sufficiently "blessed in the hunts of our Brothers and with the Members' harvest from the farm" to weather the storm; enough so, in fact, that the town attracted streams of visitors looking for something to eat. On July 20 alone, forty-six Native newcomers arrived from points north "very hungry." Town members "were shocked by the large number desiring food" and had no idea "how they would feed so many" since their "own people eat barely once a day, and others have gone to get flour from the White people." Nevertheless, the Friedenshütteners, apparently feeling a sense of collective responsibility, by evening had "collected from all our houses" donations so that enough "food appeared that together provided for our guests." Such comparative bounty and acts of generosity explain why "many wild Indians, namely from the Ohio, from Schechschequanik, Shommunk, Hallobank, Zeninga, Anahooquage and Onandago, and from Jersey" kept pouring into the town during the rest of the year and into 1770. By May of the latter year, the town determined that there was "not enough land" to sustain any more newcomers, and directed them instead to settle up the Susquehanna at Schechschiquanünk where John Roth was now ministering. That decision proved prudent since within two months Schmick was reporting that "worms and caterpillars not only ate the corn, but also the summer wheat and oats." He and others asked "where will the bread come from?"[14]

Some of it came from Bethlehem where Papunhank went often. Ever since arriving in Wyalusing in 1765, the community had maintained frequent contact with Moravian associates in and around Bethlehem. There they received essential goods, more often through trade than charity. Sometimes they brought livestock there to sell; other times it was game from their hunting expeditions. Papunhank and other Wyalusing Indians regularly hauled their deer hides and other animal products to Rose Tavern and Moravian businessman William Edmonds. With him they seemingly felt confident that the fraudulent practices of white traders about which Papunhank had long complained were not an issue.[15]

Papunhank also went to Bethlehem for other purposes. On occasion he was there to deliver or retrieve people. He apparently remained the most reliable guide for getting folks to and from Wyalusing. More important, he often went to exchange information. He rarely visited the town without interacting with Moravian officials. Sometimes he would simply deliver and pick up correspondence. Other times he was there as a messenger or an intermediary of sorts for his community. They trusted him to represent their interests well and to gather vital information about wider developments. Papunhank usually obliged since it had always been his impulse to keep abreast of events that might affect his followers' well-being. If he minded going to Bethlehem on a regular basis, he never showed it. In turn, Moravian leaders such as Nathanael Seidel and John Ettwein came to rely on Johannes to give them an informed Native perspective on Friedenshütten and other Indian towns in the upper Susquehanna. They could read missionary letters and the congregational diaries, but Papunhank offered them something else. They knew how experienced he was in Wyalusing and how responsible he had been for its re-creation, as well as how knowledgeable he was about wider Indian relations. If anyone was going to be attuned to the community and region's big picture, he was it.[16]

They also knew that as *Vorsteher* (church wardens), Johannes and Joshua Senior were largely responsible for managing the town's external affairs. Both regularly served as emissaries to the Pennsylvania government and the Six Nations. But there was no mistaking who was Friedenshütten's chief diplomat, spokesman, and town representative. Papunhank took center stage in negotiations with Penn, the Cayuga, and other Iroquois. Six Nations sachems sometimes specifically requested that he be sent to them to carry on talks. They clearly considered him to be the community's headman, even as he had been a decade earlier. And when they came in person to Friedenshütten, they typically met with town leaders in Papunhank's home. In their minds, it was the council house of Wyalusing, the place of dialogue and deliberation.[17]

Alongside all this hunting, trading, haying, couriering, and negotiating, Papunhank spent much time worshiping, singing, praying, and counseling. Communal religious activities were an everyday occurrence in Friedenshütten. When Ettwein visited in 1768, he noted that "the place has a good name among the Six Nations and elsewhere. Many Indians happen to hear the gospel here and think well of the manner of life and discipline of the Moravians." As a Native assistant and communicant member (a group that constituted about a quarter of the town's inhabitants in these years), Johannes would have been especially expected to be a disciplined, faithful participant in corporate religious gatherings. No evidence suggests that he wasn't. On a more personal basis, he regularly conversed with Schmick and a new missionary, Johann George Jungmann (he and his wife arrived in June 1769 to assist the Schmicks and remained until September 1770) on matters earthly and heavenly. That afforded them chances to hear and record details of Papunhank's spiritual commitments.[18]

Of particular note are three instances during 1770 in which Johannes counseled others. Following Sunday morning worship on March 11, Papunhank met with Job Chillaway. The two men knew each other well, having been in contact since at least the 1750s and been part of the same community for much of the past decade. On numerous occasions during the Seven Years' War, Chillaway had been Papunhank's translator, putting the Munsee's ideas into English for governors, the Provincial Council, and hosts of others. And he had been the one to relay Papunhank's vision quest narrative to Quakers. Chillaway knew Papunhank's story, idioms, and religious passions. At times he was powerfully drawn to the Christian message, as were his wife and daughter. But each time he seemed to pull back from making the type of full commitment Moravians wanted. On this day he was apparently willing to discuss with Papunhank the "Savior's love and mercy" and to consider "their souls' worthiness." According to Schmick, Johannes "with a soft heart" tenderly shared his deepest convictions with Chillaway: "I need the Savior every day, and I live blessedly in his presence from morning until evening. Yet I strive for this more and more in my heart and soul. I search for and desire nothing more than to feel and to possess as long as I live the Lord and his bloody wounds."[19]

With this same Moravian emphasis on the "bloody wounds," Papunhank explained "much regarding the Savior" to Munsee chief Newollike. He was long familiar with the Christian message having visited Nain and Wechquetank in earlier years and having heard the testimony of his brother-in-law, Anton, the long-time Native assistant in various Moravian Indian towns. Newollike confessed that "I've been to Wichlusing many times, and never really liked what I heard about the Savior. That's why I never attended a worship gathering." But on this day in July, Papunhank somehow broke down his resistance so that Newollike was ready to say, "Now I think I'm ready to go to the worship and listen to the stories about their Savior." He made good on that promise, much to the Moravians' delight.[20]

Papunhank had a third opportunity to offer spiritual counsel when he took a hunting trip with his grandson, Samuel Moor. Though a young man, Moor was likely already widowed with a two-year-old daughter. That sorrow and large responsibility may have stirred the spiritual interest he expressed to his grandfather as they spent their evenings around the fire talking about "the Savior and his great love and aid to the poor sinners, who feel this in their hearts." Papunhank told him that "without Him [Jesus] they cannot be nor are able to be blessed [saved]." Moor responded that he hoped to "experience this grace and help from our Savior" and wished to "free himself of sinfulness." When they returned to Friedenshütten, Moor asked to be baptized. Three weeks later he was, along with Billy Chillaway.[21]

Johannes's spiritual encounters with Job Chillaway, Newollike, and Samuel Moor illustrate that he remained a willing and often able religious witness. He had been doing that work for two decades, and though his message had substantially evolved, he evidently still had a knack for getting people to listen. These three Native men differed in age, power, ethnicity, and kinship relation. Yet in all cases Papunhank spoke words that resonated. Taken together, these diary passages provide glimpses of the core of his religious understanding. Most fundamentally, they reveal a religion centered on Jesus the Savior and his love for sinners. In theological terms, Johannes embraced a thoroughly Christocentric faith. He echoed his Moravian teachers' emphasis on Jesus and had become persuaded that the crucified Savior was one and the same with the creator God of his own earlier preaching. His prior language about the power of good and bad spirits within a person to shape their behavior had morphed into the conviction that sin made it impossible for anyone to save themselves. Only through the bloody wounds and sacrifice of Jesus could they be healed. There was power in that blood, a power to be possessed, a power you never stopped needing, a power Papunhank wanted to experience on a daily basis. It was the power of grace.

Family Connections

While playing these leading roles in the life of Friedenshütten, Papunhank's attachment to his Moravian community only grew stronger, especially when its ranks included more and more of his kin. Samuel Moor was one of several "new" family members in Papunhank's life between 1769 and 1772. At least this is when they begin showing up in the historical record. Kin connected to him or his wife Anna Johanna came to Friedenshütten or into the Moravian fold in these years, reinforcing familial bonds with strong religious ties. Great joy accompanied these deepened relationships and helped to cushion the loss of other loved ones and the eventual loss of Friedenshütten itself.

Sorting out the details on Papunhank's family connections once again requires some educated guesswork. When they moved to Friedenshütten, their household included Papunhank, Anna Johanna, and

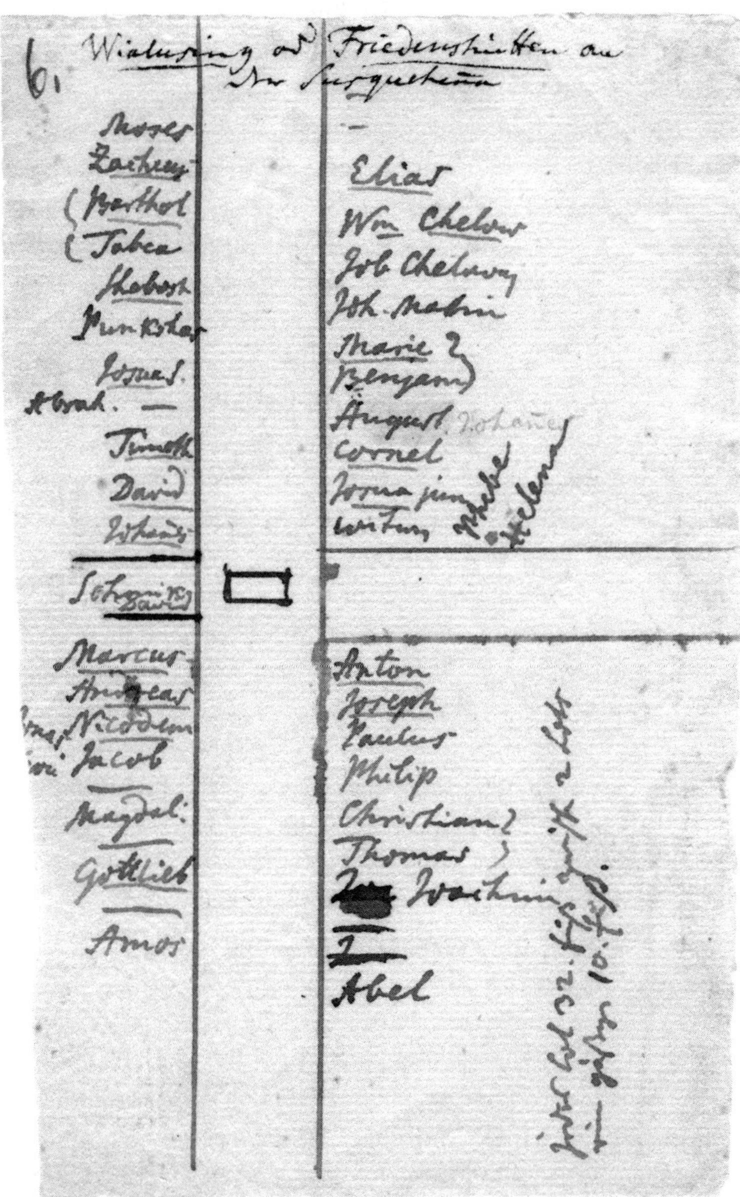

Fig. 9. Diagram of building lots in Friedenshütten (Wyalusing) compiled by Johannes Ettwein, ca. 1770. Moravian Archives, Bethlehem, Pennsylvania.

a daughter who was named Anna Paulina at her baptism in 1772. Since she married in 1779, it is likely she was born to Anna Johanna in the late 1750s or early 1760s. Her sister or half-sister, Sophia, was born in 1741, married Joshua Junior in 1764, lived across the road from her parents in Friedenshütten, and gave birth there to two daughters, Anna and Bathseba, by 1767 (see figure 9).[22] It is likely that Anna Johanna was not Papunhank's first wife and not the mother of Sophia. Anna Johanna lived until 1814, but we do not know her birth date. Odds are she was fifteen to thirty years younger than her husband. That hypothesis is supported by the fact that her grandmother appeared in Friedenshütten in 1772 when Papunhank was in his late sixties. If she was Sophia's mother, she likely lived into her nineties and had had many years between the births of her two (surviving?) daughters. The appearance of an adult grandson, Samuel Moor, in 1770 and an adult granddaughter the year before, however, make it even more likely that Papunhank had children (besides Sophia) with an earlier wife. If Moor was in his early twenties when he moved to Friedenshütten, his mother or father was likely born to Papunhank and his wife in the 1720s. Such timing is very plausible for Papunhank (born about 1705) but unrealistic for Anna Johanna. Chances are good, then, that he had experienced the loss of a wife at some point in the 1740s or 1750s. Perhaps that loss compounded the grief he felt at the passing of his father around 1750 and contributed to his religious crisis. Remarrying at some point in those years may have eased some of that pain.[23]

Might Papunhank have also had a male child in the 1760s? Within the Moravian records for Friedenshütten, there is a single reference to a son in a list of names of Indians at Wyalusing in 1765 or 1766. The catalog identified thirteen children including "Joh.Pep. son, ________ daughter." Since I have found no corroborating evidence that he had a young son in this era, this is most likely an error or possibly an orphan from one of the families in Philadelphia. If the latter, he did not remain in Papunhank's household for very long.[24]

The first addition to his kin in Friedenshütten besides granddaughters Anna and Bathseba was the arrival of an older granddaughter, her husband, and possibly three great-grandchildren in April 1769. They came with a few others from Quilutamend, an Indian village located less than ten miles northwest of Lechaweke where Papunhank likely lived and preached in the early 1750s. It is intriguing to imagine that she and possibly her parents had remained in that vicinity or returned to it at some point during the past fifteen years when warfare had subsided. More likely, though, they had only gone to that town quite recently because Moravian missionaries referred to her family as "Jersey Indians," a term typically used to refer to Delaware Indians who belonged to John Brainerd's Presbyterian congregation in New Jersey. Her name was Mary, an English Christian name that reinforces the likelihood that she had lived with and been baptized by the Presbyterians. How she and other members of her family ended up there remains a mystery. If like her brother, Samuel Moor, she was born in the 1740s, she would have been a child when her grandfather became a Munsee prophet. It is impossible to know whether she and her parents lived near him at the time or went with Papunhank when he moved his followers north of Tioga and then to Wyalusing. They were not with him when he moved to Philadelphia in 1763. In any case, she was now united or reunited with her grandfather. Given his frequent travel down the Susquehanna, he may have met them at some point after 1765 and encouraged them to move to Friedenshütten. Her small band had spent the past winter at Wechquetank, site of the former Native Moravian town, but they subsequently came, like so many others, to Friedenshütten for food. Johannes immediately gave them lodging in his cabin. His joy at their presence only grew when three weeks later her husband told Schmick that he had "decided to come and get to know Jesus better." He described himself as a "poor and sinful person, who had committed many regrettable acts . . . [and] wanted to become a different person and find salvation." Papunhank soon built them their own cabin, and indications are that they remained in the town.[25]

Late September 1769 brought another addition to the extended family. On the twenty-fourth "in the morning Joshua Jr.'s wife Sophia returned with a little baby boy. The Sisters went to see her and they both appeared well. She stated that she wished her husband would return [from hunting] so the baby could be baptized." Traditional

Native practices and gender roles regarding childbirth were apparently in play here as Sophia left the village to deliver her son and was being attended to by other women. Meanwhile, her husband was off hunting. When he arrived three days later with his father and father-in-law, he joined his wife in asking that the baby be baptized. The next night at evening worship, with Munsee and Mahican kin likely gathered around, the infant was christened and "received the name *Johannes*." Papunhank must have been touched by having a new namesake and, after a string of daughters and granddaughters, a young boy to train. Unfortunately, however, within six weeks the child was gravely ill. His father returned once again from hunting, glad he had "followed the feeling I had in my heart, which told me to return home to see what is happening with my wife and children." Four days later the young Johannes "got a severe case of convulsions" and "at midnight after a previous consecration he went gently to sleep." The heartache of losing a child and a grandchild was tragically far too common in this town as it was elsewhere among Native communities. Of the eight recorded deaths in Friedenshütten in 1769, six were young children.[26]

Alongside those deep sorrows for Papunhank came more encouraging family news from the mission outpost at Goschgoschunk. From its start in June 1768, Zeisberger encountered strong opposition there, but his small group of supporters included Papunhank's brother (Tschechquoapesek) and his wife, and Anna Johanna's sister and her husband (Gatschenis). Their kinship ties to Papunhank and Anna Johanna were likely one factor pulling them toward the United Brethren. Over the next year and a half, the two couples became more and more interested in the Christian message despite others' efforts to dissuade them: "Why do you want to believe the white people? You can see for yourselves that they are different people from us; they have quite a different skin than we have and God has not made us to live like they do." They were warned that if the Friedenshütteners moved to Goschgoschunk with their missionaries, "then we will tell their teachers to go to Hell." Undeterred, the four of them, along with blind chief Allemewi, became Zeisberger's first baptized converts on the Allegheny in December 1769 and January 1770. Gatschenis became Lucas, his wife

Paulina, and their son Israel; Tschechquoapesek became Jeremias, his wife Anna Caritas. Soon Lucas's mother and brother were asking to be baptized as well. When Schmick shared word of these baptisms with his congregation in Friedenshütten, "what joy was felt among the Members, I can't adequately describe, They uttered many an *onéowe* [great thanks] in appreciation of His grace and mercy visited upon that place, and many tears were shed, especially from Sister Rebecca for her father [Allemewi], from Br. Johannes Papunhank for his brother and from his wife Anna Johanna for her sister."[27]

With more of their kin joining the Moravians and more of their offspring coming to live in Friedenshütten, Johannes and Anna Johanna had reasons to rejoice. Within another few weeks, her uncle, aunt, and their three children moved to the town "to hear about the Savior." A year later Ameiens, another sister of Anna Johanna, was baptized as Sulamith in the west, and Sophia gave birth to a new grandchild, a girl, Salome, baptized on Good Friday.[28] All of those events were encouraging. But Papunhank must have been especially heartened by the decision of his brother to follow his religious path. Six years earlier, after perhaps a lifetime of being together and perhaps a decade of Tschechquoapesek heeding his brother's preaching, the two had split over how best to respond to the dangers of Pontiac's War. Hearing that he had become Jeremias healed that breach and gave Papunhank even more reason to pay attention to developments in the west.

Deciding to Move West

Jeremias's baptismal waters were barely dry when Zeisberger announced to his congregation that they were moving farther inland to lands along the Beaver River. A year and a half of fighting with Indian preacher Wangomen, the town's Seneca overseers, and other strong opponents in Goschgoschunk was enough. Relocating three miles away to Lawunakhannek had not markedly improved their situation, so the time had come to make a more dramatic move. Fortunately they had a place to go. Munsee chief Packanke had invited them the prior year to move to his town, Kaskaskunk (Kaskaskies or Kuskuskies or Kuskuski), and promised to let them choose their own piece of land on which to settle. He was far less interested in their Christian message than some other western Delaware headmen, but like them, he saw an opportunity to add to his numbers, and in the process, his power and prestige. For the same reasons, he was hoping that someday soon the much larger group of Friedenshütten residents would follow Zeisberger's lead and come to his town. He and other Ohio Indian leaders recognized that consolidation of Natives into more densely populated settlements might make them less vulnerable to the designs of white settlers.[29]

Meanwhile, the Six Nations had other ideas about where the Wyalusingites should end up. As noted earlier, they wanted to retain control over Indians on the Susquehanna. But in contrast to the assurances they gave one year earlier that the Wyalusingites could remain where they were, they now offered a different plan. Just as Zeisberger's troop headed to Kaskaskunk in April 1770, Gagohunt was sitting in Papunhank's house telling them that the "Chiefs of the 6 Nations think all the Indians from Hallobank, Schommunk, Schechschequanick, [and] Wichlusing should be moved to Aschcenneshik [Assinisink], to live together in a Town." Community leaders listened carefully to the proposal, reflected upon it, and then made clear they wanted no part of it:

> [To] live with other Indians in a town which does not believe in our ways and faith, this we cannot do and can't happen. We need to have a large piece of land for believers to live on alone, like the Indian chiefs in Kaskaskung have done and offered a large piece of land to Christian Indians. It's necessary, since we cannot move about every 3 or 4 years from place to place, leaving the houses we built and erecting new ones somewhere else. That would be difficult and couldn't be left in peace. We believed the 6 Nations placed us here permanently in Wichlusing to live here many years. That's why we built our houses, toiled here and were diligent. Now the land is sold. Now our uncles of the 6 Nations want us to relocate to another place, and then possibly again in another 3 or 4 years. We are not able to do this.[30]

Over the next two months, more dialogue ensued between Gagohunt and Papunhank over the Iroquois plan. The speeches quoted at the beginning of this chapter illustrate the perspective the Munsee prophet brought to those meetings. His Moravian brothers and sisters wanted to stay in Wyalusing, but if forced to move they needed sufficient land to sustain themselves. They also needed control over who lived in their community—no matter where it was—and what went on there. Moravian Indians were different. They wanted peace and quiet to live out their Christian faith and ethics unencumbered by the competing actions of nonbelieving neighbors. As Zeisberger put it rather less tactfully to Packanke in these same months, "we have rid ourselves of drinking, dancing, sacrificing, and feasting, of going to war, of the Indians' medicine and witchcraft, or worshipping strange gods, [and] lying and stealing." And they had no interest in more temporary moves, or in getting drawn into politically tricky land deals. So when the Iroquois offered them the modest sum of two dollars as payment for the lands they would lose in Wyalusing, its Natives sharply responded by saying, "We cannot accept this [money]. We had no land to sell. It is your land and therefore your money."[31]

By the end of June, Gagohunt agreed to take their message to other Six Nations chiefs, so Friedenshütten's residents breathed a sigh of relief. There the issue remained for the rest of 1770, providing a welcome respite. Schmick happily reported in December that "from the outside we have been little disturbed this year."[32] Yet Papunhank and others in the community must have continued to feel multiple pressures boring in on them. Indians to the north and west wanted them to move. That ultimately might be necessary but only acceptable if they were able to set the terms of their new living situation. There was certainly no guarantee that would happen given the power disparity between them and their overseers in New York or Ohio. Moreover, how would their current overseers, the Six Nations, react if they chose to join other Munsees and Delawares in the west? Wherever they moved, there was also no guarantee their presence would be welcomed by all or most other Indians in their new locale. The experience of Zeisberger's small congregation in Goschgoschunk made that abundantly clear.

They had already been forced to move twice, and it was not certain that their new home outside of Kaskaskunk would prove any more permanent. Meanwhile, whites in Pennsylvania, wherever they originated, were rapidly increasing in numbers, eager to get their hands on newly available lands and willing to use force for that purpose. Governor Penn had promised to look out for Friedenshütten, but he continued to have far bigger concerns. Distressing news of murders, kidnappings, and other types of raids in the Wyoming Valley regularly flowed into Friedenshütten. Deadly violence there impinged on their hunting territory and aroused fears that the conflict would spread farther north.[33] Their anxiety only intensified whenever rumors of an impending Indian war in the Ohio Country reached them. Cherokees and Senecas were once again killing one another, jeopardizing what little stability existed in the region.[34]

Friedenshütteners may have also felt pressure to move from Moravian leaders. As early as February 1769, Zeisberger wrote to Ettwein that "it has always seemed to me, as if our Indians would not stay there [Friedenshütten] long. Even if they should get the land from the governor which I do not think likely, it will become more and more difficult for them to live among the white people." That may have been more than a pragmatic observation on Zeisberger's part. As the front edge of the Moravian missionary effort, he likely wished to see its "center of gravity" move westward. That would help to bolster his evangelistic labors and enlarge the critical mass of Christian Indians in the Allegheny and beyond. His views may well have swayed Ettwein, Seidel, and other Bethlehem officials to be looking for the right moment to replant their thriving congregation in less contested lands. At the same time, it must be noted that Zeisberger remained suspicious of Ohio Indian motives in trying to attract them. As he wrote in April 1769, "As often as the Indians here on the Ohio have begun to call Indians away from the Susquehannan we have always been able to believe for sure that they do not have any good intentions, but that they must be up to something. Time will tell."[35]

Papunhank and Joshua Senior shared those concerns. When Anton sent an appeal in November 1769 urging the Friedenshütteners to move west and join them in Kaskaskunk, the two men pondered the request and then told Schmick, "Perhaps there is no good in this. . . . We are thinking that the Indians are looking for something else and perhaps when all the Indians from the Susquehanna are in Allegheny then they will make war." Convinced that "we did not place ourselves in Friedenshütten but the Savior did that," they wanted to "stay here as long as the Savior will have us and let us." To the prospect of relocating elsewhere, they replied, "What good are good land, pasture and wood to us if we cannot live in peace and quiet with each other and love the Savior." Fourteen months later in January 1771, Papunhank was still expressing those same concerns: "Why do they want us to move there? There are Brethren there now. Why won't they listen to the good words about the Savior and become converted? There are many of them, there must be something else behind all of this, which they are keeping hidden, and certainly nothing good."[36]

Papunhank likely understood Friedenshütten's predicament as a product of all these external forces pressing in upon them. But in retrospect, it is possible to see that some of its troubles were also self-made. Ironically, the community's very success threatened to subvert its survival in Wyalusing. Consider for example its comparative economic prosperity. It demonstrated the value of its lands, making them all the more appealing to white land speculators and potential settlers. White visitors were impressed with what the Moravian Indians had achieved there; they also dreamed of the profits they could make off that same property. Native visitors flocked to the town for food, both physical and spiritual. Many of them stuck around, their numbers eventually reaching levels the community believed it could not sustain. Yet Wyalusing's substantial population for an Indian town made it valuable to Native headmen elsewhere interested in enlarging their human and material resources. Bringing or keeping 150 or more peaceful Natives under their control was an attractive prospect to both the Ohio Delawares and the Six Nations. Some of those leaders were also drawn to the particular Christian message the Friedenshütteners would bring with them. It might provide the spiritual power and peaceful impulse needed to keep them well. Munsee sachem Allemewi in Goschgoschunk certainly thought so:

> The Indian priests in this district . . . will have to give up soon. The Indians do not believe in their cause any longer, and do not want to hear them anymore, but as they know that in Friedenshütten so many Indians have been converted they believe that the brethren must be offering them something different and better, and come to the conclusion that if anyone preaches the truth and the right way to happiness, it must be the brethren.[37]

Conversations over whether and where to move climaxed during the first nine months of 1771. The Six Nations remained worried about their Susquehanna Indian charges getting sucked into the Wyoming Valley conflict. Its violence intensified their desire to clear out the remaining pockets of Indians along the Susquehanna in Pennsylvania and resituate them somewhere safer and more controllable. Consequently, in late March they sent another strongly worded message to the Wyalusingites. They were particularly perturbed "because we have heard that one of your people (it was Job Chelloway) was present at the tumult between the people of Pennsylvania and New England. Their face was seen. Stay out of that mess or something very bad might occur." The Cayuga chief who delivered the message reinforced the point: "you have to abide by them or there will be dire consequences."[38]

With those reprimands and warnings still ringing in their ears, the town welcomed "the messenger Wangomen from Coschcoshing [Goschgoschunk]." He had been commissioned the prior two summers by Packanke to visit Friedenshütten but only now arrived with a letter from Zeisberger dated July 15, 1770. It stated that the western Delaware chiefs had invited all of the Susquehanna Indians to move to the Allegheny and were interested in having the Moravians "bring the words of the Gospel to them and their young people." Zeisberger's note conveyed enthusiasm for the prospect, and Wangomen, perhaps disingenuously, echoed it: "Chief Pakanke in Koschkaschung and the other Chiefs in Kekælemapæchünk [Gekelemukpechünk or Newcomer's Town] sent me here to invite all the local Indians to come to their lands and be received and embraced as friends. You will be able to select land yourselves, on which to live among other believers in peace. You may also bring your teachers with you as they are seen as being the same color."[39]

Friedenshütten now had a formal invitation to go west. Its Native leaders expressed thanks to Wangomen and those he represented but said, "We are too heavy at present to get up and go over."[40] Still, they must have been pleased at what had been promised, including the assurance that their white missionaries would not be looked upon as racial outsiders. Moravians were always insisting that their whites were not like other whites, just like they insisted that their Indians were not like other Indians.[41] For the moment, the western Delaware headmen were willing to believe them or at least claim that they did. Over the next few days, the town descended into lively debate over what to do. Men went to Schmick while women went to his wife asking for advice: "We told them to turn to the Savior prayerfully and be pious children and give everything, including this, to Him. Don't worry and let the Savior determine what is in our best interest." Those words encouraged resignation to the divine will. But they calmed very few Indian minds and souls; it's no wonder given how much more these Natives had at stake than the Schmicks. They could go back and live comfortably in Bethlehem. Moravian Indians weren't sure there was anywhere they could live comfortably. So they wrestled over the merits of the proposal, "many thought to leave, others to stay, and of course the elderly couldn't survive such a distance." Schmick found all of it to be "wasting so much of our time in useless thoughts and discussion."[42]

What Papunhank made of it all is unknown, but it is doubtful he thought the community was engaged in wasteful discussion. Evidence indicates that up to this point he was committed to keeping the community in Wyalusing. As noted before, he had plenty of reasons for wanting to remain there. Yet he also had a history of moving his people when the costs of staying put exceeded the risks of leaving. Had that point now been reached? Were their prospects in the Ohio Country sufficiently promising to take that risk?

Choices over removal bedeviled Native peoples over and over again in early America, and it only became worse in the nineteenth century. Usually there were benevolent whites telling them to go.[43] Friedenshütten proved no exception to that rule. When Bishop Nathanael Seidel visited the town with two German Moravian leaders a few weeks after Wangomen, he went so far as to declare that "it would be beneficial if some families moved to Kaschkoschkunk . . . so that as time passes more would be settled there." During his stay Seidel may have also encouraged, if not persuaded, the congregation to defer to the decision of Bethlehem officials about their removal. He made it an important agenda item for summer meetings since the future of Moravian missions in the Northeast once again hung in the balance. He called Zeisberger back to Bethlehem from the Ohio Country for the first time in three years to consult on the matter. The missionary spoke in favor of having the Indians of Friedenshütten and Schechschiquanünk join him in the west in spite of rising tides of disorder there. Frequent death threats, suicides, killings, and other disturbances shook Kaskaskunk, and Packanke seemed unable to do anything about them. That was hardly the sort of place you would want to bring Moravian Indians. But Zeisberger already had his sights set on moving all of them to the Muskingum Valley where Chief Netawatwees was ready to welcome them with land, protection, and Natives eager for Christian teaching. He had told Zeisberger as much when the missionary visited his town in March. Those potential benefits appeared very attractive when weighed against the legal realities of the Treaty of Fort Stanwix, vigilante warfare in the Wyoming Valley, white settlers inching closer with bottles of rum in hand, and Six Nations' pressure to consolidate their communities with non-Moravian towns. Little wonder, then, why Bethlehem, and divine providence, sided with Zeisberger and decided it was a good idea for them to move.[44]

Officials commissioned Zeisberger to deliver that "advice" to Friedenshütten and Schechschiquanünk on his way west in early September. Following the morning service on Friday the sixth, he shared with the community a letter from Seidel. In it he told them that "the Savior approved [most likely by the use of the lot] their request to move to the Ohio, and that they would have the blessing of those in Bethlehem as well." Had the congregation actually made such a request? Whatever the case, he advised them that "they should consider such a big decision thoroughly and ahead of time." He had sent Zeisberger to help them talk it through since he had much "experience with such things and is familiar with that area and its situation." "Much discussion ensued" as they considered various proposals about how and when such a move could be orchestrated. How, for example, would they have sufficient food during their first few months there? Memories of their subsistence crisis during their first months in Wyalusing must have come rushing back. When Zeisberger suggested that "he would have 10 acres near Lagundo-Utenünk planted with corn" before they arrived, "all previous concerns suddenly disappeared. It was decided then and resolved that everyone from here and Schechschequanik would journey together to the Ohio . . . next Spring in May."[45]

At long last the decision had been made. Zeisberger was noticeably pleased, and why not?[46] He had gotten the result he was looking for. His personal reassurances no doubt helped sway those Moravian Indians less inclined to believe that leaving Wyalusing was the right thing to do. Papunhank may have been among their number. Now he and others closed ranks with those eager to move and formed a united front that began to prepare for the next chapter in their life together.

A Poisonous Episode

Two weeks later those ranks fell apart. Like a wildfire, accusations suddenly flew through Friedenshütten that Johannes Papunhank was a witch. He possessed a "powerful and terrible poison," *Máchtapasseèk*, and used it to sicken and even kill friends and neighbors. It was evil and unless he got rid of it, his accusers were ready to get rid of him.[47] Some of them eventually went to his home and "intended to drag him out and kill him."[48] Never before had Papunhank faced such overt opposition from within his own community. Even in the turmoil of early 1763 when many in Wyalusing had decided to stop listening to his preaching, no one in the community had threatened his life.

Where did this intense animosity come from, who was involved, and why was it happening?

The immediate source of contention was a wave of illness and death in Friedenshütten that began in May and continued into September. It was nothing like the epidemics of 1764 in Philadelphia, but enough people were sick, and with a few dying, it made them wonder who or what was responsible. Healing remedies were doing little good. Apparently some more powerful "medicine" was at work here. Delawares and Munsees traditionally believed that some shamans had the ability to harm others through supernatural means including secret poisons. Living with German Moravians would not have necessarily disabused them of that idea since these Europeans were not of one mind on whether shamans could possess such powers. Perhaps Papunhank did. He had long ago testified to Job Chillaway and others that during his adult vision quest his manitou had given him special knowledge of the "Virtues, and Nature of Several Herbs, Roots, Plants & Trees and the different Relation they had one to another." Ever since then he had likely practiced healing arts, including providing medicine to Billy Chillaway's wife, Job's sister-in-law, after she was bitten by a copperhead snake the summer before. She recovered, but had Papunhank now turned his powers to more sinister ends? His accusers thought so and insisted that he had possessed the poison "many years ago and likely still has some." Such a claim seemed credible to some Friedenshütteners because it came from none other than Job Chillaway. Few if any in the town had known Papunhank longer or been more familiar with his spiritual work in the years before he became a Moravian.[49]

Oniem, possibly a shaman himself, joined Job in lashing out against Johannes. Both men had recently suffered great personal losses. Chillaway's wife had become gravely ill in May and spent the next few weeks suffering from consumption and seeking to confirm her salvation. She was "in a very pious state of longing for the Savior and His precious gifts of grace and mercy," and was baptized on Pentecost Sunday, May 19, along with her sister-in-law, Billy's wife, but sadly died four weeks later. Oniem's sister Lea and her husband Jonas became sick in August and died within three days of one another. Nine days later, Gottlieb, a seventeen-year-old orphan who spent most of his life as part of Job Chillaway's household, also passed away.[50] Amid these heartbreaking events, Job and Oniem must have wondered why Papunhank the healer had failed them so miserably. Or was this no failure at all but instead a manifestation of his evil powers? Had he singled them out for punishment? Was this his way of getting back at Chillaway for one transgression or another: jeopardizing their relationship with the Six Nations by showing up in the Wyoming Valley? Failing to become a baptized convert? Negotiating with the Pennsylvania government for a land title to Wyalusing without the town's authorization?

Whatever Papunhank's reasons for attacking their families, Chillaway and Oniem privately circulated their concerns about him and found some sympathetic listeners. Most surprising among them were Joshua Senior and his wife Bathsheba. As longtime Moravian converts and close associates of Papunhank in work and marriage, they might have been expected to be among the first to defend him against such serious accusations. Instead, Joshua refused to be dissuaded of their truth by Schmick when they conferred privately about the matter and then publicly accused Johannes and two others in the community of having the poison on September 23 at a town meeting. He seems to have believed Papunhank was guilty even before Chillaway and Oniem came back from Zeninga and Hallobank claiming that chiefs there had confirmed Papunhank's possession of the poison. Joshua's willingness to believe the worst in this moment likely stemmed from both ethnic and personal reasons. As noted before, he and other Mahicans in Friedenshütten periodically felt marginalized and lorded over by the Delaware/Munsee majority in the town, led by Papunhank. They likely worried that the same would happen again in the Ohio Country. Joshua may have resented the wide authority given the Munsee reformer, especially since he had been a Moravian far longer and been one of Papunhank's spiritual teachers on his early visits to Nain. The new wave of disease may have also brought back memories of the large number of Mahican deaths in Philadelphia in contrast to the Wyalusingites there who escaped unscathed. They were tempted to think that Papunhank may have been responsible for those outcomes as well as for the recent losses. Joshua and Bathsheba had long talked about poison as the source of their people's harm. Whether they or Chillaway or Oniem first floated the possibility that Papunhank was the supplier, they all now believed it. As the community looked ahead to life farther west, they concluded that it best chasten the one responsible for its misery and keep him from having the same kind of power there that he had here.[51]

Munsee clan conflicts may have also underlay the controversy. It is possible that Oniem spoke for the more militant and generally anti-Christian Wolf phratry against Turkey clan member Papunhank. They attacked him "for his failure to restore a land base in ceded territory with the help of the Moravians and for having surrendered to their social and political control." In other words, Papunhank had accommodated too much. The recent decision to abandon Friedenshütten made clear that his strategy of partnering with Moravians, the Pennsylvania government, and the Six Nations to secure a homeland for Munsees in the east had not worked. Munsees needed a different approach and new leadership.[52]

Some combination, then, of grief over lives lost, worries over their future in the west, ethnic tensions, clan rivalries, power struggles, and personal resentments led some town members to employ ancient beliefs to explain current events. The notion that some malevolent person or force was responsible for their woes was not so hard to believe among people desperate to make sense of familial and communal losses. And Papunhank, as suggested above, was a logical target. But he would have none of it. He was quick to deny their damning accusations. When confronted with them at the public gathering on the twenty-third he exclaimed, "Everything you say is a lie. Just listen; when I was baptized, I was cleansed of Satan and his works through the Savior's blood, and I rest in his wounds, protected from all such evil; I have been freed from this." Whatever hold evil or Satan might have had on him before his conversion was over, he claimed; he now simply wanted to live in communion with the loving Savior. Moreover, he had never knowingly had the poison and certainly didn't have it now.[53]

Most of the community believed him, but the matter was far from settled. His opponents rallied that night on the other side of the Susquehanna and screamed insults across the water. Invoking traditional Delaware and Munsee beliefs, they claimed that "the man who gave it [the poison] to him would appear and convince him to give it up. If he refuses, he will die." Hearing such prophecies and threats, Papunhank defiantly yelled back, "I've already told you, I have no such thing, and that is the truth. God knows this, so let your Indian come. I'm certain no Indian will come and convince me of such a story." In the next few days, no Indian visitant appeared. Instead Papunhank, Schmick, and Roth sent well-known go-between Joseph Peepy and another Native from Schechschiquanünk to the sachems in Zeninga and Hallobank to verify Chillaway and Oniem's claims. They returned on October 1 with the news that all the chiefs there categorically denied saying that Papunhank had poison. They had spoken with Chillaway and Oniem when they had visited recently but had said no such things about Papunhank or anyone else. As a result, they were "surprised" and "saddened by the words and the lies" the two had spread. According to Peepy, they were so troubled that such statements were attributed to them that they wept as they exonerated Papunhank and described the whole affair as the "work of the devil."[54]

Rumblings and divisions over the accusations persisted, but gradually reconciliation came to the community. Chillaway and Oniem weren't immediately ready to give up their beliefs about Papunhank but had increasingly few allies and were widely ridiculed. Even the town's young people came to Papunhank's defense and "threatened with harsh words those who would do him harm." Back on September 24, less than twenty-four hours after the original accusations had been made, some of the accusers were already having second thoughts. Three of them, Joshua Senior, Elias, and Daniel, came to Schmick and asked that "the congregation might no longer speak of this troubling matter." Over the next few days, Joshua was not sure what to think about Papunhank or his own Christian faith, so even before Peepy returned he left on a hunting trip that brought him eventually to Bethlehem. There he consulted with Seidel and others about the affair and apparently gained some peace of mind. He returned to Friedenshütten and on October 27, with a contrite spirit, confessed to the congregation, asked for forgiveness, and "declared that from now on he does not want to have anything else to do with such deceitful matters and tales." A week later "he joined us in Holy Communion, after he had first reconciled himself especially with Brother Johannes." It took Bathsheba three additional months to reach the point of "asking forgiveness for the sadness created by her participation in the whole affair of the poison and the damage it did to her faith." The gathered members responded by singing to her in Mahican, "Lord forgive us our manifold sins as we ourselves forgive."[55]

Papunhank must have been pleased to hear those words of confession, but they alone could not heal the deep wound he had suffered. It was one thing to be attacked by an unbelieving outsider like Oniem. That might be expected, especially if Oniem were a shaman himself accustomed to working with the mysteries of curses and cures. It was another thing to have his longtime associate, neighbor, and translator, Job Chillaway, turn against him. Yet he could not have been completely surprised that Job was among his chief accusers. The two men had had mounting conflicts in recent months. First, they had disagreed over Chillaway's application to get title to the Wyalusing lands. Then Papunhank leveled a series of complaints to Schmick which he hoped would be passed on to the governor about Chillaway's actions in the Wyoming conflict, which not only reflected badly on Wyalusing as a whole but included bringing a New England settler to live in his house. The colonist had now fenced ten acres, depriving others of using that land to pasture cattle. The Munsee worried that this was the first step in Chillaway bringing in more whites, grabbing more land for his exclusive use (he had already "taken 4 farms for himself"), and "act[ing] like their master here."[56] Still, was all that reason enough for Chillaway to think that Johannes was an evil sorcerer?

Worse yet for Papunhank, baptized communicants had joined with the accusers. The controversy did not simply pit nonbelievers versus believers. Instead, some of his Moravian brothers and sisters, including his son-in-law's parents, Joshua Senior and Bathsheba, perhaps some of his closest friends, believed that he was capable of nothing less than murder. How could they think these things after all he had done for this people—all the sacrifices made, all the kindnesses shown, all the dangers endured, all the tasks performed, all the evidences of his Christianity demonstrated? Hadn't he built up enough trust with them to receive the benefit of the doubt when his character was being attacked so violently? Schmick's unwavering support and belief in his innocence likely cushioned these blows, as did his participation in the daily round of religious services that went on despite the community upheaval. But in early October the missionary acknowledged how hard an experience it had been: "Dear Johannes and his wife have had a difficult time for 8 days and it has deeply hurt us, them, and all who have had no part or belief in it." Even once vindicated, feelings of betrayal must have persisted. Everyone knew how much Papunhank abhorred wickedness. His fervor for doing the right thing and wanting others to act righteously long predated his turn to Christianity. To now be falsely accused of gross wrongdoing discouraged him and left him vulnerable to wanting to repay evil for evil. He would have to work hard to repress feelings of self-righteousness, bitterness, resentment, and a desire for revenge. In the end, his apparent openness to reconciling with Joshua within a few weeks testifies to his forgiving nature and the strength of his character. And his words in the midst of the crisis testify to the solace his Christian faith provided: "If it be His will, and I be taken from this life through these lies, I will have lost nothing. I will be redeemed in an instant from all peril. I will proceed to my Savior. I would regret only leaving my wife and child." That said, it is hard not to imagine that he and Anna Johanna more than once uttered words during this affair akin to what Plains Indians exclaimed in the next century: "Our hearts fell to the ground."[57]

Final Days on the Susquehanna

If his courage occasionally faltered in the dark days of that autumn, by winter Papunhank was back in "good health and spirits" exercising whatever leadership the community needed.[58] Much of its energies over the next six months were poured into preparing for the move west.

Alongside the organizational and physical labor that required, there was still more diplomatic work to be done. At the eleventh hour, the Six Nations made one more bid to keep the Susquehanna Indians under their control. Meanwhile, persistent foes—hunger and land-hungry whites—returned in the spring, more evidence that however painful, the day had come for Friedenshütteners to move on.

As the advance guard of Moravians in the west, David Zeisberger and his young missionary colleague John Heckewelder spent the fall of 1771 and the early months of 1772 getting ready for the arrival of the migrants from Friedenshütten and Schechschiquanünk. Their roughly 200 people would add substantially to the 125 Indians now at Zeisberger's mission on the Beaver River. Questions remained as to whether Lagundo Utenünk (called Friedensstadt by the Moravians) was the right place for them all to live. Interference from unruly neighboring Indians and revelations that Delawares in the region did not actually own the land on which they were living (it was Seneca land) made them increasingly uneasy. In January Packanke finally handed over a wampum belt from Netawatwees after more than a year of delay with the message that all the Moravians were welcome to resettle in the Muskingum Valley. With that word, sentiment in Lagundo Utenünk swung strongly in favor of moving farther west. They made no official decision, however, until Zeisberger and three of his Native assistants, including Papunhank's brother-in-law, Lucas Gatschenis, went to Gekelemukpechünk in March to scout the area and to discuss with the chief the particular wants and needs of the Brethren. As before, the missionary highlighted their desire "to live by ourselves," and expressed the promise to "endeavor to be at peace with everyone." When Netawatwees warmly reciprocated with assurances of good land, separation from other Natives, and interest in hearing the gospel, Moravian minds were settled. Within a few weeks, they were loading canoes and packing horses on their way to yet another new home.[59]

Back in Friedenshütten, leaders finalized plans in February and March about how the move would be made. Most residents would depart together in late May or June, split into two groups. A party led by John Ettwein would travel by land; another under John Roth and his wife would go by water. They would transport people and goods first to Lagundo Utenünk and remain there until adequate provision could be made for them in the Muskingum Valley. Bethlehem officials promised their support and urged the town to send representatives to Philadelphia to lobby the governor and legislature for compensation for the buildings they had constructed at Wyalusing. They chose Papunhank and Joshua Senior for that assignment but instructed them to go first to Schechschiquanünk to deal with a more pressing matter.[60]

There they would meet with Cayuga and Mohawk chiefs and settle once and for all relations with the Six Nations. In January the Iroquois requested that Wyalusing send delegates to Chemung to talk with them. Papunhank and Cornelius, another older Munsee convert, were commissioned to go but they stopped en route when they heard reports of a possible murder there. A few days later, a messenger arrived with three belts of wampum and a last-ditch plea to area Delawares and Munsees. It began by asking "forgiveness for the blood shed in the previous war." The Six Nations hoped that memories of their destruction of Susquehanna River towns including Wyalusing in 1764 could now be suppressed. They went further and expressed the hope that from now on, Delawares, Munsees, and the Six Nations could be "one body, one vein and blood in our affairs." All that led up to their main point:

> Uncles in Schommunk, Hallobank, Wichlusing and Schechschequanünk! We want to speak from the heart now and tell you something which brings joy to you and to us. Uncles! We give to you the land on the *Tiaogu* [Tioga], an excellent piece of land, on which you should reside. And when you have lived there long enough, you can sell it and receive flour for it. Uncles! This land we give to you in order to make amends now for that which happened earlier and had been so difficult.[61]

The Six Nations' offer sought to heal old wounds, but it was too little and too late and failed to guarantee to the Moravian Indians what they really wanted—relative separation from other Natives, almost total isolation from whites, and a permanent homeland. Consequently, Friedenshütten's representatives had their negative response ready within twenty-four hours. But the opportunity to voice it did not come until early April. By that point the Six Nations had requested another meeting, and the community understood the importance of going to "listen to them and tell them our firm resolution to move to Allegena." To remain silent "would not bode well" for them: "the 6 Nations would be insulted if we moved from Wichlusing without telling them." Chances are Papunhank counseled this wise course of action. He had long navigated relations with the Six Nations carefully. This was no time to deviate from that pattern. He therefore went with Joshua Senior up river and heard the Iroquois repeat their offer of a new dwelling place for them and other Susquehanna Indians. That evening the two Moravians delivered their answer:

> Uncles! You know that the land of Wichlusing on which we have lived for the last 7 years was sold to the white man. We heard this, were quiet, and waited 2 years for you to come and tell us it had happened. But no one came. From Allegana however, we received last summer words from our friends there, the Chiefs, as follows: my friends, I will come to you. I'll take you by the hand and will lead you to our land. Here you may choose some land to your liking, living there in peace and quiet since your land of Wichlusing has been sold. We accepted this offer and promised to move there. We cannot go back on our word and handshake. We are moving to be among familiar Indians. These are your and our friends both. The house and fire there you already know. Uncles! You come too late. We do thank you for your generous offer and consideration.

Those words expressed the frustration and resolve of the Friedenshütteners. Iroquois choices had put them in a precarious position. They were now making their own choice to entrust their future independence to a different set of uncles. With resignation, the Six Nations accepted their decision but couldn't resist sending them on their way with one final warning and prophesy: "Consider well beforehand whereto you wish to move, so that you don't regret it. There may be death there and it might not go well there for you."[62]

With one diplomatic assignment completed, another one could begin. Johannes and Joshua now traveled to Philadelphia to appeal to the governor and legislature and to hold a private meeting with influential Quakers. From there they would go to Bethlehem to consult with Moravian leaders. For Papunhank, it must have brought back strong memories of earlier years when he was shuttling around trying to maintain firm alliances to ensure his people's peace and security. Those purposes were still at play for him in 1772; the more immediate concern, however, was getting financial help. Governor Richard Penn heard their plans to move and request for compensation for the improvements they had made at Wyalusing, but he claimed that only the colony's proprietors (his two brothers) could determine if they were entitled to payment. He also lamented that they were leaving Pennsylvania at this time rather than a year from now since it "may be injurious to the Government and the interest of the Proprietaries," a reference perhaps to Penn's concerns about who would settle in the vacated Wyalusing lands. He may have also regretted losing the Wyalusing Indians for their potential diplomatic value. Though nothing came of it, during the prior summer an advisor to his brother had proposed using the "neutral" Indians at Wyalusing as envoys with the Connecticut settlers who were holding a group of Pennsylvanians hostage. Appeals to the assembly went a bit better; they formally thanked the legislature for its past provision and care, especially during their Philadelphia captivity, and for "the present" it was now providing. The meeting with Friends yielded even more fruit. They supplied $100 to assist with the upcoming journey, a means of renewing their "old friendship" and planting seeds for greater Quaker connections to Ohio Indians.[63]

As their departure date approached, the Moravians once again dealt with two old nemeses, insufficient food and bothersome whites. Throughout May, hunger became "an unwelcome and powerful visitor." Supplies of corn had been exhausted, so community members went out looking for wild potatoes, beans, and anything else they could find to eat, much as they had done during their first weeks in Wyalusing in 1765. Pained with hunger, the town was in no mood for the colonists who showed up from Wyoming eager to "purchase the *Saal* (meeting house) and two other houses. We told them it was not mannerly of them and they were behaving poorly." Even worse, some white traders in the area engaged anew in fraud. They were using "lead Dollar coins" to buy Indian horses and cattle.[64] Papunhank must have shaken his head in disgust at renewed attempts to cheat Natives.

Perhaps that distasteful reality made it a bit easier for him to come to final terms with exiting Wyalusing. Nevertheless, it must have been hard to leave the place behind. All things considered, he had built a good life there. Giving it up was a sacrifice and a disappointment. He was frustrated to be once again forced out of his home and lands by the machinations of more powerful whites and Natives. He had seen that pattern occur over and over again for Munsees, Delawares, and other Indians in his sixty-plus years. Accommodating to new realities would be nothing new. But it got tougher as he got older, and what lay ahead in the west might require even more change than past moves. He was certainly going to be out of his geographical comfort zone there. Whatever opportunities the Muskingum Valley might afford, leaving Wyalusing probably felt like a defeat. There no one had worked harder than him to make the community a success, and a success it was. Materially speaking, its Indians including Papunhank were comparatively well-off. He had two log cabins (no other Native had more than one), a garden, and a stable. Impressive as that was, it almost certainly meant less to him than the peace, security, and relative independence he had helped Friedenshütten enjoy for the past seven years. Those assets in turn facilitated the community's religious prosperity, despite the uncertainties that filled their larger world. The fledgling refugee congregation of 1765 had more than doubled in size, baptizing over a hundred persons and enlarging its communicant base.[65] It had also spawned two new Moravian Indian communities in Schechschiquanünk and Lagundo Utenünk. Papunhank took pride in that growth and likely took heart in knowing that in the Ohio Country all those brothers and sisters would be joined together. Moreover, they included more and more of his kin. Their recent choices to become baptized Christians almost certainly were influenced by his choice to pursue that path and to stick with it. Many of them had listened to his prophetic voice before 1763 and were now following his lead again. In that way, as in so many others, he played a large role in the perpetuation and growth of Moravian Indian Christianity.

Papunhank's own identity as a Moravian Indian Christian had dramatically deepened during his Friedenshütten years. At least since his adult vision quest, the Munsee's spirituality was of the emotional, passionate variety. Encounters with the supernatural were no mere intellectual exercises. Among the United Brethren, he found a home where that could continue. Whether gazing upon religious art, confessing his sins, counseling others, or contemplating the Savior's wounds, his tears flowed freely. They were an expression of his tender spirit and devotion to Jesus. Other scholars have proposed that many Native males were drawn to Jesus as the ultimate martyred warrior who endured his cruel treatment with stoic fortitude.[66] However true that was for Papunhank, it seems equally likely that he found in Jesus the ultimate peacemaker, the one who turned away from violence and war and demonstrated through his wounds the power of love to heal the world. Papunhank loved to hear and speak and feel that truth. How fitting then, that the baptism of his daughter, Anna Paulina, was one of the final acts in Friedenshütten. As she was baptized "in Jesus' death . . . our hearts burned with piety and our gratitude for such a blessed day in our lives of faith was indescribable. With tear-soaked cheeks we recognized Him for this most blessed of church ceremonies in our community."[67] Papunhank's cheeks were still wet when four days later he left Wyalusing forever.

7

Ohio Endings

Two years into their Ohio Country sojourn in 1774, Papunhank and other Moravian Indians struggled to hold onto their fleeting hopes of finding a peaceful, quiet homeland. Wars and rumors of war once again shook their worlds with fear and uncertainty, an all too familiar reality for Native peoples within early America. Now angry Shawnees and Mingos fought Virginians in a conflict known as Lord Dunmore's War. Natives resented white intrusions into their prized hunting grounds south of the Ohio River, an access ceded to colonials by the Six Nations in the Treaty of Fort Stanwix. From late 1773 on, Shawnee leaders endeavored to enlist Native allies in their fight. The Delawares at Gekelemukpechünk were high on their list.

Thanks to the peace advocacy of Moravian Indian brothers, however, Netawatwees and the Delaware Council refused to join the hostilities. That at least is how David Zeisberger explained that moment's diplomatic dynamics:

> When they [the Shawnee] first began acting with hostility toward the White people, they had surely not imagined things would be like this, but had believed they would be able to get the *Delaware* on their side. This might well have happened if it were not for both of our *Towns* [Schönbrunn and Gnadenhütten], because fear would have moved them to join them. We recently had evidence enough of this when *Captain White Eye* [war captain of the

Delaware Council, a peace proponent, and a Moravian ally] was gone for so long. He also realizes that we are a good support for him; if it were not for the Brothers he could not reach his goal of keeping the *Delaware* at peace.[1]

Zeisberger's account points to the ongoing peace work of Native Brethren whether or not it was an accurate assessment of Moravian influence on Delaware decision-making. Not surprisingly, Papunhank remained in the middle of it. In mid-July 1774 he was one of four Native Moravians summoned to consult with the council on whether the Indians living in Gekelemukpechünk and in the two Moravian towns "should flee or remain since 8 parties of *Shawnee* had gone out to murder." They responded that they would stay put "as long as we could until we see that there was really danger. We would keep the peace recently concluded with the [Six] *Nations*. If we fled now, it would look like we were not standing firmly." Three days later, White Eyes came to Schönbrunn "to talk with our wisest Indian Brothers and consider what was best for the *Delaware Nation* and both of our *Towns*, and also what they still had to say to the *Virginians* about the *Shawnee*, because they could not quite figure it out in *Gekelemukpechünk*."[2] The Moravians welcomed White Eyes' mediating efforts and shared with him their hopes for peace. Likely drawing on Papunhank's diplomatic wisdom and his role as overseer of external affairs for the community, White Eyes delivered a message to the Virginians at Pittsburgh the following week that extolled the peaceable character of the Indians living in Gekelemukpechünk, Schönbrunn, and Gnadenhütten. He explained that all white troops should avoid Delaware towns since the Shawnees had abandoned that area. If an expedition against the Shawnees was forthcoming, the militia had no need to intimidate or endanger other Native communities.[3]

Papunhank would have preferred, of course, that all parties lay down their arms sooner rather than later. War remained for him a very bad option, even when grievances were legitimate. Odds are he understood Shawnee and Mingo frustration. He knew what it was like to live with the consequences of decisions made by other Natives and whites. And he could certainly empathize with their anger over the unprovoked murders of at least nine or ten of their villagers in May 1774. Their quest in the current conflict for some greater autonomy from the sometimes heavy hand of the Iroquois Confederacy, the maneuverings of British and colonial officials, and the seemingly inexorable push of white settlement was another expression of the longstanding Indian quest for independence in the Ohio Country begun in the Seven Years' War and bound to continue for another generation.[4]

Coming to the Muskingum Valley in the summer of 1772 embodied the Moravian Indians' own continued quest for independence. Papunhank and other community leaders brought no illusions that their move to Ohio would free them completely from others' oversight. But in leaving Friedenshütten and Schechschiquanünk they had made a conscious choice to link their futures to the western Delawares and the promises of their chiefs, and to leave behind the protection and prodding of the Six Nations and the Pennsylvania government. They were weary of the political intrigue and diplomatic hedging that had long left their status along the Susquehanna in limbo. They hoped that they were not in for more of the same in their new locale. But they were not that fortunate. They soon discovered that promises made to woo them west became harder to sustain and honor once Moravians and their white teachers had moved to the region.

So alongside staying out of war, Native Brethren once again struggled to gain clear rights to their new homelands during their first years in Ohio. Those were familiar battles for Papunhank. He had been fighting them for much of his adult life, just like his Munsee ancestors. Their search for a secure home had begun at least as early as the arrival of Europeans in their lands in the late sixteenth century. Now two hundred years later, the struggle continued. By 1772 it had sapped much of Papunhank's energy and perhaps even his will to live. No wonder he reportedly said "a number of times during the journey [from Friedenshütten to Ohio] that if he reached the destination and the Indian congregation was well established again, he would gladly lay his bones down to rest."[5] The Creator afforded him a bit more time, however. Long enough, in fact, to witness in the last six months of his life much of what he had longed for, prayed for, and worked for. Plenty of storm clouds were gathering on other horizons in May 1775, but for Johannes Papunhank the sun shone rather brightly as he finally did lay down his bones.

Moving West

Seven years after their difficult trudge to Wyalusing, Moravian Indians migrated again in June and July of 1772. More than two hundred of them slogged their way through a largely unfamiliar portion of the Pennsylvania woods on foot or in canoes, with cattle and horses in tow. They went first to the mission outpost at Lagundo Utenünk on the Beaver River. From there most of them would soon travel to the Muskingum River and join the small band of Native believers sent ahead by Zeisberger earlier that spring to initiate the Moravian presence in Ohio and grow food for the later migrants. All of them were once more starting over, with no guarantees that life would be better or even as good as what they had left behind.

If the eight-week journey was any indication of what the future held, the Moravians were in for a hard time. Once in Lagundo Utenünk, John Ettwein tried to put a good face on the whole enterprise, expressing "praise and gratitude to the Lord, on arriving here, for all His mercies and goodness vouchsafed to us thus far on this memorable journey." But even he couldn't help but recite a litany of misfortunes that had befallen them along the way: a measles outbreak, rattlesnakes everywhere (he claimed they killed close to fifty), bad weather, biting gnats and mosquitoes, interfering whites, complaining Indians (especially about there being no flour, corn, or beans), screaming children, insufficient food, poor trails, impassable swamps, and uncooperative animals. It was a wonder no one was seriously injured or killed, for "among the rocks, and the broken timbers, we fell countless times. Sister Roth fell from her horse four times—once with her child [a ten-month-old] into a bog, up to her middle, and once into the bushes backwards from her horse, with her child, and once she hung on the stirrup." Such experiences left her husband writing on June 28, "For me this was a real Job's day:

one misfortune after the other befalling me, so that the eyes of both myself and my wife overflowed."[6]

Papunhank's survival skills were considerably better than those of the Roths, but even for him, the journey was demanding. He spent much of it doing what he always did in the woods—hunting. Along with one companion, he took on the responsibility of providing an almost daily supply of meat for the travelers, bagging 150 deer in all, though only three bears (perhaps an indication that the bear population was already in significant decline in western Pennsylvania). Hard work that often required him to be out and about while others rested, hunting for the group likely gave him a sense of personal satisfaction and self-importance. The community was once again literally dependent upon him for its sustenance. His reward came in seeing "the great joy of the hungry" whenever he arrived back in camp with fresh kills.[7]

Whatever the physical challenges, a different element of the trip may have distressed Papunhank even more. Recurring ethnic tensions between Mahican Moravians and Delaware and Munsee Brethren resurfaced. Members of the latter tribes may not have harbored any ill will toward the Mahicans. But the Mahicans, and most especially Joshua Senior, remained uneasy about the relationship. He wanted to ensure that things would be different in their new home. He was apparently still reeling from the troubles of the prior autumn and still resenting what he considered the maltreatment of his people by the Delaware/Munsee majority (including Papunhank as one of its principal leaders). Consequently, during the journey he sent "messages and belts to the Chiefs [Netawatwees in Gekelemukpechünk] in the name of the Mahicans" and thereby "started separate negotiations" with the western Delawares. Joshua wanted their approval to establish a second Moravian town in the Muskingum basin where Mahicans would have the largest say. This idea had already been floated to authorities in Bethlehem, and the white missionaries had discussed it several times among themselves in Lagundo Utenünk in the two weeks following their arrival. On August 17, though Joshua had yet to arrive with a third and final group of migrants from the Susquehanna, the missionaries decided that they did "not object, indeed would like it if his Mahicans and some Delawares would start a separate settlement." It is unknown whether Papunhank supported that pragmatic plan. It's likely, however, that he was more disappointed by Joshua's attitude than his actions. Their restored friendship in the aftermath of the poison accusations had clearly not alleviated the Mahican's conviction that his people had not and would not get a square deal if they were once again a minority in a Delaware-dominated town. They wanted more autonomy to do things their way and in their language, one more Indian quest for independence.[8]

Navigating intertribal relations among Moravian believers was clearly going to remain one of the issues facing Brethren leaders in the Ohio Country. Who was going to serve in those leadership positions was determined while the more than three hundred Indian Brethren were briefly clustered at Lagundo Utenünk. When the decisions had been finalized, Papunhank and his kin figured prominently among those given special authority. Leaders selected his nuclear family to be among the first to move to Schönbrunn, or in the Delaware language, Welhik Thuppeck, a name meaning "lovely spring." Once there, his instructions were to go almost immediately to meet with Netawatwees and the Delaware Council in Gekelemukpechünk and serve as the principal spokesperson for all the migrating Moravians. He and Nathanael Davis were also appointed to be the lay heads of the Schönbrunn congregation and to serve with six other men as the Board of Overseers for Schönbrunn and Lagundo Utenünk. Those eight persons plus an additional seventeen Native men and women, including Papunhank's wife, Anna Johanna, and four others of their kin, would be the Helpers' Conference (Native church assistants) for both places. Johannes would also serve on a committee charged with translating into the Delaware language more of the Bible, as well as the Lord's Prayer.[9]

With those assigned responsibilities, Papunhank trekked five more days, arriving in Welhik Thuppeck with his family on August 23. According to Ettwein, the prospective settlement had

> a very beautiful location in a plain, some 10 miles in length and several miles in breadth near one very large spring and several other

> fine small ones. They, together, give rise to a creek, on which one can paddle during most of the year right up to the settlement itself and the Muskingham river is a stretch of very rich bottom land, more than half a mile wide and probably 5 miles long, suitable for Indian corn; it is covered almost entirely by walnut and locust trees.[10]

The missionary was clearly impressed with the transportation and agricultural advantages of the site. Those were no mere luxuries, as Papunhank well knew from his years in Wyalusing and other spots along the Susquehanna. Adequate food supplies would be essential for the viability of the new Moravian towns, a truth made plainer when word greeted them in Schönbrunn of a terrible famine ravaging the broader region that summer. Many starving Ohio Valley Indians looking for food had drifted into the tiny settlement set up by the vanguard of Native Brethren.[11]

No time was to be lost then in establishing a more permanent town. Forty lots were plotted and perpendicular streets staked out within the first couple of days, much on the model of Friedenshütten. An experienced town planner, Papunhank likely helped supervise the operation. The meeting house would stand at the intersection of two short roads, with the two missionary cabins placed adjacent to it, one on each side. Papunhank's plot was the next one to the left, his brother Jeremias's the next one to the right, followed by his brother-in-law Lucas's. Together they surrounded the missionary enterprise, literal visual reminders of the core place Johannes and his kin held within this new phase of Moravian outreach. The family's growing numbers made the same point. Even before he had arrived, in late June Lucas's sister brought her family of ten from Gekelemukpechünk to live there. Then in early August, Lucas and Paulina's newborn daughter, Anna, became the first person baptized at the new settlement. She was the first fruits in what Native Moravians hoped would be their long-term homeland.[12]

A Moravian Vision

To secure that homeland, the newly arrived Moravian leaders went promptly to see Netawatwees and his council. Contrary to the claims of one historian, who described their meeting as "nothing more than a courtesy call" to the Delaware headmen in keeping with "Indian protocol and good manners," the Native Brethren brought a crucial agenda to Gekelemukpechünk.[13] They were there to secure further assurances of their right to settle in the area, live and worship as they pleased, and be protected from outside forces. Their prior experiences in Pennsylvania, and particularly in Friedenshütten, made them especially anxious to get those matters settled. Enormous amounts of time and energy, not to mention stress and worry, had gone into their repeated negotiations with the Six Nations before and after the Treaty of Fort Stanwix. Even if they had ultimately had to move, being attentive to those relations had at least given them seven relatively peaceful, prosperous years. No one knew or understood those diplomatic lessons better than Papunhank. He'd been at it for the past quarter century, carving out spaces for his communities to persist in worlds very often filled with violence and hatred. He was long accustomed to using the power of ritual and word to gain favor and broker peace.

No surprise then that Papunhank was chosen to make the Moravians' case at Gekelemukpechünk. Disappointed no doubt because the whole town was coming off a four-day drinking binge and only four chiefs were there to hear his speech, Papunhank nevertheless proceeded according to longstanding Native protocols. Seated in a circle on the floor of Netawatwees's house, he began by presenting a series of wampum belts that ritually "wiped their eyes and cleaned their ears, so that they might see and hear us well" (words reminiscent of the Iroquois' Woods Edge Ceremony). He then brought greetings from all the new migrants, acknowledged receipt of the chief's messages inviting them to move west, and expressed thanks "for the piece of land which they had set aside for the believers." The Munsee made sure they knew that the Christian Indians had brought their white teachers with them in accord with the invitation offered. He also indicated that they had already begun to build at Welhik Thuppeck and might in the future establish another nearby settlement or two. Papunhank then laid out some Moravian expectations: The Brethren depended on there being no other Indians allowed to settle "within the borders of their district." Such people might harm their cattle. Worse yet, they might injure Moravian children amid drunken escapades. Next he acknowledged that the chiefs had already heard from Zeisberger about how the Brethren lived, but he wanted them to hear it again, this time from the mouth of a fellow Native. As historian David Silverman has written about Mohegan preacher Samson Occom in another context, "the resonance of [his] words extended from his status as a fellow Indian and his employment of Indian protocol. In Indian country, a message was only as strong as the identity of the messenger and the way in which it was delivered." What followed, as Ettwein transcribed it, was a précis of Moravian Indian belief and practice:

> We believe in the true and only God and hear His Word gladly; we hear it gladly every day, and therefore we have our teachers to live with us. We love peace with everyone and never want to get involved in any war. Because we know the harm that rum works, therefore we will not tolerate any to be brought upon our land or into our settlements. We do not have any special chiefs in our town, but we are all Brethren. When you wish to send words to us, send them to the Brethren in Welhik-Tuppeek; and call us the Brethren. When you hear anything evil of us, do not believe such lies, but ask us, and we will tell you the truth. Whenever the chiefs [in Gekelemukpechünk] have some good undertaking in hand, we will gladly help with it and contribute to it, as others do. Never be concerned about the white Brethren among us; there never will be many among us, and you shall receive word concerning those who do live among us, and be informed why they are with us.[14]

However much abbreviated in Ettwein's recording, Papunhank's speech conveyed the essentials of his people and demonstrated he still had his diplomatic and oratorical knack. In a "solemn and manly style," he told the gathered chiefs the Native Moravians were devout believers in one God, accustomed to daily worship and heedful of missionary instruction. They were lovers of peace and averse to war.

They knew the evils of the alcohol trade, practiced a kind of political equality that would not compete with others' authority, were honest and trustworthy, could be counted upon to pay tribute, and would not aid white encroachment into the region. All this was intended to allay Delaware fears and to persuade them that the Brethren would be an asset rather than a threat to their community's well-being. That was an argument Moravians would have to keep making to Ohio Indians for years to come. For now, though, Killbuck Senior, speaking on behalf of his father Netawatwees, expressed delight that the Moravians had finally moved to the area. He explained that the chiefs had approved of the plan for the newcomers to build several towns, indicated that they had rechosen the lands the Moravians would be able to use because their initial choice would not allow for the isolation the Brethren preferred, and would respond more fully to the Moravians' message when the whole council sobered up and met.[15]

With the formal meeting concluded, Papunhank seized the opportunity for some additional private conversation "with the two oldest chiefs" (one of them was probably Netawatwees). The three elder statesmen likely shared stories of their peoples' struggles and joys. But it was also a chance for Papunhank to move from diplomat to evangelist. Acting the part of the ardent preacher once more, he "spent a long time" relating "his life and preaching as a heathen to the chiefs" and then "told them what he now believes and had experienced as truth."[16] For Papunhank, his own spiritual journey was the most powerful witness to the veracity of Moravian claims. The passion and vibrancy of his Christian commitment, as well as his natural impulse to preach, came pouring forth that afternoon. He earnestly wanted the Delaware headmen to know his story and in the process, to know who and what these Moravian Indians and their god were all about. Gaining their ear was the first step in gaining their hearts. And gaining their hearts was essential both for the eternal state of their souls and the more immediate plight of Moravians in Ohio. In this case, diplomacy and evangelism were two sides of the same coin.

Back in their camp for the night, Papunhank still wasn't quite finished talking. There the prior evening he "unexpectedly had found his father's sister." Encountering his elderly aunt must have brought back a flood of memories—his father's death, his vision quest, his long years of preaching, and his embrace of Moravian Christianity. Perhaps this is why he was so eager to share his story with the Delaware chiefs. It was fresh on his mind and heart. He couldn't help but tell of the divine work in his life. As a result, "the old folks [in this village] heard more about God and His Word on these two evenings than they probably had heard in their life before." If Papunhank needed any more inspiration, he may have found it in learning that King Beaver—Tamaqua—had resided in this town near the end of his life. His legacy of peacemaking would have been another reminder to the Munsee prophet of all that had passed and what was needed to make a home in this new place far from anywhere he had been before.[17]

Whether Moravians should be allowed to make a home in this new place was a point of dispute among Delaware leaders. Up until his death in 1769, Tamaqua had supported admitting white missionaries and Native Christian believers into their lands. But others disagreed. Influenced by active nativist prophets in the 1760s, they wished to resist any incursions of white religion and culture. That meant keeping Moravian Indians, and more especially their white teachers, away. By 1772 they had plenty of evidence that when you let the Brethren in, divisions would follow. Munsee towns along the Beaver River had been saddled with conflict ever since Zeisberger showed up in 1770. As his preaching drew off handfuls of men and women, including key advisors such as Glikhican, local headman Packanke saw his power diminished. Disagreements ensued within Munsee settlements and between them and those living at the mission outpost (Lagundo Utenünk). Amid those conditions, anyone would have been hard pressed to deem the Moravian presence a success.[18]

So the opposition had good reasons to be skeptical about welcoming Brethren to the Muskingum Valley. Yet in the long run they lost the argument. Historians of Ohio Indians have identified a range of factors why "most Indian leaders on the upper Ohio looked sympathetically on the efforts of the Moravian communities and preferred to allow them to settle nearby." Kinship ties may have been one factor.

Bonds of blood linked many Native Moravians, including Papunhank, to Delawares and Munsees in the region. Moreover, at a time when headmen of those peoples were trying to consolidate disparate groups into single Delaware and Munsee "nations" for the sake of protecting their autonomy against colonial expansion, it made sense to be as inclusive as possible. What Moravians brought with them was also not to be discounted. Their pacifism made them a voice for peace, even if their presence created internal divisions. They also possessed considerable spiritual power that could be added to what the Ohio Indians already wielded, especially in combatting new rounds of disease that afflicted the region in the early 1770s. They might provide economic assistance as well. Supplies of game and white trade goods were diminishing in the upper Ohio. Native headmen began to recognize that their communities would soon need to rely more heavily upon farming. White Eyes, for example, championed greater Delaware adoption of European ways including farming techniques. Moravians practiced a more intensive agriculture that produced higher yields. They also raised livestock. Learning such practices might help Ohio Indians ward off repeats of the 1772 famine. And Brethren opposition to the increasingly rampant and destructive liquor trade might help them ward off another killer.[19]

It would take some time before these advantages were clear enough to prompt the Delaware Council to endorse fully having Moravians as their neighbors. In the meantime, Papunhank and his fellow migrants set about making the Muskingum their home.

Defining the Community

Indian Christianity took many forms in early America. From Mohawk Catholics in New France and Chumash Catholics in Alta California to Mahican Congregationalists and Wampanoag Baptists in southern New England and Delaware Presbyterians in New Jersey, indigenous peoples made Christianity their own. Much like Africans on both sides of the Atlantic, Natives across the sixteenth, seventeenth, and eighteenth centuries adapted the Christian faith to their own needs and purposes. Never merely passive recipients of an alien "colonial" religion, even in cases where physical force was applied, they indigenized Christianity. Though the imperial context in which many Indians were introduced to Christianity must be kept in mind, how much Native Americans internalized of what others strove to pass on of their faith depended ultimately on indigenous peoples' decisions. They controlled their own hearts and minds. In many instances, certain theological themes, religious practices, and biblical stories resonated with particular Indian peoples and became important to their formulations of the gospel. As a result, many different varieties of Native Christianity developed. Papunhank's story confirms that in eighteenth-century New York and Pennsylvania, for example, Mahicans and Delawares were drawn to Moravian Christianity especially by its openness to dreams and prophetic visions, singing, graphic religious art, and belief in the power of blood.

Indian Brethren therefore brought their own expressions of Moravianism to the Ohio Country in the early 1770s. Their ranks ranged from longtime converts (stretching back to the mission at Shekomeko, New York, in the 1740s) to families who had just recently embraced the faith on the Allegheny. Together in Schönbrunn and Gnadenhütten (the second Moravian town established after Joshua Senior and other Mahicans had arrived), they constructed communities imbued with the distinctive values and ways of Native Moravian believers. Their rhythms of life, work, and worship pulsed with all the hopes and fears that accompanied their move much farther into Indian territory. As in Friedenshütten, their whole world was at stake. While they shared with their white teachers the desire to see other Natives become Christian, much more than the success of Moravian evangelism hung in the balance for them. Their future and their children's future depended on securing a homeland in which peace and freedom to live and believe as they wished prevailed. Delaware, Munsee, and Mahican Brethren wanted a kind of autonomous sanctuary. That goal animated most everything they did in the next several years, even as it had among countless other Indian communities.[20]

Autonomy for them did not mean disconnection from wider political realities. On the contrary, from this point on, Native Moravian towns were to be established "only where the missionaries had received explicit invitations."[21] Nor did it mean severing ties with distant Moravian overseers. Yet unlike their situation in Friedenshütten, Bethlehem was not within easy reach. Separated now by hundreds of miles, contact with Moravian leaders became predictably much less frequent, dependent on letters and reports reaching them typically via Fort Pitt. An important political, military, and economic enclave, it, too, was going through a crucial transformation. Just as the Moravians arrived in Ohio, the British chose to withdraw from that post. They dismantled the fort in the fall of 1772 and left the adjoining town of Pittsburgh to defend itself. Pittsburgh was a bustling settlement with thousands of migrants making their homes in the area or passing through on their way to points farther west. It was also contested ground because with the removal of imperial authority, Pennsylvanians and Virginians argued over to which colony the region rightly belonged.[22] Such fury made Pittsburgh a far different type of focal point for Brethren communication and information gathering than quiescent Bethlehem or even Philadelphia had been. All that meant that the new Moravian towns had to operate more independently than their predecessors.

Most likely for that reason, community leaders were especially anxious to put down in writing what was expected of all residents. Drawing on prior drafts formulated at Lagundo Utenünk earlier in the month, on August 29 Zeisberger, Ettwein, and Heckewelder came to agreement with the Native assistants, including Papunhank, on a set of statutes and rules to govern town behavior. Though similar sets of rules likely guided earlier Native Moravian settlements, it appears that this was the first time they were codified and recorded in the mission diaries. Because extant manuscript versions of the code differ, there is some confusion over what the original document included. Nevertheless, a clear sense of Moravian boundaries emerges. Community members were to worship only the Christian god, observe the Sabbath, and refrain from all of the following: traditional Native feasts and dances, drunkenness, trading liquor, murder, assault, theft, whoring, adultery, polygamy, witchcraft, and dishonesty.[23]

It is tempting to read this list of prohibitions as a blatant and somewhat desperate effort of Euro-American missionaries to exercise pervasive social control over their Indian charges. They were understandably nervous (Ettwein in particular seems to have been especially worried) about what would become of their mission congregations in this new place so far removed from Bethlehem and much closer to large numbers of "wild Indians." But as historians Carola Wessel and Hermann Wellenreuther have effectively pointed out, "Indians who [were already a part of or] who asked for admission to the mission congregation knew what they were getting into and what they were expected to give up. Present-day critics who argue that Christian missions were mechanisms of oppression and social control underestimate the intelligence and awareness of the tribes."[24] Surely that describes Papunhank's choices well. He had rejected many of these practices for himself and his band *before* joining the Moravians. Contact with Native and white Christians may have influenced his decisions in the 1750s, but the main inspiration came from the fruits of his adult vision. Embracing Moravianism in the 1760s confirmed much of what the prophet already thought and practiced. He was not bowing to the dictates of white imperialists; he was following the judgments of his mind and the leanings of his heart. He and hundreds of other Native Moravians had become committed Christians not as an act of capitulation to colonialism but as a means of coping with some of its most trying effects.

Residents of Schönbrunn and Gnadenhütten further established their towns during the remainder of 1772 and throughout 1773. Their white teachers—Zeisberger, Heckewelder, the Jungmanns, the Roths (as of May 1773), and the Schmicks (as of August 1773)—clearly exercised important leadership responsibilities within the settlements. But as had been true in Friedenshütten, there was no mistaking these places as anything other than *Indian* towns, even if some opponents disagreed. The communities certainly operated by a different set of rules, had different style houses, practiced a different type of agriculture, and engaged in very different rituals and ceremonies than Natives at Gekelemukpechünk. That was enough to convince some Indians that they wanted no part of what the Moravians were offering. When, for example, some of the Native Brethren went to Gekelemukpechünk to buy corn, "they found the Indians . . . involved in sacrifices and celebrations. One of them told some of our people that they should not hold out any hope that he would give up that way of life and accept our way of life. He wanted to retain his brown skin and not become white."[25] On the other hand, those very Moravian differences were one factor drawing a steady flow of Native visitors to the Brethren villages. Outsiders were often very curious to learn more about life among the Indians there and were drawn as well by the powerful commonalities they shared with Native Moravians—ties of kinship, clan, language, diet, gender roles, hunting and sugar-making practices, and hopes for a secure, peaceful homeland. These Natives and their settlements had not simply become white.

Visitors found there two well-ordered towns about ten miles apart with roughly three hundred men, women, and children collectively by the end of 1773. The remaining Moravians at Lagundo Utenünk had migrated to the Muskingum that spring and helped build the log homes, church, schoolhouse, and fences that gave the settlements physical definition. As in prior mission towns, the Brethren categorized residents into four groups: communicants, baptized noncommunicants, candidates for baptism, and Natives approved to live in the village as long as they abided by community rules. So, for example, the Schönbrunn diary noted in December 1773 that 184 persons lived there, of whom 106 were baptized, 78 were unbaptized (mostly young children), and 50 were communicants. All were welcome to attend the daily morning and evening worship services, which featured short meditations on the Watchword for the day and lots of singing. Resident missionaries gave more formal sermons on Sundays and typically held Communion services every six weeks or so on a Saturday evening. Papunhank and other Native helpers came strictly from the communicant ranks and as noted before, served a variety of roles including doing one-on-one evangelism, informing newcomers of community statutes, leading religious services in the absence of the missionaries, and banishing those unable or unwilling to comply. Such a short litany of the religious activities that filled the days and weeks of Native Moravians hardly does justice to the lives they carved out in their new locale. But it at least serves as a reminder that a range of spiritual disciplines were woven into the fabric of community life alongside the daily demands of producing food, raising children, and caring for the sick.[26]

The contours of Papunhank's life in these years likely followed such patterns. Family duties, community responsibilities, and religious participation filled most of the aging prophet's hours. As always, personal joys and sorrows intermingled with wider political and social concerns. Zeisberger's brief memoir of Johannes noted that he initially found aspects of his new Ohio environment very challenging: "In the beginning he did not like it here very much. Things here were a bit too lively for him and he was not used to hearing the savages utter so many lies, blasphemies, and words of abuse about us." If an accurate characterization, Papunhank's distress likely paralleled the discomfort he experienced in 1767 when he accompanied Zeisberger on his first evangelistic mission to Indians in western Pennsylvania at Goschgoschunk. There, too, he had been disturbed by the hostile behavior and language of Natives resolute in their opposition to the good news he believed he was bringing. From his perspective, their unruly lives represented so much of what needed to change among Indians. Through the years his prophetic message had won over some. But the reactions of opposing Ohio Delawares, Munsees, and Shawnees to the Moravian presence made clear how much more remained to be done. And they indicated that the Brethren would have to fight, however peaceably, for their place in the Muskingum. Papunhank may have been understandably dispirited by that prospect. How many times had he already done the same thing for his company? Would they lose out once more and be forced to move again? Would the story turn out any differently here from what his people, the Munsees, and his religious community, the Moravians, had been experiencing for generations? If Papunhank had his doubts, who could blame him?[27]

Missionary Competitors

However uncertain he may have been about their future, news of the Moravian arrival in the Ohio Country prompted other Euro-

American Christian bodies to imagine that this was the time when they, too, could win Native converts. Chances are that they had already heard that the Delaware Council in 1771 and again in 1772 had made requests to Philadelphia Quakers asking for white missionaries and schoolteachers to be sent.[28] The Ohio Indians therefore seemed prime candidates to receive evangelists who could advance God's kingdom and perhaps in the process pave a peaceful path for white settlers to follow. David Zeisberger had no interest in the latter prospect, but as always, he was similarly concerned with bringing the gospel to more groups of Natives. Within weeks of arriving at Schönbrunn he was off to the south of Gekelemukpechünk evangelizing Shawnees. For the next year he paid them periodic visits, hoping to gain permission to establish a Moravian post in their midst. But their interest in him and Christianity ran hot and cold and in the end, nothing came of his efforts.[29] That should have been a lesson to other white missionaries. Even someone as experienced and skilled as Zeisberger didn't always get the responses he wanted. He well knew that the sizeable enclave of Indian Christians in Schönbrunn and Gnadenhütten represented the fruit of decades of Moravian labors, not the instant results of a one-off encounter.

Nevertheless, a series of white missionaries visited. Baptist David Jones came first. His initial foray into the Ohio Country during the summer of 1772 found few Delawares at home and a council reluctant to grant him permission to be there. Six months later he turned his attention to the Shawnees at Chillicothe but left after two weeks following physical threats and being told by Othaawaapeelethee that the Shawnees "had lived a long time as they now do, and liked it very well, and he and his people would live as they had done." Jones then went back to the Delawares and spent another twelve days in frustrating negotiations that by the end left him saying, "My continuance here was very disagreeable." His visit to Gnadenhütten was more promising; he found that the Indians' "conduct in time of worship is praise-worthy. Their grave and solemn countenances exceed what is commonly seen among us at such times." According to the Schönbrunn diary, Jones "praised and lauded the work of the Brothers among the

Indians and said we had done more than they would manage in their whole lives." Yet, in Jones's account, when he asked Zeisberger if he could preach to the congregation there, the Moravian "replied with some appearance of indifference, that an opportunity might be had in the morning." Jones thought it was "probable he was a little afraid to countenance me, lest some disciples be made." Perhaps that was a tongue-in-cheek remark. Still, Jones demurred in his journal that he had no such objective. If serious, his comment suggests how naive he was about evangelizing Indians or the bonds that bound Zeisberger and the Native Moravians together. Jones got his chance to preach the next day and "such was the spiritual delight enjoyed, that it seemed no small compensation for my troubles and hardships endured." As he departed the area, no Natives followed him on his way. Nonetheless, he left upbeat, willing to tell anyone who would listen on his journey home that the Moravians had formed "a true Christian congregation in the Indian country."[30]

Presbyterian David McClure wasn't any more successful or any more astute in his missionary labors in northeastern Ohio. Arrived at Gekelemukpechünk in September 1772, McClure prepared for his new ministry. He was barely unpacked, however, when he discovered that his stay was to be short-lived. The Delaware Council decided that it would be best for all concerned if McClure returned home and told him so within two weeks of his arrival. During that time, area Natives had already been communicating the same message to the missionary in less formal ways. For much of the fortnight, for example, a good portion of the community indulged in a "drunken frolic," hardly the sort of welcome McClure was hoping for. He did manage to preach on several occasions to Indian audiences, but he found most of his listeners disinterested or confused by what he said or didn't say.[31]

Delaware resistance to McClure was expressed perhaps most tellingly in a series of objections raised by the speaker of the council (probably Killbuck Senior). First he wondered why the "Almighty *Monetho*" (Manitou), who was creator of all things and father of all peoples, would send the Bible to whites and not to Indians. He argued that in lieu of the Bible, "the Great Monetho has given us knowledge here, (pointing to his forehead) & when we are at a loss what to do, we must *think*." Second, he objected that "if we take your religion, we must leave off war, and become as women, and then we shall be easily subdued by our enemies." Finally, the council worried about their land if they allowed McClure to stay. He might attract more white settlers to Ohio, a dim prospect indeed. As the speaker put it, "the white people, with whom we are acquainted, are worse, or more wicked than we are, and we think it better to be such as we are than such as they are."[32]

Exasperated by it all, McClure soon left town, but not before telling the Delawares that "they would have no more good fortune if they did not accept the Gospel. God would send judgment upon [their city] and eradicate them from the face of the earth." At least that is what he was reported to have said, according to Zeisberger, who heard it from Native Moravian, Joseph Peepy, McClure's translator. Peepy told other Moravians about the Presbyterian's ill-advised tactics: he "talked very carelessly. For example, he . . . said often that the Indians had so much beautiful and good land, but it was lying in waste and they did not use it because they were lazy people who did not want to work and resented the White people using it. In a few years all the land would be taken away from them. The White people would establish cities and towns there and drive the Indians away or even destroy them." Peepy concluded that McClure said these and "other such things, so it [is] no wonder that they [the Delawares] sent him away."[33] Zeisberger, Papunhank, and other Native Moravians no doubt agreed.

Like Jones, McClure's visit to the Ohio Country was a failure except that he, too, found much to admire in Moravian methods and results. He marveled at the worship services he attended in Lagundo Utenünk. They were filled with short sermons, and in their congregational singing "they all, young & old bore a part, & the devotion was solemn & impressive. . . . Their hymns [sung in the Delaware language] are prayers addressed to Jesus Christ, the lamb of God, who died for the sins of men." He went away convinced that

> the Moravians appear to have adopted the best mode of Christianizing the Indians. They go among them without noise or

> parade, & by their friendly behavior conciliate their good will. They join them in the chace, & freely distribute to the helpless & gradually instill into the minds of individuals, the principles of religion. They then invite those who are disposed to hearken to them, to retire to some convenient place, at a distance from the wild Indians, & assist them to build a village, & teach them to plant & sow, & to carry on some coarse manufactures.[34]

At least McClure was a good student if not a savvy missionary.

Not to be outdone, Philadelphia-area Friends got in on the action in the Ohio Country in 1773 as well. They sent three emissaries—John Parrish, John Lacey, and Zebulon Heston—to visit Gekelemukpechünk in July hoping to reestablish Quaker-Delaware contacts. Friends had had very few opportunities to maintain close relations with any Indians since the days of Pontiac's War almost a decade earlier. But recent events had begun to change that prospect. As noted earlier, Netawatwees had sent requests in 1771 and again in November 1772 to Pennsylvania's governor requesting Friends to send a minister and schoolteacher. Quakers had reportedly responded that "they did not see how anyone could live with them to instruct them and their children unless they led an orderly life. The elders would have to begin, and then the children would follow." A greater openness to fulfilling the chief's request emerged after an exchange of letters with Papunhank in the spring of 1773. Besides thanking Friends for their recent gifts to aid their migration, the Native Moravians reported that they were well settled at Welhik Thuppeck, having been kindly received by the western Delaware chiefs, and rejoicing that "many come to hear the Word of God." That was enough to prompt the Friends' Meeting for Sufferings to send out Parrish and his associates with an accompanying letter to Netawatwees and Papunhank, the two men they viewed as able to clear a way for them. Quakers probably overestimated Papunhank's current authority, but that was an understandable error given their past history with him.[35]

Papunhank was away when the Quaker trio visited, so they had to rely instead on his grandson, Samuel Moor, to translate for them during their five days of meetings with Delaware leaders at Gekelemukpechünk. Perhaps because of their historical ties, the Quakers got a friendlier hearing from the chiefs than Jones or McClure. But the council's response nevertheless showed that in negotiating with any outsiders, including the Moravians, its primary concerns were more strategic than spiritual. As Zeisberger rather cynically observed, "The Indians are not as concerned with hearing the Gospel as with acquiring gifts through this and profiting materially, under the guise of good intentions." The chiefs told the Friends that they should not only send preachers but craftsmen who could teach them various trades. More important, they wanted their aid in sending several of their men to England to get from King George III permanent guarantees to their lands. Netawatwees had made the same appeal to Governor John Penn eight months earlier. Penn avoided the request by telling him to take it up with Sir William Johnson. The three Quakers could do no better than Penn, only offering vague promises in return.[36]

Before leaving for Philadelphia the Friends, like Jones and McClure before them, visited Schönbrunn and Gnadenhütten and came away impressed. John Lacey noted that the "Indians treated us very kindly" and Parrish reported that "a number of them sent their Love to Friends, in Philadelphia." The Schönbrunn diary attributed to them even more positive reactions: "They [the Quakers] looked around the site and they liked it. In the evening service they were also pleased with our Indian Brothers and Sisters, whose order and reverence they praised."[37]

Native Moravians' decorous manner, peaceful appearance, and pious behavior often seemed to strike a resonant chord with Euro-Americans, at least during times of peace. Whites seldom failed to comment on it, with a certain surprise in their voices. Encountering Indians on the frontier who eased rather than intensified their considerable fears was a welcome relief. In the cases of Jones, McClure, and the three Friends, it didn't convince them or their sponsoring bodies that more was to be done right away to missionize Ohio Indians. But it did persuade them that what Native and white Moravians had accomplished was something worthy of respect and admiration.

Papunhank certainly thought so too, but there was little time to be complacent. Too many critical concerns pressed in upon the Moravian communities during 1773 and even more so in 1774 to allow him or other town leaders to relax. High on their list was securing a more formal endorsement of the Moravian presence in the Muskingum Valley from Netawatwees, White Eyes, and the Delaware Council. By mid-1773 those headmen had made no definitive response to the Brethren's appeals made the prior summer and fall for such recognition. Reports coming out of Gekelemukpechünk suggested it might never happen. In February, for example, the prospect of losing council member Echpalawehund to the Moravians stirred opposition against them. According to Zeisberger, opponents "foresee that if he comes to us, others will follow. Now they do not want this to happen . . . so they are considering ways to control the situation and stop it." One approach was to send the missionaries away. Opponents insisted that the Native Brethren had no need of their white teachers since they had been learning from them for decades. Moreover, some non-Moravians claimed that they "could not live as peacefully as before, because now they always have to hear how various things they did were not right and were sinful, and that their sacrifices and everything they did to please God was useless." On the other hand, the council determined on February 28 that their town could impose stricter order upon its residents without any help from the Moravians: "they had decided they would lead a better life from now on, that they would admonish and punish the young people for their disorderly and bad life. From now on they would completely forbid and put an end to drinking, dancing, gaming, and such vices, and if anyone brought *Rum* there . . . they would destroy the kegs and pour the *Rum* out onto the floor." They wondered, "Why should we also not be able to live as the Indian believers, without having teachers here." In response, some of the Moravian Indians were ready to issue an ultimatum to Netawatwees, insisting that if their missionaries were forced out, they would leave as well. But Zeisberger counseled a wait-and-see attitude and encouraged Echpalawehund to remain a part of the council.[38]

By June Papunhank could not wait any longer. He went with a handful of other Indian Brothers to make their case once again to Netawatwees. This time Isaac Glikhican did most of their talking. A former warrior captain among the Delawares in western Pennsylvania and brother of the Indian prophet Wangomen, he was accustomed to the finesse characteristic of a Delaware Council meeting. In this case, however, he sinned boldly and minced no words. After reminding the headmen of their invitation to the Brethren to join them in the Ohio Country, he spoke about Moravians' Christian commitments, disavowed any knowledge about poison (Moravians were once again rumored to possess it), asked them to send along a string and a belt of wampum they had brought to the Shawnees and Wyandots, and informed them that the Mahicans living in Gnadenhütten would soon get a permanent missionary of their own. Netawatwees acknowledged that he had not forgotten about the Moravians' request but explained that the council had not "been able to reach a conclusion." In the meantime, he thought it was "unnecessary for my grandchildren the *Mohicans* to fetch their teacher. They have enough teachers and if they bring more here then they will preach the same thing to them and nothing different from what they are preaching." A few days later, though, following some additional lobbying by Isaac and Joshua Senior, the chief relented and gave permission for another white minister to come. That provided some consolation to an otherwise frustrated set of Native Brethren tired of Netawatwees's mixed messages.[39]

Given a green light, Papunhank, Willhelm, Nicolaus, and Joshua Senior set off on June 10 to retrieve their old missionary friends, the Schmicks, from Bethlehem. They were to come to minister at Gnadenhütten among many familiar Mahicans, whose language and spiritual journeys they knew well. The expedition lasted two months, time enough for Johannes to get a respite from the irritations of Ohio diplomacy and employ his well-honed guiding skills. It was no coincidence that he would be the one selected by the community to make such a trip. Everyone knew he could fend for himself and handle whatever physical or diplomatic challenges were encountered along the way. They also knew that he was probably more than willing to go. Not only did he know the Schmicks well from their years together in Philadelphia and Friedenshütten, but he likely relished the opportunity to be back in the Pennsylvania woods and to renew friendships in Bethlehem and with Natives along the way. As in years past, he carried letters back and forth, a courier service he was long used to performing. During the trip home, his hunting and trading of skins provided the group with food. His typical self-sacrificial attitude was also on display. Johannes Jungmann, whose parents were serving at Schönbrunn, was part of the traveling entourage back to the Ohio Country and noted in his journal how "Nicolaus started to pity his horse, because it had to carry two sacks, and he threw one of them down. I did not know, what to do, and offered him, to carry the sack, but good Johannes did not let me do so; he himself carried it for quite a stretch alternately with Wilhelm, until we rested at noon, when they divided this cargo and loaded it on their horses, and marched on."[40]

The trek to Bethlehem was actually Papunhank's second major trip that spring. Back in late March he had gone with John Heckewelder to Lagundo Utenünk to help move the hundred or so remaining Moravian Indians and the Roth family from there to Ohio (see figure 10). On that journey, Papunhank had the misfortune of getting lost while out hunting on his own. Heckewelder later noted that a Native companion "had the good luck to find him at the distance of five or six miles, with a fine deer that he had killed." Once back in camp, "the sight of these two men dragging a large deer along was truly joyful to us, as well on account of the recovery of our lost friend, as of the meat that he brought." For Heckewelder, the incident was one more illustration that "Indians never despair, not even in the worst of times and under the severest trials; when placed in difficult situations they never use discouraging language, but always endeavour to raise their spirits and prevent them from sinking, under the hardships or dangers to which they are exposed." That may have been an overly sanguine view of Native emotions, but it speaks to the resilience that Papunhank and other Pennsylvania and Ohio Indians repeatedly displayed in the mid-eighteenth century when trials seemed to confront them at every turn.[41]

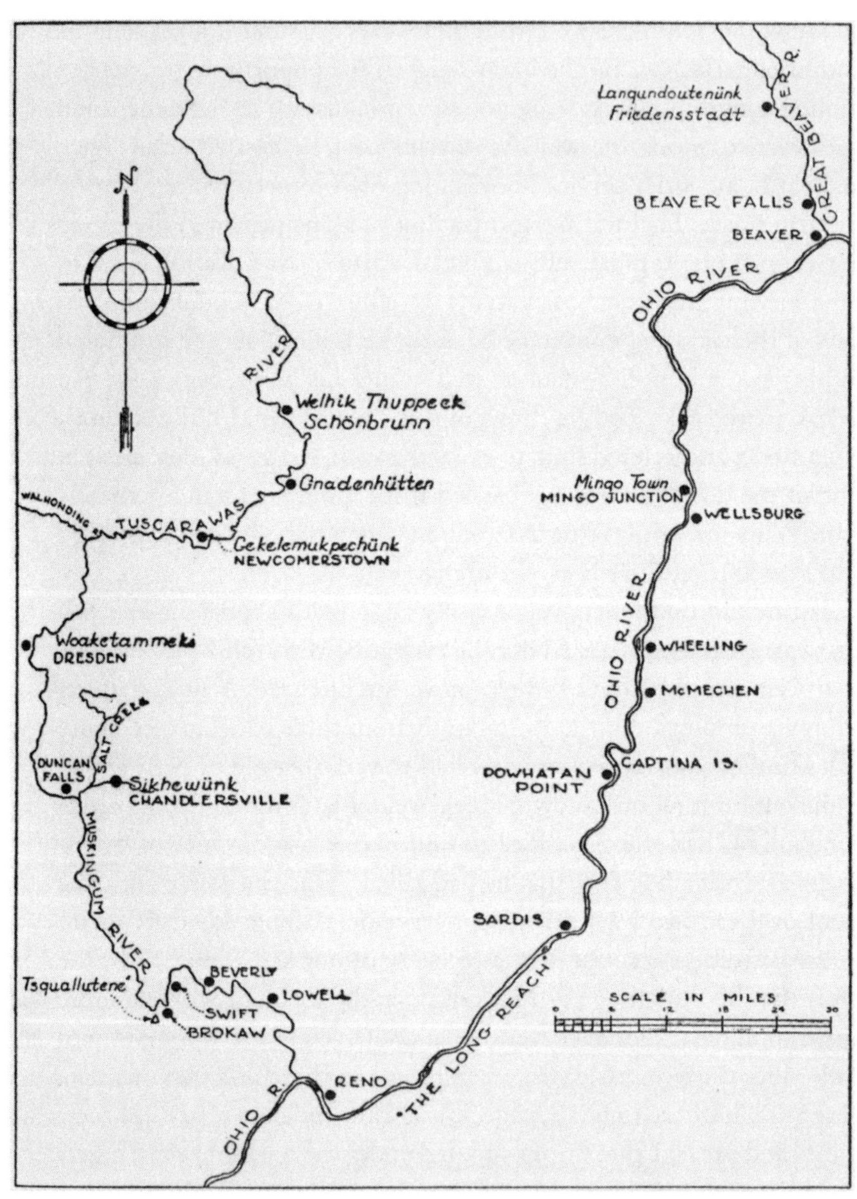

Fig. 10. Map of river route of John Heckewelder's party from Friedensstadt on the Great Beaver River to Schönbrunn on the Tuscarawas, April 13–May 5, 1773. Courtesy of Ohio History Connection.

Papunhank's resilience was rooted in his long years of adapting to troubling pressures. His heartfelt religious faith clearly bolstered his capacity to cope. That spring marked ten years since his confession of Christian belief and baptism, and more than twenty years since he had commenced preaching. If he was growing old and tired in other ways, it wasn't evident in his willingness to continue testifying to the truth he had found. While briefly at Lagundo Utenünk, according to John Roth,

> after the early service a couple of our Brothers Joh. Pepunh. and Nathanael Davis gave the sweetest message about the hope we have and the foundation of our Salvation to a couple of strangers who wanted to hear about the Gospel. The former [Papunhank] said among other things: "why should we not believe? The word that is preached to us is proven in us; we feel it," and the other, "as soon as I sought the Savior with all my heart, I found him; whatever I have asked him for, I have received. I continue to become more blessed. Sometimes my heart burns like a flaming fire with love and emotion. It is true what the believers sing and say."[42]

Such Native spiritual confidence warmed Roth's heart, but apparently did not make him particularly easy to work with. Within weeks of the Roths' arrival in Schönbrunn, Zeisberger wrote to Nathanael Seidel in Bethlehem that he had "already seen enough times that Jungmann [the other resident missionary there] and Roth would not get along." And that was not all: "For that matter the same might be said for Jungmann and Schmick . . . I personally have had no difficulties with either Jungmann or Roth. I have nothing against them, except that I believe Jungmann is a poor preacher. His sermons are full of such nonsense and absurd things. . . . It is a disgrace and an embarrassment." Roth had the same low opinion of Jungmann's preaching, also calling it "nonsense," and suggesting that a "shoemaker [Jungmann's trade] should stay at his workbench and busy himself with that which is familiar." That was enough to prompt Jungmann to inform Seidel that "I have come to fear him. I want to be free of him." He insisted that he had been a "loyal worker," even though "my wife and I are both worn out." Efforts to make amends with Roth had been rebuffed. Schmick had no better luck. Once he got to Gnadenhütten, he found the Roths greedy and only grudgingly willing to hand over material objects, animals, and crops needed to sustain the newcomers.[43]

How much of this soap opera, detailed in the letters he carried to and from Bethlehem, Papunhank knew about is impossible to say. He may have picked up signs of tension during the few weeks between late March and mid-August (early May to early June) when he was actually in Schönbrunn. If so, it may have been another incentive for him to leave town as soon as he could, especially if he thought Schmick might be able to mediate the situation. Whatever the case, any knowledge of internal missionary squabbles would have been disturbing, particularly at a moment when Native Brethren were working overtime to persuade the powers that be in Gekelemukpechünk not only to let them keep the white teachers they already had but to add another missionary couple.

Furthermore, Moravian Indians had bigger worries to attend to in the summer of 1773. News arrived in late June that Cherokees had resumed fighting with western tribes along the Wabash River. Those events were part of a complex web of Indian and imperial relations that at best, Moravians understood only partially. They feared, rightly as it turned out, that some larger conflagration was on the horizon.[44] Meanwhile, disease was ravaging the region: "A bad cough [whooping cough] has been raging in this entire area. Since spring it has taken more than 50 children in Gekelemukpechünk alone, and now it has also appeared among our children here." Four died within a week in mid-July. Then a deadly fever (perhaps yellow fever) hit in August. Many were afflicted to the point of death, including longtime Native assistant Anton. Johann Jungmann barely survived his bout with it and worried about how all of this was affecting the Native Brethren:

> There are so many suffering from fever and the children have whooping cough. Some have died, one after another. This is such a terrible shock for our Indians to witness. . . . I hope our Indians

> notice that we white Brothers also are dying. We can't let them think we were the ones who led only their children to slaughter through these illnesses.[45]

Jungmann's fears weren't unfounded. When disease and death hit communities, people naturally looked for explanations. As in Friedenshütten two years earlier, poison seemed a plausible culprit to some Indians. Moravians had heard talk of it ever since they had arrived in the Muskingum. Back in March, Zeisberger "confronted the old Magician story" in Gnadenhütten "in the person of none other than old Josua." Joshua's wife "Bathsheba was ill and this was supposed to have been done by Jeremias [a different Jeremias from Papunhank's brother], the son of Bartolomäus, who had hexed her; in Friedenshütten it was supposed to be Johannes. Now since he doesn't live with them, it had to be someone else." By mid-August Zeisberger and the other missionaries determined that "as far as the poison story and similar things are concerned, we must be on our guard and prevent anything from coming into our congregations in order to ensure that this whole affair becomes totally extinct." They agreed to "ridicule these things as fables and demonstrate on all occasions that there is nothing to the whole affair." That proved easier said than done. Within a few weeks, a woman who had recently moved to Schönbrunn was accused by other Natives of possessing poison. Fortunately, in Zeisberger's view, she "revealed her innocence [and] we were thus spared many unpleasantries."[46]

Homeland uncertainties, missionary disputes, poisonous threats, deadly disease—all those "unpleasantries" beset the Moravian towns in 1773. And Papunhank did not escape their direct touch, most tragically on the night of September 9 when Nathanael, his infant grandson, "became ill and was afflicted with an attack of the palsy, and toward evening he went quickly to his eternal home." Johannes and Anna Johanna made their way to Gnadenhütten to comfort Sophia and Joshua Junior, Nathanael's parents, who were "affected . . . all the more because it [his death] had come so unexpectedly." With broken hearts, they buried "the small body of the departed" the next evening.[47]

War Once More

Fears that there would be more bodies to bury in God's Acre gripped the two Moravian towns the next spring and persisted for much of 1774. The problem now was war rather than disease. As noted earlier, the withdrawal of overt British authority at Fort Pitt (and also at Fort De Chartres on the Mississippi River) as a cost-saving measure opened the door for other governments and private parties to try to fill the power vacuum. British officials' hopes of keeping the western frontier of their North American empire quiescent had been repeatedly dashed since the end of the Seven Years' War. Almost immediately, Native irritations boiled over into Pontiac's Rebellion. In subsequent years, efforts to hold colonial speculators and squatters at bay were less and less successful, much to the chagrin of Ohio Indians. British imperial control in the west was evaporating, an ominous development for Brethren Indians, and a foretaste of the wider collapse of British rule that lay ahead.[48]

At first in 1774, conflict in the Ohio Valley pitted Virginians against Pennsylvanians in a flurry of competing land claims. When the latter colony failed to take concrete steps to provide for the protection of whites near Pittsburgh, Virginia's lieutenant governor, Lord Dunmore, sanctioned the raising of a militia company under the command of John Connolly. Its presence added to the political and legal squabbles that racked the frontier and threatened to turn the verbal war into a hot one. Dunmore might have imagined that given his position, his aggressive steps could be a way to reassert British authority in the region. But they instead served only to fuel his private material acquisitiveness and the very type of frenzied white territorial expansion British policy had sought to restrain. Naturally, Ohio Indians grew leery of what was happening, and before long a few isolated instances of violence broke out. Dunmore and Connolly seized the opportunity those skirmishes provided to redirect antagonism away from fellow whites toward Natives. Squashing Shawnee and Mingo warriors, and the towns they came from, could then be portrayed as acts of self-defense rather than what they really were—a means to coerce more Native land cessions and clear the way for waves of migrating settlers.[49]

All of this distressed residents of Schönbrunn and Gnadenhütten on several fronts. Most immediately they worried about their own safety. As events unfolded between April and October, they were eerily reminiscent of the dangers faced amid Pontiac's War and the Paxton Boys crisis. Now as then the Moravian towns' liminal position outside of both Native and white communities made them vulnerable to attack from either side. Angry Shawnees and Mingos bent on avenging the deaths of relatives, along with their Munsee allies, might decide that Indians unwilling to join them in the fight, and more especially white missionaries who lived among them, were legitimate targets. Gnadenhütten went so far as to post armed guards to protect the Schmicks and others. On the other hand, when Zeisberger reported in May that "we now hear that there is supposed to be a gang of White people on the *Ohio* who committed the murders against these Indians, as happened in the previous war in *Pennsylvania*," he explicitly invoked the troubling memory of a time when frontier whites lumped Native Brethren with all other Indians as enemies. On that occasion the Pennsylvania government provided the necessary protection to keep them alive. That option no longer existed, so instead they appealed to the chiefs in Gekelemukpechünk. But Zeisberger was not optimistic: "the *Chiefs* cannot protect us; they have no power or force. We must expect our help and protection from the Lord alone." At the end of June, he reiterated those points. They were

> mostly worried that gangs of White people might possibly be formed to go out against the Indians. This would be the most dangerous thing for us because people like this are not under anyone's command, and we have nothing to fear now from the Indians, who are most likely to seek protection from us and believe they are safe with us. . . . Redeem Israel, O God, out of all his troubles and protect us from all sin and earthly turmoil.[50]

The earthly turmoil of Dunmore's war threatened more than individual Moravian lives. The stability and well-being of the entire region was at stake. Native Brethren well knew the disruptions and suffering that widespread violent conflict brought. Distress in 1774 over the war, therefore, extended beyond concern for their immediate safety to broader worries about its destructive potential. Limiting the scope of its damage meant for convinced pacifists like Papunhank doing more than lying low or hiding out, at least when opportunity afforded itself. In the waning years of the Seven Years' War, he had sought ways to facilitate the resumption of peace and security in Pennsylvania. Now he joined with other leaders from Schönbrunn and Gnadenhütten in active peacemaking efforts designed to keep the conflict from spreading. As described at the beginning of this chapter, Moravian Indians pleaded with other Natives to stay at peace rather than joining Shawnee and Mingo warriors in their retaliatory attacks. The Moravian diplomats' primary audience was the Delaware chiefs at Gekelemukpechünk, but they also made appeals to Shawnees who had not yet participated in the fighting. White Eyes principally carried the Moravians' diplomatic torch. Though not one himself, he was sympathetic to the Brethren cause and a close associate of Isaac Glikhican. As a member of the Head Council at Gekelemukpechünk and its leading war captain, he was well positioned to advise Netawatwees and to represent Delaware interests to whites and Indians alike.[51]

In this case, White Eyes' peace advocacy coincided with what most others wanted including the Wyandots, Cherokees, and other southern Indians. During the early 1770s Shawnee leaders in Ohio had tried to construct a Native alliance against the terms of the Treaty of Fort Stanwix. Neither British officials in America—specifically Sir William Johnson and his nephew and successor Guy Johnson—nor the Six Nations were enthused by that prospect since it undermined their claims to authority over the region. They sent their own emissary, Kiashuta, to the Ohio to persuade as many headmen as would listen to remain neutral and to convince the Delawares to play their traditional role of mediator. Most obliged but not all. John Logan, the son of famous Oneida go-between Shickellamy (discussed in chapter 1), had seen too many of his close kin murdered to bury the hatchet. Still, the diplomacy of White Eyes, Kiashuta, and others succeeded in minimizing the size of the war parties. Even key Shawnee chief

Cornstalk chose to keep his people out of the fray. All that meant that the Shawnee alliance was smaller and weaker than it might have been. That was good for the cause of peace, or more precisely, the cause of limiting the carnage. But it also served the expansionist aims of Lord Dunmore. He had fewer and weaker opponents with which to contend in clearing a way for more white speculation and settlement. Moreover, there was still enough Indian pushback for him to justify launching a mass assault on Shawnee towns along the Scioto River in September 1774. Though the major battle of Point Pleasant was somewhat inconclusive, Dunmore achieved his goal—a treaty in which Shawnees relinquished their hunting rights south of the Ohio River, leaving those parts (Kentucky) to land-hungry Virginians.[52]

How fully Papunhank understood the costliness of this peace is difficult to gauge. He wanted neither a broader war nor a massive influx of whites. In working against the former, he and other peace advocates may have facilitated the latter. But White Eyes and other Delawares were certain that greater armed resistance to Dunmore's ambitions would have only broadened the scope of death and suffering on both sides and done little in the long run to slow down colonial expansion because Indians, however united, were bound to lose that fight.[53]

For the time being, whites seemed primarily headed to Kentucky and other points to the southwest so the Muskingum seemed as good a place as any to call home. That became much clearer by November 1774 after peace and stability were restored. During the prior six or seven months, Native Moravians had good reason to wonder whether they would ever gain clear rights to live at Schönbrunn and Gnadenhütten. Amid the war, Netawatwees and the Delaware Council were even more reluctant to decide whether the Brethren could stay and even more anxious to deny responsibility for inviting them in the first place. Association with Moravians could prove fatal or at least politically damaging. Warring Shawnees, Munsees, and Mingos accused Delawares at Gekelemukpechünk of being "Virginians" and "Shwonnak" (a white man or friends of the whites) when they failed to join the fight. Having white missionaries in their midst or nearby made them especially suspect. In April Zeisberger summarized the situation: "The *Chief* [Netawatwees] is worried for his life because he is accused, and rightfully, of having called us; he fears that all guilt will be placed on his head and things will not turn out well for him in the end. Therefore he is now trying to save himself and squirm his way out of this matter by saying he did not do it." Things were no better two months later:

> There was a council gathering of the *Delaware Nation* from this entire area. Our Indian Brothers once again offered a *Belt of Wampum* in the name of both of our Towns, because as long as we have been here we still do not know how things stand between them and us. No *Chief* wants to acknowledge that he called us White Brothers here, and we have thus not yet been recognized or accepted in Indian country for the reason we are actually here. Presumably we have only been tolerated because they think if they drive us away our Indians will not remain either. Sooner or later they will find a suitable occasion to drive us away, which many people would like to see.

By mid-July Netawatwees was encouraging the Moravians (unsuccessfully) to move their women and children elsewhere, and in mid-August the council seemed ready to force them to move until White Eyes offered a stirring defense.[54]

Circumstances grew dire enough in September for the Moravians to think more seriously about moving. Besides the war's events, their numbers were beginning to exceed their space. Many newcomers had come during the summer, some as war refugees, so that Schönbrunn in particular was beginning to burst at the seams. There were a "great many inconveniences" when there were "so many and numerous Indians together in one place, first of all because they keep so many cattle and then also because the peoples are so different from each other and do not fit well together. Thus it would be good if they could be spread out a bit." Zeisberger's hope of starting another mission town among the Shawnees was no longer viable, so instead he floated the idea to his superiors of establishing a settlement in Cuyahoga farther north in

Ohio. It was "supposed to be a lovely area not far from Lake Erie . . . there they would have the Wyandots and Chippewas as neighbors. We would be more useful there than here because it is quite out of the way." Perhaps for all of these reasons, "several of our Indian Brethren would like to go there, especially Johannes."[55]

At first blush it seems very surprising, if not shocking, that Papunhank would be among those wanting to move again. He had endured the stresses and strains of so many prior moves; it is hard to imagine he would want to do it again. Just two years earlier, he had come to the Muskingum Valley with high hopes that it would be the long-term peaceful homeland he and his communities had sought for decades. Why would he already be giving up on it and imagining that life would be better somewhere else? Much of any explanation would seem to lie in his hatred of war and its accompanying dangers and destruction. By early September he likely knew that Dunmore was on the move with seven hundred men. It was easy to think that things were bound to get much worse for area Natives before they got any better. Maybe now was the time to get further out of harm's way. He had retreated effectively with his people in the 1750s. Current circumstances in his mind may have called for a similar strategy. Moreover, the Chippewas and Wyandots might prove easier to work with than the western Delawares had so far. And there might be more room for different tribal peoples to cluster together in separate enclaves to reduce some of their friction.

Ultimate decisions on where to live were now out of Papunhank's hands, but he still likely pondered all those possibilities as he set off with John Heckewelder and two other Natives for another trip to Bethlehem on September 14.[56] Heading east as Dunmore headed west was as good a symbolic act as any to express his frustration with the war and his desire to distance himself as much as possible from future violence. Community members may have even encouraged him to go. It would give him a way to serve, more time along familiar Pennsylvania trails, and a chance to be back with old friends in Bethlehem. It might even afford enough days to pass for wider events to take a more positive turn.

A Final Homeland

By the time Papunhank arrived back in Schönbrunn on November 12, events had indeed turned. First and foremost, the fighting was over, a treaty had been formulated, and peace was on the way to being concluded. That grand news had come just six days earlier. The Moravians rejoiced that "the air was cleared and the heavy, oppressive feeling we had experienced despite all confidence and childlike trust in the Savior, disappeared. How could we praise Him and thank Him adequately for this? Our tongues are too few and even if every beat of our heart were an expression of gratitude and every breath a song of praise, it would not suffice."[57] No doubt Papunhank shared in that relief and rejoicing. It alleviated much of the anxiety he felt for himself, his kin, and his people.

Nevertheless, the matter of where the Moravians could live remained unresolved. But there was important news on that front as well. Upon returning to Gekelemukpechünk from Dunmore's expedition in early November, White Eyes was determined to resolve the issue once and for all. Speaking ostensibly on behalf of the Brethren, he denounced Netawatwees for his actions on the matter. In particular, he was furious with the chief for a message he had sent to the Shawnees that White Eyes had intercepted in which Netawatwees denied ever inviting the Moravians to the Ohio Country and insisted that the Delawares "would never accept God's word, much less live" like them. All council members knew Netawatwees had broken appropriate protocol. During a time of war, he had no authority to send such a message without it first being approved by White Eyes, the community's leading war captain. Moreover, White Eyes expressed great sorrow over the content of the message and said he wanted "to remove himself from everything and have nothing more to do with the *Chief's Affairs*." He then walked out of the meeting but later that day sent Netawatwees a series of demands:

> Brothers and their Indians who have accepted God's word and become believers should have freedom of conscience in Indian country. They should be their own people and live separately. Anyone who wanted to accept God's word and become a believer

should have the freedom to do so. The nonbelievers should also live separately, but not hinder the believers in any way, and see them as their friends who share a bond as one *Nation*.

Netawatwees wasn't pleased with White Eyes' critique and retorted with "harsh accusations" against the Moravians, including the well-worn claim that they possessed poison and harbored "bad people and sorcerers." He also told them that any decision about the lands they occupied would depend on the Wyandots because they had given the Delawares the land in the first place.[58]

Zeisberger found all of this both troubling and hopeful, and Papunhank likely concurred. The missionary noted, "We sit like the bird on the branch, with no certain or lasting home, and the longer we are constantly restless and fleeting, the more difficult it becomes." He lamented what he now saw as the deceitful scheme of the Delaware chiefs to lure the Moravians to the Ohio Country and then "chase their teachers away . . . [and] subdue the Indian believers." On the other hand, he was thankful for having a powerful advocate in White Eyes. When the two met privately on November 16, the Indian confided that there was still opposition to the Moravians being there, but that he would threaten to leave the council and thereby destroy Netawatwees's power if the believers were not granted their freedom. White Eyes' longer-term hope was that he could get a "district of land" set apart for the Moravians and that other Indians would be moved farther away from them. A month later he reported that a large council would be held soon to discuss the matter further, and the Moravians should plan to send some Brothers to it. White Eyes also told them that when things were settled for the Moravians, he planned to go to England to straighten out the Delaware land claims "so that no one would ever stain their land with blood and the White people would never drive them out." Like so many other Indians, he wanted to find a means to secure a peaceful, autonomous, permanent homeland.[59]

Two more months passed before the Brethren got the word they had long been waiting for. Netawatwees, White Eyes, and other members of the council came to Gnadenhütten to deliver the message personally. They summoned representatives from Schönbrunn to join them, and Papunhank was appropriately one of the five who went. Closely gathered together in Joshua Junior's home on February 27, the Native Moravians held their breath as Netawatwees prepared to speak. He began in traditional Indian fashion by laying belts of wampum before them and then declared "you can live peacefully, for all the land presented to us by the Delamattenoes [Wyandots] was given to you too. You as well as we have part in it, and righteous claim." Righteous claim—those were sweet words to hear in any language. And there was more. The Delawares at Gekelemukpechünk were moving ten or fifteen miles away to Goschachgünk to establish a new settlement so the Moravians would have more space to spread out. Furthermore, the Brethren should feel free to start another town since their numbers kept growing. The chief also indicated that no public verbal attacks on the Moravians would be tolerated, the Delaware leadership was open to receiving Moravian Christianity, and White Eyes would take a wampum belt to "London and request the King to sanction their possession of the land and with his hand take hold of the other end of the Belt in order to prevent white people from settling on this land or taking it away. In this way, the Indians would not become involved in arguments or war in trying to drive the white people away." Finally, the Delaware chiefs promised not to sell any of the land, but rather it was to remain "their and their descendants' property for hunting and settling (in order to live on it in peace and quietness)."[60]

The following day White Eyes went with Papunhank and the other Schönbrunn representatives to their town and delivered the same "happy and welcome news." Zeisberger and the rest of the community listened in awesome wonder as

> the *Chief*, in the presence of his *Councellors* . . . told our Indians he was in favor of the Brothers and their work; from now on they would also support this; they would accept God's word; the Indian believers and their teachers should enjoy complete freedom in Indian country and enjoy equal rights and privileges. The country was now open to us and the Indian believers would have as much

right and participation in the country as the nonbelievers. Any Indians who wanted to turn to the Brothers and become believers would be free to do so and would not be stopped.[61]

With those words it was clear that White Eyes had won the day. As a result, the Moravians had seemingly gained the recognition and acceptance they had been striving for ever since planning their move to the Ohio Country. What a cause for celebration and thanksgiving! Whether Netawatwees had had a change of heart or he had simply been previously voicing the objections of others, the pro-Moravian forces on the council had prevailed. That didn't mean that their opposition was eliminated. But it gave the Brethren a standing and an endorsement from the Delaware Council that they had been seeking for a long time. In the weeks that followed, the council's decisions were communicated to Indians near and far. Even Captain Pipe, one of the staunchest opponents of the Moravians on the council, had spread the word to the Beaver River towns, reportedly announcing that "anyone who wanted to go to the Brothers to hear God's word and to become a believer was free to do so." From Zeisberger's perspective, this was "more evidence that not only the *Chiefs* know this among themselves, but all the Indians know. We can now enjoy this and see the fruits of it daily, because we are not aware that they are acting improperly toward us at all; they are all friendly and very courteous."[62]

Within a span, then, of three to four months between November 1774 and March 1775, peace had been restored and Native Moravians had secured a substantial measure of autonomy, freedom, and respect. They had a homeland. How long it would last no one knew. But surely they were entitled to a few innocent, even naive, moments of imagining that here finally, they had a peaceful place of their own to live out what they understood to be God's call upon them and to pass on this space and this faith to their children and their children's children.

No one had more of a right to entertain such thoughts than Johannes Papunhank. His life's work—or at least the last twenty-five years of it—was choosing peace over war and leading communities dedicated to that principle. Their perennial struggle within the exigencies of mid-eighteenth-century early America was finding somewhere to call home. That was a quest shared with dozens of indigenous peoples. Some other Native leaders for practical reasons similarly believed that peace was the best and only viable means for achieving that goal. But overall, relatively few Indians and even fewer Euro-Americans embraced the values, attitudes, lifestyles, and ideological pacifism Papunhank cultivated first among his followers and later among fellow Moravians. They ran too much against the grain and were frankly too hard. They allowed little room for self-aggrandizement, revenge, or hate. Those commodities were in ample supply within the Munsee prophet's world and as a result, all his efforts reaped merely modest gains against them. And they left Papunhank's people—whoever composed that group at any particular moment—repeatedly searching for a secure space to stay. Like indigenous peoples across the continent, they wanted to retain or regain a measure of sovereignty, an element of independence. Here in the Ohio Country Papunhank may have let himself believe that dream had finally been realized. If it was not quite the Promised Land, it was at least a place where war had ended, wider authorities had endorsed their right to be there, Brethren towns were growing, and some of their opposition was moving farther away. Could he hope for much more than that? No wonder Zeisberger claimed that after his return from Bethlehem in November, Papunhank "came to like it here better than all the other places and he was content."[63]

Several events in March and April 1775 likely buoyed Papunhank's spirits even further. His large number of kin living in Schönbrunn and Gnadenhütten expanded with the birth and baptism of a new nephew, Paulus, son of Lucas and Paulina. A Native woman preacher who had always insisted that what the Moravians preached "was all lies . . . was now convinced otherwise and actually wanted to become a believer." It was a "good spring" for the annual boiling sugar operations, and those involved returned with a "very plentiful" supply. Drunken Indians arrived with "horseloads of *Rum*" but had it confiscated and only returned to them on their way out of town. Schönbrunn and Gnadenhütten sent wampum belts to the Wyandots and other western Indians in gratitude for their lands and as a way of indicating that the "Indian believers have now been accepted and are recognized and respected as their friends." The new town of Goschachgünk followed the Moravian model of urban design when laying out its streets and houses. An Easter weekend service, focused on the wounds of Jesus, drew "more Indian strangers here than there had ever been, and our Meeting Hall, which can easily hold 300 people, was too small. Many were powerfully moved and touched." And though there was "famine everywhere among the [other] Indians, because last year they were always busy thinking more about fleeing than planting," the Moravian communities were well supplied with food.[64]

Seeing kin and Native preachers enter the Moravian fold, practicing the customary labors of spring, controlling the flow of liquor, employing diplomacy to good ends, spreading Brethren orderliness, feeling with hundreds of others the sufferings of Christ, providing for the physical needs of friend and stranger—all those had been passions of Papunhank. They had been some of the major experiences and responsibilities of his later adult life. Observing them now in the wake of so much other good news likely brought comfort to his soul if not to his body.

That body was finally wearing out. The harsh demands of travel caught up with him. He had become ill on his final trip east the prior fall and according to Zeisberger, had "never really recovered since then." In early May "he got pains in his side and began coughing, which really bothered him." It was likely some sort of respiratory infection, perhaps pneumonia. Whatever the cause, he endured twelve more days of pain during which "he only talked about how he wanted to die and he did not want to get well again." On the one hand, that seems a surprising sentiment for a man as determined as Johannes, especially when there was so much to be thankful for that spring. On the other hand, he may very well have thought what better time to finish his life journey. So much of what he had striven for had come to fruition, if only temporarily. Why wait to see it dissolve once again? Instead of grasping onto life, he simply asked those gathered around him "to send his greetings to all the Brothers and Sisters in Bethlehem, and . . . said he loved everyone and did not hold anything against anyone." With that he died on May 15, 1775.[65]

The hundreds that processed to his burial place the next day included four generations of his kin. Wife Anna Johanna, brother Jeremias, daughters Sophia and Anna Paulina, grandson Samuel Moor, and great-granddaughter Louisa were just some of the more prominent family members mourning his loss. In one way or another, Papunhank had shepherded all of them to this place and time. They had followed his lead into Moravianism and to the Ohio Country. They had embraced the pacifism he had long preached. They had clung to the flock that he as much as anyone had helped sustain. They were part of his legacy, a legacy of peacemaking, community-building, sacrificial service, and prophetic word.

Epilogue

Three months after Papunhank's death, Englishman Nicholas Cresswell wandered into Schönbrunn with trader John Anderson. His travels that summer through Virginia, Pennsylvania, and the Ohio Country were closely recorded in his journal, including explicit details about his various and sundry sexual escapades. In fact, on the night prior to reaching Schönbrunn he had graciously accommodated the sexual advances of a "young, Handsom & Healthy" Native woman. Hardly the pious sort, then, Cresswell had few expectations when he entered the Moravian town. He was soon impressed, though, by what he saw as he walked about the Native Brethren settlement: "It is a pretty town consisting of about Sixty houses built of Loggs and covered with Clapboards. It is regularly layed out in three spacious streets which meet in the Center where there is a large meeting house built of Loggs Sixty foot square covered with Shingles, Glass in the windows and a Bell, [and] a good plank floor with two rows of forms." Perhaps at Anderson's urging, Cresswell went back to the meeting house that evening for the Moravian service. Surprised by what he had seen earlier in the day, what he encountered now came as even more of a shock:

> Never was I more astonished in my life. I expected to have seen nothing but Anarchy and Confusion as I have been taught to look upon these beings with contempt. Instead of that, here is the greatest regularity order, and Decorum, I ever saw in any place

> of Worship in my life. With that Solemnity of Behaviour and Modest, Religeous deportment [they] would do Honnor to the first religious Society on earth. And put a Bigot or Enthusiast out of countenance.
>
> The parson was a Dutchman [German] but preached in English. He had an Indian interpreter that explained it to the Indians by sentences. They sing in the Indian language. The men sits in one row of Forms and the women on the Other with Children in the front each Sex comes in and goes out on their side the house. The Old men sits on each side the parson. Treated with Tea Coffee & Broiled Bacon at supper the Sugar they make themselves out of the sap of a certain tree.[1]

What Cresswell described were scenes familiar to Papunhank. Though no longer with them, it is easy to imagine him milling amid the ranks gathered that night, talking and singing and eating. Those were routines he had grown accustomed to in his last decade. Their very presence in the Ohio Country was due in no small part to him. For the past eleven years, he had poured mind, body, and soul into making Native Brethren communities peaceful and secure so that Indians could live in accord with what he believed God intended. That same goal had animated his life ever since his adult vision quest reoriented his priorities. Over the following twenty-five years, his actions and words testified to his lasting commitment to peace. Together they reverberated across the hills and valleys of Pennsylvania, drawing Natives to his side. But they also inspired reformist Quakers to strive harder for peace and justice, saved Moravian outreach to Indians, and persuaded some government officials to work with him to extend a measure of protection to vulnerable Natives. Those achievements were noteworthy in a world in which the tide of events and attitudes flowed so strongly in the opposite direction. Papunhank's main concern had never been to change white attitudes about Native Americans. For the most part, his strong impulse was to keep virtually all Euro-Americans at a distance. But if the fruit of his labor, embodied in the work, play, and worship that went on in Schönbrunn and Gnadenhütten, could alter white views during and after his lifetime, as apparently they did in Cresswell's case, he surely wouldn't have minded, particularly if it meant that peace had more of a chance.

That's just what Anthony Benezet also hoped when in 1784 he used Papunhank to illustrate the quality of Indian character. By that point prospects were increasingly dim for a future in which both Natives and whites could flourish in the new United States. The Quaker reformer endeavored to halt or at least slow down the torrent of Indian-hating that accompanied the gaining of American independence and had already wreaked havoc upon numerous Indian peoples. He hoped that rehearsing Papunhank's story would open white eyes to the kind of person the Munsee had been and other Indians could become. A generation later, other writers similarly held up the prophet as a model Christian convert and as one who in his own words "desired to do justice, to love God and to live in peace."[2]

Unfortunately for Indians in eighteenth-century America, such high-minded aspirations were no guarantee that all would be well. In fact, acting upon those ideals often provoked conflict rather than harmony. Papunhank's life demonstrated that point over and over. The commitments he made and the stances he took netted him multiple foes. Even Zeisberger acknowledged that point in Papunhank's *lebenslauf*: "His heart was firmly attached to the Savior and the Unity, and he endured sufficient tests of this. But he had many enemies among the Indians who accused him of various bad things. They particularly accused him of having the poison about which the Indians have made so much, and this caused him many difficult hours."[3] Papunhank's perceived spiritual power made him a threat to Native religious competitors and an easy scapegoat when tragedy befell Native communities. But Indians were not his only adversaries; plenty of whites also took issue with him. Calling out traders for their fraudulent practices, barring purveyors of liquor from selling their wares, receiving aid from Quakers while frontier settlers suffered, holding back the tide of white settlement in the upper Susquehanna—all this and more had made Papunhank the object of scorn, hostility, and death threats. Just being admired by some whites in this era was reason enough for other whites to hate him or at least distrust him. They couldn't or wouldn't believe that Papunhank's intentions for peace were genuine. They had to be duplicitous. Their Indian hating had reached the point of making it intellectually impossible to imagine such a peace-loving Native.[4]

It is tempting to think that Papunhank aroused so much opposition because he was unusual in facing so many momentous choices in the years from the Seven Years' War to the American Revolution. But in fact those choices were common for Indians living across the continent during those tumultuous decades. Decisions had to be repeatedly made about where to live, how to hold onto homelands, whether to fight, where to find power, how to subsist, whose ways to follow, and how to be safe. Papunhank was an "ordinary" Indian in having to confront those types of issues. Dozens of other Native peoples and Native leaders had to do the same as they navigated the challenges and opportunities imperial contests, territorial expansion, and racial antipathy presented.

On the other hand, Papunhank may rightly be seen as quite uncommon and extraordinary in the paths he chose. If his life likely followed the typical patterns of his Munsee people in his first four or five decades, as has been suggested here, thereafter he went his own way. Adult vision quests were not rare among mid-Atlantic Indians, but they were sufficiently unusual to gain the attention of whole communities and required substantial courage on the part of the individual to seek out a potentially life-changing encounter with the supernatural. Prophets were born of such experiences, and their numbers were growing in the region when Papunhank felt his own call to preach. Still, it was only a handful of men and women who spoke a prophetic word, garnered followings, and convinced other Indians to heed their wisdom. Their spiritual power made them charismatic—and dangerous. Most all of them championed a return to ancestral ways. Papunhank followed suit but kept his options open to a greater degree than others. He agreed that whites were ruining Native lives through corruption, deceit, greed, and aggression, and was bolder than others in speaking truth directly to the seats of colonial power. Yet he saw the value in well-crafted communication with Euro-American authorities and thought blanket rejections of all things white ill advised. Most essentially, he believed that violence was not an appropriate means for resolving conflicts or achieving his goals. Here more than anywhere, Papunhank set his own course even as he perpetuated and enlarged an older Native peacemaking tradition. His pacifism was neither accidental nor incidental. Once persuaded that the Creator longed for humanity to be at peace, he resolutely opposed war whatever the consequences. That meant navigating through a host of difficult circumstances from the 1750s to the 1770s when a resort to fighting was the more straightforward and popular choice. He shared with other Munsees, Delawares, and Shawnees the goal of independence in Pennsylvania and Ohio and was frustrated as much as they with the long history of European encroachments upon Native autonomy. Yet he refused to condone warfare as the solution. In his view, other strategies could yield more fruitful results, at least for the comparatively small numbers of Indians under his leadership. Convincing even them of the wisdom of his choices was no easy task, however. They challenged his authority and most ultimately parted ways with him when war came right into their village. By that point in 1763, Papunhank had already made the crucial decision to unite with Moravians. His willingness to court the favor of both Quakers and the United Brethren during the prior five years had been another significant departure from other Delaware prophets. Moravian and Friends' peace testimonies were sufficiently akin to his to make them viable allies and in the case of the former, his eventual partners in seeking a secure home. German missionaries were instrumental in bringing him into their fold, but the main attraction was the likeminded Natives with whom he and his family could share life, work, and worship. Hundreds of other Indians made that same choice to become Moravian Christians in the mid-eighteenth century, including some of Papunhank's earlier charges and many of his kin. Nevertheless, that decision was an uncommon one, uncommon enough to leave most Indians and whites bewildered.

Perhaps that is why Papunhank has remained an obscure and virtually forgotten figure. He bewilders us. He fits poorly or not at all into the categories constructed for eighteenth-century Indians. A Delaware prophet who inspired peacemaking rather than war? A nativist willing to embrace Christianity and maintain that commitment till the end? An outspoken critic of white political and economic practices highly admired by leading Pennsylvanians? A Native war refugee protected by some whites against the violent intentions of other whites? An Indian whose life may be sufficiently reconstructed to write his biography? Then and now, Johannes Papunhank stands out as an extraordinary man, a countercultural individual whose story forces us to broaden our notions of whom and what Indians could be and do in early America.

His story also invites us to dig deeper into the lives of other Natives too long presumed to be anonymous and unrecoverable. Among those hidden figures are many of Papunhank's kin. Moravian records and other colonial documents allow for at least glimpses, and sometimes rather full views, of their lives before and after Papunhank's death. His passing in May 1775 was only one of the events that month that turned their worlds upside down. Two weeks later news arrived of the shots fired at Lexington and Concord. The Munsee prophet would likely have known something about the rising imperial tensions of 1774–75 in the wake of Lord Dunmore's War and his travels east to Bethlehem. But whether he had any inkling of a coming revolution and war for independence is impossible to know. For his kin and other Native Brethren, those developments meant reiterating their commitment to peace and political neutrality. It also meant abandoning their homes in Schönbrunn in early 1777 for temporarily safer havens at Gnadenhütten and Lichtenau, a new mission town founded in 1776 but abandoned in 1780 just before American troops burned the village down. In remaining neutral, the Moravian Indians joined in 1775 and 1776 with the most prominent leaders of the various Ohio Indian peoples who sought to use diplomacy to weather the storm of the imperial crisis and the further advance of white settlement. Small groups of Mingos, Shawnees, Delawares, and Wyandots considered that approach too passive, however, and initiated raids on frontier outposts. In a pattern reminiscent of earlier conflicts, those attacks precipitated white anger and a willingness to use violence against any Indians who happened to be handy. The resulting atrocities perpetrated upon innocent Natives had dire results by late 1777 and early 1778: "the Ohio Indians abandoned neutrality *en masse* and chose instead to fight." By that point the British were actively recruiting Indian allies in the Ohio Valley to war on western settlers. Colonists of all stripes including loyalists responded by organizing militia units to defend their communities. Fueled by grief, fear, suspicion, and a burning desire for revenge, militiamen came to despise all Indians regardless of what they professed. Those feelings only intensified over the course of the conflict. Meanwhile, warring Indians now fighting on the British side looked upon any Natives unwilling to join them as potential spies for the enemy. Mistrusted by all parties, then, peace-loving Native Moravians were once again caught in the crossfires of early American violence. Their wholesale massacre in March 1782 in Gnadenhütten by colonial militia seems an almost inevitable outcome of a generation of disturbing events.[5]

It would be naive to imagine that Papunhank, had he lived, could necessarily have done anything to prevent the tragic horrors that befell three generations of his offspring that bloody morning. Yet it is still worth pondering whether his diplomatic skills and love of peace might have made some type of difference, for it was precisely this eventuality that he had labored so long and so hard to avoid. The dream of finding a secure homeland where he could live in peace with likeminded Natives amid the turmoil and terrors of mid-eighteenth-century America animated the final twenty-five years of his life. In the end, the wonder is not that so many of his people were brutally murdered but that largely through his courage, perseverance, wisdom, and vision so many of them had managed to survive as long as they did.

Notes

Abbreviations

AMP August Mahr Papers, Ohio History Connection Library, Columbus, Ohio.

BDHP Bethlehem Digital History Project, http://bdhp.moravian.edu/home/home.html.

FAM Friendly Association Minutes, 1760–64, ser. 7, box 18, folder 11, Cox-Parrish-Wharton Papers, Historical Society of Pennsylvania, Philadelphia.

FAP Friendly Association for Regaining and Preserving Peace with the Indians by Pacific Measures, Records of the Philadelphia Yearly Meeting Indian Committee, Quaker and Special Collections, Haverford College, Haverford, Pennsylvania.

HSP Historical Society of Pennsylvania, Philadelphia, Pennsylvania.

JEP John Ettwein Papers, Moravian Archives, Bethlehem, Pennsylvania.

MAB Moravian Archives, Bethlehem, Pennsylvania.

MDP Merle Deardorff Papers, Warren Historical Society, Warren, Pennsylvania.

MMDZ Wellenreuther, Hermann, and Carola Wessel, eds. *The Moravian Mission Diaries of David Zeisberger, 1772–1781*. Translated by Julie Tomberlin Weber. University Park: Pennsylvania State University Press, 2005.

MPCP Hazard, Samuel, ed. *Colonial Records. Minutes of the Provincial Council of Pennsylvania, from the Organization to the Termination of the Proprietary Government*. 16 vols. Harrisburg, PA: Theo. Fenn, 1838–53.

PA Hazard, Samuel, et al., eds. *Pennsylvania Archives*. 1st–9th series. Philadelphia and Harrisburg: State of Pennsylvania, 1852–1949.

PFP Pemberton Family Papers, Quaker and Special Collections, Haverford College, Haverford, Pennsylvania.

RIM Records of the Indian Missions, Moravian Archives, Bethlehem, Pennsylvania.

WJP Sullivan, James, et al., eds. *The Papers of Sir William Johnson*. 14 vols. Albany: University of the State of New York, 1921–65.

Introduction

1. Congregational diary of First Moravian Church of Philadelphia, December 1, 1761–June 30, 1764, February 6, 1764, MC Phila 1.8, MAB, translated by Edward Quinter. My thanks to Scott Paul Gordon for sharing this new translation with me.
2. Key works on Moravians in early America include Atwood, *Community of the Cross*; Fogelman, *Jesus Is Female*; Sensbach, *Rebecca's Revival*; Merritt, *At the Crossroads*; and Wheeler, *To Live Upon Hope*.
3. Eighteenth-century sources offer many spellings of Papunhank's name including Papunhang, Papoonan, Papounan, Papounhan, Papunhan, Papunham, Papunchay, Papunehang, Papunahung, Papanohal, Papoonhoal, and Paypunehay.
4. Daniel P. Barr, "Did Pennsylvania Have a Middle Ground?," 337–63, provides a helpful overview of recent scholarship on the declining fortunes of Indians in Pennsylvania during the 1700s.
5. Pearl, "'Our God, and Our Guns,'" 59–68; Spero, *Frontier Country*, 148–69, quote on 159.
6. Atwood, "Understanding Zinzendorf's Blood and Wounds Theology," 31–47; Linford D. Fisher, "'I Believe They Are Papists!'" 410–37; Rubin, *Tears of Repentance*, 197–237.
7. Papunhank's vision of peace conforms well with what sociologist Johan Galtung labels "positive peace." See the summary of Galtung's views in Goode, "Relevance of Peace," 4–5.
8. Silver, *Our Savage Neighbors*, 104.
9. The label "prophet" is appropriately ascribed to Papunhank for several reasons, even though Euro-Americans appear not to have begun using that term for Indian religious reformers until around 1800 (I am indebted to Jennifer Graber for this observation). As chapter 2 will explain, Papunhank may very well have understood his divine call following his adult vision quest as fulfilling the role of a prophet. Moreover, though

he did not predict the future (one traditional notion of what a prophet does), he experienced visions and proclaimed a message that called governments and society to account. It was thoroughly and consistently "prophetic" in its demands for peace, social and economic justice, and spiritual renewal.

10. [Benezet], "Account of Behaviour & Sentiments," 482.
11. [Benezet], *Some Observations on Indian Natives*, 35. Benezet had earlier almost certainly made reference to Papunhank's story, though he did not refer to him by name, in his preface to *Plain Path to Christian Perfection*. Frost, "Anthony Benezet," 5, 15n18.
12. Benezet to John Ettwein, April 12, 1784, JEP, 128.
13. [Benezet], *Some Observations on Indian Natives*, 24.
14. [Benezet], *Some Observations on Indian Natives*, 32, 33, 36. A new interpretation of the Gnadenhütten massacre as state-sponsored warfare is offered in Rob Harper, *Unsettling the West*, 137–44.
15. Silverman, "Racial Walls," 183; Plank, "Peace, Imperial War, and Revolution," 135 (narrative histories of peace quote); Loskiel, *History of the Mission*, pts. 2 and 3; *John Papunhank, a Christian Indian.*
16. Key works on the eighteenth-century Indian prophets include Dowd, *Spirited Resistance*; Anthony F. C. Wallace, "New Religions among the Delaware"; Charles Hunter, "Delaware Nativist Revival"; Champagne, "Delaware Revitalization Movement"; Cave, "Delaware Prophet Neolin"; Cave, *Prophets of the Great Spirit*; Irwin, *Coming Down from Above*; and Jacobs, "Native American Prophetic Movements."
17. Silver, *Our Savage Neighbors*; Schutt, *Peoples of the River Valleys*; Merritt, *At the Crossroads*; Grumet, *Munsee Indians*; Goode, "Dangerous Spirits"; Kenny, *Peaceable Kingdom Lost*; Kaiser, "Munsee Social Networking"; White, *Middle Ground.*
18. Plank, *John Woolman's Path*; Erben, *Harmony of the Spirits*; Olmstead, *David Zeisberger*; Slaughter, *Beautiful Soul of John Woolman*; Pickett, "A Religious Encounter."
19. Dowd, *Spirited Resistance*, xviii, 20–21, 31–32; Cave, *Prophets of the Great Spirit*, 15; Goode, "Dangerous Spirits," 258–83.
20. Key works include Linford D. Fisher, *Indian Great Awakening*; Martin and Nicholas, *Native Americans, Christianity*; Silverman, *Faith and Boundaries*; Silverman, *Red Brethren*; Leavelle, *Catholic Calumet*; Andrews, *Native Apostles*; and Wheeler, *To Live Upon Hope.*
21. Merrell, "Some Thoughts."

22. Recent examples include Julie A. Fisher and Silverman, *Ninigret*; Marsh, *Lenape among the Quakers*; Oberg, *Professional Indian*; and Pulsipher, *Swindler Sachem*.
23. Anthony F. C. Wallace, *King of the Delawares*; Fullagar and McDonnell, "Introduction," 17.
24. Axtell, *Indian Peoples of Eastern America*, xix–xxi; Julie A. Fisher and Silverman, *Ninigret*, ix–x.
25. For two examples of biographies about people who also left few sources behind, see Collison, *Shadrach Minkins* and Corbin, *Life of an Unknown*.
26. Friedenshütten diary, January 1–December 31, 1768, April 24, 1768, box 131, folder 5, RIM, translated for author by Edward Quinter.
27. Tishcohan was the uncle of later Delaware leader Teedyuscung. Merritt, *At the Crossroads*, 326–27.
28. Schussele erroneously depicted Zeisberger preaching to the Goschgoschunk Natives around a campfire due to a mistaken secondary source he had read. The event actually took place in the council house. Michel, "Christian Schussele," 260–61.
29. Richter, "Framework for Pennsylvania Indian History," 236–61; Calloway, "Red Power," 145–62.
30. Key works include Merrell, *Into the American Woods*; Merritt, *At the Crossroads*; Matthew C. Ward, *Breaking the Backcountry*; Pencak and Richter, *Friends and Enemies in Penn's Woods*; Steven Harper, *Promised Land*; Schutt, *Peoples of the River Valleys*; Silver, *Our Savage Neighbors*; Kenny, *Peaceable Kingdom Lost*; Moyer, *Wild Yankees*; Spero, *Frontier Country*. The mid-Atlantic region has typically been used to designate the geographical area that included the colonies of New York, New Jersey, Pennsylvania, and Delaware. Whether it is a useful designation or construct is questioned in Richter, "Mid-Atlantic Colonies, R.I.P."
31. Historian Paul A. W. Wallace commented perceptively on these matters more than two generations ago: "Contrary to the white man's all-but-ineradicable belief, the Indians were not, as a rule, trigger-quick in the matter of revenge. It was a constitutional maxim . . . of the Six Nations that bloody provocation was not to be responded to in kind unless it were three times repeated. A close student of Indian revenges will be surprised to find how long, how patiently, and often with what genuine (and generous) tact, Indians of whatever nation sought to keep the peace." Paul A. W. Wallace, "John Heckewelder's Indians," 502.
32. Goode, "Relevance of Peace," 3.
33. McConnell, *A Country Between*, 115, 121, 127, 142–44, 183, 203, 238.

34. Wheeler, *To Live Upon Hope*, 107.
35. Examples of later Native leaders of the nineteenth and twentieth centuries who continued to express some of these ideas may be found in Martínez, *American Indian Intellectual Tradition*. The phrase "right order" comes from Goode, "Relevance of Peace," 5.
36. Sellers, "History, Memory, and the Indian Struggle," 714–42; Midtrød, *Memory of All Ancient Customs*, 133–36; Eustace, *Passion Is the Gale*, 290, 321–31; Goode, "Dangerous Spirits," 258–83; Duval, *Independence Lost*, 17–18. Other recent works that detail Native peacemaking strategies include Rushforth, *Bonds of Alliance*; Richter, *Ordeal of the Longhouse*; Juliana Barr, *Peace Came*; and multiple essays in Goode and Smolenski, *Specter of Peace*.
37. Examples of excellent studies of Indian-European relations outside the mid-Atlantic include Duval, *Native Ground*; Juliana Barr, *Peace Came*; and Witgen, *Infinity of Nations*.
38. Marsden, *Jonathan Edwards*, 10.

1. The Munsees' World

1. *MMDZ*, 272; author visit to Schoenbrunn Village, May 2014. The Moravian town was reconstructed as a historic site in the early twentieth century in present day New Philadelphia, Ohio, and is administered by the Ohio History Connection (formerly the Ohio Historical Society).
2. *MMDZ*, 272–73. In this published version, Zeisberger lists the baptism date incorrectly as 1762. Merritt, *At the Crossroads*, 317–20, provides another translation of the *lebenslauf* and has Zeisberger listing the baptism as occurring in 1760. Close examination of the original document by the author revealed that the digit in question was in fact a "3," so Zeisberger did have the date of Papunhank's baptism accurate after all. Schönbrunn diary September 12, 1774–May 30, 1775, May 16, 1775, box 141, folder 6, RIM.
3. Nathaniel Holland to Israel Pemberton Jr., October 16, 1760, 4:43, FAP.
4. "Post, 1760," 48.
5. For one excellent overview of these transformations, see Calloway, *New Worlds for All*.
6. On the final point, see Calloway, *Pen and Ink Witchcraft*.
7. Grumet, *Munsee Indians*, 4.
8. Grumet, *Munsee Indians*, 3–11, 105–6; Otto, *Dutch-Munsee Encounter*, 4–5, 16, 38–39; Kraft, "Settlement Patterns," 102, 105; Goddard, "Delaware Language," 103–10; Weslager, *Delaware Indians*, 37, 42–47; and Becker,

"Cultural Diversity," 93–95. There has been considerable disagreement among scholars on how best to understand and use labels such as Munsees, Lenapes, and Delawares. For a good summary of views on the subject, see Otto, *Dutch-Munsee Encounter*, 20n7.

9. Otto, *Dutch-Munsee Encounter*, 10, 17–19, 106–76, quote on 124; Merwick, *Shame and Sorrow*, 237–59.
10. Grumet, *Munsee Indians*, 173, 220; Folts, "Westward Migration of Munsee Indians," 33–35.
11. Midtrød, *Memory of All Ancient Customs*, 18, 53, 86, 103, quote on 53; Grumet, *Munsee Indians*, 20, 61, 71–72, 104–5.
12. Grumet, *Munsee Indians*, 173–74, 208–12; Kraft, "Settlement Patterns," 113–14.
13. Grumet, *Munsee Indians*, 173.
14. Grumet, *Munsee Indians*, 175.
15. Shannon, *Iroquois Diplomacy*, 55–63; Weslager, *Delaware Indians*, 103–4; Grumet, *Munsee Indians*, 201–5; and Midtrød, *Memory of All Ancient Customs*, 126–42. Excellent treatments of the Covenant Chain are provided in Richter, *Ordeal of the Longhouse* and Jennings, *Ambiguous Iroquois Empire*.
16. Folts, "Westward Migration of Munsee Indians," 32–35; Grumet, *Munsee Indians*, 205–12, 226–27; Midtrød, *Memory of All Ancient Customs*, 144–46, 152–54; Kraft, "Settlement Patterns," 102; Merritt, *At the Crossroads*, 30; and Kaiser, "Munsee Social Networking," 146–47.
17. Folts, "Westward Migration of Munsee Indians," 34–35.
18. Grumet, *Munsee Indians*, 238; Midtrød, *Memory of All Ancient Customs*, 140–42.
19. Midtrød, *Memory of All Ancient Customs*, 144; Kenny, *Peaceable Kingdom Lost*, 11–15; Weslager, *Delaware Indians*, 155–71.
20. Grumet, *Munsee Indians*, 155, 257.
21. Otto, *Dutch-Munsee Encounter*, 148–55; Merwick, *Shame and Sorrow*, 237–59; Midtrød, *Memory of All Ancient Customs*, 1–121.
22. Grumet, "Sunksquaws, Shamans, and Tradeswomen," 45, 52; Midtrød, *Memory of All Ancient Customs*, 151.
23. Grumet, *Munsee Indians*, 199, 216, 221, 351n34, 363n45, 376n32; Midtrød, *Memory of All Ancient Customs*, 148, 253n12.
24. Wolley, "Two Years Journal," 1:27–28; Grumet, *Munsee Indians*, 348–49n21; Axtell, *Indian Peoples of Eastern America*, 3.
25. Grumet, *Munsee Indians*, 348–49n21, quote on 348 from original land deed as cited by Grumet.
26. Grumet, *Munsee Indians*, 20–21, 155, quotes on 20 and 21; Becker, "Cultural Diversity," 93–94.

27. Merritt, *At the Crossroads*, 328–29; Grumet, *Munsee Indians*, 155, 355n25, 364n4; Midtrød, *Memory of All Ancient Customs*, 162–63. Merritt provides a genealogical tree showing Shabash as Mamanuchqua's grandson.
28. Grumet, *Munsee Indians*, 348n21, 376n32; [Benezet], "Account of the Behaviour & Sentiments," 484; Ettwein, "Brother Ettwein's Account," 264.
29. Grumet, "Taphow," 24.
30. Grumet, "Minisink Settlements," 218; "At a Conference with Indians, August 5, 1761," *MPCP*, 8:634.
31. Grumet, *Munsee Indians*, 257. For excellent accounts of the Shekomeko mission, see Dally-Starna and Starna, "Introduction," 1:1–73, and Wheeler, *To Live Upon Hope*, 67–171.
32. Kraft, "Settlement Patterns," 102; Midtrød, *Memory of All Ancient Customs*, 146–47; Folts, "Westward Migration of Munsee Indians," 33–34.
33. Paul A. W. Wallace, *Indians in Pennsylvania*, 140; Midtrød, *Memory of All Ancient Customs*, 146, 156–57; Kaiser, "Munsee Social Networking," 149; Faull, "From Friedenshütten to Wyoming," 87; Paul A. W. Wallace, *Indian Paths of Pennsylvania*, 83–84; William A. Hunter, "John Hays' Diary," 65, 67n24.
34. Axtell, *Indian Peoples of Eastern America*, 31; Heckewelder, *History, Manners, and Customs*, 117; Schutt, "Female Relationships," 93.
35. Friedenshütten diary, January 1,1770–December 31, 1770, September 23, 1770, box 131, folder 7, RIM, translated for author by Edward Quinter; Heckewelder, *History, Manners, and Customs*, quote on 116; Schutt, "Female Relationships," 93; Paul A. W. Wallace, *Indians in Pennsylvania*, 62; Axtell, *Indian Peoples of Eastern America*, 42–43. Moravian missionary Johann Jacob Schmick wrote down in the Friedenshütten diary for September 23, 1770, a very detailed description of how this sacred rite was conducted based on what some Moravian Indians told him.
36. Heckewelder, *History, Manners, and Customs*, 245–48, quote on 247; Axtell, *Indian Peoples of Eastern America*, 32; Schutt, "Female Relationships," 93; Paul A. W. Wallace, *Indians in Pennsylvania*, 63.
37. Axtell, *Indian Peoples of Eastern America*, 103; Reichel, "Wyalusing and the Moravian Mission," 192–93; Schutt, *Peoples of the River Valleys*, 16–20; de Schweinitz, *Life and Times of Zeisberger*, 80–81; Paul A. W. Wallace, *Indians in Pennsylvania*, 32–33, 36–37.
38. Becker, "Cultural Diversity," 96–99; Kenny, *Peaceable Kingdom Lost*, 20–21; Weslager, *Delaware Indians*, 174–75; Merrell, *Into the American Woods*, 25, 54, 157, 225–27, 232–33.
39. Schutt, *Peoples of the River Valleys*, 79–86; Becker, "Cultural Diversity," 93; Paul A. W. Wallace, *Indians in Pennsylvania*, 112–13. Midtrød, *Memo-*

ry of All Ancient Customs, 161–66, describes how the growing numbers of whites prompted similar migrations among Hudson Valley Indians in the early- to mid-eighteenth century.

40. Hinderaker, "Declaring Independence," 107–8; McConnell, "Peoples 'In Between,'" 94–102; Jennings, *Ambiguous Iroquois Empire*, 45, explains that the terms "uncle" and "nephews" were used by Indians to refer to "the ordinary tributary relationship, involving an obligation to protect, on the one side, and a reciprocal obligation to heed counsel on the other."
41. Kenny, *Peaceable Kingdom Lost*, 41–46; Merrell, "Shickellamy," 233; Schutt, *Peoples of the River Valleys*, 86–90; Grumet, *Munsee Indians*, 245–49, quote on 249; Steven Harper, *Promised Land*, 70–94; Steven Harper, "Making History," 217–33; Jennings, *Ambiguous Iroquois Empire*, 328–40, 388–97; Merritt, *At the Crossroads*, 41–49.
42. Schutt, *Peoples of the River Valleys*, 87–89; Kenny, *Peaceable Kingdom Lost*, 46–49; Grumet, *Munsee Indians*, 249–50; Steven Harper, *Promised Land*, 82; Jennings, *Ambiguous Iroquois Empire*, 342–46; "Canasatego's Speech," *MPCP*, 4:575–79.
43. Historians have long debated the meanings of Delawares being called "women." For a list of works on the topic, see Kenny, *Peaceable Kingdom Lost*, 248n18. Also see Jennings, *Ambiguous Iroquois Empire*, 44–46, 48–49, and Grimes, *Western Delaware Indian Nation*, 1–27.
44. Schutt, *Peoples of the River Valleys*, 92. Italics in original.
45. Merrell, "Shickellamy," 227–57, quote on 240; Merrell, *Into the American Woods*, 54–56, 77–79, 193.
46. Merrell, "Shickellamy," 227–57, quote on 250.
47. Grumet, *Munsee Indians*, 251–55; Grigg, *Lives of David Brainerd*, 72–79; Pointer, *Encounters of the Spirit*, 110; Kenny, *Peaceable Kingdom Lost*, 49; Weslager, *Delaware Indians*, 187–94.
48. Jennings, *Ambiguous Iroquois Empire*, 350–51, defines the Ohio Country as beginning with the "Allegheny tributary of the Ohio River (the tributary itself was often called the Ohio River) and extended indefinitely westward to merge with an equally vague 'Illinois country.'"
49. Hinderaker, "Declaring Independence," 108–9; Shannon, *Iroquois Diplomacy*, 125–28; McConnell, *A Country Between*, 60–62; Matthew C. Ward, *Breaking the Backcountry*, 24; Grimes, *Western Delaware Indian Nation*, 51.
50. Hinderaker, "Declaring Independence," 110–13; Shannon, *Iroquois Diplomacy*, 129–30; McConnell, *A Country Between*, 69–80.
51. Matthew C. Ward, *Breaking the Backcountry*, 24–29; Shannon, *Iroquois Diplomacy*, 131–33; McConnell, *A Country Between*, 77–80.

52. McConnell, "Pisquetomen and Tamaqua," 279.

53. McConnell, *A Country Between*, 70–71; Shannon, *Iroquois Diplomacy*, 130; Matthew C. Ward, *Breaking the Backcountry*, 29–30.

54. Kenny, *Peaceable Kingdom Lost*, 51–52; McConnell, *A Country Between*, 80–112.

2. Becoming a Prophet

1. [Benezet], "Account of Behaviour & Sentiments," 484. Papunhank's testimony was first published in London in *An Account of a Visit Lately Made to the People Called Quakers in Philadelphia, by Papanahoal, an Indian Chief* and then in the 1803 pamphlet, *An Account of the Behavior and Sentiments of some well disposed Indians, mostly of the Minusing Tribe*. There are several extant versions of the original manuscript, each containing variations from the others. Brookes used Huntington Library Manuscript 824 ("Some Account of the Behaviour & Sentiments of a Number of Well-Disposed Indians," Huntington Library, San Marino CA), but made some edits of his own. Huntington Library Manuscript 8249 is likely an earlier, rougher draft of this account. The Historical Society of Pennsylvania in Philadelphia houses two other manuscript versions of this text: "Some Remarks made by a Person who accompanied Papunahoal and the other Indians on their way home as far as Bethlehem [1760]," box 11C, folder 5, Society Miscellaneous Collection; and "Some Account of the Visit of the Friendly Indians to Philadelphia, 1760," box 10, Gilbert Cope Collection. Two more manuscript versions of "Some Remarks made by a Person who accompanied Pawpoonahoal & the other Indians from Philadelphia as far as Bethlehem on their way" are in the Allinson Family Papers, box 8, Indians folder, Quaker and Special Collections, Haverford College, Haverford, PA. Other printed versions of the text may be found in Grumet, *Journey on the Forbidden Path*, 129–32, and Irwin, *Coming Down from Above*, 375. Irwin follows the lead of anthropologist Grumet in proposing that the original manuscript was written by Indian-sympathizer Charles Thomson rather than Benezet. But this seems unlikely given Benezet's firsthand access to the source materials used to write the manuscript, his personal correspondence at the time that indicated his familiarity with the manuscript, and evidence that some of the drafts of the manuscript are in Benezet's handwriting. Plank, "Quaker Reform and Evangelization," 183, 185, supports the view that Benezet was the author.

2. For an excellent case study of the challenges of transcribing and translating Indian speeches, see Merrell, "'I desire.'"

3. Dowd, *Spirited Resistance*, xiii.
4. Dowd, *Spirited Resistance*, xiii, 2; Charles Hunter, "Delaware Nativist Revival," 40; Merritt, *At the Crossroads*, 91–92; White, *Middle Ground*, 279–81.
5. Irwin, *Coming Down from Above*, 111–12. As explained in chapter 1, manitous or *manitouwak* were the spirits who populated nature. The purpose of a vision quest was to have a manitou appear and offer its aid and protection, and thereafter to function as a guardian spirit.
6. Dowd, *Spirited Resistance*, xiii–xv, 2–3, 16; Charles Hunter, "Delaware Nativist Revival," 40, 47.
7. Moravian missionary David Zeisberger made one of the first attempts to assess the phenomenon of Indian preachers in the late 1770s. He had been observing and interacting with them for the prior thirty years during his ministry work in Pennsylvania, New York, and Ohio. He dated their emergence to the late 1740s, but it seems likely that some had begun preaching sooner than that. Zeisberger, "History of Indians," 133–36.
8. Dowd, *Spirited Resistance*, 29; White, *Middle Ground*, 281; David Brainerd, "Related Correspondence," 576.
9. Edwards, "Life of Brainerd," 329–30. Moravian August Spangenberg's 1745 journal describes a similar Native response from Shickellamy to Brainerd at Shamokin, Pennsylvania, in June 1745. See "Spangenberg's Journal, 1745," 7.
10. Thomas Brainerd, *Life of John Brainerd*, 233–35; Cave, *Prophets of the Great Spirit*, 11–14; Dowd, *Spirited Resistance*, 30; Irwin, *Coming Down from Above*, 126–27.
11. As quoted in Merritt, *At the Crossroads*, 90. Zeisberger, "History of Indians," 133, noted the separate "paths to heaven" theology of the Indian preachers.
12. Post, "Journal, 1760," 56–61, quotes on 58 and 56; Hays, "Diary, 1760," 73; Zeisberger, "History of Indians," 133; Dowd, *Spirited Resistance*, 32; Cave, *Prophets of the Great Spirit*, 16; Charles Hunter, "Delaware Nativist Revival," 42–43. The town of Assinisink is often rendered "Assinsink" in various primary and secondary sources.
13. Dowd, *Spirited Resistance*, xviii, 19; Anthony F. C. Wallace, "Delaware Indian Religions," 7–8.
14. Dowd, *Spirited Resistance*, 19.
15. Mancall, *Deadly Medicine*, 63–84, 107; Heckewelder, *History, Manners, and Customs*, 261–67; Goode, "Dangerous Spirits," quote on 262; Merrell, *Into*

the American Woods, 86–87, 99–100; Weslager, *Delaware Indians*, 201–4; [Benezet], "Account of Behaviour & Sentiments," 484.

16. Heckewelder, *History, Manners, and Customs*, 269–74; Axtell, *Indian Peoples of Eastern America*, 199–200, 216–19.
17. [Benezet], "Account of the Behaviour & Sentiments," 484; Grumet, *Munsee Indians*, 17; Heckewelder, *History, Manners, and Customs*, 163–65.
18. Cave, *Prophets of the Great Spirit*, 3; Irwin, *Coming Down from Above*, 108–12.
19. Irwin, *Coming Down from Above*, 108, notes that within Delaware cosmology, Kishelëmukòng had created them, their lands, and all the animals and plants within it, and given it to them. I believe this name for the creator is an Unami word rather than a Munsee word.
20. Weslager, "Delaware Indian Name Giving," 139; [Benezet], "Account of Behaviour & Sentiments," 484; Cave, *Prophets of the Great Spirit*, 27–30; Irwin, *Coming Down from Above*, 110–12.
21. [Benezet], "Account of Behaviour & Sentiments," 484.
22. [Benezet], "Account of Behaviour & Sentiments," 484; Heckewelder, *History, Manners, and Customs*, 224–26; Irwin, *Coming Down from Above*, 106–12.
23. [Benezet], "Account of Behaviour & Sentiments," 484.
24. Dowd, *Spirited Resistance*, 31.
25. Irwin, *Coming Down from Above*, 112.
26. [Benezet], "Account of Behaviour & Sentiments," 484; "Spangenberg's Journal, 1745," 12, 13.
27. Jon Butler, *Awash in a Sea of Faith*; Linford D. Fisher, *Indian Great Awakening*; Dowd, *Spirited Resistance*, 23–46. Dowd applied the term "Great Awakening" to the rise of the nativist prophets.
28. Post, "Journal, 1760," 48.
29. Hays, "Diary, 1760," 111.
30. [Benezet], "An Account of Papunahung's Second Visit, 1761," 486. Papunhank shared this information during his second extended visit with Quakers, which they once again documented extensively. As with his first visit to Friends in 1760, multiple manuscript accounts of their interactions in 1761 are extant. The account in Brookes's *Friend Anthony Benezet* is once again based on Huntington Library Manuscript 824. "Some account of a Visit divers Friends made to the Indians at the time of the Treaty of Easton, taken by one of the Company as follows, 1761" is part of another Huntington manuscript, 8249, [pp. 12–18], and contains material not contained in Brookes's published version. Other manuscript accounts

that overlap and, in some cases, duplicate, what is contained in the Huntington manuscripts include "Report of the Trustees of the Friendly Association who attended the Indian Treaty of Easton," 4:139–52, FAP; John Woolman, "The Substance of some Conversation with Paponahoal the Indian Chief at AB's in presence of Jo. W—n Ab etc.," 13:23, Pemberton Family Papers, HSP; and Quaker Journal (attributed to Susanna [Hatton] Lightfoot), Easton, PA 1761, Quaker Collection, William Clements Library, University of Michigan, Ann Arbor, MI. A published version of the "Some account of a Visit divers Friends made to the Indians" manuscript may be found in Amos W. Butler, "Visit to Easton," 267–74. Butler found his copy of this manuscript in the possession of the Bristol and Somersetshire Friends Meeting, Bristol, England.

31. [Benezet], "Account of Behaviour & Sentiments," 480, 483, quotes on 483.
32. These themes are discussed especially well in W. R. Ward, *Protestant Evangelical Awakening* and Winiarski, *Darkness Falls.*
33. Ettwein, "Report of the Journey," 35, 109n89; Faull, "From Friedenshütten to Wyoming," 87. Lechaweke was also known as Hazivok and as Asserughne.
34. Paul A. W. Wallace, *Indians in Pennsylvania*, 107–8; Ettwein, "Report of the Journey," 35.
35. Grumet, *Munsee Indians*, 20.
36. Grumet, *Munsee Indians*, 22.
37. Wyalusing is spelled or referred to by many different names in eighteenth-century sources including Machachlosung, Machemihilusing, M'chwihilusing, Quialoosing, and Chwihilusing. For clarity sake, I will use Wyalusing except in direct quotes. "Frederick Post's Relation of What Passed between Him and the Quaker," in Grumet, *Journey on the Forbidden Path*, 117–18. Post reported the same information in a letter to Israel Pemberton dated May 20, 1760: Christian Frederick Post to Israel Pemberton, May 20, 1760, 3:521, FAP; "Post's Report," *PA*, 1st ser., 3:742–44; Craft, *History of Bradford County*, 12; author visit to Wyalusing, PA, in June 2013. Among recent historians, Dowd, *Spirited Resistance*, 31; Grumet, *Munsee Indians*, 257; and Merritt, *At the Crossroads*, 84, endorse the 1752 date for Papunhank's arrival in Wyalusing. In a previously edited volume, *Journey on the Forbidden Path*, 47n9, Grumet asserted that Papunhank settled Wyalusing in 1758.
38. Post, "Journal, 1760," 48; Hays, "Journal, 1760," 49. The original Post journal may be found at Christian Frederick Post diary, 1760, HSP.
39. "Journal of Moses Tatamy and Isaac Hill [Still] to Minisinks, 1758," *PA*, 1st ser., 3:504–8. Historians who endorse the later founding date (1758)

for Papunhank's settlement at Wyalusing include Kaiser, "Munsee Social Networking," 155, and William A. Hunter, "John Hays' Diary ," 67n24.

40. Daniel P. Barr, "'Road for Warriors,'" 1, 3 (quote); Grimes, *Western Delaware Indian Nation*, 76–89; Matthew C. Ward, *Breaking the Backcountry*, 30, 36–44; Preston, *Braddock's Defeat*; Anderson, *Crucible of War*, 94–110.
41. Hinderaker, "Declaring Independence," 116–17. Matthew C. Ward, *Breaking the Backcountry*, 45–46, explains that "the raids on the backcountry formed a central part of French military strategy." Outnumbered and out-resourced, "the French were thus prepared to equip and provision Indian war parties, hoping to neutralize the British war effort and to compel the British colonies to seek peace rather than to agitate for war."
42. Loskiel, *History of the Mission*, pt. 2, 164.
43. Hinderaker, "Declaring Independence," 117; Kenny, *Peaceable Kingdom Lost*, 71; Matthew C. Ward, *Breaking the Backcountry*, 56–57, 64; Camenzind, "Violence, Race," 204 (quote).
44. Kenny, *Peaceable Kingdom Lost*, 71–72.
45. Loskiel, *History of the Mission*, pt. 2, 165, 169.
46. Loskiel, *History of the Mission*, pt. 2, 164–71; Kaiser, "Munsee Social Networking," 155; Kenny, *Peaceable Kingdom Lost*, 75; Weslager, *Delaware Indians*, 229, 231. Matthew C. Ward, *Breaking the Backcountry*, 71, notes that the violence was especially intense in Northampton Country, Pennsylvania (the area east of the North Branch of the Susquehanna River) where "over four times as many settlers were killed as taken captive."
47. Kenny, *Peaceable Kingdom Lost*, 59, 75; Shannon, "War, Diplomacy, and Culture," 85–89.
48. Shannon, *Iroquois Diplomacy*, 146–59.
49. Loskiel, *History of the Mission*, pt. 2, 165.
50. Loskiel, *History of the Mission*, pt. 2, 165; Camenzind, "Violence, Race," 205–8, 216, quote on 216; Camenzind, "From Holy Experiment"; Weiser as quoted in Kenny, *Peaceable Kingdom Lost*, 75.
51. As quoted in Matthew C. Ward, *Breaking the Backcountry*, 64.
52. William A. Hunter, "Moses (Tunda) Tatamy," 264; William A. Hunter, "John Hays' Diary," 65, 67n24; Post, "Journal, 1760," 44.
53. William A. Hunter, "John Hays' Diary," 65, 67n24; Weslager, *Delaware Indians*, 230; "Journal of Tatamy and Hill [Still]," 507.
54. Kenny, *Peaceable Kingdom Lost*, 65–68; Hinderaker, "Declaring Independence," 115–16; Preston, "'Make Indians of Our White Men,'" 281–88.
55. [Benezet], "Account of Behaviour & Sentiments," 482.
56. [Benezet], "Account of Behaviour & Sentiments," 482.

57. [Benezet], *Account of Behavior and Sentiments*, 10. I have quoted here from the 1803 published version of Papunhank's testimony because this text is misquoted in Brookes's version.

58. [Benezet], "Account of Behaviour & Sentiments," 482, 484; Dowd, *Spirit of Resistance*, 33–35, 136–47, quote on Neolin on 34; Dowd, *War under Heaven*; Cave, "Delaware Prophet Neolin"; Irwin, *Coming Down from Above*, 129–32, 177–94; Edmunds, *Shawnee Prophet*.

59. Kaiser, "Munsee Social Networking," 148, 150, 150n23, 155, quotes on 148; Heckewelder, *History, Manners, and Customs*, 253.

60. Grumet, *Munsee Indians*, 71–72, 95, 99, 117–18, 134, 140–41, 144, 158, 173.

61. Marsh, *Lenape among the Quakers*, 97–98. Marsh suggests, and Patrick Spero concurs, that area Indians and the Pennsylvania government forged a peaceful relationship through these means down to the 1720s. Spero, *Frontier Country*, 49–70.

62. Eustace, *Passion Is the Gale*, 290, 321–331, quote on 290. For wider treatments of condolence ceremonies, see White, *Middle Ground* and Richter, *Ordeal of the Longhouse*.

63. Charles Hunter, "Delaware Nativist Revival," 40, 47; Champagne, "Delaware Revitalization Movement," 120–21; Cave, *Prophets of the Great Spirit*, xi, xiii, 3–6, 37–38, 43; Irwin, *Coming Down from Above*, 126–33; White, *Middle Ground*, 279–81. Other Christian themes noticeable in various Indian prophets include the notion of heaven and hell, some type of sacred scripture, and belief in the need for salvation. Indian prophets often turned these Christian ideas to their own purposes.

64. Anthony F. C. Wallace, "New Religions among the Delaware," 8; Dowd, *Spirit of Resistance*, 31; Cave, *Prophets of the Great Spirit*, 15; White, *Middle Ground*, 279–80; and Irwin, *Coming Down from Above*, 127, all support the idea that Papunhank absorbed ideas from Christian groups.

65. *An Epistle from our Yearly-Meeting*; Frost, "William Penn's Experiment," 577–605; Merrell, *Into the American Woods*, 119; Spady, "Colonialism and Penn's Treaty," 30–39; Preston, "Squatters, Indians," 184–89; Sellers, "History, Memory, and the Indian Struggle," 714–42.

66. Unlike other European Christian bodies in the colonies, Friends had not yet engaged in formal missionary outreach to Natives. That is not to say, however, that Quakers were not committed to or engaged in evangelization of non-Quakers. Reformist Friends in particular, who were intent on revitalizing the movement through stricter discipline, were among the most avid Quaker evangelists. Their contacts with Papunhank in the

early 1760s may be seen as one expression of their outreach. See Plank, "Quaker Reform and Evangelization," 177–91.

67. Minutes for Council held in Philadelphia, October 19, 1756, and Council held at Newcastle, October 21, 1756, *MPCP*, 7:292–93, 295; Anthony Benezet to Jonah Thompson, April 24, 1756, in Brookes, *Friend Anthony Benezet*, 220; Kenny, *Peaceable Kingdom Lost*, 76–82; Silver, *Our Savage Neighbors*, 98; Camenzind, "Violence, Race," 215.
68. Silver, *Our Savage Neighbors*, 98–103; Marietta, *Reformation of American Quakerism*, 92–93, 135–36, 157–58, 188–89; James, *A People among Peoples*, 178–92; Bauman, *For the Reputation of Truth*, 77–125; Camenzind, "From Holy Experiment," 161–204; Thayer, "Friendly Association," 356–76; Jennings, *Empire of Fortune*, 339, 375.
69. As noted earlier, Moravian theology and preaching in this era emphasized the blood and wounds of Jesus Christ for human salvation. Atwood, "Understanding Zinzendorf's Blood and Wounds Theology," 31–47.
70. The purpose of the first trip was to gain Iroquois Confederacy permission to resettle Indians from their Shekomeko mission to the Wyoming Valley. Other trips hoped to establish mission work among the Six Nations. "Spangenberg's Journal, 1745," 5–16; Beauchamp, *Moravian Journals*, 24–105; Olmstead, *David Zeisberger*, 37–40. Zeisberger made three other substantial trips and stays in Onondaga in 1752, 1753, and 1754.
71. As quoted in Merritt, *At the Crossroads*, 132.
72. Loskiel, *History of the Mission*, pt. 2, 78–81, 91, 119, 120–22, 148, 153, quote on 122.
73. Ettwein, "Report of the Journey," 35. Craft, *Historical Discourse*, 123, states that the diary of the Bethlehem Moravian congregation for July 7, 1760, noted that Papunhank and his people had heard Brethren preach the gospel five or six years earlier.
74. Merritt, *At the Crossroads*, 156–59; Hamilton, *John Ettwein*, 164, quoting Zinzendorf from 1756.
75. Burkholder, "Neither 'Kriegerisch' nor 'Quäkerisch,'" 158–61; Jennings, *Ambiguous Iroquois Empire*, 350.
76. Nain diary extracts [written by Augustus Spangenberg], entries for August 14, August 26, August 27, and August 29, 1758, box 125, folder 1, item 10, RIM, translated for author by Roy Ledbetter.
77. Anthony F. C. Wallace, "Delaware Indian Religions," 8. As noted earlier, many of the prophets drew upon elements of Christian belief and refashioned them for their own purposes. At the same time, most of them

preferred to keep Christians themselves at arm's length as part of their message to keep apart from the corrupting influence of Euro-American peoples and ways.

78. [Benezet], "Account of Behaviour & Sentiments," 483.
79. "Journal of Tatamy and Hill [Still]," 507; Post, "Journal, 1760," 50; Hays, "Diary, 1760," 47.
80. Scholars of the Delaware prophets have consistently interpreted their rise as coming in response to the crises faced by their peoples in the mid-eighteenth century. Charles Hunter, "Delaware Nativist Revival," 40; Dowd, *Spirited Resistance*, 18–19; Champagne, "Delaware Revitalization Movement," 107–26; Cave, *Prophets of the Great Spirit*, xi; Irwin, *Coming Down from Above*, 124.
81. Schutt, *Peoples of the River Valleys*, 115–16.
82. [Benezet], "Account of Papunahung's Second Visit, 1761," 491.
83. [Benezet], "Account of Papunahung's Second Visit, 1761," 488–89.
84. As Dowd, *Spirited Resistance*, 30–31, 41–42, explains, many of the nativist prophets preached a "separate creation" theology in which they argued that God had created Indians, blacks, and whites separately and there were different paths for them to follow toward salvation. White, *Middle Ground*, 282, suggests that this theology was implicit in some of Papunhank's language, but the quoted passage here points strongly in this other direction. For another Indian leader with similar views to Papunhank, see Wheeler, "Hendrick Aupaumut," 228.

3. Building Alliances

1. Diary of the Brethren Dav. Zeisberger and Nathanael the Indian, June 10–July 10, 1763, June 26, box 227, folder 10, RIM, translated for author by Roy Ledbetter.
2. Eustace, *Passion Is the Gale*, 90–95, notes that colonial Americans often doubted the sincerity or authenticity of Indian emotional expressions, but in this case Zeisberger showed no such doubts in his journal entry. For their part, Natives often "expressed great concern about the emotional sincerity of Europeans" (91).
3. Papunhank's phrase here, at least as recorded by Zeisberger, bore a striking resemblance to the words he used in a conversation with Friend Moales Pattison three years earlier regarding his sense that the Quakers spoke "good words" that were the "true voice" of God. He was clearly searching for some more definitive spiritual resting place in the early 1760s.

4. A number of recent students of Native American interactions with Christianity have pointed out the limitations of the term "conversion" when characterizing the complexity of Indian responses to Christian faith and institutions. In particular, they have noted the totalizing connotations of the word "conversion" with respect to the nature of the religious and cultural change Indians who chose to associate with Christianity may have experienced. On the other hand, to use alternative terms such as "affiliated with" or "associated with" can leave the impression that such Indians should not be considered fully Christian. In this case, I have employed the term because I think it fairly represents how Papunhank looked upon the significance of the religious choice he made at this point in his life. I believe he understood that he was entering into a new level of relationship with the Moravians and into a new way of understanding and experiencing his relationship with a supreme being. See the discussion of "conversion" in Linford D. Fisher, *Indian Great Awakening*, 86–89.
5. Richter, "Framework for Pennsylvania Indian History," quote on 250; Hinderaker, "Declaring Independence," 105–25. Moyer, *Wild Yankees*, 18–23, makes a similar argument about Indians in the Wyoming Valley and more broadly in Northeast Pennsylvania during the 1750s and 1760s.
6. Kenny, *Peaceable Kingdom Lost*, 86–89; McConnell, *A Country Between*, 124–26; Daniel P. Barr, "Victory at Kittanning?," 5–32.
7. In Pennsylvania, as elsewhere in British North America, the lieutenant governor was the chief executive in the colony since Crown-appointed governors remained in Britain. As a result, lieutenant governors were often referred to and thought of simply as governors.
8. Schutt, *Peoples of the River Valleys*, 15–16; Kenny, *Peaceable Kingdom Lost*, 83–86; Merritt, *At the Crossroads*, 208–10, 215–16; Anthony F. C. Wallace, *King of the Delawares*, 103–15, 124–36.
9. Anthony F. C. Wallace, *King of the Delawares*, 56–102; Kenny, *Peaceable Kingdom Lost*, 92; Matthew C. Ward, "'Peaceable Kingdom' Destroyed," 265–67. Since Papunhank's following appears to have grown in size in the late 1750s, it seems reasonable to conclude that the vast majority supported his strategies.
10. "Substance of Conferences between Several Quakers in Philadelphia and the heads of the six Indian nations [April 19–25, 1756]," 1:103, 107, 111, 115, FAP; Daiutolo, "Role of Quakers," 7–8.
11. Steven Harper, *Promised Land*, 92–94, 103–14; Merritt, *At the Crossroads*, 224–25. Friends referred to the planting of the Pennsylvania colony as a "holy experiment," particularly in regard to establishing peaceful and just

relations between the area's indigenous population and the European newcomers.

12. Anthony F. C. Wallace, *King of the Delawares*, 108–15, 137–44, 158–60; Kenny, *Peaceable Kingdom Lost*, 84–97; Merritt, *At the Crossroads*, 224–31, 235–36; Steven Harper, *Promised Land*, 107–14; Daiutolo, "Role of Quakers," 10–21.
13. As quoted in Gerona, "Imagining Peace," 55.
14. Anthony F. C. Wallace, *King of the Delawares*, 184–91; Daiutolo, "Role of Quakers," 22.
15. William Denny to Sir William Johnson, December 6, 1756, *WJP*, 9:565 (quote); Steven Harper, *Promised Land*, 112–14; Merrell, "'I desire,'" 777–826; Kenny, *Peaceable Kingdom Lost*, 94, 97; Schutt, *Peoples of the River Valleys*, 116–17; Minutes for Council held in Easton, July 28, 1757, *MPCP*, 7:678. Charles Thomson served as Teedyuscung's clerk and wrote a pro-Delaware account of their grievances and the various Easton treaties: *An Inquiry into the Causes of the Alienation of the Delawares and Shawanese Indians from the British Interest.*
16. Kenny, *Peaceable Kingdom Lost*, 97, 101; Steven Harper, *Promised Land*, 112–14; Merritt, *At the Crossroads*, 256–57; Jennings, *Empire of Fortune*, 346–48, 384–87; Anthony F. C. Wallace, *King of the Delawares*, 161–207.
17. Schutt, *Peoples of the River Valleys*, 114–16, quote on 115. Eustace, *Passion Is the Gale*, 322–30, argues that one of those challenges was getting Euro-American negotiators to conform to Native diplomatic protocols, including the condolence ceremonies with which Indians wished to begin treaties.
18. Schutt, *Peoples of the River Valleys*, 118; McConnell, "Pisquetomen and Tamaqua," 273–89; McConnell, *A Country Between*, 126–27; Grimes, *Western Delaware Indian Nation*, 88.
19. McConnell, *A Country Between*, 127–35; McConnell, "Pisquetomen and Tamaqua," 285–88; Kenny, *Peaceable Kingdom Lost*, 97–105. Post made two key journeys to the west to negotiate with the western Delawares. See "The Journal of Christian Frederick Post, from Philadelphia to the Ohio . . . [July 15, 1758–September 20, 1758]" and "The Journal of Christian Frederick Post, on a message from the Governor of Pennsylvania, to the Indians on the Ohio . . . [October 25, 1758–January 10, 1759]," in Thwaites, *Early Western Travels*, 185–233, 234–91. For Post's diplomatic role in 1758–59, see Champion, "Christian Frederick Post," 308–25.
20. Minutes of Council held at Easton, October 7–26, 1758, *MPCP*, 8:174–223; Kenny, *Peaceable Kingdom Lost*, 105–11; Merritt, *At the Crossroads*, 250–

52, 256–57; Daiutolo, "Role of Quakers," 23–25; McConnell, *A Country Between*, 132, 137–41.

21. Nain diary extracts, August 8, 1758, box 125, folder 1, item 10, RIM, translated for author by Roy Ledbetter; "Journal of Moses Tatamy and Isaac Hill [Still] to Minisinks, 1758," *PA*, 1st ser., 3:504–8, quote on 507; Grumet, *Munsee Indians*, 265.
22. Minutes of Conference held at Burlington, August 7–8, 1758, *MPCP*, 8:156–61, quote on 158; Grumet, *Munsee Indians*, 265–66; Jennings, *Empire of Fortune*, 389–90, 398–400.
23. Papunhank and his family arrived on August 14 and departed on the twenty-ninth. At the Moravian Archives in Bethlehem, Pennsylvania, there are two "versions" of the Nain congregational diary during its years of existence from 1757 to 1763. The full diaries are "housed" physically at the end of each year or six-month period of the Bethlehem congregational diaries for these years (volumes 17 through 26 of the Bethlehem diary). All materials drawn from them were translated for the author by Edward Quinter. Extracts from the Nain diary, written most likely by Augustus Spangenberg, are in box 125 of RIM. The extracts often summarize, paraphrase, or condense the original diary entries. All materials drawn from them were translated for the author by Roy Ledbetter.
24. The names used here for Papunhank's family members are their Christian names given at their later baptisms. Their Munsee names are not known. Sophia was baptized in 1764, Anna Johanna was baptized in 1766, and Anna Paulina was baptized in 1772. Because Anna Johanna lived until 1814, some uncertainty exists as to whether she was Sophia's mother. It is also uncertain whether Anna Paulina was alive at this time, though her baptism in 1772 makes it likely since younger children were not typically baptized except as infants or on their deathbeds. See chapter 6 for further discussion of these family connections. The Nain diary entry for August 29 also indicates that a sister of either Papunhank's or his wife was also with them in Nain. Nain diary, August 29, 1758, in Bethlehem diary, vol. 19, MAB. Many of Nain's residents were Mahican converts who had moved to Pennsylvania from the earlier missions in Shekomeko, New York, and western Connecticut. Some of them had lived at Gnadenhütten until the 1755 attack by hostile Indians forced them to remove to Bethlehem. The Indian town of Nain was founded to accommodate many of these refugee Natives.
25. Loskiel, *History of the Mission*, pt. 2, 189, "full proof of their repentance" quote; Nain diary, August 14 and August 27, 1758, MAB; Nain diary

extracts August 27 [misdated August 26] and August 29, 1758, RIM. The extracts writer may have editorialized the last comment a bit since a more literal translation of the diary statement might be that Papunhank and his family "quietly and orderly took their leave from here" (translation by Edward Quinter). Nanhun was an early Mahican convert to Moravianism, being baptized as Joshua on September 15, 1742. Thereafter he was almost always referred to by Moravians as Joshua Senior. Hartzell, "Joshua, Jr," 1. For more on Joshua Senior, see Wheeler, "Imagined Mohican-Moravian Lebenslauf," 29–44.

26. Hartzell, "Joshua, Jr.," 2. Joshua was a communicant Moravian, having participated in his first Communion in February 1758.
27. Minutes of Council held at Easton, October 8, 1758, *MPCP*, 8:176; McConnell, *A Country Between*, 113, 134; Jennings, *Empire of Fortune*, 406–9.
28. Six Nations' relations with Johnson and the British were in fact extremely complex, as noted in Jennings, *Empire of Fortune*, 413–17.
29. On Moravian recovery efforts, see Loskiel, *History of the Mission*, pt. 2, 177–90.
30. Kaiser, "Munsee Social Networking," 155.
31. Minutes from the Lancaster Treaty of 1762 imply that some type of agreement giving Papunhank's company the right to be in Wyalusing had been made. Minutes of Conference at Lancaster, August 24 and August 27, 1762, *MPCP*, 8:757–58, 770.
32. Anthony F. C. Wallace, *King of the Delawares*, 228; Hays, "Diary, 1760," 49. In 1760 Hays reported that there were sixty men in Wyalusing's council. With younger men, women, and children, plus "outsiders" who were living at the town, the estimate of three hundred to four hundred total residents seems reasonable. A year later, Quakers were informed that there were about three hundred people living at Wyalusing. "Some account of a Visit divers Friends made to the Indians at the time of the Treaty of Easton, taken by one of the Company as follows, 1761" [12], Huntington Library Manuscript 8249, Huntington Library, San Marino, CA. Plank, *John Woolman's Path*, 138, and Goode, "Dangerous Spirits," 272, estimate that only about half of Wyalusing's population adhered to Papunhank's teachings. But that figure strikes me as too low until late 1762 and early 1763, when a crisis of religious authority occurred in the town.
33. Nain diary, July 1, July 2, July 3, July 5, July 8, July 9, July 12, and July 13, 1759, in Bethlehem diary 1759, vol. 20, MAB. Other people from Wyalusing visited Nain in August, some staying as long as two months. Nain diary, September 26, 1759, in Bethlehem diary 1759, vol. 20.

34. Nain diary, August 13, 1759, in Bethlehem diary 1759, vol. 20.
35. Shannon, "War, Diplomacy, and Culture," 87–89; Anthony F. C. Wallace, *King of the Delawares*, 234–35; Hornor, "Intimate Enemies," 162–85; Matthew C. Ward, "Redeeming the Captives," 161–89.
36. Merritt, *At the Crossroads*, 250–52, 256–57, 306n49; Daiutolo, "Role of Quakers," 23–24; Kenny, *Peaceable Kingdom Lost*, 92–97, 105–11; Anthony F. C. Wallace, *King of the Delawares*, 192–222. Activist Quakers remained in contact with Teedyuscung until his death in 1763.
37. Minutes of Council held in the State House, July 12, 1760, *MPCP*, 8:488, 490; Israel Pemberton to Christian Frederick Post, May 6, 1760, folder 2, PFP.
38. Post, "Journal, 1760," 48; Hays, "Journal, 1760," 47; Post to Israel Pemberton, May 20, 1760, 3:521, FAP.
39. Minutes of Council held at Philadelphia, April 3, 1760, *MPCP*, 8:468–71.
40. Post, "Journal, 1760," 48. It seems very likely that Post intentionally chose a biblical text that squared with his diplomatic mission and demonstrated Christian support for the peace commitments of Papunhank's band. Post was a sometime Moravian missionary whom Papunhank may have met or at least heard about during his visits to Nain. If not before, the two met when Post visited Wyalusing in the fall of 1759.
41. Post, "Journal, 1760," 48, 50; Hays, "Journal, 1760," 49, 53; Hays, "Diary, 1760," 49. Hays kept both a journal and a rougher draft diary during the diplomatic mission.
42. Post, "Journal, 1760," 51, 52, 48, 47, 109; Hays, "Diary, 1760," 111.
43. Wechquetank diary 1760, August 16, 1760, box 124, folder 1, item 5, RIM, translated for author by Roy Ledbetter; Olmstead, *David Zeisberger*, 113; Loskiel, *History of the Mission*, pt. 2, 191.
44. FAM, July 11, 1760; [Benezet], "Account of Behaviour & Sentiments," 479.
45. "Minutes of meetings with a delegation of Minisink, 2 Nanticokes & 3 Delawares from an Indian Town called Mahachloosen about 50 or 60 miles above Wyoming on the Susquehannah, July 11–16, 1760," [1–8], Huntington Library Manuscript 8249; Minutes for Council held at the State House, July 11, 1760, and July 12, 1760, *MPCP*, 8:484–88; [Benezet], "Account of Behaviour & Sentiments," 479–81; Goode, "Dangerous Spirits," 269–72 ("alcohol as a moral corruption" quote on 271); Merritt, *At the Crossroads*, 84–85; Plank, *John Woolman's Path*, 159.
46. "Minutes of meetings with a delegation of Minisink," [4–8]; Minutes of a Council held in the State House, July 12, 1760, *MPCP*, 8:488–89; [Benezet], "Account of Behaviour & Sentiments," 481–82; O'Toole, *White Savage*, 234; Merritt, *At the Crossroads*, 85.

47. Minutes of a Council held in the State House, July 16, 1760, *MPCP*, 8:490–91; Minutes of a Conference with the Indians, August 5, 1761, *MPCP*, 8:634–35.
48. Minutes of a Council held in the State House, July 12, 1760, *MPCP*, 8:489–90; "Some Account of the Behaviour & Sentiments of a Number of Well-Disposed Indians," Huntington Library Manuscript 824, Huntington Library; [Benezet], "Account of Behaviour & Sentiments," 481–82. Papunhank was by no means alone in opposing the liquor trade. Many Indians did so in early America, though on the whole, their efforts were not effective. Mancall, *Deadly Medicine*, 101–29; Goode, "Dangerous Spirits," 265–68.
49. [Benezet], *An Account of a Visit*. Benezet and Pemberton spread the word quickly on Papunhank's visit to other Friends and religious colleagues, including Moravian leader Augustus Spangenberg and Schwenkfelder leader Christopher Schultz. The latter had the report translated into German. Anthony Benezet to Augustus Spangenberg, July 19, 1760, box 211, folder 1, RIM; Erben, *Harmony of the Spirits*, 286–89. Erben suggests that Papunhank became nothing less than "the spiritual center around which revolved Quaker and Schwenkfelder religious visions and activism for peace" (289).
50. FAM, Aug. 7, 1760.
51. [Benezet], "Account of Behaviour & Sentiments," 484–85.
52. [Benezet], "Account of Behaviour & Sentiments," 483.
53. The quote is taken from Huntington Library Manuscript 824 rather than from Brookes's printed version. For whatever reason, Brookes omitted the word "wrong" from before the word "voice." Other manuscript versions of the text cited in chapter two, endnote one, include the word "wrong."
54. Plank, *John Woolman's Path*, 158, notes that Quaker accounts of Papunhank "emphasized the ways in which he resembled them, while neglecting possible differences. Their eagerness to project their own beliefs onto Papunhank was obvious." Plank, "Peace, Imperial War, and Revolution," 143–44, suggests that Papunhank may have been one of the sources Anthony Benezet drew upon for his antislavery arguments. Merritt, *At the Crossroads*, 127, suggests that the different readings Post (a Moravian) and Quakers gave to Papunhank's religious faith makes plain that neither understood the syncretic nature of Papunhank's religion at this time. While this is certainly a possibility, the different readings also likely resulted from the different theologies and spiritual practices of these

two Christian bodies as well as from the different needs they had at that moment.

55. Plank, *John Woolman's Path*, 137, argues that Quakers had interpreted the war as a "providential trial," and Papunhank became a "sign of promise" that times were improving.

56. Pointer, *Encounters of the Spirit*, 122–24.

57. Nain diary, July 19 and July 20, 1760, in Bethlehem diary 1760, vol. 22, MAB. Six months later in February 1761, a Moravian Indian visited Papunhank and heard him speak at an evening gathering. He then reported back to Bethlehem that because Papunhank "didn't make any mention of Jesus' blood and wounds, to him this seemed right away clear proof of Papunhank's lack of agreement with the Brethren in Bethlehem. When they [Papunhank and his people] were there [Bethlehem] it was mere pretense." Nain diary, February 13, 1761, in Bethlehem diary 1761, vol. 23, MAB. Merritt, *At the Crossroads*, 5–7, 51–52, 61–64, examines the importance of alliance-building for Indians and whites alike, and on 91–92 and 98 identifies the possible benefits for Indians of alliances with white Christian groups. Plank, *John Woolman's Path*, 138, emphasizes Papunhank and his band's desire to show "the perceived affinity between their own beliefs and Quakerism." For two valuable discussions of other Indian leaders who similarly navigated their people's relations with Christianity and the regnant political bodies, see Dally-Starna and Starna, "Introduction," 1:1–73, and Wheeler, "Hendrick Aupaumut," 225–49.

58. Merritt, *At the Crossroads*, 127; Nain diary, August 12, 1761, in Bethlehem diary 1761, vol. 24, MAB; Bethlehem diary 1760, July 21, 1760, vol. 22, MAB; Nain diary, August 14, August 15 (last two quotes from this day), and August 26, 1761, in Bethlehem diary 1761, vol. 24, MAB.

59. Schutt, *Peoples of the River Valleys*, 94–149, discusses the Delawares' strong propensity to function as mediators and to forge alliances with other Native peoples and Euro-Americans. Also see Schutt, "Tribal Identity," 378–98.

60. William Edmonds to Israel Pemberton, July 19, 1760, folder 1, PFP; John Fothergill to James Pemberton, November 2, 1761, 34:111, and John Hunt to Israel Pemberton Jr., November 13, 1761, 15:71, PFP; Nathaniel Holland to Israel Pemberton Jr., September 12, 1760, 4:27; Nathaniel Holland to Israel Pemberton Jr., September 17, 1760; Nathaniel Holland to Israel Pemberton Jr., October 16, 1760 (second and following quotes from this letter); Nathaniel Holland to Israel Pemberton Jr., October 30, 1760; Nathaniel Holland to Israel Pemberton Jr., May 21, 1761 (first quote from

this letter); and Israel Pemberton's Accounts of the Friendly Association, April 7, 1761, all 4:27, 35, 43, 47, 63, 115, and 83, FAP; Plank, *John Woolman's Path*, 159.

61. Nathaniel Holland to Israel Pemberton Jr., December 29, 1760, 4:63, FAP.
62. FAM, July 29, 1761, July 30, 1761, August 10, 1761; Israel Pemberton Jr.'s Accounts of the Friendly Association, 4:241, FAP.
63. [Benezet], "Account of Papunahung's Second Visit, 1761," 485–87; Minutes of a Conference with the Indians, August 5 and August 11, 1761, *MPCP*, 8:634–35, 649; Israel Pemberton to Mary Pemberton, August 4, 1761, 4:153, FAP. Iroquois insistence that Papunhank attend likely indicates their assumption of sovereignty over the lands his company inhabited.
64. Israel Pemberton to Mary Pemberton, August 4, 1761, 4:153, FAP; [Benezet], "Account of Papunahung's Second Visit," 485–86. Plank, *John Woolman's Path*, 158–59, speculates that Friends found Papunhank's hand gestures and loud volume un-Quaker-like and perhaps disturbing. He notes that later published accounts of this event toned down these details.
65. "Some account of a Visit" [12–17; quotes on 12], Huntington Library Manuscript 8249; Israel Pemberton to Mary Pemberton, August, 7, 1761, 4:163, FAP; Plank, *John Woolman's Path*, 139. Originally from Ireland and a minister at seventeen, Susanna Hatton lost her first husband, Joseph Hatton, in 1759, and married Pennsylvania farmer Thomas Lightfoot in 1763. Larson, *Daughters of Light*, 223, 241–42, 312.
66. "Some account of a Visit," [13, 16].
67. "Some account of a Visit," [17].
68. [Benezet], "Account of Papunahung's Second Visit," 485–87; "Some account of a Visit," [12–16]; Plank, *John Woolman's Path*, 158–59.
69. Silver, *Our Savage Neighbors*, 104–5.
70. [Benezet], "Account of Papunahung's Second Visit," 489; Plank, "Peace, Imperial War, and Revolution," 142 ("inclusive peace" quote), 153 ("kinship of all people" quote). This portion of Benezet's account was based on John Woolman's manuscript "The Substance of some Conversation with Paponahoal the Indian Chief at AB's in presence of Jo. W—n Ab etc.," 13:23, PFP. Goode, "Dangerous Spirits," 278, suggests that "Papunhank connected with his Quaker partners through the language of religious revivalism."
71. [Benezet], "Account of Papunahung's Second Visit," 489–90. The account also noted that Curtis's testimony was in a style "very much like that of Friends."

72. "Substance of some Conversation with Paponahoal"; Miller, "'Nature Hath a Voice," 43; Plank, *John Woolman's Path*, 144, 158; John Hunt to Israel Pemberton Jr., November 13, 1761, 15:71, PFP.
73. Israel Pemberton to Mary Pemberton, August 4, 1761, 4:153, FAP; "Some account of a Visit," [15].
74. Grumet, *Munsee Indians*, 264–70, quote on 265.
75. Schutt, *Peoples of the River Valleys*, 114–15; Nain diary, August 12, August 14, August 15, and August 28, 1761, in Bethlehem diary 1761, vol. 24, MAB. Many of Papunhank's people visited Nain during August before and after the Easton treaty. While at Nain, Papunhank's faith was critiqued by both German missionary Johann Jacob Schmick and his Indian assistant, Joachim.
76. "Some account of a Visit," [14, 17]; quote on [14]; Plank, *John Woolman's Path*, 159.
77. "Some account of a Visit," [18]. This manuscript includes two paragraphs detailing events in the months following the Treaty of Easton and the Friends' meetings with Papunhank's band in Philadelphia in August. Eustace, *Passion Is the Gale*, 322–25; Papunehayl, Job Chilliway, and David Owens to [government officials?], September 15, 1761; Nathaniel Holland to Israel Pemberton, September 30, 1761; Papunehang to Governor Hamilton, October 2, 1761; Governor James Hamilton to Papoonan of Wighlusing, October 12, 1761; The Governor's Answer to Papounham and the Indians at Wighalousing, October 12, 1761, all 4:191, 195, 223, 235, 236, FAP. During the war, some Mingos who had earlier moved to the Ohio Country moved back eastward into Pennsylvania.
78. "Some account of a Visit," [18].
79. Israel Pemberton to Tonquakena, October 31, 1761, 4:239, FAP; FAM, October 1, 1761; Nathaniel Holland to Israel Pemberton, November 12, 1761, 4:243, FAP.
80. Israel Pemberton and the Friendly Association to Papunehang, March 20, 1762; and Israel Pemberton's Accounts of the Friendly Association, 4:271, 267, 367, FAP; FAM, June 3, 1762, September 2, 1762; "Account of the Easton Treaty with the Indians [June 15–27, 1762]," Friendly Association Records, 1758–62, Friends Historical Library, Swarthmore College, Swarthmore PA; Steven Harper, *Promised Land*, 114–21; Daiutolo, "Role of Quakers," 27–29, quote on 29; Anthony F. C. Wallace, *King of the Delawares*, 239–51; Kenny, *Peaceable Kingdom Lost*, 115–22; Merritt, *At the Crossroads*, 257–61. Some Quakers of the Friendly Association had presumably interacted with Papunhank at Lancaster and in September,

that body voted to provide his people with more material assistance. But thereafter few if any direct contacts seem to have been made until the following summer.

81. Minutes at a Conference with Northern Indians, held at Lancaster, August 24 and August 27, 1762, *MPCP*, 8:757–58, 770.
82. Names of Indians at Treaty at Lancaster, 1762, *PA*, 1st ser., 4:90; Merritt, *At the Crossroads*, 260; Kenny, *Peaceable Kingdom Lost*, 115–16. The other Wyalusing Indians listed as attending the Lancaster Treaty were Wanoadea, Tunkghoak, Newoale, Wajeathu, Sakimoamos, Tutulas, Loapeghk, Queghkoau, Claghkolen, Keshashink, Woayaghk, Maghmenekoneyr, Mosawoapamech, Meshkus, Uleweeghkomen, and Kuwoghwolau. I list them here as one small way of countering their anonymity in historical memory.
83. Nain diary extracts, October 31, 1762, box 125, folder 3, item 2, RIM, translated for author by Roy Ledbetter.
84. Nathanael, a Moravian Indian, reported in June 1762 that he had had "many opportunities there [Wyoming] to speak with joy to some of the Indians there, especially Augustus and Papunhank, about the blessedness in Jesus' Wounds." Nain diary extracts, June 8, 1762, box 125, folder 3, item 1, RIM, translated for author by Roy Ledbetter.
85. Loskiel, *History of the Mission*, pt. 2, 196. Papunhank would presumably have similarly wanted to remain a religious teacher in Wyalusing if Quakers had sent several of their own to supply his town.
86. Brief Report of the Visit of the Brethren David Zeisberger and Anton the Indian up the Susquehanna as far as Machemihilusing [Wyalusing], May [16–29], 1763, box 227, folder 9, entry for May 24, 1763, RIM, translated for author by Roy Ledbetter; Anthony F. C. Wallace, *King of the Delawares*, 252–66; Middleton, *Pontiac's War*, 57, 65–99. Zeisberger noted that as many as half of the town's people had left "last Spring" (1762?) and moved twenty miles away, presumably for a variety of reasons including religious dissatisfaction. But Wallace, *King of the Delawares*, 262, notes that the attack on Wyoming prompted some of its residents to flee to Wyalusing. So there was likely a fair amount of fluidity in the community's population at this increasingly uncertain time.
87. Brief Report of the Visit of Zeisberger and Anton, May 1763, May 22, 1763. Zeisberger's version of the community's divisions came via Delaware translator and Wyalusing resident Job Chillaway. He happened upon the Moravians en route to Wyalusing and filled them in on what was going on there.

88. Brief Report of the Visit of Zeisberger and Anton, May 1763, quotes from entries for May 23 and May 24. Moravians had long wanted to send someone to evangelize the Wyalusingites. Anton himself had expressed that desire in August 1760. Wechquetank diary, August 16, 1760, box 124, folder 1, item 5, RIM, translated for author by Roy Ledbetter.
89. Diary of the Brethren Dav. Zeisberger and Nathanael the Indian from their Journey and Stay in Chwihilusing [Wyalusing], June 10–July 10, 1763, box 227, folder 10, quotes from entry for June 20, RIM, translated for author by Roy Ledbetter.
90. David Zeisberger to Nathanael Seidel, June 18, 1763, box 229, folder 2, item 2 (quote), RIM, translated for author by Roy Ledbetter; Diary of Zeisberger, June 10–July 10, 1763, June 16 1763; Moulton, *Journal of Woolman*, 122–34, quote on 134.
91. Moulton, *Journal of John Woolman*, 134; Slaughter, *Beautiful Soul of John Woolman*, 250–61; Pickett, "A Religious Encounter," 77–92; Plank, *John Woolman's Path*, 161–66; Olmstead, *David Zeisberger*, 113–15.
92. John Woolman to Israel Pemberton, June 27, 1763, and John Pemberton to Israel Pemberton, July 2, 1763, in Gummere, *Journal and Essays of Woolman*, 91–93; Slaughter, *Beautiful Soul of John Woolman*, 262; Plank, *John Woolman's Path*, 166.
93. FAM, July 7 and July 21, 1763; Anthony Benezet to Sir Jeffrey Amherst, July 1763, in Brookes, *Friend Anthony Benezet*, 248–53, quote on 252.
94. Diary of Zeisberger, June 10–July 10, 1763, quotes from entry for June 20; Zeisberger to Seidel, June 18, 1763; Olmstead, *David Zeisberger*, 113–15; Loskiel, *History of the Mission*, pt. 2, 206–7; Merritt, *At the Crossroads*, 304, suggests that Papunhank's motives for joining the Moravians included the fact that he had kin among them, but I have not been able to confirm this link at this point in his life. Zeisberger told his supervisor in Bethlehem, Nathanael Seidel, in his June 18 letter that Papunhank had "declared himself against the Quakers" in his decision to join with the Moravians. Zeisberger also claimed that Woolman had tried to convince the Natives that denominations didn't matter, to which Papunhank had responded that God had "now pointed them to the Brethren" and they were content with that decision.
95. Diary of Zeisberger, June 10–July 10, 1763, quotes from entries for June 21 and June 24.
96. Wheeler, *To Live Upon Hope*, 105–32, quotes on 106 and 125; Diary of Zeisberger, June 10–July 10, 1763, June 26, 1763. Also see Merritt, *At the Crossroads*, 89–121, for an excellent discussion of why Delaware Indians

were attracted to Moravianism. She emphasizes the role of dreams in bringing Indians and Moravians together, but like Wheeler concludes that it was "the power inherent in the body and blood of Christ [that] seemed to be what most attracted Indians to the Moravian faith" (112).

97. Diary of Zeisberger, June 10–July 10, 1763, quotes from entry for July 5.

4. Captives Together

1. "1765 Address of the Christian Indians at the Barracks in Philadelphia to Governor John Penn [March 19, 1765]," BDHP, http://bdhp.moravian.edu/personal_papers/letters/indians/1765indianaddress.html. The address may also be found in *PA*, 4th ser., 4:170–71.
2. "An Address of Christian Indians in Nain and Wechquetank to Governor Hamilton, July 27, 1763," box 124, folder 7, item 1, RIM. The Moravian mission town of Pachgatgoch, Connecticut, was still in existence but was already in serious decline by the early 1760s. It closed officially in October 1770.
3. Middleton, *Pontiac's War*, 57–66, 129–34; Merritt, *At the Crossroads*, 273–78; Silver, *Our Savage Neighbors*, 60–64; Olmstead, *David Zeisberger*, 116–19; Dowd, *War under Heaven*, 194–95; on the final incident, Kenny, *Peaceable Kingdom Lost*, 128–29, notes that Presbyterian minister John Elder wrote to Governor Hamilton on September 30 proposing that a group of western settlers (those who became the Paxton Boys) take an expedition to Wyoming and Wyalusing to pursue enemy Indians. They proceeded without waiting for Hamilton's okay but turned back after encountering the massacre at Wyoming.
4. Governor James Hamilton to Timothy Horsfield, August 10, 1763, box 124, folder 7, item 3, RIM. Horsfield had drawn up a list of characteristics to distinguish Christian Indians from "wild Indians": "Distinguishing Christian Indians from 'wild' Indians," box 124, folder 7, item 4, RIM; see a discussion of the list in Olmstead, *David Zeisberger*, 117.
5. Wechquetank diary, English version, September 5, September 20, October 6, and October 10, 1763, box 124, folder 4, item 4, RIM.
6. Peter Boehler to Governor James Hamilton, October 10, 1763, BDHP, http://bdhp.moravian.edu/personal_papers/letters/indians/1763boehler.html.
7. Plan for Protecting . . . October 1763, box 124, folder 7, item 5, RIM.
8. Kenny, *Peaceable Kingdom Lost*, 133. Both white and Native Moravians constantly asserted their innocence. See various documents relating to Moravian sales of gunpowder to Indians in the summer and fall of 1763 in box 125, folder 5, items 1, 2, 3, 4, and 6, RIM.

9. Frederick Marshall to Lewis Weiss, November 3, 1763, BDHP, http://bdhp.moravian.edu/personal_papers/letters/indians/1763marshall.html.
10. Merritt, *At the Crossroads*, 280–81; Petition of Schmick to Penn, November 9, 1763, BDHP, http://bdhp.moravian.edu/personal_papers/letters/indians/1763schmick.html.
11. Bethlehem diary, November 16, 1763, trans. Katherine Carté Engel, BDHP, http://bdhp.moravian.edu/community_records/bethlehem_diary/16nov1763.html; *PA*, 4th ser., 4:134, provides a list of the heads of households who came to Philadelphia from the two Indian towns.
12. "Journal Kept at Fort Augusta, 1763," July 29, 1763, *PA*, 2nd ser., 7:439; Wechquetank diary, September 14 and September 21, 1763; Minutes of Council held at Philadelphia, September 17, 1763, *MPCP*, 9:44–46, 66–68, quotes on 46 and 68; FAM, 1760–64, October 6, 1763, ser. 7, box 18, folder 11. In early October officers at Fort Augusta received word that Papunhank had also told the governor in September that "the Indians are Universally Joined against us, and are Determined to attack our fort." "Journal Kept at Fort Augusta, 1763," October 5, 1763, *PA*, 2nd ser., 7:446.
13. Col. James Irvine to Gov. Penn, November 23, 1763, *PA*, 4th ser., 4:138. Penn was not unique in taking actions to protect noncombatant Indians. In 1755 Governor Jonathan Belcher of New Jersey had taken a number of steps to safeguard them including having them register with the government, swear loyalty, and wear a red ribbon around their necks. Most of the Indians in question lived at the Christian Indian communities of Cranbury and Bethel. Marsh, *Lenape among the Quakers*, 138–39; Becker, "New Jersey Haven," 326–28.
14. Irvine to Gov. Penn, November 23, 1763, 138.
15. FAM, 1760–64, November 29, 1763; William Johnson to Cadwallader Colden, January 12, 1764, *WJP*, 4:288; Petition by Lewis Weiss to the Pennsylvania General Assembly, December 23, 1763, box 124, folder 6, item 16, RIM; Statement on events relating to Stinton murder quoting a number of persons to prove Renatus innocent [1764], box 124, folder 6, item 17, RIM; *MMDZ*, 485; Matthew Smith, *Declaration and Remonstrance*; Craft, *History of Bradford County*, 12, 16.
16. Frederick Marshall Journal, November 25, 1763, box 217, folder 14, RIM.
17. Minutes of Conference held at Philadelphia, December 1, 1763, *MPCP*, 9:77–78. The governor had sent a message with Curtis to Wyalusing in October asking Papunhank to communicate with the Six Nations living in southern New York the Pennsylvania government's interest in getting Six Nations' cooperation in curbing Indian violence. Now Papunhank

was reporting the Six Nations' response that they would send their fuller message to the Pennsylvania government via Sir William Johnson, but for now were willing to say that they were interested in living with the English in friendship. Newollike's message was that he and his people had been gravely threatened by the warring Indians for supporting the English.

18. Minutes of Council held at Philadelphia, December 10, 1763, *MPCP*, 9:86–87.
19. Minutes of Council held at Philadelphia, December 10, 1763, *MPCP*, 9:87–88.
20. Bernhard Grube to Nathanael Seidel, December 8, 1763, box 211, folder 16, item 22, RIM, translated for author by Roy Ledbetter; David Zeisberger to Nathanael Seidel, December 9, 1763, box 229, folder 2, item 3, RIM, translated for author by Roy Ledbetter.
21. Diary of Indian *Gemeine*, [December 1], 1763–January 4, 1764, trans. Katherine Carté Engel, BDHP, http://bdhp.moravian.edu/community_records/christianindians/provincediary/1764province.html; Johann Schmick to Nathanael Seidel, December 8, 1763, box 221, folder 9, item 4, RIM, translated for author by Roy Ledbetter.
22. Minutes of Councils held at Philadelphia, December 20 and December 21, 1763, *MPCP*, 9:93–96; Governor John Penn address to the Assembly Concerning several Indian conferences and the late murder of six friendly Indians at Conestogoe Manor, December 21, 1763, *PA*, 4th ser., 3:252–53; Middleton, *Pontiac's War*, 134.
23. Penn to the Assembly, *PA*, 4th ser., 3:252–53; Pearl, "'Our God, and Our Guns,'" 59–68; Spero, *Frontier Country*, 148–69; Kenny, *Peaceable Kingdom Lost*, 130–46; Merritt, *At the Crossroads*, 282–92; Silver, *Our Savage Neighbors*, 175–83.
24. FAM, November 21, November 22, and November 29, 1763; Friendly Association to James Ervin [Irvine], November 22, 1763, FAP, 4:375.
25. Diary of Indian *Gemeine*, [December 1], 1763–January 4, 1764, December 29 and December 31, 1763, and January 2, 1764; Journal of Frederick Marshall, October 28, 1763–January 18, 1764, December 31, 1763 and January 1, 1764, box 217, folder 14, item 1, RIM, translated for author by Roy Ledbetter; Silver, *Our Savage Neighbors*, 183.
26. Bernhard Grube to Nathanael Seidel, January 4, 1764, box 211, folder 16, item 24, RIM, translated for author by Roy Ledbetter.
27. Heckewelder, *Narrative of the Mission*, 80–82; "Diary of the Indian *Gemeine*," [December 1,] 1763–January 4, 1763, January 2, 1764; Olmstead, *David Zeisberger*, 126–27; John Penn to Sir William Johnson, January 5, 1764, *PA*, 4th ser., 3: 264.

28. Sir William Johnson to Cadwallader Colden, January 12, 1764, *WJP*, 4:288. In this letter Johnson informed Colden that "those of Wawiloosin [Wyalusing] (our friends) are gone chiefly to Philadelphia, and the Rest [of the Wyalusingites?] are removed to Chugnot on the Susquehanna." Chugnot or Chughnut or Choconut was an Indian town along the Susquehanna River in what is now southern New York.
29. "Diary of the Indian *Gemeinlein* on Pilgrimage, January 4–January 17, 1764," January 4 and January 5, 1764, trans. Katherine Carté Engel, BDHP, http://bdhp.moravian.edu/community_records/christianindians/diaires/amboy/1764amboy.html; Congregational diary of First Moravian Church of Philadelphia, December 1,1761–June 30, 1764, January 12, 1764, MC Phila 1.8, MAB, translated by Edward Quinter; "1764 Message by Lieutenant Governor John Penn delivered to the departing Christian Indians through William Logan [January 7, 1764]," BDHP, http://bdhp.moravian.edu/personal_papers/letters/indians/1764governor.html; Journal of Frederick Marshall, October 28, 1763–January 18, 1764, January 15, 1764. Penn's message of January 7 seems to indicate that all of the Wyalusingites went to New Jersey, but other sources indicate that only Papunhank and his family had been diverted.
30. "Travel Diary of the little Indian *Gemeine*—1764 [January 18–January 24, 1764]," trans. Katherine Carté Engel, BDHP, http://bdhp.moravian.edu/community_records/christianindians/diaires/travel/1764travel.html; Cadwallader Colden to Sir William Johnson, January 9, 1764, *WJP*, 11:12–13; Thomas Apty to John Penn, January 11, 1764, *PA*, 4th ser., 4:157; William Franklin to John Penn, January 12, 1764, *PA*, 4th ser., 4:157–58; Thomas Gage to Sir William Johnson, January 12, 1764, *WJP*, 4:293; Dowd, *War under Heaven*, 195–96; Olmstead, *David Zeisberger*, 127.
31. Journal of Frederick Marshall, October 28, 1763–January 18, 1764; January 15, 1764, includes quote from James; Congregational diary of First Moravian Church of Philadelphia, January 12, January 14, and January 21, 1764; "Diary of the Indian *Gemeine* in the Barracks in Philadelphia 1764," January 28, January 29, February 2, and February 8, 1764, trans. Katherine Carté Engel, BDHP, http://bdhp.moravian.edu/community_records/christianindians/diaires/barracks/1764/translation64.html; Bernhard Grube to Nathanael Seidel, February 9, 1764, box 211, folder 16, item 26, RIM, translated for author by Roy Ledbetter. Papunhank's joy at returning to Philadelphia may have also been due to being reunited with the other Wyalusingites. In a speech to the New Jersey Council and General Assembly printed in the March 1, 1764, issue of the Pennsylvania *Gazette*,

Governor Franklin indicated that a small number of refugee Indians had remained in New Jersey with his permission and under his protection, but these Natives were probably not the Wyalusingites. Instead, they were Hannah Freeman and four other Lenape women from Chester County, Pennsylvania. They had fled to New Jersey in late 1763 or early 1764 and apparently took up residence "somewhere near the Quaker stronghold of Woodbury." Hannah remained there for the next seven years before returning to Pennsylvania. Marsh, *Lenape among the Quakers*, 134–41, quote on 141; Becker, "New Jersey Haven," 330.

32. "Diary of the Indian *Gemeine* in the Barracks," February 4–February 9, 1764; Grube to Seidel, February 9, 1764 (quote); "Remonstrance from the Frontier Inhabitants to Governor John Penn, February 13, 1764," *MPCP*, 9:138–42; Heckewelder, *Narrative of the Mission*, 84–86; Silver, *Our Savage Neighbors*, 185–90, 202–26; Kenny, *Peaceable Kingdom Lost*, 147–202; Merritt, *At the Crossroads*, 288–94; Daiutolo, "Role of Quakers," 28–29. Many of the key pamphlets of the verbal war may be found in Dunbar, *Paxton Papers*.

33. Heckewelder, *Narrative of the Mission*, 85–88, quote on 85; "Diary of the Indian *Gemeine* in the Barracks," January 31, February 1, February 3, February 16, February 17, and February 21, 1764, quote on January 31; Memorial of several Discources, which John Jacob Schmick . . . hath lately had with Pompunagh, February 3, 1764, *MPCP*, 9:135–36, quote on 135; Minutes of Council, February 14, 1764, *MPCP*, 9:136–37. Back in January, colonial official William Logan had expressed similar worries about what other Indians would make of the Conestoga killings and similar hopes that the refugee Indians, en route to New York, would be ambassadors of peace. That plan fizzled when the Indians were turned away at the border. William Logan to David Zeisberger, January 11, 1764, BDHP, http://bdhp.moravian.edu/personal_papers/letters/indians/1764logan.html.

34. Johann Jacob Schmick to Nathanael Seidel, February 16, 1764, box 221, folder 9, item 8, RIM, translated for author by Roy Ledbetter; Minutes of Council, February 14, 1764, *MPCP*, 9:136–37.

35. Congregational Diary of First Moravian Church of Philadelphia, February 21, 1764; Heckewelder, *Narrative of the Mission*, 88, quote on 88.

36. Bernhard Grube to Peter Boehler, February 20, 1764, box 211, folder 16, item 28, RIM, translated for author by Roy Ledbetter; Schmick to Seidel, February 16, 1764, quotes from this letter; Johann Jacob Schmick to Nathanael Seidel, February 21, 1764, box 221, folder 9, item 9, RIM, translated for author by Roy Ledbetter. Political discussions between key offi-

cials regarding what to do with the refugee Indians were brisk through late March and early April and may be followed in William Johnson to John Penn, January 20, 1764, *WJP*, 11:17–19; William Johnson to John Penn, February 9, 1764, *PA*, 4th ser., 4:162–63; John Penn to Sir William Johnson, February 17, 1764, *WJP*, 4:327–28; William Johnson to John Penn, February 27, 1764, *WJP*, 4:343; William Johnson to Cadwallader Colden, February 28, 1764, *WJP*, 4:345–46; Thomas Gage to William Johnson, March 8, 1764, *WJP*, 4:357–58; Thomas Gage to John Penn, March 9, 1764, *MPCP*, 9:170–71; William Johnson to Thomas Gage, March 16, 1764, *WJP*, 4:368; and Thomas Gage to William Johnson, March 26, 1764, *WJP*, 4:377. Gage proposed that the Indians be removed to Burlington, New Jersey, but nothing came of that idea. White Moravians in Philadelphia heard in early March that Johnson was willing to take the refugees but that the governor and assembly of New York had rejected the plan. Congregational Diary of First Moravian Church of Philadelphia, March 9, 1764.

37. "Diary of the Indian *Gemeine* in the Barracks," March 25, 1764; David Zeisberger to Nathanael Seidel, box 229, folder 2, item 30, RIM, translated for author by Roy Ledbetter.
38. "An Indian Congress [March 4–5, 1764]," *WJP*, 11:88–90, quote on 90; "Journal of Indian Affairs [March 5–23, 1764]," *WJP*, 11:106–9; William Johnson to Thomas Gage, April 16, 1764, *WJP*, 11:132; "Journal of Indian Affairs [May 21–31, 1764]," *WJP*, 11:208–9, quote on 209; "Journal of Indian Affairs [June 15–July 3, 1764]," *WJP*, 11:252–53. In March Johnson estimated that 185 Natives had come from Otseningo. That group included former Wyalusingites and other residents of the town.
39. "Diary of the Indian *Gemeine* in the Barracks," April 2, April 5, April 7, and April 12, 1764, quote from April 12; Johann Jacob Schmick to Nathanael Seidel, April 12, 1764, box 221, folder 9, item 11, RIM, translated for author by Roy Ledbetter; David Zeisberger to Nathanael Seidel, April 15, 1764, box 229, folder 2, item 5, RIM, translated for author by Roy Ledbetter. Zeisberger spent ten weeks in Philadelphia with the refugees from early March through mid-May. The Grubes and Schmicks remained with them for the entire sixteen months. Another Moravian missionary, Johann Roth, also spent short periods of time there.
40. "Diary of the Indian *Gemeine* in the Barracks," May 5 and May 17, 1764.
41. "Diary of the Indian *Gemeine* in the Barracks," January 27, January 29, February 24, February 25, March 9, April 19, April 20, May 7, May 9, June 10, and June 11, 1764, quotes from April 20; Johann Jacob Schmick to Nathanael Seidel, February 9, 1764, box 221, folder 9, item 7, RIM, trans-

lated for author by Roy Ledbetter; Johann Jacob Schmick to Nathanael Seidel, April 22, 1764, box 221, folder 9, item 12, RIM, translated for author by Roy Ledbetter. For more on the role of singing and hymnody within Moravian Indian communities, see Wheeler and Eyerly, "Songs of the Spirit," 1–25.

42. "Diary of the Indian *Gemeine* in the Barracks," February 3, February 21, March 25, June 11, and June 26, 1764; Schmick to Seidel, February 21, 1764, quote from this letter. The wedding occurred on June 26, the one-year anniversary of Papunhank's baptism.

43. "Diary of the Indian *Gemeine* in the Barracks," January 29, February 10, February 11, February 12, February 18, February 26, April 1, April 30, May 6, quotes from February 26 and May 6; "Distinguishing Christian Indians from 'wild' Indians," [August 1763], box 124, folder 7, item 4, RIM. According to Grube, British Captain Schlosser told him on February 1 that the Moravian Indians "were completely different Indians than I have seen in Indians country." Schlosser may have been referring to both their behavior and their appearance. "Diary of the Indian *Gemeine* in the Barracks," February 1, 1764.

44. Johann Jacob Schmick to Nathanael Seidel, May 6, 1764, box 221, folder 9, item 13, RIM, translated for author by Roy Ledbetter; Grube to Seidel, December 8, 1763; Schmick to Seidel, December 8, 1763; "Diary of the Indian *Gemeine* in the Barracks," February 17, March 2, March 5, April 24, April 30, May 1, and May 10, 1764, quotes on March 5; Bernhard Grube to Nathanael Seidel, June 6, 1764, box 211, folder 16, item 35, RIM, translated for author by Roy Ledbetter.

45. Among numerous references to sickness and death, see "Diary of the Indian *Gemeine* in the Barracks," February 7, February 12, February 17, February 26, April 2, May 9, May 15, June 16, June 19, June 30, July 20, July 31, August 25, and August 31, 1764; Johann Jacob Schmick to Nathanael Seidel, May 21, 1764, box 221, folder 9, item 15, RIM, translated for author by Roy Ledbetter; Johann Jacob Schmick to Nathanael Seidel, July 25, 1764, box 221, folder 9, item 17, RIM, translated for author by Roy Ledbetter.

46. Bernhard Grube to Nathanael Seidel, July 5, 1764, box 211, folder 16, item 40, RIM, translated for author by Roy Ledbetter; "Diary of the Indian *Gemeine* in the Barracks," August 14, August 16, October 14, October 20, and November 13, 1764; Johann Jacob Schmick to Nathanael Seidel, November 12, 1764, box 221, folder 9, item 21, RIM, translated for author by Roy Ledbetter.

47. "Diary of the Indian *Gemeine* in the Barracks," December 20, 1764. A further report on their journey is recorded in "Diary of the little Indian *Gemein* currently in the barracks in Philadelphia, 1765," January 5, 1765, trans. Katherine Carté Engel, BDHP, http://bdhp.moravian.edu/community_records/christianindians/diaires/barracks/1765/translation65.html.

48. "Diary of the Indian *Gemeine* in the Barracks," June 19, June 30, and July 11, 1764, quote from June 30; Bernhard Grube to Nathanael Seidel, July 18, 1764, box 211, folder 16, item 41, RIM, translated for author by Roy Ledbetter; Johann Jacob Schmick to Nathanael Seidel, July 25, 1764, box 221, folder 9, item 17, RIM, translated for author by Roy Ledbetter.

49. Bernhard Grube to Nathanael Seidel, August 26, 1764, box 211, folder 16, item 45, RIM, translated for author by Roy Ledbetter; Bernhard Grube to Nathanael Seidel, September 2, 1764, box 211, folder 16, item 46, RIM, translated for author by Roy Ledbetter; Johann Jacob Schmick to Nathanael Seidel, August 24, 1764, box 221, folder 9, item 18, RIM, translated for author by Roy Ledbetter, says that Joshua Senior had acted as a "tempter" to Papunhank so that now he "was also confused." Zeisberger had moved to Christiansbrunn, outside of Bethlehem, following his departure from Philadelphia in May. He had stayed at the single Brethren house there before.

50. Bernhard Grube to Nathanael Seidel, September 19, 1764, box 211, folder 16, item 47, RIM, translated for author by Roy Ledbetter.

51. "Diary of the Indian *Gemeine* in the Barracks," July 17, 1764; Schmick to Seidel, August 24, 1764; Johann Jacob Schmick to Nathanael Seidel, January 13, 1765, box 221, folder 9, item 22, RIM, translated for author by Roy Ledbetter; Bernhard Grube to Nathanael Seidel, February 3, 1765, box 211, folder 16, item 52, RIM, translated for author by Roy Ledbetter. Bathsheba was Joshua Senior's second wife. His first wife (Joshua Junior's mother), Salome, had deserted him in 1747. Hartzell, "Joshua, Jr.," 1.

52. "Diary of the Indian *Gemeine* in the Barracks," February 12, February 26, June 23, June 25, and November 12, 1764; Bernhard Grube to Nathanael Seidel, November 26, 1764, box 211, folder 16, item 50, RIM, translated for author by Roy Ledbetter; Schmick to Seidel, January 13, 1765.

53. Grube to Seidel, November 26, 1764 (quote); "Diary of the Indian *Gemeine* in the Barracks," November 12 and November 27, 1764.

54. Schutt, "Tribal Identity," 378–80, 391. Schutt's argument is weakened by her failure to note the intertribal marriage between Papunhank's daughter Sophia (Munsee) and Joshua Junior (Mahican), Bathsheba and

Joshua Senior's son that helped bind these two families and two ethnic groups together. In December 1763 Grube noted another potential source of division—the Moravian Indians were coming from two communities (Nain and Wechquetank) and now were being thrown together. He argued that he and Schmick should have joint oversight of all the Indians, rather than maintaining leadership over only those who had been with them in their respective communities. Grube to Nathanael Seidel, December 8, 1763.

55. "Diary of the Indian *Gemeine* in the Barracks," March 1, April 3, June 21 (first quote), July 11, July 23, and July 24, 1764; Bernhard Grube to Nathanael Seidel, May 23, 1764, box 211, folder 16, item 34, RIM, translated for author by Roy Ledbetter; Bernhard Grube to Nathanael Seidel, June 21, 1764, box 211, folder 16, item 37, RIM, translated for author by Roy Ledbetter; Grube to Seidel, November 26, 1764 (all other quotes).

56. "Diary of the Indian *Gemeine* in the Barracks," October 14 ("wilderness again" quote) and October 20, 1764 ("have patience" quote); Grube to Seidel, August 26, 1764; Johann Jacob Schmick to Nathanael Seidel, November 12, 1764, box 221, folder 9, item 21, RIM, translated for author by Roy Ledbetter. Schmick had been willing in August to meet with the governor twice more to convey messages from Papunhank. "Diary of the Indian *Gemeine* in the Barracks," August 14 and August 16, 1764.

57. "Proclamation of Peace with the Delaware and Shawanese Indians," *PA*, 4th ser. 3:293–94; "Diary of the Indian *Gemeine* in the Barracks," December 4, December 6, December 20, December 25 (second quote), December 28, and December 29, 1764; "Diary of the little Indian *Gemein*, 1765," January 5, 1765 (first quote).

58. According to the congregational diary, when Papunhank and the others returned in December, they were imagining that in the spring they would move to two settlements: one at Wyalusing and the other "a few miles north of Wajomick [Wyoming]." But that plan seems to have soon dissolved. "Diary of the Indian *Gemeine* in the Barracks," December 20, 1764. "Diary of the little Indian *Gemein*, 1765," January 5, January 17, January 24, and February 5, 1765; Bernhard Grube to Nathanael Seidel, January 13, 1765, box 211, folder 16, item 51, RIM, translated for author by Roy Ledbetter; Schmick to Seidel, January 13, 1765; Bernhard Grube to Nathanael Seidel, February 3, 1765, box 211, folder 16, item 52, RIM, translated for author by Roy Ledbetter; Johann Jacob Schmick to Nathanael Seidel, February 7, 1765, box 221, folder 9, item 23, RIM, translated for author by Roy Ledbetter; Heckewelder, *Narrative of the Mis-*

sion, 90–92; Loskiel, *History of the Mission*, pt. 2, 230; Olmstead, *David Zeisberger*, 130–31.

59. "Diary of the little Indian *Gemein*, 1765," January 18, 1765; Schmick to Seidel, February 7, 1765; Johann Jacob Schmick to Nathanael Seidel, March 2, 1765, box 221, folder 9, item 24, RIM, translated for author by Roy Ledbetter.
60. Schmick to Seidel, March 2, 1765; "Diary of the little Indian *Gemein*, 1765," March 15, 1765.
61. "1765 Address of Christian Indians to Penn." Papunhank was one of four Indians who signed the letter.
62. Schmick and Joshua Senior expressed their thanks to Fox in person. According to the congregational diary, Fox "with wet eyes . . . said: I have done what I could because I knew these were innocent people. What concerns you, however, I would have gladly done more, but had no orders for it." "Diary of the little Indian *Gemein*, 1765," March 19, 1765. For Quaker involvement, see "Diary of the Indian *Gemeine*," [December 1,] 1763–January 4, 1764, December 30, 1763, January 2 and January 3, 1764; "Diary of the Indian *Gemeine* in the Barracks," February 11, 1764; FAM, February 2, 1764; Friendly Association Expenses, 1764–76, Cox-Parrish-Wharton Papers, box 18, folder 13, HSP; Heckewelder, *Narrative of the Mission*, 92.
63. Sloan, "'Time of Sifting," 3–22; Marietta, *Reformation of American Quakerism*, 194–202.
64. I include in this number all those who went. Not all of them were "Moravian" in the sense of being baptized. "Diary of the little Indian *Gemein*, 1765," March 20, 1765; Andrews, *Native Apostles*, 103–5. Sample Moravian accounts include Loskiel, *History of the Mission*, pt. 3, 1–18; Heckewelder, *Narrative of the Mission*, 90–92; Olmstead, *David Zeisberger*, 130–45. Interestingly, two nineteenth-century histories accorded Natives a bit larger role in shaping the refugees' fate and the continuation of Moravian missions: de Schweinitz, *Life and Times of Zeisberger*, 308, and Reichel, "Wyalusing and the Moravian Mission," 189.

5. From Prophet to Guardian

1. Travel Diary of Brother Schmick and David Zeisberger with the Indian Brothers and Sisters from Nain and Wechquetank to the Susquehanna and Machilusing [Wyalusing] from April 3 to May 24, 1765, box 131, folder 1, RIM, translated for author by Roy Ledbetter.
2. Wheeler and Hahn-Bruckart, "Eighteenth-Century Trail of Tears," 45–46, 54; Brief Report of the Visit of the Brethren David Zeisberger

and Anton the Indian up the Susquehanna as far as Machemihilusing [Wyalusing], May [16–29], 1763, box 227, folder 9, entry for May 23, 1763, RIM, translated for author by Roy Ledbetter.

3. Schutt, "Tribal Identity," 383, agrees that the white Moravians endorsed Papunhank's authority but then argues that they placed too much authority in his hands. In doing so they "unwittingly undermined their plans to create a unified Christian community" through concentrating more power in a single individual than was common among Natives and by privileging Munsee-Delaware leadership over Mahican. In my view, given Wyalusing's circumstances, the missionaries had little choice but to support Papunhank's leading place in the community and overall, that choice had more positive than negative effects.
4. Kenny, *Peaceable Kingdom Lost*, 205–16; Spero, *Frontier Country*, 170–96; Matthew C. Ward, "'Peaceable Kingdom' Destroyed," 269–72.
5. "Diary of the little Indian *Gemein*, 1765," January 17, February 5, March 22, March 31, and April 2, 1765. A *band* or *bande* was a Moravian term for a time of close fellowship among two or more believers.
6. Travel Diary of Schmick and Zeisberger to Machilusing, April 3 to May 24, 1765, April 4, April 5, April 8, April 9, and April 11, 1765; Paul A. W. Wallace, *Indian Paths of Pennsylvania*, 88–89, 187–90; Olmstead, *David Zeisberger*, 137–38; de Schweinitz, *Life and Times of Zeisberger*, 309–10.
7. Travel Diary of Schmick and Zeisberger to Machilusing, April 3 to May 24, 1765, April 11, April 13, April 14, April 17, April 19, and April 20, 1765.
8. Travel Diary of Schmick and Zeisberger to Machilusing, April 3 to May 24, 1765, April 23, April 24, April 25, April 26, and April 30, 1765.
9. Travel Diary of Schmick and Zeisberger to Machilusing, April 3 to May 24, 1765, April 25 and May 4, 1765; Kenny, *Peaceable Kingdom Lost*, 206–13. Word may have also reached them about another uprising occurring that spring in southern Pennsylvania. Frontier settlers known as the Black Boys were contesting imperial Indian policy, especially the resumption of trade with western Indians. Spero, *Frontier Country*, 170–87.
10. Travel Diary of Schmick and Zeisberger to Machilusing, April 3 to May 24, 1765, May 8 and May 9, 1765; Loskiel, *History of the Mission*, pt. 2, 233–34.
11. Travel Diary of Schmick and Zeisberger to Machilusing, April 3 to May 24, 1765, May 9, May 10, May 13, May 14, May 15, and May 20, 1765; Schutt, "Tribal Identity," 383.
12. David Zeisberger to Nathanael Seidel, June 23, 1765, box 229, folder 2, item 9, RIM, translated for author by Julie Tomberlin Weber; Travel Diary

of Schmick and Zeisberger to Machilusing, April 3 to May 24, 1765, May 21, 1765 [misdated as May 22]; Friedenshütten [Wyalusing] diary May 21, 1765–January 20, 1766, May 21 and May 31, 1765, box 131, folder 2, RIM, translated for author by Roy Ledbetter; Nazareth Diary 1760–69 extracts, July 18, 1765, trans. Tilde Marx, https://www.moravianchurcharchives.org/eLibrary/Nazareth%20Diary%201760-1769.pdf. The Pennsylvania government supplied flour for the Wyalusingites to help them until their own harvest. They were still picking up some of it in July 1765.

13. The Moravian Archives in Bethlehem and the Wyalusing Valley Museum placed a new historic marker on the site of Friedenshütten in recent years. A stone pillar had been built there to mark the location in the 1870s by the Moravian Historical Society.
14. David Zeisberger to Nathanael Seidel, May 19, 1765, box 229, folder 2, item 6, RIM, translated for author by Roy Ledbetter; Jordan, "Annals of Friedenshuetten," in *The Moravian*, February 24, 1886, diary entries for June 4 and June 24, 1765; Reichel, "Wyalusing and the Moravian Mission," 185–86, 213; Friedenshütten [Wyalusing] diary January 21, 1766–December 31, 1766, May 6, May 12, and May 13, 1766, box 131, folder 3, RIM, translated for author by Roy Ledbetter; Loskiel, *History of the Mission*, pt. 3, 1–2. Over a three-month span in 1886 in issues of the Moravians' weekly denominational newspaper, *The Moravian*, John Jordan provided translated excerpts from the Friedenshütten diary from 1765 through 1772. Copies of this newspaper may be found at the Moravian Archives in Bethlehem. Faull, "Mapping a Mission,"107–16, reproduces and analyzes a detailed map of the town done in 1768 by Georg Wenzel Golkowsky, a cartographer in Bethlehem. He based his map on a drawing done by John Ettwein during his visit to Friedenshütten in May 1768.
15. "Distinguishing Christian Indians from 'wild' Indians"; Nazareth diary 1760–1769 extracts, July 18 and August 15, 1765; Reichel, "Wyalusing and Moravian Mission," 193–94, 202; Jordan, "Annals of Friedenshuetten," in *The Moravian*, February 24, 1886, diary entry for June 17, 1765, March 10, 1886, diary entry for May 1, 1766; Friedenshütten [Wyalusing] diary, October 12, 1765 (quote); May 17, 1766.
16. Travel Diary of Schmick and Zeisberger to Machilusing, April 3 to May 24, 1765, May 12 and May 13, 1765. The white visitor left the following day.
17. Friedenshütten [Wyalusing] diary, May 17, 1766 (Paxtons) and February 2, 1766 (Nanticokes); Loskiel, *History of the Mission*, pt. 3, 15. "Strange" is one way of translating the German word *Fremden* that the Moravians used often in reference to outsiders or non-Moravian visitors. In Frie-

denshütten some were temporary visitors, others were long-term residents who were unbaptized members of the community. On Nanticoke burial practices, see Shaffer, "Nanticoke Indian Burial Practices," 141–62.

18. Key works addressing how Indians could be Native and Christian include Martin and Nicholas, *Native Americans, Christianity*; Linford D. Fisher, *Indian Great Awakening*; Andrews, *Native Apostles*; Merritt, *At the Crossroads*, 89–128; Leavelle, *Catholic Calumet*; Silverman, *Faith and Boundaries*; Silverman, *Red Brethren*; and Wheeler, *To Live Upon Hope*.
19. Friedenshütten [Wyalusing] diary, September 21, September 22, October 13, November 24, December 19, December 31, and Memorabilia, 1765; Jordan, "Annals of Friedenshuetten," in *The Moravian*, March 3, 1886, diary entry for August 22, 1765; David Luther Roth, *Johann Roth*, 25, 196; Frank, "Spiritual Life in Schönbrunn Village," 35n22 (quote on Native assistants' duties); Wellenreuther and Wessel, "Introduction," MMDZ, 63–65; "Memorandum about the Indian Matters from our dear brother David Zeisberger, when he was leaving Bethlehem, concerning the work among the Indians in the future, Bethlehem 4th March, 1764," box 315, folder 3, item 5, RIM, translated for author by Roy Ledbetter (from context clues, it is possible that this document was written in March 1765 rather than March 1764); Friedenshütten [Wyalusing] diary, August 17, 1766.
20. David Zeisberger to Nathanael Seidel, June 25, 1766, box 229, folder 2, item 19, RIM, translated for author by Julie Tomberlin Weber; Loskiel, *History of the Mission*, pt. 3, 4 ("large acquaintance" quote); Zeisberger to Seidel, June 23, 1765; Friedenshütten [Wyalusing] diary, June 2 and Memorabilia, 1765; Friedenshütten [Wyalusing] diary, Memorabilia, 1766; Friedenshütten diary, Memorabilia, 1767, box 131, folder 4, RIM, translated for author by Roy Ledbetter.
21. Friedenshütten [Wyalusing] diary, August 2, August 4, and August 7, 1765.
22. David Zeisberger to Nathanael Seidel, September 22, 1765, box 229, folder 2, item 13, RIM, translated for author by Julie Tomberlin Weber; David Zeisberger to Nathanael Seidel, October 20, 1765, box 229, folder 2, item 14, RIM, translated for author by Julie Tomberlin Weber; Friedenshütten [Wyalusing] diary, November 24, 1765.
23. Friedenshütten [Wyalusing] diary, September 14, 1766.
24. David Zeisberger to Nathanael Seidel, January 20, 1766, box 229, folder 2, item 15, RIM, translated for author by Julie Tomberlin Weber. The congregational diaries from Wyalusing from December 1765 and January 1766 relay the stories of many individuals experiencing one form or another of

spiritual awakening. On "exercised bodies" during the Great Awakening, see Winiarski, *Darkness Falls*, 209–30.

25. Friedenshütten [Wyalusing] diary, January 3, 1766; Friedenshütten [Wyalusing] diary, English translation [item 2], February 6, 1766.
26. Wheeler, *To Live Upon Hope*, 116–32, discusses how Mahican men in Shekomeko adopted Moravian rituals and poured into them new meanings rooted in their Native heritage.
27. Friedenshütten [Wyalusing] diary, July 13, July 21, and August 10, 1766. Wheeler, *To Live Upon Hope*, 170, points up that at least in the case of Mahicans, women were "often slower to turn to the Christian practice introduced by Moravian missionaries, in part because it was perceived as a possible threat to women's religious power."
28. Travel Diary of Schmick and Zeisberger to Machilusing, April 3 to May 24, 1765, May 15, 1765; Shannon, *Iroquois Diplomacy*, 167. This boundary line was a preview of what would be more firmly established at the 1768 Treaty of Fort Stanwix.
29. Friedenshütten [Wyalusing] diary, June 12 (second quote) and June 27 (third quote), 1765; David Zeisberger to Nathanael Seidel, [June 2?, 1765], box 229, folder 2, item 8, RIM, translated for author by Julie Tomberlin Weber; Zeisberger to Seidel, June 23, 1765 (first quote); David Zeisberger to Nathanael Seidel, June 30, 1765, box 229, folder 2, item 10, RIM, translated for author by Julie Tomberlin Weber; Schutt, "Tribal Identity," 385; Olmstead, *David Zeisberger*, 139. The Andastes had occupied the Susquehanna Valley until sustained warfare with the Iroquois in the seventeenth century drove them out and decimated their numbers. As noted earlier, Johnson and the Six Nations were already negotiating a boundary line that would sell off the Susquehanna Valley to Pennsylvania. That deal was finalized in the Treaty of Fort Stanwix in 1768.
30. Zeisberger to Seidel, June 30, 1765; Loskiel, *History of the Mission*, pt. 3, 6; Friedenshütten [Wyalusing] diary, July 20 and July 21, 1765; David Zeisberger to Nathanael Seidel, July 8, 1765, box 229, folder 2, item 11, RIM, translated for author by Julie Tomberlin Weber.
31. David Zeisberger to Nathanael Seidel, September 22, 1765, box 229, folder 2, item 13, RIM, translated for author by Julie Tomberlin Weber; David Zeisberger to Nathanael Seidel, October 20, 1765 (quotes from this letter), box 229, folder 2, item 14, RIM, translated for author by Julie Tomberlin Weber; David Zeisberger to David Nitschmann and Nathanael Seidel, April 8, 1766, box 229, folder 2, item 18, RIM, translated for author by Julie Tomberlin Weber; Schutt, "Tribal Identity," 386, sug-

gests that the two Indians believed that their prior residence at Wyalusing (Papunhank) and Tunkhannock (Anton) gave them grounds to claim that they "could forego further applications for permission to live along the North Branch of the Susquehanna." Her article posits deep divisions along tribal lines within the Moravian Indian community. By early 1766 Zeisberger was reporting that Joshua was getting along much better with the community, and with his wife, but by April Joshua was "now deserted and no one wants to have anything to do with him." The missionary even suggested that Joshua wanted to create his own town and believed he had the support of Moravian officials in Bethlehem for such a venture. David Zeisberger to Nathanael Seidel, January 26, 1766, and David Zeisberger to Nathanael Seidel, February 14, [17]66, box 229, folder 2, items 16 and 17, RIM, translated for author by Julie Tomberlin Weber; Zeisberger to Nitschmann and Seidel, April 8, 1766 (quote).

32. Zeisberger to Seidel, January 26, 1766; Friedenshütten [Wyalusing] diary, March 7, March 12, March 18, April 3, April 5, April 11, and April 23, 1766. According to the Moravian diary, Newollike soon regretted his decision because he feared he would lose "Credit or Honor" for failing to help them (April 3, 1766). But on the seventeenth the Brethren also heard that Newollike was badmouthing them. Echgohund (or Achcohunt or Achgohunt) was the chief at Schechschiquanünk, a village located further north on the Susquehanna River about twenty-four miles above Wyalusing. On April 11 he offered his services as an intermediary, but the community went in a different direction.
33. Zeisberger to Nitschmann and Seidel, April 8, 1766.
34. "Journey to Cajuga," in Beauchamp, *Moravian Journals*, 219–21; Jordan, "Annals of Friedenshuetten," in *The Moravian*, March 10, 1886, diary entry for May 1, 1766.
35. Jordan, "Annals of Friedenshuetten," in *The Moravian*, March 10, 1886, diary entry for May 1, 1766.
36. For sample discussions of these types of diplomatic intrigues, see Julie A. Fisher and Silverman, *Ninigret*, 41–44, 54–55, 68–69, and Merrell, *Into the American Woods*, 101, 202–5, 209–10.
37. Diarii from the Provincial Synod kept in Bethlehem from May 30th till June 4th, 1766, American Provincial Synod Results 1764–1768, MS English, MAB; Zeisberger to Seidel, June 25, 1766.
38. Friedenshütten [Wyalusing] diary, July 21 (first quote), July 24, July 25, 1766; Johann Jacob Schmick to Nathanael Seidel, August 18, 1766 (all other quotes), box 221, folder 10, item 1, RIM, translated for author by Julie

Tomberlin Weber. Schmick's August 18 letter makes clear that there had been other sources of conflict along tribal lines in the community including efforts by Anton either to keep believing Mahicans from having contact with visiting Indians or to keep non-Mahican and Mahican believers in the community separated. Either way, he was reproved for his actions. Fortunately, by this point the Brothers had reached "an understanding and are reconciled through the Savior's special presence and grace."

39. Jordan, "Annals of Friedenshuetten," in *The Moravian*, March 10, 1886, diary entry for June 23, 1766; Schutt, "Tribal Identity," 388–89; David Luther Roth, *Johann Roth*, 25; Johann Jacob Schmick to Nathanael Seidel and the Oeconomats-Conferenz, [October 15–19?, 1766], box 221, folder 10, item 2, RIM, translated for author by Julie Tomberlin Weber; Johann Jacob Schmick to Nathanael Seidel, October 20, 1766, box 221, folder 10, item 3, RIM, translated for author by Julie Tomberlin Weber. The Oeconomats-Conferenz was created in the mid-1760s as a new supervising board for all ecclesiastical affairs within the American Moravian Church. Peucker, *Time of Sifting*, 152–53. Schmick and Zeisberger's falling out was temporary. By November 14, 1766, Schmick reported to Seidel that he and Zeisberger had had "a thorough discussion" about the matters that divided them in early November and that now "the entire matter has been put aside as you requested, buried, and should also be completely forgotten by us." Johann Jacob Schmick to Nathanael Seidel, November 14, 1766, box 221, folder 10, item 4, RIM, translated for author by Julie Tomberlin Weber. When Zeisberger returned the following September en route to the Allegheny, Schmick and the whole town were "overjoyed" to see him. Friedenshütten diary, September 24, 1767.

40. "Journey to Onondaga and Cayuga, by David Zeisberger and Gottlob Senseman, October, 1766," in Beauchamp, *Moravian Journals*, 223–36, quotes on 223, 230, and 236; Olmstead, *David Zeisberger*, 143–45.

41. Johann Jacob Schmick to Nathanael Seidel, February 24, 1767, box 221, folder 10, item 7, RIM, translated for author by Julie Tomberlin Weber; Friedenshütten diary, January 11, January 19, January 20, and February 23, 1767; Johann Jacob Schmick to Nathanael Seidel, February 22, 1767, box 221, folder 10, item 6, RIM, translated for author by Julie Tomberlin Weber. Schutt, *Peoples of the River Valleys*, 113, 130, 135–38, equates Hallobank with Wapwallopen, a Munsee town south of Wyoming in Pennsylvania. But this seems highly unlikely. Instead, see the map of Munsee towns in chapter 1 (figure 6) from Folts, "Westward Migration of Munsee Indians," 32.

42. The Watchword was the daily text or texts set by United Brethren officials for Moravian devotional use and preaching. It was comparable to a lectionary.
43. Friedenshütten diary, January 1, January 5, January 18, February 14, March 5, April 16, and May 10, 1767; Schmick to Seidel, February 22, 1767.
44. Friedenshütten diary, April 5 (first quote), April 7, April 17, May 18, May 30 (second quote), June 13, and July 14, 1767; Johann Jacob Schmick to Nathanael Seidel, June 5, 1767, box 221, folder 10, item 9, RIM, translated for author by Julie Tomberlin Weber. Papunhank and his wife often functioned as caregivers. For example, in January 1768 they took the widow Phoebe into their home when she became ill. Friedenshütten diary January 1, 1768–December 31, 1768, January 13, 1768, box 131, folder 5, item 1, RIM, translated for author by Roy Ledbetter. Merritt, *At the Crossroads*, 112–13, discusses how and why the emphasis on Christ's bloody sacrifice resonated with Native men and women.
45. Friedenshütten diary, July 22 and August 3, 1767.
46. Friedenshütten diary, September 24 and September 25, 1767; Hulbert and Schwarze, "Diary of Zeisberger's Journey," 8–9.
47. Hulbert and Schwarze, "Diary of Zeisberger's Journey," 10–20, quotes on 11 and 20; *MMDZ*, 485; Schutt, *Peoples of the River Valleys*, 129.
48. Friedenshütten diary, November 10, 1767.
49. Hulbert and Schwarze, "Diary of Zeisberger's Journey," 21, 23, quote on 21.
50. Hulbert and Schwarze, "Diary of Zeisberger's Journey," 21–30 (quotes on 21, 23, 28, and 29). Olmstead, *David Zeisberger*, 149–53, describes the encounter with Wangomen in detail. Dowd, *Spirited Resistance*, 32, 37–38, identifies Wangomen as the Assinisink Prophet described in chapter 2. Papunhank may have met Wangomen before, since the latter man had lived previously at Assinisink and had on at least one occasion heard Zeisberger preach in Wyalusing. Allemewi's daughter, Rebecca, had been baptized by Schmick on June 7, 1767, at Friedenshütten. Friedenshütten diary, June 7, 1767.
51. Friedenshütten diary, January 1–December 31, 1768, May 2, May 3, May 8, and May 9, 1768, box 131, folder 5, item 2, English translation, RIM; Faull, "From Friedenshütten to Wyoming," 92–93; Johann Jacob Schmick to Nathanael Seidel, May 15, 1768, box 221, folder 10, item 14, RIM, translated for author by Julie Tomberlin Weber; Loskiel, *History of the Mission*, pt. 3, 28. When opportunity arose, Papunhank continued his evangelistic activities within Friedenshütten, as in July 1768 when to a group of Cayuga he "testified to how sweet it is to him and the other Indians here that they

not only hear good words about the Savior but also feel His Love in their hearts." Friedenshütten diary, July 18, 1768.

52. On bountiful harvests, growing numbers of livestock, feeding visitors, and comparative healthiness, see Friedenshütten [Wyalusing] diary, October 26, 1765; Friedenshütten [Wyalusing] diary, August 12, October 19, November 1, and Memorabilia, 1766; Friedenshütten diary, May 6, May 7, May 9, May 20, September 21, September 22, October 17, and Memorabilia, 1767; and Friedenshütten diary, February 22 and August 22, 1768. For the town's building structures, see Memorabilia at end of the Friedenshütten diaries for 1766, 1767, and 1768. On the expansion of the chapel and the adding of a belfry and bell, see Friedenshütten diary, September 8, September 12, September 17, and September 19, 1768. For the Indians' request for having religious art adorn the chapel walls, see Johann Jacob Schmick to Nathanael Seidel, June 19, 1768, box 221, folder 10, item 15, RIM, translated for author by Julie Tomberlin Weber. On the arrival and impact of the religious paintings, see Friedenshütten diary, July 6, July 18, and October 10, 1768, and Friedenshütten diary, January 1–December 31, 1769, May 8 and July 21, 1769, box 131, folder 6, RIM, translated for author by Roy Ledbetter. Among the very numerous examples of Native spiritual interest in the spring of 1768, see Friedenshütten diary, English translation (item 2), February 1, February 13, February 20, February 21, March 28, March 30, April 1, April 2, April 5, April 11, and April 13, 1768. In "Report of the Journey," 40–42, Ettwein noted the town's favorable reputation among the Six Nations and others and provided a detailed description of its physical layout. Schutt, *Peoples of the River Valleys*, 136, notes the comparative advantages of living in Friedenshütten.

53. Merrell, *Into the American Woods*, 304–5; Schutt, *Peoples of the River Valleys*, 130–31; Spero, *Frontier Country*, 187–93; Friedenshütten diary, English translation (item 2), February 8 and February 16, 1768; J[ohn] A[rbo] to [Pennsylvania government], March 14, 1768, JEP; John Penn, "To the Magistrates of Cumberland County Directing the Arrest of one Frederick Stump," January 19, 1768, *PA*, 4th ser., 3:350–51; John Penn, "Proclamation directing the arrest of one Fredrick Stump," January 19, 1768, *PA*, 4th ser., 3:355–56; John Penn, "To our Indian Brethren at Wighaloosin, on the River Susquehanna," January 28, 1768, *PA*, 4th ser., 3:368–70; [Second] Proclamation directing the arrest of Frederick Stump and his servant, March 16, 1768, *PA*, 4th ser., 3:387–89; Jordan, "Annals of Friedenshuetten," in *The Moravian*, March 31, 1886, diary entry for March 3, 1768.

54. Sir William Johnson to the Bretheren of Wialosing & the Big Island, March 18, 1768, box 221, folder 10, item 4, RIM; Friedenshütten diary, April 5, 1768; Schmick to Seidel, June 5, 1767; McConnell, *A Country Between*, 225–29, 244–45. Johnson had earlier written to Penn in mid-February commending him for "the measures you are taking for the relief of the Indian Grievances the necessity for which appears daily more obvious." The two leaders also organized a condolence council at Fort Pitt in the west in late April and early May in an effort to persuade other Indians not to retaliate for the Stump murders. Sir William Johnson to Gov. Penn, February 18, 1768, *PA*, 1st ser., 4:290, and Sir Wm. Johnson to Gov. Penn, February 29, 1768, *PA*, 1st ser., 4:293–94; Minutes of the Conferences held at Fort Pitt, in April and May, 1768, *MPCP*, 9:514–43.
55. Zeisberger to Nitschmann and Seidel, April 8, 1766; Schmick to Seidel, June 19, 1768; Schutt, "Tribal Identity," 383–88.
56. Friedenshütten diary, April 3 and April 24, 1768; McConnell, *A Country Between*, 244–48; Sir William Johnson to Gov. Penn, January 15, 1767, *PA*, 1st ser., 4:261–62; Extract from a Report of the Lords of Trade to the Earl of Shelbourne, December 23, 1767, *PA*, 1st ser., 4:281; Shannon, *Iroquois Diplomacy*, 167; Spero, *Frontier Country*, 193–96.
57. Friedenshütten diary, June 19, June 20, July 18 (Gagohunt quotes), and July 19 (Papunhank quote), 1768; Johann Jacob Schmick to Nathanael Seidel, August 14, 1768, box 221, folder 10, item 16, RIM, translated for author by Julie Tomberlin Weber. During his June visit, Echgohund had tried to convince them to bring back those who had been sent to Goschgoschunk but they refused. A draft of their response to Echgohund may be found at "Message of Wichilusing Indians to Chief Achgohunt," [1768], JEP, 1352, translated for author by Roy Ledbetter. Echgohund's message was disturbing enough to prompt them to send a delegation including Papunhank to Bethlehem to consult with Nathanael Seidel about what to communicate to the Cayuga chief directly. They returned on July 6 and informed Echgohund on the seventh that Bethlehem had authorized supplying his town with a Moravian minister. John Roth would begin work there in 1769. Residents in Schechschiquanünk had been requesting that a Moravian missionary come live there since 1767.
58. Friedenshütten diary, September 17, September 18, and September 23, 1768; Johann Jacob Schmick to Nathanael Seidel, September 18, 1768 (quotes from this letter), box 221, folder 10, item 17, RIM, translated for author by Julie Tomberlin Weber; Schutt, "Tribal Identity," 390.

59. Johann Jacob Schmick to Nathanael Seidel, [September 26, 1768] (quote), box 221, folder 10, item 18, RIM, translated for author by Julie Tomberlin Weber; Friedenshütten diary, September 24 and September 25, 1768.
60. Friedenshütten diary, November 9, 1768; Johann Jacob Schmick to Nathanael Seidel, November 15, 1768, box 221, folder 10, item 19, RIM, translated for author by Julie Tomberlin Weber. Chillaway had decided back on September 18 to go, which according to Schmick, "suited us because that way someone from our settlement would be present there." Friedenshütten diary, September 18, 1768. Schmick's letter to Seidel in November reported that Chillaway insisted that efforts to get the community to send representatives to the treaty had been purely orchestrated by Abraham and Indians in Schechschiquanünk who wanted to "lead our Brothers in Wichlusing into the old Indian ways again, to make a covenant with them and then to get power over them again and to follow their *Commandments*."
61. Friedenshütten diary, September 25, 1768.
62. Friedenshütten diary, November 9 and November 10, 1768; Schmick to Seidel, November 15, 1768; "Deed determining the Boundary Line between the Whites and Indians," in O'Callaghan, *Documents Relative to Colonial History*, 8:135–37; John Penn to the Assembly Concerning the result of the treaty lately held by Sir William Johnson at Fort Stanwix, January 16, 1769, *PA*, 4th ser., 3:402–5; Shannon, *Iroquois Diplomacy*, 167–68. The cession included not only the land on which Friedenshütten stood but the town's main hunting grounds near Wyoming, Tunkhannock, and Shamokin.
63. Friedenshütten diary, December 5, 1768; McConnell, *A Country Between*, 251–53; White, *Middle Ground*, 351–53.
64. David Zeisberger to Nathanael Seidel, August 9, 1768, box 229, folder 2, item 28, RIM, translated for author by Julie Tomberlin Weber.

6. New Trials

1. Friedenshütten diary January 1, 1770–December 31, 1770, May 20, 1770, box 131, folder 7, item 1, RIM, translated for author by Edward Quinter.
2. Friedenshütten diary, June 24, 1770.
3. Friedenshütten diary, June 14, 1770; Friedenshütten diary January 1, 1771–January 31, 1772, April 16, 1771, box 131, folder 8, item 1, RIM, translated for author by Edward Quinter. In the first instance, the visitors were Indian agent George Croghan and a recent immigrant from Ireland, Dr. Forbus: "They toured our little community and worship house . . . [and]

were impressed and got to see many houses. . . . The visitors were amazed by the singing of the members and children and by their attentiveness and demeanor." Even Native visitors were impressed. When Delaware prophet Wangomen saw the town in April 1771, he commented that "there isn't any other such Indian village like this, with so many things both inside and outside the dwellings and so much livestock." Friedenshütten diary, April 30, 1771.

4. Loskiel, *History of the Mission*, pt. 3, 65.
5. Friedenshütten diary, January 1, 1769–December 31, 1769, January 1, 1769, box 131, folder 6, RIM, translated for author by Julie Tomberlin Weber; Message of some of the People call'd Quakers in Philadelphia to Netalwelman, King & Headman of the Delaware Indians and his Council, March 10, 1767, 4:391, FAP; McConnell, *A Country Between*, 225–32; Wellenreuther, "White Eyes," 142. Schutt, *Peoples of the River Valleys*, 138–39, notes that Killbuck had kin in the town—his mother's sister and her sons. This Killbuck, sometimes known as John Killbuck or Killbuck Sr., is not to be confused with his son, also known as Killbuck or Gelelemend and eventually as William Henry. Presbyterians would keep trying to gain permission to establish a mission among the Ohio Delawares. John Brainerd wrote to them in 1767 expressing his desire to "tarry with you sometime if it be agreeable to you." Five years later David McClure spent two weeks at Newcomer's Town but was told by its council that he was not welcome to stay longer. "John Brainerd to Natotwhalaman, King of the Delawares," August 6, 1767, 4:395, FAP; McClure, *Diary of David McClure*, 80–83.
6. Friedenshütten diary, January 7, 1769, translated for author by Julie Tomberlin Weber; Lewis Weiss to the Honorable John Penn, November 28, 1768, box 131, folder 11, item 3, RIM.
7. "Petition of Several Indians to His Honor the Governor [John Penn], February 7, 1769," in Reichel, "Wyalusing and the Moravian Mission," 213–14.
8. "Petition of Several Indians."
9. Friedenshütten diary, January 31, February 12, February 14, March 7, and July 26, 1769, translated for author by Edward Quinter (all additional translations from 1769 diary done for author by Edward Quinter); "A Letter to the Honorable John Penn [from Johann Jacob Schmick], February 13, 1769," in Reichel, "Wyalusing and the Moravian Mission," 215; "John Penn to Papoonham and the Rest of the Wyaloosing Indians, June 21, 1769," in Reichel, "Wyalusing and the Moravian Mission," 216. Indi-

ans living twenty-four miles north at Schechschiquanünk sent a similar petition to Penn and sent a representative with Papunhank and Joshua to Philadelphia. Penn sent them similar assurances. Moravian missionary John Roth and his wife had just begun to serve in that town, so it functioned as a kind of outpost of the work in Friedenshütten. "Petition of Samuel Davis in behalf of himself and his friends the Indians to John Penn, February 7, 1769," in Reichel, "Wyalusing and the Moravian Mission," 215.

10. "The Indians' Reply to John Penn, August 1769," in Reichel, "Wyalusing and the Moravian Mission," 216–17; Friedenshütten diary, June 10 and June 11, 1769; Johann Jacob Schmick to John Ettwein, June 13, 1769, JEP, 515, translated for author by Roy Ledbetter; Johann Jacob Schmick to John Ettwein, January 10, 1769, JEP, 501, translated for author by Roy Ledbetter; Kenny, *Peaceable Kingdom Lost*, 217–20; Moyer, *Wild Yankees*, 23–31; Spero, *Frontier Country*, 199–206; Reichel, "Wyalusing and the Moravian Mission," 204. On the surveyor issue, see Johann Schmick [?] to John Penn [?], [1769], JEP, 1080. In this letter Schmick protested his innocence to the governor regarding accusations made by some land-hungry whites that he "had stirred up a number of Indians, to hinder a Surveyor to do his Duty." Following the Fort Stanwix Treaty, the Penns acted rapidly to lay hold of the newly acquired lands in the Wyoming Valley by hiring land speculators like Charles Stewart to survey the land, bring in settlers, set up trading posts, and keep out Connecticut "intruders."
11. Friedenshütten diary, March 27, 1769.
12. Friedenshütten diary, April 21 and May 7, 1769; Johann Jacob Schmick to John Ettwein, May 22, 1769 (quote from this letter), JEP, 514, translated for author by Roy Ledbetter. Schutt, *Peoples of the River Valleys*, 137–38; White, *Middle Ground*, 351. According to Schmick (Friedenshütten diary, April 21, 1769), the old Cayuga claimed that the Six Nations had told Johnson that "Indians need deer, bear, beaver, and other animals that live in the forest and in the streams and lakes. That is the wealth from which they also live, and the hides and furs they sell to your people. From it they purchase blankets, powder, lead, and other necessary goods for their physical needs." The importance of maintaining fruitful trading relationships was a longstanding Iroquois diplomatic appeal. It carried less weight with the English by the late 1760s.
13. Faull, "From Friedenshütten to Wyoming," 92, 95, 96; Friedenshütten diary, July 1, July 15, September 27, and November 10, 1769; Frieden-

shütten diary, March 5, March 19, June 14, October 17, November 11, and December 15, 1770; Friedenshütten diary, August 13, August 16, and December 3, 1771.

14. Friedenshütten diary, May 7, July 20, July 21, and Memorabilia, 1769; Friedenshütten diary, May 13, July 7, and July 10, 1770. By year's end in 1770, Schmick was able to report that through God's provision of "good hunting results" and a "blessed harvest," the "terrible damage" done by the worms had been overcome. Friedenshütten diary, Memorabilia, 1770.

15. Johann Jacob Schmick to John Ettwein, October 9, 1770, JEP, 524, translated for author by Roy Ledbetter; Friedenshütten diary, January 16, February 14, and August 28, 1769; Friedenshütten diary, April 20 and October 17, 1770; Friedenshütten diary, September 27, 1771. For one occasion when Schmick appealed to Ettwein and their Bethlehem overseers for new clothes for some of the town's poor, see Schmick to Ettwein, May 28, 1769.

16. Friedenshütten diary, March 7 and August 28, 1769; Friedenshütten diary, June 5, June 15, September 10, October 10, October 17, and October 31, 1770; Friedenshütten diary, January 15, May 21, June 1, and December 3, 1771; Johann Jacob Schmick to John Ettwein, June 4, 1770, JEP, 521, translated for author by Roy Ledbetter; Johann Jacob Schmick to John Ettwein, January 7, 1771, JEP, 525, translated for author by Roy Ledbetter.

17. As *Vorsteher*: Friedenshütten diary, April 20, 1771; as diplomat: Friedenshütten diary, February 12, March 7, and June 11, 1769; Friedenshütten diary, May 11–May 20 and June 19–June 30, 1770; Friedenshütten diary, January 21 and January 26, 1772; Friedenshütten diary February 2, 1772–June 10, 1772, March 30 and April 14, 1772, box 131, folder 9, item 1, RIM, translated for author by Edward Quinter; on meetings at Papunhank's home: Friedenshütten diary, April 29, 1770; Friedenshütten diary, March 27, 1771.

18. Ettwein, "Report of the Journey," 95. Ettwein could be more critical of the Native Christians. According to his biographer, he was distressed by the lack of outward evidences of piety among the Christian Indians in their daily household activities, as well as by some of their economic and financial dealings. He minded the fact that Indians were not always as responsible as he wanted them to be in paying back loans or debts owed to missionaries or the missions. Ettwein liked to see signs of Christian Indians acting industriously and in accord with Euro-American cultural practices. He took such actions as signs of true conversion. His

bent toward wanting Christian Indians to "civilize" according to Euro-American ways stood in contrast with earlier Moravian leaders. Hamilton, *John Ettwein*, 90, 94–96. In 1769 there were 45 communicants out of a total of 178 persons in Friedenshütten. In 1770 there were 47 communicants out of 172 persons, and in 1771 there were 48 communicants out of 151 persons. These numbers included both adults and children. The communicants were all adults.

19. Friedenshütten diary, March 11, 1770. For an earlier instance of Chillaway's spiritual interest, see Friedenshütten diary, September 11, 1768. On his wife's religious interest, see Friedenshütten diary, July 30, 1769. On his daughter's interest in baptism, see Friedenshütten [Wyalusing] diary August 17, September 12, September 21, and November 23, 1766. "Register of Persons," MMDZ, 585, suggests that Chillaway was never baptized.
20. Friedenshütten diary, July 20 and July 23, 1770. Newollike would eventually be baptized as Augustinius on May 12, 1774, in Schönbrunn, Ohio. MMDZ, 193.
21. Friedenshütten diary, December 15, 1770; Friedenshütten diary, January 6, 1771; MMDZ, 120–21, 121n122, 600. Chillaway was renamed Willhelm.
22. Friedenshütten List of Indian families and their properties, box 131, folder 10, item 5, RIM.
23. Valuable biographical data on many Moravian Indians may be found in "Register of Persons," MMDZ, 573–600. Reichel, "Wyalusing and the Moravian Mission," 213; Friedenshütten diary, March 25, 1772. Anna Johanna had a sister, Paulina, who bore six children between 1769 and 1777. Even if she were a considerably younger sister, the chances are that Anna Johanna was only in her thirties or early forties by that point.
24. Catalog of names of Nain, Wechquetank, and Machelusing Indians [1765 or 1766], box 125, folder 4, item 25, RIM.
25. Friedenshütten diary, April 25, April 30, May 21 (quote), May 25, and Memorabilia, 1769; MMDZ, 119, 119n116. The end of the year summary for 1769 ("Memorabilia") stated that "seven people arrived to stay here from Jersey, namely 2 widows, a woman and her husband, 3 children, a single man, and a single woman." Schmick twice referred to these people as coming from Jersey, as does the December 25, 1772, Schönbrunn diary entry. Mary formally became a member of that congregation on that date in 1772. Her husband's comments to Schmick suggest he was already familiar with the Christian message, more evidence that they had been part of Brainerd's town. For the location of Quilutamend, see Ettwein's 1768 map in Faull, "From Friedenshütten to Wyoming," 87–88.

26. Friedenshütten diary, September 19, September 20, September 24, September 27, September 28, November 10, November 12, November 14, and Memorabilia, 1769. On Native birthing practices see Axtell, *Indian Peoples of Eastern America*, 3–4.
27. David Zeisberger to Matthew Hehl, July 22, 1768, box 229, folder 2, item 27, RIM, translated for author by Julie Tomberlin Weber; Johann Jacob Schmick to Nathanael Seidel, September 18, 1768, box 221, folder 10, item 17, RIM, translated for author by Julie Tomberlin Weber; Goschgoschunk diary, February 25–September 7, 1769, April 7, April 17 (first two quotes) , and April 19, 1769, English translations by Tilde Marx, MDP; Goschgoschunk diary, September 9, 1769–April 16, 1770, November 13, November 15, November 17, December 3, December 19, and December 24, 1769, and January 20 and January 21, 1770, English translations by Tilde Marx, MDP; Friedenshütten diary, April 26, 1770 (last quote); David Zeisberger to Matthew Hehl, December 30, 1769–February 21, 1770, English translation, box 229, folder 3, item 10, RIM.
28. Friedenshütten diary, May 5, 1770; Lagundo Utenünk (Friedensstadt) diary, April 17, 1770–February 27, 1771, February 9, 1771, English translation by Tilde Marx, MDP; David Zeisberger to Nathanael Seidel, March 10, 1771, Letter VIII, English translation by Tilde Marx, MDP; Friedenshütten diary, March 29, 1771.
29. Zeisberger to Seidel, August 9, 1768; Goschgoschunk diary, January 26, March 27, April 7, April 11, May 2, July 1, and July 10, 1769; Goschgoschunk diary, April 17, 1770; Olmstead, *David Zeisberger*, 154–67; Rob Harper, *Unsettling the West*, 11–12.
30. Friedenshütten diary, April 29, 1770.
31. Friedenshütten diary, May 11, May 15, May 20, June 18, and June 19 (second quote), 1770; Lagundo Utenünk (Friedensstadt) diary, May 5, 1770 (first quote); Olmstead, *David Zeisberger*, 169–70.
32. Friedenshütten diary, June 30 and Memorabilia, 1770.
33. "Minutes of Council held at Philadelphia, January 15, 1770 and Minutes of Council held at Philadelphia, October 20, 1770," in *MPCP*, 9:645–46, 94–97; Friedenshütten diary, October 23 and November 10, 1769; Friedenshütten diary, May 9, 1770; Moyer, *Wild Yankees*, 28–31.
34. Goschgoschunk diary, February 14 and March 3, 1770; Lagundo Utenünk (Friedensstadt) diary, July 30, 1770; McConnell, *A Country Between*, 258–59, 262, 265–66.
35. David Zeisberger to John Ettwein, February 27, 1769 (first quote), Letter I, English translation by Tilde Marx, MDP; Goschgoschunk diary,

April 11, 1769 (second quote). Two months later Zeisberger conferred with Allemewi, whether "in his opinion the Chiefs in the West had good intentions in inviting all the Indians of their nation [Delawares] here, or whether they had anything secret in mind. He replied that he thought their intentions to be good, because they were really peacefully minded, and did not wish for another war." Goschgoschunk diary, June 16, 1769.

36. Johann Jacob Schmick to John Ettwein, November 6, 1769, JEP, 517, translated for author by Roy Ledbetter; Schmick to Ettwein, January 7, 1771.

37. Goschgoschunk diary, June 16, 1769. Some Stockbridge Indians (mostly Mahicans) were among the Native visitors drawn to Friedenshütten by its Christian character. They had asked the Six Nations for permission to move to the new Moravian town in 1765 but were turned down. Small groups of them came to Friedenshütten in 1770 and 1771 persuaded it offered a better option than accepting the invitation from Shawnee Indians in Ohio to move there. Friedenshütten diary, September 30, 1770; Friedenshütten diary, June 17, June 23, June 24, June 26, and July 28, 1771; Friedenshütten diary, May 5, 1772; Frazier, *Mohicans of Stockbridge*, 176–77.

38. Friedenshütten diary, March 25, April 24, and April 29, 1771. Chillaway defended his actions, claiming that Pennamite forces "had kept him a prisoner" lest he reveal their plans to the New Englanders. The Cayuga chief seems to have been satisfied with this explanation. Johann Jacob Schmick to John Ettwein, April 21, 1771, JEP, 526, translated for author by Roy Ledbetter.

39. Lagundo Utenünk (Friedensstadt) diary, July 14 and July 15, 1770. As a frequent opponent of Zeisberger and Christianity, Wangomen had likely found a range of excuses for not conveying Packanke's message to this large group of Christian Indians during the prior two years. For Packanke's request to Wangomen in 1769, see Goschgoschunk diary, July 1, 1769.

40. Friedenshütten diary, April 30, 1771. This is John W. Jordan's translation, perhaps better called a paraphrase, contained in Jordan, "Annals of Friedenshuetten," in *The Moravian*, April 21, 1886, diary entry for April 30, 1771.

41. For one example, see Zeisberger's dialogue with Wangomen in Goschgoschunk diary, April 12, 1770.

42. Friedenshütten diary, May 3, 1771.

43. For an excellent account of another group of Christian Indians in this same period wrestling with whether to move (in their case from southern New England to Oneida lands in New York), see Silverman, *Red Brethren*.

44. Friedenshütten diary, May 20, 1771; Lagundo Utenünk (Friedensstadt) diary, May 27, June 26, July 14, August 2, August 7, and August 15, 1771; Olmstead, *David Zeisberger*, 179; Loskiel, *History of the Mission*, pt. 3, 64–65; de Schweinitz, *Life and Times of Zeisberger*, 369–70. By that point in 1771, Zeisberger also knew that time might be of the essence in moving to the Muskingum Valley since they might have Christian competition there. He had heard in June that Netawatwees's messenger to Philadelphia, Killbuck Jr., had just returned from asking Quakers to send a preacher to them. The Friends agreed and promised to send some of their people within two months' time. Lagundo Utenünk (Friedensstadt) diary, June 24, 1771. On the other hand, a strong group opposed to Christianity emerged in Newcomer's Town following Zeisberger's visit there.
45. Friedenshütten diary, September 6, 1771. According to the Lagundo Utenünk (Friedensstadt) diary for July 15, 1771, Wangomen returned from his time at Friedenshütten and Schechschiquanünk with letters from Schmick and Roth that described many things about life there. But the entry does not indicate what these towns had decided about the invitation to come west.
46. Friedenshütten diary, September 6, 1771.
47. Friedenshütten diary, September 23, 1771.
48. John Roth to Nathanael Seidel, October 15, 1771, box 221, folder 7, item 16, RIM, translated for author by Edward Quinter.
49. White, *Middle Ground*, 331–32; [Benezet], "Account of Behaviour & Sentiments," 484; Friedenshütten diary, August 18 and August 20, 1770. Once a Moravian, Papunhank's healing practices would have been limited to employing herbal and plant remedies acceptable and perhaps even familiar to Euro-Americans. Whether prior to that time his healing practices included more controversial methods is not known. Illness was quite common in Friedenshütten in prior years but seems to have been especially bad in this stretch during 1771. For one description of sickness in the town in 1770, see Johann Jacob Schmick to John Ettwein, September 13, 1770, JEP, 523, translated for author by Roy Ledbetter.
50. Friedenshütten diary, May 15, May 17 (quote from this date), May 19, June 1, June 17, August 30, September 2, September 10, and September 11, 1771; Johann Jacob Schmick to Nathanael Seidel, September 25, 1771, box 221, folder 11, item 10, RIM, translated for author by Julie Tomberlin Weber.
51. Friedenshütten diary September 23, 1771; Schmick to Seidel, September 25, 1771; Schutt, "Tribal Identity," 391–92. Joshua had been baptized in 1742, Bathsheba in 1743.

52. Kaiser, "Munsee Social Networking," 156–57.
53. Friedenshütten diary September 23, 1771; Schmick to Seidel, September 25, 1771.
54. Friedenshütten diary September 23, October 1, and October 2, 1771; Schmick to Seidel, September 25, 1771; Johann Jacob Schmick to Nathanael Seidel, October 2, 1771, box 221, folder 11, item 11, RIM, translated for author by Julie Tomberlin Weber; John Roth to Nathanael Seidel, September 30, 1771, box 221, folder 7, item 15, RIM, translated for author by Edward Quinter.
55. Friedenshütten diary, September 24, September 28, October 6 (quote from young people), and October 27, 1771; Johann Jacob Schmick to Nathanael Seidel, November 5, 1771, box 221, folder 11, item 12, RIM, translated for author by Julie Tomberlin Weber; Friedenshütten diary, January 19, 1772.
56. Johann Jacob Schmick to John Ettwein, April 22, 1771, JEP, 527, translated for author by Roy Ledbetter.
57. Schmick to Seidel, October 2, 1771 (first quote); Friedenshütten diary, September 24 (second quote), September 29, and October 1–5, 1771; Calloway, *Our Hearts Fell*. Only for Sunday, October 6, did the diary report an interruption to the normal pattern of worship: "We had to postpone our events because wild Indians with rum came last night. They camped along the Susquehanna and drank heavily and caused commotion. Oniem and Michael were drawn to this."
58. Friedenshütten diary, December 3, 1771.
59. Lagundo Utenünk (Friedensstadt) diary, January 1, 1772–April 12, 1772, January 5, January 10, January 13, January 27, March 26, March 30, and April 12, 1771, English translations by Tilde Marx, MDP; Olmstead, *David Zeisberger*, 182–89. Fourteen people from Friedenshütten had already moved to Lagundo Utenünk back in October 1771. Friedenshütten diary, October 11, 1771.
60. Friedenshütten diary, January 26, February 10, February 28, February 29, March 2, March 10, March 30, and June 10, 1772. Worn out by their missionary labors, the Schmicks had requested and received permission to return to Bethlehem rather than moving west, and did so in early May.
61. Friedenshütten diary, January 22 and February 8, 1772 (quotes from this date); Schechschequanunk diary, January 1, 1772–May 3, 1772, January 28, 1772, box 133, folder 4, RIM, translated for author by Julie Tomberlin Weber; Johann Jacob Schmick to John Ettwein, February 10, 1772, JEP, 531, translated for author by Roy Ledbetter.

62. Friedenshütten diary, March 30 and April 4, 1772; Schechschequanunk diary, March 31, 1772.
63. "Richard Penn to the Indians at Wyaloosing, May 15, 1772," in Reichel, "Wyalusing and the Moravian Mission," 219–20; Minutes of Council held at Philadelphia, August 8, 1771, 9:754, *MPCP*; Christian Indians of Wialusing and Sheshecunnuck to the Honorable Representatives of the Freemen of the Province of Pennsylvania, May 16, 1772, 4:459, FAP; A Conference with Papunehang, Joseph Peepy, Joshua & John Martin from the Indians at Wyaloosing & Sheshequanunk now about to remove to the westward of the Ohio, May 16, 1772, 4:463, FAP; Philadelphia Friends to Papunehang & others of the Delaware nation, August 8, 1772, 4:467, FAP. The precise amount of the "present" provided by the assembly is not clear, but Ettwein had reported a few months earlier that some white Moravians had been privately speaking with assembly members and prominent Quakers (Abel James and Joseph Fox) about providing "a gift for your great journey." Ettwein had been told by those power brokers that it would be helpful if some deputies were sent from Wyalusing to Philadelphia to meet with government officials and prominent Friends well acquainted with Papunhank from years past. Hence the trip in May 1772. John Ettwein to the Missionaries at Friedenshütten, [late 1771 or early 1772], JEP, 1040, translated for author by Roy Ledbetter. Moravian bishop Nathanael Seidel had sent a letter to Richard Penn back in October 1771 congratulating him on his appointment and informing him of the Wyalusing Indians' plans to move to the west. Address of welcome to Richard Penn from the Unitas Fratrum, October 24, 1771, JEP, 1582.
64. Friedenshütten diary, May 7, May 11, May 12, May 18, May 22, May 23, and June 7, 1772.
65. "An Enumeration of the Indian Families residing at Friedenshuetten and of the Improvements belonging to each, 1771," in Reichel, "Wyalusing and the Moravian Mission," 217–19; Friedenshütten diary, Memorabilia 1771; "Status of the Indian Mission on the Susquehanna, at the time of the exodus, June 1772," in Reichel, "Wyalusing and the Moravian Mission," 220–22.
66. Merritt, *At the Crossroads*, 112–13; Wheeler, *To Live Upon Hope*, 107–8.
67. Friedenshütten diary, June 7, 1772.

7. Ohio Endings

1. *MMDZ*, 217–18. On White Eyes' crucial leadership role among the Ohio Delawares in the 1770s, see Wellenreuther, "White Eyes," 139–61.
2. *MMDZ*, 216–17.

3. Wellenreuther, "White Eyes," 145; [White Eyes' Speech], July 23, 1774, William H. Smith, *St. Clair Papers*, 1:331–33.
4. White, *Middle Ground*, 357–65; Hinderaker, "Declaring Independence," 105–25; Rob Harper, *Unsettling the West*, 50–66.
5. *MMDZ*, 273.
6. Ettwein and Roth, "Diaries of Ettwein and Roth," 118–53 (Ettwein quotes on 158 and 160; Roth quote on 135). Another translation of Roth's diary, with substantial annotations, is in [Johann Roth], "Diary of a Moravian Indian Mission Migration," 247–70.
7. Ettwein and Roth, "Diaries of Ettwein and Roth," 142.
8. Ettwein and Roth, "Diaries of Ettwein and Roth," 134; "Protocol of the Conference at Langundo-Utenünk on 12 August 1772," in *MMDZ*, 556; "Protocol of the Conference at Langundo-Utenünk on 17 August 1772," in *MMDZ*, 558; Schutt, "Tribal Identity," 392.
9. "Protocol 12 August 1772," 555; "Protocol 17 August 1772," 558–59; Ettwein, "Brother Ettwein's Account," 259–60.
10. Ettwein, "Brother Ettwein's Account," 261.
11. *MMDZ*, 95–97.
12. Ettwein, "Brother Ettwein's Account," 261; John Ettwein, "Plan of the Settlement of Schönbrunn [1772]," in *MMDZ*, 645, shows the location of these plots; Olmstead, *David Zeisberger*, 194, 196–97; *MMDZ*, 98, 100–101.
13. Olmstead, *David Zeisberger*, 194. At their meeting on August 12, the missionaries had determined that a group would go to Gekelemukpechünk "in order to salute the Chief there and have talks with him." "Protocol 12 August 1772," 555.
14. Ettwein, "Brother Ettwein's Account," 262–63; Silverman, "To Become a Chosen People," 261. Ettwein presented the portion of Papunhank's speech here quoted as a quotation in his journal account. Ettwein of course received it in translation from Munsee to German, and it has subsequently been translated into English. In those ways it was considerably removed from Papunhank's own voice. Yet its consistency with his longstanding convictions makes it a reliable representation of his message.
15. Loskiel, *History of the Mission*, pt. 3, 81; Ettwein, "Brother Ettwein's Account," 263.
16. Ettwein, "Brother Ettwein's Account," 263–64.
17. Ettwein, "Brother Ettwein's Account," 261, 264.
18. McConnell, *A Country Between*, 226–28; Hinderaker, *Elusive Empires*, 180.
19. Hinderaker, *Elusive Empires*, 180–82 (quote on 180); McConnell, *A Country Between*, 228–29; "Introduction," *MMDZ*, 22, 68–69; Paul A. W.

Wallace, *Thirty Thousand Miles*, 98, 102; Grimes, *Western Delaware Indian Nation*, 168–70, 183. Wellenreuther, "White Eyes," 149–55, explains that White Eyes envisioned gaining a legal title to the land the Delawares occupied in the Ohio Country from the British king or later the Continental Congress in exchange for "accepting an energetic program of acculturation and adaptation to European notions of civilization and orderly life" (150). He even advocated creating a town of whites next to the Delawares' chief town so that Natives could learn European methods. Netawatwees and the council rejected White Eyes' plan in January 1776, including its implication that non-Moravian white Christians be allowed to settle in the region.

20. Gnadenhütten was located on the site where Tamaqua had previously lived, a fitting spot for Indians wishing to continue his peace legacy. Mahicans constituted a majority in the town, but some Delawares were present. Joshua Senior served as one of its principal Native leaders. Joshua Junior, Sophia, and their children lived there. Papunhank and Anna Johanna visited Gnadenhütten regularly and in general, there was frequent exchange between the two Moravian towns.
21. "Introduction," *MMDZ*, 59.
22. Hinderaker and Mancall, *At the Edge of Empire*, 155–57. In light of the British withdrawal, Governor Richard Penn sent two messages to the Pennsylvania Assembly in early 1773 asking for their approval to create a garrison of twenty-five to thirty men to man Fort Pitt to protect whites in the region from Indian attack. *PA*, 4th ser., 3:537–39.
23. *MMDZ*, 102; Olmstead, *David Zeisberger*, 195. My summary of the statutes and rules draws upon the shorter list found in the Lagundo Utenünk mission diary for September 1772 as translated by August Mahr in "Schoenbrunn Diary," Appendix IV, 185–89, MSS Coll. 215, box 4, folder 19, AMP (also printed in Olmstead, *David Zeisberger*, 195, 347–48), and the longer list found in the JEP, 1634, and printed in Heckewelder, *Narrative of the Mission*, 122–24. *MMDZ*, 563–64, also prints this longer version.
24. "Introduction," *MMDZ*, 68.
25. *MMDZ*, 129.
26. *MMDZ*, 178. Much more extensive descriptions of religious life in the two Moravian towns may be found in Frank, "Spiritual Life in Schönbrunn Village," 20–38, "Introduction," *MMDZ*, 59–71, and Olmstead, *David Zeisberger*, 194–213. Watchwords were scriptural texts for each day selected by Moravian leaders in Herrnhut, Germany, and then sent to North America. *MMDZ*, 96n26. Evening services were not always held; it depended

upon, among other things, what person was available to conduct them, what other matters needed attention, and how many Indians were present within the town at that moment.

27. Minutes from a meeting of the resident missionaries in August 1773 provide further clues to the concerns that absorbed community time and attention—at least the missionaries' time and attention. As usual, navigating relations with local and regional authorities was at the top of the list. In the missionaries' opinion, the Delaware chiefs were to be given their due but not to the point of being exploited by them. Zeisberger and the others also believed that religious practices should be comparable in both towns so that their flock would see their community as one body, not two. Hunting expeditions were to be encouraged for the food and clothing they generated, but the recently baptized shouldn't stay away too long lest they stray from the faith. Similarly, young people should be urged to marry young lest their urges lead them to "get involved in bad things." And rumors of poison possession and use among the Brethren needed to be extinguished. "Conference held at Schönbrunn on 19 August 1773," in *MMDZ*, 559–63.
28. Wellenreuther, "White Eyes," 147–48.
29. *MMDZ*, 108–14, 122–24, 127, 133, 164–73; David Zeisberger to Nathanael Seidel, January 26, 1773, box 229, folder 4, item 5, RIM, translated for author by Edward Quinter; David Zeisberger to Nathanael Seidel, March 21, 1773, box 229, folder 4, item 6, RIM, translated for author by Edward Quinter.
30. Jones, *Journal of Two Visits*, 28–32, 46–84 (Othaawaapeelethee quote on 64), 90–103 (quotes on 102, 93–94, and 95); Heckewelder, "Canoe Journey," 290 (final quote).
31. McClure, *Diary of David McClure*, 61–79. I discuss McClure's encounter with the Delawares at greater length in Pointer, *Encounters of the Spirit*, 199–203.
32. McClure, *Diary of David McClure*, 80–81.
33. *MMDZ*, 108.
34. McClure, *Diary of David McClure*, 50, 51. Ettwein's account of McClure's positive impression of the Moravian town conformed to the Presbyterian's diary: "[He] attended an evening and a morning devotion, which were held in the Indian tongue. He lodged with us and could not praise highly enough the reverence shown by old and young, and the beautiful singing. He said, they had not known anything of this mission." Ettwein, "Brother Ettwein's Account," 268.

35. Minutes of a Council held at Philadelphia, May 7–13, 1771, *MPCP*, 9:735–42; Message of Netawatwees to Governor John Penn, November 26, 1772, *MPCP*, 10:61–64; *MMDZ*, 120; [Philadelphia Friends] to Papunehang & others of the Delaware Nations, August 8, 1772, 4:467, FAP; John Papunehang et al. to Israel Pemberton, March 21, 1773, Jonah Thompson Collection, HSP; Philadelphia Yearly Meeting Minutes for Meeting for Sufferings for Pennsylvania and New Jersey, Minute Book One, 1755–75, 388–91, Quaker and Special Collections, Haverford College, Haverford, PA; [Philadelphia Friends] to Netawattwalemun and John Papunehang, July 8, 1773, folder 2, PFP. John Ettwein kept Philadelphia Friends abreast of events in the west. See for example John Ettwein to [Abel] James and [Henry] Drinker [July 17, 1773], 4:487, FAP.
36. Lacey, "[Journal of] John Lacey 1773," 152–53; Parrish, "[Journal of] John Parrish 1773," 154–55; Ettwein to James and Drinker [July 17, 1773]; *MMDZ*, 150–51 (Zeisberger quote); Message of Netawatwees to Governor John Penn, November 26, 1772, *MPCP*, 10:61–64; *MMDZ*, 120. According to Zeisberger, on the last request, "the Quakers attempted to decline such a suggestion, and said they were sorry to say it wasn't in their power to make it happen. But the Indians threatened them with violence, and forced them to at least agree to the last proposal." David Zeisberger to Nathanael Seidel, August 26, 1773, box 229, folder 4, item 10, RIM, translated for the author by Edward Quinter. In a subsequent letter Zeisberger expressed concern about the advantages Quakers might gain should they ever aid the Delawares in getting to England: "Now I've had a thought and I wish to pose a question—should we not become involved somehow or observe what is happening, or even arrange something through our agents and connections in England? Why should the Quakers be the ones who have the privilege to send missionaries among the Indians? They are after all a sect, which has neither baptism nor communion. They will establish paganism and support it. Aren't we able to protest to the clergy of the Church in England, especially if they interfere with our locations?" David Zeisberger to Nathanael Seidel, October 21, 1773, box 229, folder 4, item 11, RIM, translated for author by Edward Quinter.
37. Lacey, "[Journal of] John Lacey 1773," 152; Parrish, "[Journal of] John Parrish 1773," 155; *MMDZ*, 151.
38. *MMDZ*, 126, 131–32, 135, quotes on 131–32; David Zeisberger to John Ettwein, March 20, 1773, JEP, 718, translated for author by Roy Ledbetter; Zeisberger to Seidel, March 21, 1773.

39. *MMDZ*, 142–45, quotes on 144; Diary of the Little Indian Congregation at Gnadenhütten on the Muskingum from May 1 to June 7, 1773, June 1 and June 7, 1773, trans. August Carl Mahr, MSS Coll. 215, box 5, folder 1, AMP; Olmstead, *David Zeisberger*, 160, 206–9.
40. *MMDZ*, 145, 152–53; Johannes Jungmann Travel Diary, July 20–August 16, 1773, from Bethlehem to Schonbrunn, July 22, July 26, July 27, July 30, and July 31, 1773, quote on July 31, trans. August Carl Mahr, MSS Coll. 215, box 4, folder 18, AMP.
41. Heckewelder, *History, Manners, and Customs*, 197–98. Heckewelder's journal of the trip back to Schönbrunn may be found in Heckewelder, "Canoe Journey," 283–98.
42. Lagundo Utenünk (Friedensstadt) diary, January 1–April 24, 1773, April 2, 1773, box 137, folder 4, RIM, translated for author by Julie Tomberlin Weber.
43. David Zeisberger to Nathanael Seidel, June 9, 1773, box 229, folder 4, item 8, RIM, translated for author by Edward Quinter; Johann Georg Jungmann II to Nathanael Seidel, August 27, 1773, box 217, folder 7, item 9, RIM, translated for author by Edward Quinter; Johann Jacob Schmick to John Ettwein, August 30, 1773, JEP, 532, translated for author by Roy Ledbetter. With the Schmicks' arrival, the Roths were redeployed to Schönbrunn but ran into problems there as well. According to the congregational diary, the whole family was sent back to Bethlehem in May 1774 for their own safety as war was about to break out. But back in January, Zeisberger had sent Seidel a blistering attack on Roth, insisting that neither the Indian believers nor his missionary colleagues could stand him. Hence, all seemed eager to have the Roth family leave. David Zeisberger to Nathanael Seidel, January 28, 1774, box 229, folder 4, item 12, RIM, translated for author by Edward Quinter.
44. *MMDZ*, 146, 146n214.
45. *MMDZ*, 149 (first quote), 154, 157; Zeisberger to Seidel, August 26, 1773; Jungmann to Seidel, August 27, 1773 (second quote).
46. David Zeisberger to John Ettwein, March 20, 1773, JEP, 718, translated for author by Roy Ledbetter; "Conference held at Schönbrunn on 19 August 1773," 563; *MMDZ*, 159.
47. Diary of the Little Indian Congregation at Gnadenhütten on the Muskingum from August 16 to October 22, 1773, September 9 and September 10, 1773, trans. August Carl Mahr, MSS Coll. 215, box 5, folder 3, AMP.
48. Hinderaker and Mancall, *At the Edge of Empire*, 160; Hinderaker, *Elusive Empires*, 194–95; Matthew C. Ward, " 'Peaceable Kingdom' Destroyed," 269–72.

49. McConnell, *A Country Between*, 268–77; Hinderaker and Mancall, *At the Edge of Empire*, 157–60; Hinderaker, *Elusive Empires*, 189–95; Downes, *Council Fires*, 152–78; Olmstead, *David Zeisberger*, 214–29.

50. Diary of the Little Indian Congregation at Gnadenhütten on the Muskingum from February 16 to May 19, 1774, May 14 and May 16, 1774, trans. August Carl Mahr, MSS Coll. 215, box 5, folder 5, AMP; *MMDZ*, 190–94, 197, 199–200, 210, 211, quotes on 191, 192, and 211; John Heckewaelder to John Ettwein, May 24, 1774, JEP, 248, translated for author by Roy Ledbetter; Loskiel, *History of the Mission*, pt. 3, 93–97. According to the Gnadenhütten diary, Schmick received intelligence on May 16 that two Mingo warriors had come to kill him and his wife on the fourteenth but turned away when they saw two armed Indian guards. On the failure of the Pennsylvania government to secure control over this territory, see Spero, *Frontier Country*, 206–22.

51. *MMDZ*, 164–65, 190–97, 201–7, 213–18, 610–11; Wellenreuther, "White Eyes," 143–45, 148.

52. White, *Middle Ground*, 351–65; McConnell, *A Country Between*, 274–79; Hinderaker and Mancall, *At the Edge of Empire*, 158–60; Olmstead, *David Zeisberger*, 221–30; Downes, *Council Fires*, 154–56; Wellenreuther, "White Eyes," 142–47. White Eyes accompanied Dunmore's troops on their march to the Shawnees in hopes of softening colonial treatment of hostile Natives. Pennsylvania governor John Penn also strongly encouraged the Delawares to remain at peace and to mediate with the Shawnees. See Penn's "Message to the Chiefs and Warriors of the Delaware Indians," *MPCP*, 10:204–5, and Arthur St. Clair to Governor Penn, August 25, 1774, William H. Smith, *St. Clair Papers*, 1:341.

53. *MMDZ*, 226n501; Rob Harper, *Unsettling the West*, 66–67, 79–83.

54. *MMDZ*, 187–88, 204–7, 215–16, 224, 235, quotes on 188 and 205; Olmstead, *David Zeisberger*, 229–30.

55. David Zeisberger to Nathanael Seidel, September 13, 1774, box 229, folder 4, item 20, RIM, translated for author by Roy Ledbetter. Zeisberger made the same points in his letter to John Ettwein, September 12, 1774, JEP, 722, translated for author by Roy Ledbetter.

56. *MMDZ*, 229.

57. *MMDZ*, 243.

58. *MMDZ*, 238–41; Olmstead, *David Zeisberger*, 230–32.

59. *MMDZ*, 241–42, 245, 249–50. Wellenreuther and Wessel, *MMDZ*, 245n553, suggest that White Eyes' threat to leave the council had teeth: "Since Netawatwees as chief needed the consent of the whole Council, the abdi-

cation of White Eyes would have deprived him of the consent of White Eyes and his supporters. Such a development would have destroyed his basis for acting as chief." Wellenreuther, "White Eyes," 149, argues that White Eyes' notion of Delaware autonomy included independence from the Six Nations.

60. Diary of the Little Indian Congregation at Gnadenhütten on the Muskingum from September 1, 1774 to February 28, 1775, February 25, February 26, and February 27, 1775, trans. August Carl Mahr, MSS Coll. 215, box 5, folder 7, AMP. Johann Schmick, the Gnadenhütten diarist, reported the same news to John Ettwein the next day in a letter: Johann Jacob Schmick to John Ettwein, February 28, 1775, JEP, 537, translated for author by Edward Quinter.
61. *MMDZ*, 259–60. Wellenreuther and Wessel, *MMDZ*, 259n599, argue that the phrase "they would accept God's word" is best understood as meaning that the Delawares would accept the presence of the white missionaries in their midst.
62. *MMDZ*, 262.
63. *MMDZ*, 273.
64. *MMDZ*, 262–69.
65. *MMDZ*, 272–73; Diary of the Little Indian Congregation at Gnadenhütten on the Muskingum from May 1, 1775 to September 28, 1775, May 15 and May 16, 1775, trans. August Carl Mahr, MSS Coll. 215, box 5, folder 9, AMP. According to Loskiel's history, Papunhank, with characteristic humility, told Schmick shortly before his death that "I go to our Savior as a poor sinner, for I am the poorest and worst of all, and have nothing to plead but the blood of Christ. His righteousness is my wedding dress." Loskiel, *History of the Mission*, pt. 3, 109.

Epilogue

1. Cresswell, *A Man Apart*, 91 (August 26 and August 27, 1775).
2. [Benezet], *Some Observations on Indian Natives*, 24–37; "A Remarkable Indian Minister," 178.
3. *MMDZ*, 273.
4. Merrell, *Into the American Woods*, 88–92, discusses the opposition Christian Indians faced from whites and other Natives alike. Liam Riordan makes a similar point in "'Complexion of My Country,'" 108–10.
5. Hinderaker, *Elusive Empires*, 207–16, quote on 210; Olmstead, *David Zeisberger*, 266, 308, 330–34.

Bibliography

Manuscripts and Archives

Friends Historical Library, Swarthmore College, Swarthmore PA
Friendly Association Records, 1758–62
Historical Society of Pennsylvania, Philadelphia
Christian Frederick Post Journal 1760
Cox-Parrish-Wharton Papers
Gilbert Cope Collection
Jonah Thompson Collection
Pemberton Family Papers
Portrait of Tishcohan by Gustavus Hesselius
Society Miscellaneous Collection
Huntington Library, San Marino CA
Huntington Library Manuscripts
Moravian Church Archives, Bethlehem PA
Christian Schussele, *The Power of the Gospel*, painting
Congregational Diary of First Moravian Church, Philadelphia
Congregational Diary of Moravian Church, Bethlehem
Congregational Diary of Moravian Church, Nain
Diarii of the American Provincial Synod, 1764–68
John Ettwein Papers
The Moravian
Records of the Indian Missions
Ohio History Connection, Columbus
August C. Mahr Papers
Quaker and Special Collections, Haverford College, Haverford PA

Allinson Family Papers
Friendly Association for Regaining and Preserving Peace with the Indians by Pacific Measures, Records of the Philadelphia Yearly Meeting Indian Committee
Pemberton Family Papers
Philadelphia Yearly Meeting Minutes for Meeting for Sufferings for Pennsylvania and New Jersey
Warren Historical Society, Warren PA
Merle Deardorff Papers
William Clements Library, University of Michigan, Ann Arbor
Quaker Collection

Published Works

Anderson, Fred. *Crucible of War: The Seven Years' War and the Fate of Empire in British North America, 1754–1766*. New York: Vintage, 2001.

Andrews, Edward E. *Native Apostles: Black and Indian Missionaries in the British Atlantic World*. Cambridge MA: Harvard University Press, 2013.

An Epistle from our Yearly-Meeting in Burlington, For the Jerseys and Pennsylvania. Philadelphia, 1722.

"A Remarkable Indian Minister." *Christian Disciple* 6 (1818): 178.

Atwood, Craig. *Community of the Cross: Moravian Piety in Colonial Bethlehem*. University Park: Pennsylvania State University Press, 2012.

———. "Understanding Zinzendorf's Blood and Wounds Theology." *Journal of Moravian History* 1, no. 1 (2006): 31–47.

Axtell, James, ed. *The Indian Peoples of Eastern America: A Documentary History of the Sexes*. New York: Oxford University Press, 1981.

Barr, Daniel P. "Did Pennsylvania Have a Middle Ground? Examining Indian-White Relations on the Eighteenth-Century Pennsylvania Frontier." *Pennsylvania Magazine of History and Biography* 136, no. 4 (October 2012): 337–63.

———. "'A Road for Warriors': The Western Delawares and the Seven Years War." *Pennsylvania History* 73, no. 1 (Winter 2006): 1–36.

———. "Victory at Kittanning? Reevaluating the Impact of Armstrong's Raid on the Seven Years' War in Pennsylvania." *Pennsylvania Magazine of History and Biography* 131, no. 1 (January 2007): 5–32.

Barr, Juliana. *Peace Came in the Form of a Woman: Indians and Spaniards in the Texas Borderlands*. Chapel Hill: University of North Carolina Press, 2007.

Bauman, Richard. *For the Reputation of Truth: Politics, Religion, and Conflict among the Pennsylvania Quakers, 1750–1800*. Baltimore: Johns Hopkins University Press, 1971.

Beauchamp, William M., ed. *Moravian Journals relating to Central New York, 1745–66*. Syracuse NY: Onondaga Historical Association, 1916.
Becker, Marshall J. "Cultural Diversity in the Lower Delaware River Valley, 1550–1750: An Ethnohistorical Perspective." In *Late Woodland Cultures of the Middle Atlantic Region*, edited by Jay F. Custer, 90–101. Newark: University of Delaware Press, 1986.
———. "A New Jersey Haven for Some Acculturated Lenape of Pennsylvania during the Indian Wars of the 1760s." *Pennsylvania History* 60, no. 3 (July 1993): 322–44.
[Benezet, Anthony.] *An Account of a Visit Lately Made to the People Called Quakers in Philadelphia, by Papanahoal, an Indian Chief.* London: S. Clark, 1761.
———. "An Account of Papunahung's Second Visit to Friends the 4th of the 8th Month, 1761." In Brookes, *Friend Anthony Benezet*, 485–92.
———. *An Account of the Behavior and Sentiments of some well disposed Indians, mostly of the Minusing Tribe*. Stanford NY: Daniel Lawrence, 1803.
———. "An Account of the Behaviour & Sentiments of a Number of Well-Disposed Indians Mostly of the Minusing Tribe." In Brookes, *Friend Anthony Benezet*, 479–85.
———. *A Plain Path to Christian Perfection*. Philadelphia: Joseph Crukshank, 1772.
———. *Some Observations on the situation, disposition, and character of the Indian Natives of this continent*. Philadelphia: Joseph Crukshank, 1784.
Bethlehem Digital History Project. http://bdhp.moravian.edu/home/home.html.
Brainerd, David. "Related Correspondence." In Jonathan Edwards, *The Life of David Brainerd*, edited by Norman Pettit. Vol. 7 of *The Works of Jonathan Edwards*, 555–90. New Haven: Yale University Press, 1985.
Brainerd, Thomas, ed. *Life of John Brainerd*. Philadelphia: Presbyterian Publication Committee, 1865.
Brookes, George S. *Friend Anthony Benezet*. Philadelphia: University of Pennsylvania Press, 1937.
Burkholder, Jared S. "Neither 'Kriegerisch' nor 'Quäkerisch': Moravians and the Question of Violence in Eighteenth-Century Pennsylvania." *Journal of Moravian History* 12, no. 2 (Fall 2012): 143–69.
Butler, Amos W. "A Visit to Easton." *Indiana Magazine of History* 32, no. 3 (September 1936): 267–74.
Butler, Jon. *Awash in a Sea of Faith: Christianizing the American People*. Cambridge MA: Harvard University Press, 1992.
Calloway, Colin G. *New Worlds for All: Indians, Europeans, and the Remaking of Early America*, 2nd ed. Baltimore: Johns Hopkins University Press, 2013.

———. *Our Hearts Fell to the Ground: Plains Indian Views of How the West Was Lost*. Boston: Bedford/St. Martins, 1996.

———. *Pen and Ink Witchcraft: Treaties and Treaty Making in American Indian History*. New York: Oxford University Press, 2014.

———. "Red Power and Homeland Security: Native Nations and the Limits of Empire in the Ohio Country." In *Facing Empire: Indigenous Experiences in a Revolutionary Age*, edited by Kate Fullagar and Michael A. McDonnell, 145–62. Baltimore: Johns Hopkins University Press, 2018.

Camenzind, Krista. "From Holy Experiment to the Paxton Boys: Violence, Manhood, and Peace in Pennsylvania during the Seven Years' War." PhD diss., University of California, San Diego, 2002.

———. "Violence, Race, and the Paxton Boys." In Pencak and Richter, *Friends and Enemies in Penn's Woods*, 201–20.

Cave, Alfred. "The Delaware Prophet Neolin: A Reappraisal." *Ethnohistory* 46, no. 2 (Spring 1999): 265–90.

———. *Prophets of the Great Spirit: Native American Revitalization Movements in Eastern North America*. Lincoln: University of Nebraska Press, 2006.

Champagne, Duane. "The Delaware Revitalization Movement of the Early 1760s: A Suggested Reinterpretation." *American Indian Quarterly* 12, no. 2 (Spring 1988): 107–26.

Champion, Walter T., Jr. "Christian Frederick Post and the Winning of the West." *Pennsylvania Magazine of History and Biography* 104, no. 3 (July 1980): 308–25.

Collison, Gary. *Shadrach Minkins: From Fugitive Slave to Citizen*. Cambridge MA: Harvard University Press, 1998.

Corbin, Alain. *Life of an Unknown*. Translated by Arthur Goldhammer. New York: Columbia University Press, 2001.

Craft, David. *Historical Discourse of the Wyalusing Presbyterian Church, Delivered September 5, 1869*. Towanda PA: Bradford Reporter, 1870.

———. *History of Bradford County, Pennsylvania with Illustrations, 1770–1878*. Philadelphia: Everts, 1878; rep. ed. Bradford PA: Bradford County Historical Society, 1992.

Cresswell, Nicholas. *A Man Apart: The Journal of Nicholas Cresswell, 1774–1781*. Edited by Harold B. Gill Jr. and George M. Curtis III. Lanham MD: Lexington Books, 2009.

Daiutolo, Robert, Jr. "The Role of Quakers in Indian Affairs during the French and Indian War." *Quaker History* 77, no. 1 (Spring 1988): 1–30.

Dally-Starna, Corinna, and William Starna, trans. and ed. *Gideon's People: Being a Chronicle of an American Indian Community in Colonial Connecticut*

and the Moravian Missionaries Who Served There. 2 vols. Lincoln: University of Nebraska Press, 2009.
———. "Introduction." In Dally-Starna and Starna, *Gideon's People*, 1–73.
de Schweinitz, Edmund. *The Life and Times of David Zeisberger*. Philadelphia: Lippincott, 1870; rep. ed. New York: Arno Press, 1971.
Dowd, Gregory Evans. *A Spirited Resistance: The North American Indian Struggle for Unity, 1745–1815*. Baltimore: Johns Hopkins University Press, 1992.
———. *War under Heaven: Pontiac, the Indian Nations, & the British Empire*. Baltimore: Johns Hopkins University Press, 2002.
Downes, Ralph. *Council Fires on the Upper Ohio: A Narrative of Indian Affairs in the Upper Ohio Valley until 1795*. Pittsburgh PA: University of Pittsburgh Press, 1940.
Dunbar, John R. *The Paxton Papers*. The Hague: Martinus Nijhoff, 1957.
Duval, Kathleen. *Independence Lost: Lives on the Edge of the American Revolution*. New York: Random House, 2015.
———. *The Native Ground: Indians and Colonists in the Heart of the Continent*. Philadelphia: University of Pennsylvania Press, 2007.
Edmunds, R. David. *The Shawnee Prophet*. Lincoln: University of Nebraska Press, 1985.
Edwards, Jonathan. *The Life of David Brainerd*. Edited by Norman Pettit. Vol. 7 of *The Works of Jonathan Edwards*. New Haven: Yale University Press, 1985.
Erben, Patrick. *A Harmony of the Spirits: Translation and the Language of Community in Early Pennsylvania*. Chapel Hill: University of North Carolina Press, 2012.
Ettwein, John. "Brother Ettwein's Account of His Visit in Langunto-Utentink, on the Beaver Cr., and Welhik Tuppeek, on the Muskingum River." In *John Ettwein and the Moravian Church during the Revolutionary Period*, edited by Kenneth Hamilton, 258–73. Bethlehem PA: Times Publishing, 1940.
———. "Report of the Journey of John Ettwein, David Zeisberger, and Gottlob Senseman to Friedenshuetten and their stay there, 1768." Edited and translated by Archibald B. Hulbert and William N. Schwarze. *Ohio Archaeological and Historical Quarterly* 21 (1912): 32–42.
Ettwein, John, and Johann Roth. "Diaries of Johann Ettwein and Johann Roth of the Migration from Friedenshuetten, Pa. (Wyalusing) to Friedenstadt, Pa. (Langundoütenunk)—1772." In *Johann Roth: Missionary* by

David Luther Roth, edited by Frederick G. Roth and translated by John W. Jordan, 118–53. Greenville PA: Beaver Printing Co., rev. ed., 1988.

Eustace, Nicole. *Passion Is the Gale: Emotion, Power, and the Coming of the American Revolution*. Chapel Hill: University of North Carolina Press, 2008.

Faull, Katherine. "From Friedenshütten to Wyoming: Johannes Ettwein's Map of the Upper Susquehanna (1768) and an Account of His Journey." *Journal of Moravian History* 11 (Fall 2011): 82–96.

———. "Mapping a Mission: The Origins of Golkowsky's Map of Friedenshütten, Pennsylvania." *Journal of Moravian History* 7 (Fall 2009): 107–16.

Fisher, Julie A., and David J. Silverman. *Ninigret, Sachem of the Niantics and Narragansetts: Diplomacy, War, and the Balance of Power in Seventeenth-Century New England and Indian Country*. Ithaca NY: Cornell University Press, 2014.

Fisher, Linford D. "'I Believe They Are Papists!': Natives, Moravians, and the Politics of Conversion in Eighteenth-Century Connecticut." *New England Quarterly* 81, no. 3 (September 2008): 410–37.

———. *The Indian Great Awakening: Religion and the Shaping of Native Cultures in Early America*. New York: Oxford University Press, 2012.

Fogelman, Aaron S. *Jesus Is Female: Moravians and Radical Religion in Early America*. Philadelphia: University of Pennsylvania Press, 2008.

Folts, James D. "The Westward Migration of the Munsee Indians in the Eighteenth Century." *New York State Museum Bulletin* 506 (2005): 31–47.

Frank, Albert H. "Spiritual Life in Schönbrunn Village." *Transactions of the Moravian Historical Society* 26 (1990): 20–38.

Frazier, Patrick. *The Mohicans of Stockbridge*. Lincoln: University of Nebraska Press, 1992.

Frost, J. William. "Anthony Benezet: The Emergence of a Weighty Friend." *Quaker History* 103, no. 2 (Fall 2014): 1–17.

———. "William Penn's Experiment in the Wilderness: Promise and Legend." *Pennsylvania Magazine of History and Biography* 107, no. 4 (October 1983): 577–605.

Fullagar, Kate, and Michael A. McDonnell. "Introduction." In *Facing Empire: Indigenous Experiences in a Revolutionary Age*, edited by Kate Fullagar and Michael A. McDonnell, 1–24. Baltimore: Johns Hopkins University Press, 2018.

Gerona, Carla. "Imagining Peace in Quaker and Native American Dream Stories." In Pencak and Richter, *Friends and Enemies in Penn's Woods*, 41–62.

Goddard, Ives. "The Delaware Language, Past and Present." In *A Delaware Indian Symposium*, edited by Herbert C. Kraft, 103–10. Anthropological Series Number 4. Harrisburg: Pennsylvania Historical and Museum Commission, 1974.

Goode, Michael. "Dangerous Spirits: How the Indian Critique of Alcohol Shaped Eighteenth-Century Quaker Revivalism." *Early American Studies* 14, no. 2 (Spring 2016): 258–83.

———. "Introduction: The Relevance of Peace in Early American History." In Goode and Smolenski, *Specter of Peace*, 1–29.

Goode, Michael, and John Smolenski, eds. *The Specter of Peace: Rethinking Violence and Power in the Colonial Atlantic*. Leiden, Netherlands: Brill, 2018.

Gordon, Scott Paul. "The Paxton Boys and Edward Shippen: Defiance and Deference on a Collapsing Frontier." *Early American Studies* 14, no. 2 (Spring 2016): 319–47.

Grigg, John A. *The Lives of David Brainerd: The Making of an American Evangelical Icon*. New York: Oxford University Press, 2009.

Grimes, Richard S. *The Western Delaware Indian Nation, 1730–1795: Warriors and Diplomats*. Bethlehem PA: Lehigh University Press, 2017.

Grumet, Robert S., ed. *Journey on the Forbidden Path: Chronicles of a Diplomatic Mission to the Allegheny Country, March–September, 1760*. Transactions of the American Philosophical Society, vol. 89, part 2. Philadelphia: American Philosophical Society, 1999.

———. "The Minisink Settlements: Native American Identity and Society in the Munsee Heartland, 1650–1778." In *The People of Minisink: Papers from the 1989 Delaware Water Gap Symposium*, edited by David G. Orr and Douglas V. Campana, 175–250. Philadelphia: Mid-Atlantic Region of the National Park Service, 1991.

———. *The Munsee Indians: A History*. Norman: University of Oklahoma Press, 2009.

———. "Sunksquaws, Shamans, and Tradeswomen during the 17th and 18th Centuries." In *Women and Colonization: Anthropological Perspectives*, edited by Mona Etienne and Eleanor Burke Leacock, 43–62. New York: Praeger, 1980.

———. "Taphow: The Forgotten 'Sakemau and Commander in Chief of all those Indians inhabiting northern New Jersey.'" *Bulletin of the Archaeological Society of New Jersey* 43 (1988): 23–28.

Gummere, Amelia Mott, ed. *The Journal and Essays of John Woolman*. New York: Macmillan, 1922.

Hamilton, Kenneth. *John Ettwein and the Moravian Church during the Revolutionary Period*. Bethlehem PA: Times Publishing, 1940.

Harper, Rob. *Unsettling the West: Violence and State Building in the Ohio Valley*. Philadelphia: University of Pennsylvania Press, 2018.

Harper, Steven. "Making History: Documenting the Walking Purchase." *Pennsylvania History* 77, no. 2 (Spring 2010): 217–33.

———. *Promised Land: Penn's Holy Experiment, the Walking Purchase, and the Dispossession of the Delawares, 1600–1763*. Bethlehem PA: Lehigh University Press, 2006.

Hartzell, Lawrence W. "Joshua, Jr.: Moravian Indian Musician." *Transactions of the Moravian Historical Society* 26 (1990): 1–19.

Hays, John. "John Hays' Diary, May 17–June 28, 1760." In Grumet, *Journey on the Forbidden Path*, 35–115.

———. "John Hays' Journal, May 17–June 28, 1760." In Grumet, *Journey on the Forbidden Path*, 35–115.

Hazard, Samuel, ed. *Colonial Records. Minutes of the Provincial Council of Pennsylvania, from the Organization to the Termination of the Proprietary Government*. 16 vols. Harrisburg PA: Theo. Fenn, 1838–53.

Hazard, Samuel, John Linn, William Egle, George Reed, and Thomas Montgomery, eds. *Pennsylvania Archives*. 1st–9th series. Philadelphia and Harrisburg PA: State of Pennsylvania, 1852–1949.

Heckewelder, John. "A Canoe Journey from the Big Beaver to the Tuscarawas in 1773: A Travel Diary of John Heckewaelder." Edited and translated by August C. Mahr. *Ohio State Archaeological and Historical Quarterly* 61 (1952): 283–98.

———. *History, Manners, and Customs of the Indian Nations Who Once Inhabited Pennsylvania and the Neighboring States*. 1819. Reprint, New York: Arno Press, 1971.

———. *A Narrative of the Mission of the United Brethren among the Delaware and Mohegan Indians, from Its Commencement, in the Year 1740, to the Close of the Year 1808*. 1820. Reprint, New York: Arno Press, 1971.

Hinderaker, Eric. "Declaring Independence: The Ohio Indians and the Seven Years' War." In *Cultures in Conflict: The Seven Years' War in North America*, edited by Warren R. Hofstra, 105–25. Lanham MD: Rowman & Littlefield, 2007.

———. *Elusive Empires: Constructing Colonialism in the Ohio Valley, 1673–1800*. New York: Cambridge University Press, 1997.

Hinderaker, Eric, and Peter C. Mancall. *At the Edge of Empire: The Backcountry in British North America*. Baltimore: Johns Hopkins University Press, 2003.

Hornor, Elizabeth. "Intimate Enemies: Captivity and Colonial Fear of Indians in the Mid-Eighteenth Century Wars." *Pennsylvania History* 82, no. 2 (Spring 2015): 162–85.

Hulbert, Archer B., and William N. Schwarze, trans. and ed. "Diary of David Zeisberger's Journey to the Ohio, called in Delaware the Allegene, from Sept. 20th to Nov. 16th, 1767." *Ohio Archaeological and Historical Quarterly* 21, no. 1 (January 1912): 8–32.

Hunter, Charles. "The Delaware Nativist Revival of the Mid-Eighteenth Century." *Ethnohistory* 18, no. 1 (Winter 1971): 39–49.

Hunter, William A. "John Hays' Diary and Journal of 1760." *Pennsylvania Archaeologist* 24, no. 2 (August 1954): 63–83.

———. "Moses (Tunda) Tatamy, Delaware Indian Diplomat." In *Northeastern Indian Lives, 1632–1816*, edited by Robert S. Grumet, 258–72. Amherst: University of Massachusetts Press, 1996.

Irwin, Lee. *Coming Down from Above: Prophecy, Resistance, and Renewal in Native American Religions*. Norman: University of Oklahoma Press, 2008.

Jacobs, Lyn R. "Native American Prophetic Movements of the Eighteenth and Nineteenth Centuries." PhD diss., Syracuse University, 1995.

James, Sydney V. *A People among Peoples: Quaker Benevolence in Eighteenth-Century America*. Cambridge MA: Harvard University Press, 1963.

Jennings, Francis. *The Ambiguous Iroquois Empire: The Covenant Chain Confederation of Indian Tribes with English Colonies from Its Beginnings to the Lancaster Treaty of 1744*. New York: W. W. Norton, 1984.

———. *Empire of Fortune: Crowns, Colonies, and Tribes in the Seven Years War in America*. New York: W. W. Norton, 1988.

John Papunhank, a Christian Indian of North America: A Narrative of Facts. Dublin: Christopher Bentham, 1820.

Jones, David. *A Journal of Two Visits Made to Some Nations of Indians on the West Side of the River Ohio in the Years 1772 and 1773*. 1774. Reprint, New York: Arno Press, 1971.

Jordan, John W., trans. and ed. "The Annals of Friedenshuetten on the Susquehanna, with John Ettwein's Journal of the Removal of the Mission to Friedenstadt." In *The Moravian*, February 24–May 19, 1886.

Kaiser, Siegrun. "Munsee Social Networking and Political Encounters with the Moravian Church." In *Ethnographies and Exchanges: Native Americans, Moravians, and Catholics in Early North America*, edited by A. G. Roeber, 145–64. University Park: Pennsylvania State University Press, 2008.

Kenny, Kevin. *Peaceable Kingdom Lost: The Paxton Boys and the Destruction of William Penn's Holy Experiment*. New York: Oxford University Press, 2009.

Kraft, Herbert C. "Late Woodland Settlement Patterns in the Upper Delaware Valley." In *Late Woodland Cultures of the Middle Atlantic Region*, edited by Jay F. Custer, 102–15. Newark: University of Delaware Press, 1986.

Lacey, John. "[Journal of] John Lacey 1773." In *The Tuscarawas Valley in Indian Days, 1750–1797*, edited by Russell H. Booth Jr., 151–53. Cambridge OH: Gomber House Press, 1994.

Larson, Rebecca. *Daughters of Light: Quaker Women Preaching and Prophesying in the Colonies and Abroad, 1700–1775*. New York: Knopf, 1999.

Leavelle, Tracy Neal. *The Catholic Calumet: Colonial Conversions in French and Indian North America*. Philadelphia: University of Pennsylvania Press, 2012.

Loskiel, George Henry. *A History of the Mission of the United Brethren among the Indians of North America*. Translated by Christian Ignatius Latrobe. 3 parts. London: United Brethren Society for the Furtherance of the Gospel, 1794.

Mancall, Peter C. *Deadly Medicine: Indians and Alcohol in Early America*. Ithaca NY: Cornell University Press, 1995.

Marietta, Jack D. *The Reformation of American Quakerism, 1748–1783*. Philadelphia: University of Pennsylvania Press, 1984.

Marsden, George. *Jonathan Edwards: A Life*. New Haven: Yale University Press, 2003.

Marsh, Dawn G. *A Lenape among the Quakers*. Lincoln: University of Nebraska Press, 2014.

Martin, Joel W., and Mark A. Nicholas, eds. *Native Americans, Christianity, and the Reshaping of the American Landscape*. Chapel Hill: University of North Carolina Press, 2010.

Martínez, David, ed. *The American Indian Intellectual Tradition: An Anthology of Writings from 1772 to 1972*. Ithaca NY: Cornell University Press, 2011.

McClure, David. *Diary of David McClure, Doctor of Divinity, 1748–1820*. Edited by Franklin B. Dexter. New York: Knickerbocker Press, 1899.

McConnell, Michael N. *A Country Between: The Upper Ohio Valley and Its Peoples, 1724–1774*. Lincoln: University of Nebraska Press, 1992.

———. "Peoples 'In Between': The Iroquois and the Ohio Indians, 1729–1768." In *Beyond the Covenant Chain: The Iroquois and Their Neighbors in Indian North America, 1699–1800*, edited by Daniel K. Richter and James H. Merrell, 93–112. Syracuse NY: Syracuse University Press, 1987.

———. "Pisquetomen and Tamaqua: Mediating Peace in the Ohio Country." In *Northeastern Indian Lives, 1632–1816*, edited by Robert S. Grumet, 273–89. Amherst: University of Massachusetts Press, 1996.

Merrell, James H. "'I desire all that I have said . . . may be taken down aright': Revisiting Teedyuscung's 1756 Treaty Council Speeches." *William and Mary Quarterly*, 3rd ser., 63, no. 4 (October 2006): 777–826.

———. *Into the American Woods: Negotiations on the Pennsylvania Frontier*. New York: W. W. Norton, 1999.

———. "Schickellamy, 'A Person of Consequence.'" In *Northeastern Indian Lives, 1632–1816*, edited by Robert S. Grumet, 227–57. Amherst: University of Massachusetts Press, 1996.

———. "Some Thoughts on Colonial Historians and American Indians." *William and Mary Quarterly*, 3rd ser., 46, no. 1 (January 1989): 94–119.

Merritt, Jane T. *At the Crossroads: Indians and Empires on a Mid-Atlantic Frontier, 1700–1763*. Chapel Hill: University of North Carolina Press, 2003.

Merwick, Donna. *The Shame and the Sorrow: Dutch-Amerindian Encounters in New Netherland*. Philadelphia: University of Pennsylvania Press, 2006.

Michel, Bernard E. "Christian Schussele: Portrayer of America." *Transactions of the Moravian Historical Society* 20, no. 2 (1965): 249–67.

Middleton, Richard. *Pontiac's War: Its Causes, Course and Consequences*. New York: Routledge, 2007.

Midtrød, Tom Arne. *The Memory of All Ancient Customs: Native American Diplomacy in the Colonial Hudson Valley*. Ithaca NY: Cornell University Press, 2012.

Miller, Jay David. "'Nature Hath a Voice: John Woolman's Wilderness *Habitus*." *Religion and Literature* 45, no. 2 (Summer 2013): 27–54.

Moulton, Phillips P., ed. *The Journal and Major Essays of John Woolman*. New York: Oxford University Press, 1971.

Moyer, Paul. *Wild Yankees: The Struggle for Independence along Pennsylvania's Revolutionary Frontier*. Ithaca NY: Cornell University Press, 2015.

Nazareth Diary 1760–1769 Extracts. Translated by Mrs. Marx. https://www.moravianchurcharchives.org/eLibrary/Nazareth%20Diary%201760-1769.pdf.

Oberg, Michael Leroy. *Professional Indian: The American Odyssey of Eleazar Williams*. Philadelphia: University of Pennsylvania Press, 2015.

O'Callaghan, E. B., ed. *Documents Relative to the Colonial History of the State of New York*. 15 vols. Albany: Weed, Parsons, 1857–87.

Olmstead, Earl P. *David Zeisberger: A Life among the Indians*. Kent OH: Kent State University Press, 1997.

O'Toole, Fintan. *White Savage: William Johnson and the Invention of America*. New York: Farrar, Straus and Giroux, 2005.

Otto, Paul. *The Dutch-Munsee Encounter in America: The Struggle for Sovereignty in the Hudson Valley*. New York: Berghahn Books, 2006.

Parrish, John. "[Journal of] John Parrish 1773." In *The Tuscarawas Valley in Indian Days, 1750–1797*, edited by Russell H. Booth Jr., 154–56. Cambridge OH: Gomber House Press, 1994.

Pearl, Christopher Ryan. "'Our God, and Our Guns': Religion and Politics on the Revolutionary Frontier." *Pennsylvania History* 85, no. 1 (Winter 2018): 59–68.

Pencak, William A., and Daniel K. Richter, eds. *Friends and Enemies in Penn's Woods: Indians, Colonists, and the Racial Construction of Pennsylvania*. University Park: Pennsylvania State University Press, 2004.

Peucker, Paul. *A Time of Sifting: Mystical Marriage and the Crisis of Moravian Piety in the Eighteenth Century*. University Park: Pennsylvania State University Press, 2015.

Pickett, Ralph. "A Religious Encounter: John Woolman and David Zeisberger." *Quaker History* 79, no. 2 (Fall 1990): 77–92.

Plank, Geoffrey. *John Woolman's Path to the Peaceable Kingdom: A Quaker in the British Empire*. Philadelphia: University of Pennsylvania Press, 2012.

———. "Peace, Imperial War, and Revolution in the Eighteenth-Century Atlantic World." In Goode and Smolenski, *Specter of Peace*, 134–56.

———. "Quaker Reform and Evangelization in the Eighteenth Century." *Amerikastudien / American Studies* 59, no. 2 (2014): 177–91.

Pointer, Richard W. "'An Almost Friend': Papunhank, Quakers, and the Search for Security amid Pennsylvania's Wars, 1754–1765." *Pennsylvania Magazine of History and Biography* 138, no. 3 (July 2014): 237–68.

———. *Encounters of the Spirit: Native Americans and European Colonial Religion*. Bloomington: Indiana University Press, 2007.

Post, Christian Frederick. "Journal of Christian Frederick Post, April 21–June 30, 1760." In Grumet, *Journey on the Forbidden Path*, 35–115.

Preston, David. *Braddock's Defeat: The Battle of Monongahela and the Road to Revolution*. New York: Oxford University Press, 2015.

———. "'Make Indians of Our White Men': British Soldiers and Indian Warriors from Braddock's to Forbes's Campaigns, 1755–1758." *Pennsylvania History* 74, no. 3 (Summer 2007): 280–306.

———. "Squatters, Indians, Proprietary Government, and Land in the Susquehanna Valley." In Pencak and Richter, *Friends and Enemies in Penn's Woods*, 180–200.

Pulsipher, Jenny Hale. *Swindler Sachem: The American Indian Who Sold His Birthright, Dropped Out of Harvard, and Conned the King of England*. New Haven: Yale University Press, 2018.

Reichel, William C. "Wyalusing and the Moravian Mission at Friedenshuetten." *Transactions of the Moravian Historical Society* 1, no. 5 (1871): 179–224.

Richter, Daniel K. "A Framework for Pennsylvania Indian History." *Pennsylvania History* 57, no. 3 (July 1990): 236–61.

———. "Mid-Atlantic Colonies, R.I.P." *Pennsylvania History* 82, no. 3 (Summer 2015): 260–81.

———. *Ordeal of the Longhouse: The Peoples of the Iroquois League in the Era of European Colonization*. Chapel Hill: University of North Carolina Press, 1992.

Riordan, Liam. "'The Complexion of My Country': The German as 'Other' in Colonial Pennsylvania." In *Germans & Indians: Fantasies, Encounters, Projections*, edited by Colin G. Calloway, Gerd Gemünden, and Susanne Zantop, 97–119. Lincoln: University of Nebraska Press, 2002.

Roth, David Luther. *Johann Roth: Missionary*. Edited by Frederick G. Roth and translated by John W. Jordan. Greenville PA: Beaver Printing Co., rev. ed., 1988.

[Roth, Johann.] "Diary of a Moravian Indian Mission Migration across Pennsylvania in 1772." Edited and translated by August C. Mahr. *Ohio Historical Quarterly* 62 (1953): 247–70.

Rubin, Julius H. *Tears of Repentance: Christian Indian Identity and Community in Colonial Southern New England*. Lincoln: University of Nebraska Press, 2013.

Rushforth, Brett. *Bonds of Alliance: Indigenous and Atlantic Slaveries in New France*. Chapel Hill: University of North Carolina Press, 2012.

Schutt, Amy C. "Female Relationships and Intercultural Bonds in Moravian Indian Missions." In Pencak and Richter, *Friends and Enemies in Penn's Woods*, 87–103.

———. *Peoples of the River Valleys: The Odyssey of the Delaware Indians*. Philadelphia: University of Pennsylvania Press, 2007.

———. "Tribal Identity in the Moravian Missions on the Susquehanna." *Pennsylvania History* 66, no. 3 (Summer 1999): 378–98.

Sellers, Jason R. "History, Memory, and the Indian Struggle for Autonomy in the Seventeenth-Century Hudson Valley." *Early American Studies* 13, no. 3 (January 2015): 714–42.

Sensbach, Jon F. *Rebecca's Revival: Creating Black Christianity in the Atlantic World*. Cambridge MA: Harvard University Press, 2006.

Shaffer, Gary D. "Nanticoke Indian Burial Practices: Challenges for Archaeological Interpretation." *Archaeology of Eastern North America* 33 (2005): 141–62.

Shannon, Timothy J. *Iroquois Diplomacy on the Early American Frontier*. New York: Viking, 2008.

———. "War, Diplomacy, and Culture: The Iroquois Experience in the Seven Years' War." In *Cultures in Conflict: The Seven Years' War in North America*, edited by Warren R. Hofstra, 79–103. Lanham MD: Rowman & Littlefield, 2007.

Silver, Peter. *Our Savage Neighbors: How Indian War Transformed Early America*. New York: W. W. Norton, 2008.

Silverman, David J. *Faith and Boundaries: Colonists, Christianity, and Community among the Wampanoag Indians of Martha's Vineyard, 1600–1871*. New York: Cambridge University Press, 2005.

———. "Racial Walls: Race and the Emergence of American White Nationalism." In *Anglicizing America: Empire, Revolution, Republic*, edited by Ignacio Gallup-Diaz, Andrew Shankman, and David J. Silverman, 181–204. Philadelphia: University of Pennsylvania Press, 2015.

———. *Red Brethren: The Brothertown and Stockbridge Indians and the Problem of Race in Early America*. Ithaca NY: Cornell University Press, 2010.

———. "To Become a Chosen People: The Missionary Work and Missionary Spirit of the Brotherton and Stockbridge Indians, 1775–1835." In *Native Americans, Christianity, and the Reshaping of the American Landscape*, edited by Joel W. Martin and Mark A. Nicholas, 250–75. Chapel Hill: University of North Carolina Press, 2010.

Slaughter, Thomas P. *The Beautiful Soul of John Woolman, Apostle of Abolition*. New York: Hill and Wang, 2008.

Sloan, David. "'A Time of Sifting and Winnowing:' The Paxton Riots and Quaker Non-Violence in Pennsylvania." *Quaker History* 66, no. 1 (Spring 1977): 3–22.

Smith, Matthew. *A Declaration and Remonstrance Of the distressed and bleeding Frontier Inhabitants Of the Province of Pennsylvania*. Philadelphia: William Bradford, 1764.

Smith, William H. *The St. Clair Papers: The Life and Public Services of Arthur St. Clair*. 2 vols. 1882. Reprint, New York: Da Capo, 1971.

Spady, James O'Neil. "Colonialism and the Discursive Antecedents of Penn's Treaty with the Indians." In Pencak and Richter, *Friends and Enemies in Penn's Woods*, 18–40.

Spangenberg, A. G. "Bishop A. G. Spangenberg's Journal of a Journey to Onondaga in 1745." In Beauchamp, *Moravian Journals*, 5–24.

Spero, Patrick. *Frontier Country: The Politics of War in Early Pennsylvania*. Philadelphia: University of Pennsylvania Press, 2016.

Sullivan, James, Alexander C. Flick, Almon W. Lauber, Milton W. Hamilton, and Albert B. Corey, eds. *The Papers of Sir William Johnson*. 14 vols. Albany: University of the State of New York, 1921–65.

Thayer, Theodore. "The Friendly Association." *Pennsylvania Magazine of History and Biography* 67, no. 4 (October 1943): 356–76.

Thomson, Charles. *An Inquiry into the Causes of the Alienation of the Delawares and Shawanese Indians from the British Interest*. London: J. Wilkie, 1759.

Thwaites, Reuben G., ed. *Early Western Travels, 1748–1846*. Cleveland OH: Arthur H. Clark, 1904.

Wallace, Anthony F. C. *King of the Delawares: Teedyuscung, 1700–1763*. Philadelphia: University of Pennsylvania Press, 1949.

———. "New Religions among the Delaware." *Southwestern Journal of Anthropology* 12, no. 1 (Spring 1956): 1–21.
Wallace, Paul A. W. *Indian Paths of Pennsylvania*. Harrisburg: Pennsylvania Historical and Museum Commission, 1971.
———. *Indians in Pennsylvania*. 2nd ed. Revised by William A. Hunter. Harrisburg: Pennsylvania Historical and Museum Commission, 1981.
———. "John Heckewelder's Indians and the Fenimore Cooper Tradition." *Proceedings of the American Philosophical Society* 96, no. 4 (August 1952): 496–504.
———. *Thirty Thousand Miles with John Heckewelder*. Pittsburgh PA: University of Pittsburgh Press, 1958.
Ward, Matthew C. *Breaking the Backcountry: The Seven Years' War in Virginia and Pennsylvania, 1754–1765*. Pittsburgh PA: University of Pittsburgh Press, 2003.
———. "The 'Peaceable Kingdom' Destroyed: The Seven Years' War and the Transformation of the Pennsylvania Backcountry." *Pennsylvania History* 74, no. 3 (Summer 2007): 247–79.
———. "Redeeming the Captives: Pennsylvania Captives among the Ohio Indians, 1755–1765." *Pennsylvania Magazine of History and Biography* 125, no. 3 (July 2001): 161–89.
Ward, W. R. *The Protestant Evangelical Awakening*. New York: Cambridge University Press, 1992.
Wellenreuther, Hermann. "White Eyes and the Delawares' Vision of an Indian State." *Pennsylvania History* 68, no. 2 (Spring 2001): 139–61.
Wellenreuther, Hermann, and Carola Wessel, eds. *The Moravian Mission Diaries of David Zeisberger, 1772–1781*. Translated by Julie Tomberlin Weber. University Park: Pennsylvania State University Press, 2005.
———. "Introduction." In Wellenreuther and Wessel, *Moravian Mission Diaries*, 1–87.
Weslager, C. A. "Delaware Indian Name Giving and Modern Practice." In *A Delaware Indian Symposium*, edited by Herbert C. Kraft, 135–45. Anthropological Series Number 4. Harrisburg: Pennsylvania Historical and Museum Commission, 1974.
———. *The Delaware Indians: A History*. New Brunswick NJ: Rutgers University Press, 1972.
Wheeler, Rachel. "Hendrick Aupaumut: Christian-Mahican Prophet." In Martin and Nicholas, *Native Americans, Christianity*, 225–49.
———. "An Imagined Mohican-Moravian Lebenslauf: Joshua, Senior, 1720–1775." *Journal of Moravian History* 11 (Fall 2011): 29–44.

———. *To Live Upon Hope: Mohicans and Missionaries in the Eighteenth-Century Northeast*. Ithaca NY: Cornell University Press, 2008.

Wheeler, Rachel, and Sarah Eyerly. "Songs of the Spirit: Hymnody in the Moravian Mohican Missions." *Journal of Moravian History* 17, no. 1 (Spring 2017): 1–25.

Wheeler, Rachel, and Thomas Hahn-Bruckart. "On an Eighteenth-Century Trail of Tears: The Travel Diary of Johann Jacob Schmick of the Moravian Indian Congregation's Journey to the Susquehanna, 1765." *Journal of Moravian History* 15, no. 1 (Spring 2015): 44–88.

White, Richard. *The Middle Ground: Indians, Empires, and Republics in the Great Lakes Region, 1650–1815*. New York: Cambridge University Press, 1991.

Winiarski, Douglas L. *Darkness Falls on the Land of Light: Experiencing Religious Awakenings in Eighteenth-Century New England*. Chapel Hill: University of North Carolina Press, 2017.

Witgen, Michael. *An Infinity of Nations: How the Native New World Shaped Early North America*. Philadelphia: University of Pennsylvania Press, 2012.

Wolley, Charles. "A Two Years Journal in New York and Part of Its Territories in America." In *Historic Chronicles of New Amsterdam, Colonial New York, and Early Long Island*, edited by Cornell Jaray, 2 vols., 1: 17–97. Port Washington NY: Ira J. Friedman, 1968.

Zeisberger, David "A History of the Northern American Indians." Edited by Archer Butler Hulbert and William Nathaniel Schwarze. *Ohio Archaeological and Historical Quarterly* 19, no.1 (1910): 1–173.

Index